Policing and Violence

Policing and Violence

RONALD G. BURNS
Texas Christian University

CHARLES E. CRAWFORD
Western Michigan University

Editors

M.L. DANTZKER
Series Editor

Upper Saddle River, New Jersey 07458

Library of Congress Cataloging-in-Publication Data

Policing and violence / Ronald Burns and Charles Crawford editors.
     p. cm.—(prentice Hall's policing and . . . series)
   Includes bibliographical references.
   ISBN 0-13-028437-8
      1. Police brutality. 2. Police—Violence against. I. Burns, Ronald, 1968– II.Crawford,
   Charles, 1967– III. Series.

HV8141 .P597 2002
363.2—dc21   2001040944

Publisher: Jeff Johnston
Executive Acquisitions Editor: Kim Davies
Assistant Editor: Sarah Holle
Editorial Assistant: Korrine Dorsey
Managing Editor: Mary Carnis
Production Editor: Linda B. Pawelchak
Production Liaison: Barbara Marttine Cappuccio
Director of Manufacturing and Production: Bruce Johnson
Manufacturing Buyer: Cathleen Peterson
Art Director: Cheryl Asherman
Cover Design Coordinator: Miguel Ortiz
Cover Design: Carey Davis
Cover Photo: Alan Pappe/PhotoDisc
Marketing Manager: Jessica Pfaff
Composition: Pine Tree Composition, Inc.
Printing and Binding: Phoenix Color Corp.

Pearson Education LTD., *London*
Pearson Education Australia PTY. Limited, *Sydney*
Pearson Education Singapore, Pte. Ltd.
Pearson Education North Asia Ltd., *Hong Kong*
Pearson Education Canada, Ltd., *Toronto*
Pearson Educación de Mexico, S.A. de C.V.
Pearson Education—Japan, *Tokyo*
Pearson Education Malaysia, Pte. Ltd.

10 9 8 7 6 5 4 3 2 1
ISBN 0-13-028437-8

Contents

❖

Preface   vii

Acknowledgments   xi

Contributors' Biographical Information   xiii

Chapter 1   The Political Economy of Police Violence   1
Paul B. Stretesky

Chapter 2   Violence by and Against the Police   25
Jason T. Carmichael and David Jacobs

Chapter 3   From Report Takers to Report Makers:
Understanding the Police and Violence   52
Robert P. McNamara

Chapter 4   Situational Determinants of Police Violence   73
Ronald Burns and Charles Crawford

Chapter 5   Police Use of Deadly Force: Where We Should Be Looking   101
Steven E. Reifert

Chapter 6   Training and Police Violence   127
Kenneth W. Flynn

Chapter 7   Police Pursuits: Just One Form of Police Violence   147
Matt Welch

Chapter 8   Community Policing and Police Violence   167
Rhonda K. DeLong

Chapter 9   The International Dimensions of Violence and the Police   189
               Richard H. Ward

Chapter 10   Future Directions of Police Violence: What to Expect   214
               Gene Stephens

Chapter 11   Policing and Violence in Review: Perspectives
               from the Practitioner Turned Academic/Practitioner   228
               M.L. Dantzker

Preface

———————————————— ❖ ————————————————

Police officers must be constantly prepared to defend against, or use, force. As such, police officers need special skills and knowledge to appropriately engage in this often controversial and dangerous aspect of their job. Implications for officer misuse of violence include criminal and civil litigation, loss of public support, injury, and death. For example, recent violent incidents in New York City resulted in additional strains between minority groups and the police. In Fort Worth, Texas, an officer received a 90-day unpaid suspension after her vehicle struck and killed the driver of another vehicle as she was responding to a nonemergency disturbance call.

Police officers' use of force attracts a great deal of attention, often becoming the main story on television news shows and in the headlines of newspapers. Police violence both directly and indirectly affects a substantial portion of our society. However, we must ask, "How much do we understand about the relationship between police officers and violence?" We all have opinions regarding how much force is too much, and we all have ideas of how much violence police officers encounter, but do any of us have what could be considered an accurate understanding of *all* aspects of police violence?

Although a substantial body of research has addressed police violence, few scholarly texts have primarily focused on it. For instance, most texts addressing the history of policing glance over the foundations of police violence, while others provide limited coverage of the laws and training surrounding this aspect of the profession. Numerous texts addressing police violence tend to focus on officers and deadly force. Although this is an important aspect of police violence, such acts affect only a small number of officers, leaving a void in our understanding of *all* forms of police violence.

The purpose of this text is to provide a comprehensive account of police violence. In covering aspects ranging from the history of police violence to future directions, we hope readers will gain a more complete understanding of the concept and all that it entails. In contrast to many publications addressing police violence, this text covers acts of violence *by and against* officers. In selecting contributors who have a strong background in the various areas of police violence (including both practitioners and academics), we believe we help fill a void in the policing literature.

It is hoped that readers will use the text primarily to further understand police actions and reactions as they relate to violence. The study of police violence is not new; however, no text comprehensively covers the issue. Such coverage is of significance to a wide audience, including not only police officers, students, and academics, but citizens, researchers, policymakers, and police administrators.

For the classroom, this text would be most useful in upper-level criminology and policing courses, as well as graduate seminars dealing with critical issues in policing. The text would also be useful in professional seminars for police trainers, as well as for instructors and students in the fields of public administration/affairs, law, violence, deviance, and sociology. Additionally, organizations such as the ACLU, citizen action groups, and civilian review boards may find use for the text. Finally, researchers and policmakers outside the United States may appreciate the text for its extensive coverage of police violence.

Development of this text initially began following our work on two research articles on police use of force and a follow-up piece on suspect use of force. Through a series of conversations with colleagues such as John Hepburn, Mark Dantzker, and John Fuller, and presentations on panels at the American Society of Criminology and the Academy of Criminal Justice Sciences, we began thinking about expanding this theme and putting together a reader that focuses specifically on police violence, pulling authors from a variety of backgrounds, all united by the goal of developing a comprehensive and better understanding of the area. As we continued our research, we realized that although there were numerous articles on police violence, few books specifically address the issue at length, leaving a void for practitioners, researchers, and students.

We decided to seek out contributors we believed had a strong understanding of situational and contextual interpretations of justice actions, including police violence. In choosing both practitioners and academicians, we believe this text will fill a gap in the policing literature. The collection of 11 original chapters covering a wide variety of areas of police violence should provide readers with "one-stop shopping" for coverage of the topic.

In Chapter 1 ("The Political Economy of Police Violence"), Paul B. Stretesky documents the origins of police violence from a historical, materialistic, and dialectical perspective. He examines the political economy of police violence from a historical perspective by examining how various modes of production are related to violence by and against the police. Focusing on the dynamics of police violence over time in relation to the transformation from feudalism to capitalism in its various forms and investigating police violence from a materialistic perspective by examining productive forces and the relations of productions, Stretesky provides a thorough and insightful account of police violence.

Through examining the research surrounding violent acts by and against police officers in Chapter 2 ("Violence by and Against the Police"), Jason T. Carmichael and David Jacobs help set the foundation for a comprehensive account of police violence. Their chapter examines areas such as the coercive techniques officers use to deal with resistance and the legal provisions that regulate police use of force. The authors review the social science research on the factors that contribute to the use of force by and against officers and close by proposing an approach to reducing unwarranted violence by the police.

In exploring the reasons why police officers can feel justified in using excessive force, Robert P. McNamara describes how officers are socialized and includes an overview of the subculture of policing in Chapter 3 ("From Report Takers to Report Makers: Understanding the Police and Violence"). McNamara addresses the "nature versus nurture" debate in policing and examines police violence through frustration-aggression, social learning, and the subculture of violence theories.

Taking Carmichael and Jacobs's work in Chapter 2 a bit further, Chapter 4 ("Standard Determinants of Police Violence") provides an account of the situational factors affecting an officer's likelihood to use or be the victim of violence. In this chapter, we, Ronald Burns and Charles Crawford, present research specifically devoted to situational factors affecting police violence and provide several real-life accounts of a city being forced to re-examine police practices as a result of incidents in which situational factors played influential roles. The development of measurements of police violence (particularly as they relate to measurement of situational factors) is also discussed.

The next four chapters are written by authors with current field experience as police officers. In Chapter 5 ("Police Use of Deadly Force: Where We Should Be Looking"), Steven E. Reifert presents and questions the literature regarding deadly force. He examines, among other things, measurements of deadly force, related training issues, and why some officers use deadly force while others refrain from doing so. Reifert's occupational insight provides a refreshing deviation from traditional accounts of more academically based accounts of police use of deadly force.

Kenneth W. Flynn also draws on his experience in policing in his discussion of "Training and Police Violence" in Chapter 6. Many suggest that increased professionalization of policing begins with improved training, and that many violent encounters between citizens and suspects can be avoided through appropriate police responses. Captain Flynn highlights these arguments in his account of how police violence can be reduced through proper training. Among the training-related issues addressed are the importance of education, methods for training, training standards, and civil liability.

Television is replete with shows involving criminals trying to outrun police officers. In "Police Pursuits: Just One Form of Violence" (Chapter 7), Matt Welch demonstrates the importance of officer pursuits, and how such acts can be recognized as violence. Welch skillfully combines existing research and his experience in policing in his discussion of the types of police pursuits, legal issues and policies surrounding pursuits, frequency and dangerousness of such events, and training required to prepare officers for pursuits.

While we recognize the benefits of community policing in relation to public perception of policing, we are uncertain what impact community policing will have in many other areas of policing. As such, understanding police violence in the *community era* of policing is important as an increasing number of police departments adopt the community policing philosophy. In Chapter 8 ("Community Policing and Police Violence"), Rhonda K. DeLong addresses various aspects of community policing and how related changes will impact police violence. Among other issues, DeLong stresses the importance of effective selection, recruitment, and training of officers as many departments alter their approach to policing.

A text on police violence would be incomplete without a look at international rates of violent police-citizen encounters and explanations of the differences between countries. It is imperative that we address the impact on policing of our shift toward a global society. Drawing on decades of experience personally researching international policing, Richard H. Ward highlights the differences and similarities in police violence as it exists in various countries. In Chapter 9 ("The International Dimensions of Violence and the Police"), Ward suggests, among other things, that the most significant determinate of police violence is the country's form of government.

In Chapter 10 ("Future Directions of Police Violence: What to Expect"), Gene Stephens provides a look to the future of police violence. From the perpective of his 30 years as a futurist specializing in criminal justice and policing in particular, Stephens reviews the projections of others and describes what he believes is the future of police violence. In general, he argues that we can expect to see "more of the same" in the next few years, followed by a short period of "new" violence, and finally a "real" decrease in violence by and against police. Stephens's insightful chapter assists readers in understanding what shifts in police violence we face, and why we should expect change.

M.L. Dantzker uses Chapter 11 ("Policing and Violence in Review: Perspectives from the Practitioner Turned Academic/Practitioner") to share his understanding and interpretation of police violence based on his experience as a practitioner and an academic. Dantzker skillfully provides a sense of closure (often lacking, yet required in edited texts) by addressing the significance of police violence in everyday life, while summarizing and elaborating on the preceding chapters.

Ronald Burns
Charles Crawford

Acknowledgments

We must acknowledge numerous people for their patience, influence, contributions, and commitment. We thank all of our contributors, and many thanks go to the *Policing and . . .* series editor M.L. Dantzker and from Prentice Hall, to Kim Davies and Sarah Holle.

We wish to thank our colleagues at Texas Christian University and Western Michigan University and our graduate school "cronies" (Mike, Paul, Jeff, Marian, Tom, Lynne, Jana, Adrian, Diane, among others) and mentors (Mike Lynch, Lori Fridell, Gene Stephens, Ted Chiricos, and Gary Kleck, among others) for their inspiration and companionship.

We also wish to acknowledge the patience and support of our wives, Lisa Burns and Raeshell Crawford, and Charles's son Ryan and recognize the lifelong support of our relatives in New York and Florida. Finally, we wish to remember and acknowledge Mark Yeisley, a true friend and dedicated scholar. Thanks to everyone involved.

Contributors' Biographical Information

-- ❖ --

Ronald G. Burns received his Ph.D. from the School of Criminology and Criminal Justice at Florida State University. He is an assistant professor of criminal justice in the Department of Sociology and Criminal Justice at Texas Christian University. His most recent publications appeared in *Police Quarterly; Police Practice and Research; Crime, Law and Social Change; Studies in Symbolic Interaction; Sociological Spectrum;* and *Environment and Behavior*. His primary research interests center on police violence and media construction of crime. Recent research includes an examination of image shaping on behalf of the Food and Drug Administration and an observation of the factors related to a suspect resisting arrest.

Jason T. Carmichael currently is a Ph.D. student at Ohio State University. He does research on crime and social control. Current projects include a study of the economic and social conditions associated with variations in jail use, a study of the political and social conditions that produce a legal death penalty, and factors influencing incarceration rates across states.

Charles E. Crawford is an associate professor of sociology at Western Michigan University. He recently published in the areas of gender and sentencing, prison sexual violence, suspect resistance at arrest, and racial profiling. His current research involves the study of situational factors in police use of force and racial and pretextual stops. He conducts evaluation research for the Kalamazoo Department of Public Safety.

Rhonda K. DeLong is currently an assistant professor of criminal justice at Ferris State University. She received her Ph.D. from Western Michigan University in 1997. She is an MCOLES (Michigan Commission on Law Enforcement Standards) Instructor teaching in the law enforcement track program. Her areas of expertise include community policing; criminal investigation; and recruitment, selection, and training of police officers. She has also been a certified Michigan police officer since 1985 and is currently working with the Lawrence (Michigan) Police Department as a patrol officer.

Kenneth W. Flynn is a captain in the Fort Worth Police Department (FWPD) and has been a commissioned officer with the department for 18 years. He served as an officer, sergeant, and commander in the Patrol Division and has worked in the Criminal Investigations Division. He currently commands the Internal Affairs Division with the FWPD. Flynn has made numerous presentations to police recruit classes and citizen groups regarding police conduct and citizens' rights.

David Jacobs, professor of sociology at Ohio State University, does research on the political sociology of crime and social control and issues in political economy. Current projects include a study of the political and social conditions that lead to a legal death penalty, a court-level study of the political determinants of prison sentence length, and a study of the political and other historically contingent conditions that influence the percentage of a state's population that is incarcerated.

Robert P. McNamara is an associate professor of sociology and the director of the Center for Social Research at Furman University. He is also the director of the Greenville Social Services Training Institute in Greenville, South Carolina. He is the author of ten books: *Perspectives on Social Problems; Crossing the Line: Interracial Couples in the South,* with Maria Tempenis and Beth Walton; *Crime Displacement: The Other Side of Prevention*; *The Times Square Hustler: Male Prostitution in New York City*; *Sex, Scams and Street Life: The Sociology of New York City's Times Square; Beating the Odds: Crime, Poverty, and Life in the Inner City; Police and Policing* with Dennis Kenney; *The Urban Landscape: Selected Readings* with Kristy McNamara; *Social Gerontology* with David Redburn; and *Managing a Deviant Status: Field Research and the Labeling Perspective* with Deanna Ramey and Linda Henry. McNamara has also written five monographs on issues such as homelessness, the Viola Street community, poverty, and domestic terrorism. He has also published numerous articles on a variety of topics and has been a consultant for state, federal, and private agencies on topics such as AIDS, drug abuse, urban redevelopment, homelessness, policing and gangs, and health care. He is currently working as a consultant for the Police Executive Research Forum providing technical assistance training to police departments around the country on the problem-oriented policing model. In 1998, McNamara was named Faculty Member of the Year by the Association of Furman Students as well as by the Office of Multicultural Affairs. He was also recognized by Senator Fritz Hollings in 1997 on the floor of the United States Senate for his life and work reflected in *Beating the Odds.* McNamara holds a Ph.D. in sociology from Yale University.

Steven E. Reifert is currently a doctoral candidate in the sociology department at Western Michigan University. He holds a masters degree in public administration from Ball State University and a bachelors degree in science from Park College, Missouri. He has been in law enforcement for over 22 years, beginning his career as a special agent for the Air Force Office of Special Investigations. He has worked in a municipal department for the past 13 years as an undercover narcotics officer, community policing officer, and crime prevention officer. He is currently a sergeant in the patrol division. He is also an adjunct faculty member at Western Michigan University, where he teaches crime prevention, community policing, and ethics in criminal justice. His academic interests involve police ethics, deadly force, pursuit policies, and police/community interaction.

Gene Stephens is a professor in the College of Criminal Justice at the University of South Carolina and a consulting futurist/presenter with more than 100 organizations including the FBI Academy, the California Command College, the Law Enforcement Management Institute of Texas, the Florida Criminal Justice Executive Institute, and Police Futurists International. He is also the current criminal justice editor of *The Futurist* and the law and justice associate editor of *USA Today's* magazine. He served as editor of *Criminal Justice Review* and *Southern Journal of Criminal Justice,* as well as *Police Futurist.*

Paul B. Stretesky received his Ph.D. from the School of Criminology and Criminal Justice at Florida State University. He is currently an assistant professor in the Department of Criminology at the University of South Florida and is a former member of the Sociology Department at Colorado State University. His publications have appeared in several leading sociological and criminological journals, including *Social Problems, Social Science Quarterly, Justice Quarterly, American Political Science Review, Journal of Criminal Justice,* and the *British Journal of Criminology.* His primary research interests are in the areas of environmental and social justice.

Richard H. Ward is currently dean and director of the Criminal Justice Center and College at Sam Houston State University. He holds a doctorate in criminology from the University of California at Berkeley and served as vice president at John Jay College of Criminal Justice and vice chancellor for administration at the University of Illinois at Chicago. He has worked with criminal justice practitioners in almost 50 countries over the past 30 years and has directed numerous sponsored research projects relating to law enforcement.

Matt Welch is currently an auto theft detective with the Fort Worth Police Department (FWPD). He began his career in policing with the LaPlata County (Colorado) Sheriff's Department where he performed investigative, patrol, and jail duties. He also taught tactical driving at the regional academy. He has been with the FWPD since 1986 and, in addition to auto theft detective, has served as a field training officer, neighborhood patrol officer, background investigator, mayor's aide, and patrol officer. Welch is bicycle certified and has three certifications (NAPD, SPDI, and CLETA) as a tactical driving instructor. He was recognized in 1998 for his efforts in helping the FWPD win the National League of Cities' "Community Policing Award" for cities with populations above 250,000.

1

The Political Economy of Police Violence

Paul B. Stretesky

❖

INTRODUCTION

Picture an act of police violence in your mind's eye. What do you imagine? When most of us think about police violence, we see it as an isolated occurrence—perhaps an event that we recently read about in the newspaper or viewed on television. For many of us, acts of police violence are relatively unrelated and—above all—the result of the individual choices. We may even believe that all acts of police violence must be judged on a case-by-case basis. We rarely think of police violence as a public issue, one that is attached to the role of police as actors in the social, political, and economic system.

Drawing upon Spitzer's (1981) method of analysis provided in "The Political Economy of Policing," the purpose of this chapter is to examine police violence in the United States from a historical, materialistic, and dialectical perspective. Such an analysis aids in understanding how and why police violence has changed with the times. In this analysis, I explore the political economy of police violence from a historical perspective by examining how various modes of production are related to violence by and against the police (for a more elaborate explanation of how historical, materialistic, and dialectical approaches can be related to the study of policing institutions, see Spitzer, 1981, pp. 314–317). Rather than examine police violence as an ahistorical phenomenon (i.e., it has and does exist), this work focuses on the dynamics of police violence over time in relation to transformations from feudalism to capitalism in its various forms (e.g., laissez-faire and monopoly capitalism). One potential problem with adopting a historical perspective is that it relies on available accounts taken from others. Therefore, the validity of this work ultimately rests on the accurateness of historical accounts of police and police violence.

This chapter also investigates police violence from a materialistic perspective by observing productive forces and the relations of production (Marx, 1976/1867). As Spitzer (1981, p. 314) points out, such an analysis "stands in clear contrast to that of conventional sociology, which emphasized ideas, motives, attitudes, and beliefs as the methodological and theoretical starting points" (for a recent summary of conventional perspectives on police violence, see Worden, 1996). At times the relationship between the ruling class and police violence appears direct (e.g., thugs were hired by the manufacturing elite to attack workers during the "big stick" era [President Theodore Roosevelt's 1901 foreign policy approach]), while at other times the relationship appears more indirect (e.g., the police beating of Rodney King or the torture of Abner Louima). It is clear that throughout history police violence is not always a direct expression of the ruling class (Greenberg, 1976; see also Lynch & Groves, 1989). Rather, as this analysis shows, the history of police violence is more complicated. As Harring (1983, p. 15) points out, "it is theoretically possible to have a class society without also making it a police society." As this analysis shows, working-class interests and the interests of the semi-autonomous state have significantly influenced structures of policing and the type and amount of police violence that exist over time.

Police violence is also examined from a dialectical perspective. That is, policing institutions have changed because contradictions in those institutions cannot be solved within existing sets of relationships (Spitzer, 1981). Police do, after all, serve opposing social control functions. That is, police are expected to maintain social control through the simultaneous use of violent and nonviolent tactics. As this investigation shows, when fundamental contradictions in policing institutions intensify, changes in policing (including police reform) occur.

TOWARD A HISTORICAL DEFINITION OF POLICE VIOLENCE

Since this work is historical in nature, any definition of police must be broad enough to effectively capture changes in the policing institution over time. Therefore, I adopt Weber's (1958, p. 180) conception of police as one of many "specific staff of [individuals] who will use physical or psychological compulsion with the intention of obtaining conformity with order, or inflicting sanctions for infringement of it." This definition encompasses public, private, formal, and informal systems of policing.

It is also important to point out that I do not enter into the current debate surrounding the use of unnecessary force found in the conventional crime literature (see, for example, Klockars, 1996). Such debates are always based on legal and moral terms that tend to support the existing social structure. Instead, a critical perspective of police violence is more appropriate here: *All police violence that is the direct or indirect result of oppressive social and economic relationships is unnecessary.* My argument, then, is structural in the sense that individual acts of police violence can often be referenced to larger social and economic conditions that make people more or less likely to become the targets of police violence. Such an analysis, then, must consider that seemingly dissimilar forms of police violence are interconnected and can be referenced to larger social and economic structures. Consider the following real-life images of police violence:

> A young African American girl who is shopping with her family is suspected of taking an inexpensive item from an upscale department store. Two private security guards follow her into the parking lot and begin to question her. When the girl's father objects to the guards' questions, one of the security guards puts a chain around the father's neck and crushes his trachea.

A Hispanic man is pulled over by a state trooper late one night for speeding. The officer approaches the car and tells the man in English to keep his hands visible. The man, who does not speak English, cannot understand the officer and instead searches for his driver's license and insurance. The trooper panics because the driver does not comply with his orders. When the driver makes a "sudden movement," the trooper shoots.

A West African immigrant teenager leaves his country in search of a better life in the United States. He takes a job as a street vendor. When he is returning home from work, he is mistaken for a rape suspect wanted by police. Four members of the special police unit assigned to aggressively patrol the streets in the neighborhood where the immigrant lives determine that he is armed and poses a threat to them. They shoot at the teen 41 times, hitting him 19 of those times. Only after the young man dies do the officers discover that he was unarmed and not the person they were looking for.

Several hundred activists begin a 50-mile march for peace. Sheriffs' deputies, who are determined to stop the demonstration, use tear gas, nightsticks, and whips against the activists. Several members of the peace group are seriously injured—one activist later dies from injuries she sustained in the incident.

Two police officers respond to a report of domestic disturbance in a large urban housing project. As the officers arrive at the project and exit their patrol vehicle, they are engulfed in a shower of glass bottles and rocks that are thrown from the roof of a nearby building. One officer is struck in the eye by a piece of broken glass that bounces off the pavement. The wounded officer's partner radios for help while he assists his partner back to the car. As the officers await backup, several shots are fired in their general direction.

It is Sunday afternoon. An officer observes an African American youth shooting baskets at a public school's basketball court located in an affluent suburb just outside the city's limit. The city where the boy lives is plagued by poverty, violence, and unemployment. The officer, who works for the suburban police department, recognizes the youth as a city resident who he has previously warned to stay off this school's property. The officer loads the youth's bike into the trunk of his patrol car and then drives the boy and his bicycle back to the city. Before releasing the youth near the city court, the officer slaps the boy in the head and warns him that the next time he finds him near the school, he will "beat his ass."

These are but a few images that exist in our society today. These images are real—they are not fantasies of my, your, or someone else's imagination. Many exist in the city or area in which you live. These images are distant to us only to the extent that we refuse to recognize them as meaningful consequences of the way life is organized in modern social, political, and economic systems of production and consumption: as outcomes of class and race relations. More important, all of these images have something in common: They demonstrate how police violence can be created by the social economic and political systems in which we live. In the remainder of this chapter, police violence in the United States is examined from material, historical, and dialectical perspectives.

POLICING PRECAPITALIST SOCIETIES

The earliest types of societies were small-scale stateless societies (Michalowski, 1985). These hunting and gathering societies can be characterized by communally owned property, the absence of social classes, a minimal division of labor, and a lack of any "organized state or societal ruler" (Beirne & Messerschmidt, 1991, p. 23). Offenses and conflicts in these preclass societies were dealt with informally. Police violence did not exist because the police did not exist. However, as state societies began to develop, a set of supporting social relations also developed. The way in which law, education, family and kinship networks, government, and even crime were organized was related to the way the economic system was organized. All members of society did not, however, benefit equally from the law. Instead, classes were formed in which some members of society benefited from economic arrangements and some classes were exploited by those arrangements. In Ancient Rome, for example, large slave populations were forced to provide free labor to the ruling elite. As societies developed, systems of policing were created to ensure that the social order was maintained. Moreover, it became increasingly clear that the police would, if necessary, use force (i.e., police violence) to ensure conformity and order.

The English frankpledge system provides one of the best examples of how early policing institutions were organized to promote the social order in agricultural societies (Critchley, 1972). The frankpledge was a system of self-policing that existed during feudal times (450 A.D.–1660) and ensured collective liability for crime among a king's subjects. According to Bellamy (1973, p. 90):

> The frankpledge was the old grouping together of most men into bands of about ten for purposes of protecting public order. The sheriff had to see that all able-bodied adult males, except nobles, clergy, and some categories of freemen, were in such a group. If a member of a tithing committed an offense the other nine were supposed to ensure his appearance in court when required, even by arresting him if they believed it was necessary. A fine was the penalty for failure.

The frankpledge system, as a method of social control, fit feudalism well. The agricultural base of production during those times (when peasants where forced to farm their feudal lord's land) meant that local townships were relatively stable (Lee, 1901/1971). These conditions allowed tithing members to easily monitor one another and report any criminal behavior among their peers to the sheriff. Remarkably similar forms of self-policing are described in other early agriculturally based societies (e.g., Chinese [Hsiao, 1960], French [Greenshields, 1994], and Italian and Greek [Reith, 1952]). There are relatively few historical accounts of frankpledge violence (Bellamy, 1973; Lee, 1901/1971). Social organization at the time was hierarchical and stable and "most every kind of social bond was decided by either tradition or contract" (Canterbery, 1995, p. 22).

While the frankpledge system and other forms of self-policing largely reflect the existing mode of production, policing would change. Bellamy (1973, p. 201) argues:

> Society was becoming less rigid and status and domicile had come to change more rapidly. . . . In the later middle ages, a felon could consider himself distinctly unlucky if he was captured by the authorities. The maxim was not efficiency but financial economy, making the [frankpledge] system of public order pay for itself. A king with no proper permanent army, and who could not pay with regularity the members of his own household, was not likely to be able either to visualize or to finance an [effective] police system.

The eventual failure of the frankpledge system can largely be attributed to the economic transformation from feudalism to capitalism. As early as the 1400s, peasants were leaving the land because of diminished economic prospects. This was largely a result of a growing population, better agricultural technology that led to a surplus of food (and labor), expanding trade, the emergence of nation-states, and the enclosure movement. According to Canterbery (1995, p. 31):

> Landowners could now profit from either farming or raising sheep because the revival of trade made specialization efficient again. A land-owning noble did not have to be very clever to figure out that a lone Shepard could watch over sheep in a pasture, whereas ten or twelve laborers might be needed to grow food on the same land. Thus, much of the land that had once been open was fenced in (enclosed). The greatest loss to the smaller farmers was the common land on which they had, by [feudal] custom fed their poultry, pastured their cows, and chopped wood for fuel. Many of the peasants . . . became laborers in agriculture, . . . cottage industries, [and] . . . shops in town.

Thus, serfs and peasants who had once been forced to live on and work the king's land were now required to leave it. For the emerging capitalist class, the process of enclosure created the necessary mass of "free-laborers" needed to convert raw materials into products that could be traded or sold in the new economy. Laborers had little say about where they could go to sell their labor and thus became highly mobile—moving to places that paid wages and moving from places that did not. This slow process of change from an agricultural economy to a capitalist economy meant that the frankpledge was impractical as a system of policing. The noble class could no longer expect to maintain effective control over the serfdom through the frankpledge.

As the economy transformed from feudalism to capitalism, new social problems emerged. By most accounts, housing and social conditions such as poverty and massive unemployment produced uncontrollable crime and increasingly frequent mob riots. According to Reith (1952, p. 45), "London's underworld was always ready to pour out from its slum warrens and cellars. The latter opened on to the streets, and were led, even by respectable citizens, to the semi-destitute." To deal with these emerging disturbances to the public order, new forms of policing were established. These changes, however, brought about various forms of police violence.

One important policing effort was adopted in 1692 when the English government set up a system of monetary rewards and criminal pardons for assistance that led to the arrest of criminals (Hirschel & Wakefield, 1995). According to Spitzer (1981, p. 322):

> The peculiar relationship between weak government and disorganized community life on the one hand, and the widespread use of rewards to encourage cooperation on the other, led to the appearance of at least one type of relatively specialized group mediating between the errant masses and the ruling elite—the thief-takers.

Thief-takers were in essence private police—they had no official status and were paid by the king when their arrests resulted in a conviction. Moreover, they were often given rewards by the victim and often were allowed to keep the thief's belongings (if any existed). By most accounts, thief-takers were "just as likely to promote crime as prevent it" (Tobias, 1979, p. 46). Hirschel and Wakefield (1995, p. 70) argue that thief-takers "quickly became professional criminals and spawned a sophisticated [crime network] . . . whole districts of London were regarded as sanctuaries in which thieves and villains enjoyed almost complete immunity from prosecution" (see also Howson, 1970). Crooked thief-takers were also likely to be directly or indirectly responsible for large amounts of violence, including the deaths of people innocent of the crimes for which they were accused. According to one account, the Thief-Taker General of Great Britain and Ireland (Jonathan Wild) may have fabricated evidence that led to the execution of more than 76 people (Tobias, 1979). The demise of the thief-takers can largely be attributed to their lack of public support as "legitimate agents of social control" (see Spitzer, 1981). Thief-takers such as Wild were actually responsible for the thefts they were supposed to be preventing. The social elites of the time realized that the thief-takers could not produce the type of discipline the urban masses needed. Eventually even Wild was arrested, found guilty, and executed for collaborating with felons (Tobias, 1979, p. 15).

Another important development in policing occurred during the transformation from feudalism to capitalism—the change from the frankpledge system to the watch system. During the 14th century, the tithing man became known as the "chief pledge" and eventually the "parish constable" (Reith, 1952). Under the watch system, the parish constable was a locally elected, unpaid position, which carried with it the responsibility of apprehending people who broke the law. The watch system was, above all, a form of policing that still relied on self-accountability. The constable could appoint "watchmen" from the community to aid in policing efforts, but the entire community was still required to assist the constable in emergencies.

By the early 19th century, it was common for the appointed constable to be a member of the working class—with working-class interests (Foster, 1974). As class conflict in England began to intensify, the role of the community-appointed constable became increasingly important to both labor and the elite. According to Foster (1974, p. 56):

> Having representatives in parliament could be useful, but the basic social function of labour's organized strength was to control the police. If, beside the army, the authorities had a police force to provide local intelligence (and, in the case of prosecution, witness and evidence) the practice of extra-legal unionism would be in grave danger. So whatever else the working-class leaders might do, their first duty was to keep hold of the police.

Thus, as labor began to organize, the constable system was effectively manipulated to serve its interests. In many areas the constables refused to intervene in working-class riots (Foster, 1974). In some cases constables even protected rioters. In one such instance a British soldier, Tom Morris, described the events of October 28, 1816:

> As soon as I heard of the riot I went round, collected our men, and took them to the captain's quarters, who complimented me for my alacrity in getting the men together. The idea of having an opportunity of contending with a mob seemed most congenial to his sentiments. . . .
> The constable went with us, and proceeded to read the riot act. On some brickbats and stones being thrown at us, our brave captain gave orders to lead, and then he gave direction that we should fire among the mob, when the constable interposed and said, "There was no necessity for that yet." "Then," said the officer, "if I am not allowed to fire, I shall take my men back!" The constable's patriotic answer deserves to be recorded: "Sir," said he, "you are called upon to aid and assist the civil powers, and if you fire upon the people without my permission, and death ensues, you will be guilty of murder; and if you go away without my leave, it will be at your peril." (cited in Ereira, 1981, p. 78)

Even when constables did intervene on behalf of the elite in public disturbances and riots, they were often not effective at preventing them. Constables who were perceived to be acting against the interests of labor could be brutally attacked and killed by the mobs.

As a result, the loss of property became increasingly unacceptable to the ruling elite who could not gain control of the poor, criminal, and working classes through the watchman or thief-taking systems of policing. Moreover, "[a]s riots became increasingly frequent and formidable, . . . constables, night watchmen, and city marshals were useless" (Reith, 1952, p. 46).

In an effort to gain control of the riots, the government often turned to military force, which also proved ineffective at preventing damage. The military could not prevent the riots but simply reacted to them after the damage was done through "volley-firing or sabre charges" (Reith, 1952, p. 46). Such violence against the rioters had the potential to produce more violence and destruction of property—especially as directed at the ruling elite and its system of justice. Taylor (1997, p. 18) notes:

> In June of 1780 much of central London was in the hands of rioting crowds, who inflicted considerable damage on property, including *symbolic attacks on prisons, Banks of England and the houses of prominent figures, including magistrates and judges.* (emphasis added)

The propertied and ruling elite realized that system of policing needed to change.

POLICING AND VIOLENCE IN MODERN ENGLAND

In early 19th-century England, public order was a serious issue for elites: "Working-class mobs that destroyed property in town and country, as much as working-class radicals who advocated the end of a property-based social and political order, had to be kept in control" (Taylor, 1997, p. 39). As a result, two important changes in policing occurred in the late 18th and early 19th centuries. First, the police were centralized. The new police would be under the control of two police commissioners who were appointed by the Home Secretary. Centralization of the police diminished the power of the old locally appointed constables and increased governmental control over police. Many scholars note "centralization [of the police in 19th-century England] was consistent with wider sociopolitical trends that streamlined production, increased efficiency, and reduced costs" (Lynch & Groves, 1989, p. 84). Second, the police became proactive rather than reactive. As early as 1748, Henry Fielding, who was appointed Magistrate of Westminster and was credited with forming one of the first modern police forces (the Bow Street Runners), argued that police should *prevent* crime (Hirschel & Wakefield, 1995). As Michalowski (1985, p. 173) observes, "the creation of a preventive police force tended to shift the responsibility for crime away from the society and onto the newly created professional police." Thus, crime was no longer the result of oppressive social conditions created by new forms of production, but the result of ineffective policing systems or ineffective police that failed to control the "dangerous classes." It is interesting to note that even in today's society, we often view high crime rates as the fault of police—or give police the credit when crime rates are low. Both the centralization and proactive nature of the police are tied to capitalist forms of production and have implications for the type and target of policing violence that develop.

In 1829 Robert Peel, the Home Secretary, established the first large-scale police force in London through the Metropolitan Police Act. The act created a uniformed, organized, paid, and civil police force that consisted of approximately 800 men. Unlike the constables in the old watch system, the new police were centralized, organized along military lines, and under control of the civil government. To prevent crime, the new constables (named after the old constables of the watch system to maintain their legitimacy and put citizens' fears of a centralized police force at bay; see Taylor, 1997) would be deployed by time and place by a chief constable situated in centrally located headquarters.

One of the biggest obstacles facing the upper classes was to ensure that the new police were well disciplined and loyal to them. This would prove to be difficult task since most of the police hired during this time were members of the working classes who joined the police force for lack of better economic prospects (Miller, 1999, p. 25). The early London police, for example, stressed that the officers should be detached from the citizens they patrolled. Police were carefully screened to ensure that they were willing and able to give up their class ties. Therefore, police commissioners refused to hire men from the most oppressed occupations. Agricultural laborers, for example, had some of the lowest wages at the time and were also least likely to be hired as police officers (Miller, 1999). Once hired, the police were closely monitored and regulated to ensure strict discipline and loyalty:

> The ordinary constable was made very aware of his position both within the force and within society as a whole. He was expected to exercise self-discipline and follow codes of behavior, on and off-duty, that were not part of normal working-class culture. . . . Attendance at fairs or race meetings was also forbidden. Insofar as he appeared in the public house or at the racecourse he did so as a policeman, responsible for the enforcement of a code of behavior that was not readily accepted by many members of the working class. Debt was to be avoided, wives were to be maintained, and religion was to be properly observed. Uniforms were often required at all times. He was to be the embodiment of the social discipline that many of his masters wished to see imposed throughout society. (Taylor, 1997, p. 54)

Of the 3,400 men who joined the Metropolitan Police between 1829 and 1930, fewer than 1,000 remained 4 years later (Taylor, 1997). Many police were dismissed for drinking, sexual misconduct, and poor dress. Others were dismissed for more serious incidents including violence against superior officers (Taylor, 1997). Despite these initial setbacks, a large number of police were eventually employed across England—approximately 20,000 in 1860 and 55,000 in 1911 (Martin & Wilson, 1969).

The elite's problems were further compounded by popular responses to the new police. The new police were initially referred to as "Peel's bloody gang" by the working class (Miller, 1999, p. 13). Antipolice violence was pervasive in both urban and rural areas. Police were beaten, branded with irons, and killed (Miller, 1999; Taylor, 1997). The working class had an extreme dislike for the new police. It was not uncommon for police to be driven out of working-class communities and towns by groups of angry and violent citizens. Oftentimes such events led to immense and violent clashes between the police and citizens. Local military forces often sided with the people in these clashes, and national armed forces had to be called in to restore order. However, it is clear that the new police had a distinct advantage over the military that used lethal force—they could better control crowds through some restraint on the use of force. Prior to 1863, bobbies were instructed to conceal their batons in "tail pockets" to demonstrate to the public that they had moral authority (Miller, 1999, p. 48). It is even reported that the early police won the support of some "moderate radicals like Francis Place, who shared their concern for peaceful protests" (Miller, 1999, p. 14).

Another tactic used to separate the police from their working-class roots was to provide good pay and desirable perks. Some police were given subsidized housing (e.g., they lived in strategically located station houses), provided with free water and gas, and given uniforms to wear on and off duty. Police wages were considerably higher than wages paid by industry or agriculture (Steedman, 1984). It is clear that by the start of the 20th century, the police "had been transformed into a well disciplined body centered on a clear and growing core of career men, who had a clear view of themselves as a quasi-professional group with a distinct role and responsibility in society" (Taylor, 1997).

Little is known about the extent of police violence against citizens in England. It is clear, however, that it existed:

> Complaints about officiousness, brutality and arbitrariness can be found in most parts of the country, at one time or another. Not all were founded but others were. The fact that men in one force had to be instructed "not to use sticks to beat mobs with nor to use shortened or leaded staves (with nails or lead added), life preservers or other weapons" is indicative of the problems that could occur. (Taylor, 1997, p. 95)

Police violence against citizens, though, tended not to result in death. This is probably because early English police did not carry weapons (Miller, 1999). In colonial America, however, the story was much different.

POLICING AND VIOLENCE IN COLONIAL AMERICA

American colonists brought their ideas about policing with them from England. Early colonists policed themselves through the "brotherly-watch," which simply meant that communities were responsible for monitoring the behavior of their residents and reporting any "sexual promiscuity, drunkenness, idleness, heretical religious views, or failure to attend church" (Walker, 1998, p. 18). According to Walker (1998), high levels of public surveillance made the need for police patrols unnecessary. By the 17th century, however, many colonies had established a civil law enforcement system that replicated the systems in place in England. The night watch and constable system was established in many towns (Vila & Morris, 1999). Just as in England, early American constables were unpaid and elected. Constables were expected to maintain order and oversee the night watch.

The position of American constable in the 18th century was not well respected. Even as early as 1653, men were refusing to serve as constables even though there was a stiff monetary penalty for doing so. As Vila and Morris (1999, p. 11) point out, this had implications for the type of policing citizens in early American society could expect: "The job [of constable] was often taken by men of dubious integrity—those who took bribes, assaulted citizens, used the office to advance their personal interests, and committed numerous other crimes." Riots to lower food prices and oppose British control were common. Constables often became the target of angry mobs that perceived the early police as a symbol of exploitation and oppression. Also, it "was fairly common for a constable to be assaulted when he tried to make an arrest" (Vila & Morris, 1999, p. 10).

In rural areas the chief law-enforcement officer was the sheriff who was appointed and paid for each arrest—as were the thief-takers in England during that time. In addition, formal systems of policing were established to control black slaves who were increasingly being viewed as a threat to white society. Slavery was the dominant mode of production in early colonial America. Slaves were primarily forced to work in agriculture for the "largest 2–3 percent of the planters [who] ruled the legislatures of each of the Southern states" (Center for Research on Criminal Justice [CRCJ], 1975, p. 20). The first African slaves were shipped to America in 1619 (Clarke, 1998, p. 17). By 1780 the slave population was roughly 562,000; in 1820 it was 1,771,656. Slaves accounted for approximately 50% of the population in states such as South Carolina, Georgia, Florida, Alabama, Mississippi, and Louisiana. The large number of slaves caused many white plantation owners to fear a slave uprising. Indeed, slave revolts were not infrequent. Between the years of 1619 and 1865, 100 slave insurrections were documented—about 1 every 3 years (Clarke, 1998, p. 48; see also Berry, 1994). Nat Turner carried out one of the most feared slave rebellions of the time. In August 1831 Nat Turner instigated a revolt that grew to approximately 70 slaves. This small army killed nearly 60 whites. In an effort to stop the slave insurrection, nearly 3,000 state militia troops were sent to defeat Turner and his men. Turner was eventually captured and the slave revolt was put down. In the end more than 100 slaves were executed for their connection to the uprising. Turner himself was executed on November 11, 1831 (Berry, 1994).

In America, slave patrols made up the first form of modern policing:

> The plantation slave patrols, often consisting of three armed men on horseback covering a beat of 15 square miles, were charged with maintaining discipline, catching runaway slaves and preventing slave insurrection. In pursuing this duty, they routinely invaded slave quarters and whipped and terrorized Blacks caught without passes after curfew. (CRCJ, 1975, p. 20)

According to Clarke (1998), sheriffs' committal notices during the time indicate that police violence against blacks was not only frequent but also severe. As the threat of insurrection increased, so did the brutality of the police, as Clarke (1998, p. 51) observed: "So great was the perceived threat, that these [slave] patrollers were invested with the authority to apprehend, try, and punish any suspect as they saw fit."

POLICING AND VIOLENCE IN EARLY INDUSTRIAL AMERICA

After America gained independence from British rule, citizens were still not in favor of a formal police force. The forms of policing in America mirrored those of England between independence and the Civil War, when many state constitutions limited the size of police watches. After the Civil War, however, the "American dream," combined with political repression in Ireland and Germany, brought a large number of Irish and German immigrants to America. This large-scale immigration in the East and Northeast provided the emerging manufacturing elite with a cheap source of labor needed to run their factories and machines. Company towns grew rapidly across the United States. Under this early industrial economy, mercenary policing now "could provide a basis for establishing state order" (Spitzer, 1981, p. 323).

By all accounts, early American factory workers faced a horrendous existence. As Platt observes:

> Manufacturers took the classic laissez-faire position that workers were commodities to be purchased for the cheapest price the market offered. . . . Wages were depressed to the point that entire families had to work twelve to sixteen hour days to support themselves at a minimum level: dilapidated housing and three starchy meals a day. (CRCJ, 1975, p. 23)

In order to fight these oppressive working conditions, labor organized. By the 1890s "local working classes [were] important political forces to reckon with" (Harring, 1983, p. 25). These labor struggles did not, however, go unchallenged. The manufacturing elite engaged in a wide range of tactics aimed at "depressing the cost of labor, including union busting, increasing the supply of labor through immigration, mobilizing different segments of the work-force against each other, and lowering the skill levels required of workers" (CRCJ, 1975, p. 23). Industry also used the mercenary system of policing (i.e., private police) to control the working class. According to Spitzer (1981, p. 323):

> Under the pressure of working-class militancy in the last quarter of the nineteenth century and the unreliable and sometimes hostile reactions of local middle classes and law enforcement officials, industrialists began to look outside the local community to obtain more effective repressive controls.

Private police were paid for their policing services just as the English thief-takers. The Pinkerton police, founded by Allan Pinkerton in the early 1850s, were the most notorious private police. The Pinkerton police supplemented public police in cities such as Chicago, helped spy on the South during the Civil War, and specialized in strikebreaking. According to Weiss (1978), the Pinkertons helped suppress nearly 77 strikes by 1892.

Private police were often extremely violent (see Yellen, 1969). For instance, in response to a 22% wage cut by Carnegie Steel, workers in Homestead, Pennsylvania, decided to strike in July 1892 (Rellin, 1996). The strikers surrounded the Homestead Steel Mill. Henry Frick, hired by Andrew Carnegie to deal with the workers and their union, engaged the Pinkerton police to ensure order and protect the property at the steel mill. On July 6, 1892, 300 Pinkerton police were loaded on two steam barges that sailed up the Monongahela River toward the Homestead Steel Mill. Striking workers and their families, armed with guns, knives, and sticks, tried to prevent the Pinkertons from landing at the mill, and a violent clash between the two groups ensued. In the end, nine workers and seven Pinkerton police were killed. The local sheriff was blamed for the tragedy because he had failed to control the striking workers to the point that the Pinkerton police's services were required. Eventually the state militia was called in to put an end to the strike.

In another violent clash, the Baldwin Felts Detective Agency assisted the Colorado militia in suppressing a coal miner strike in Ludlow (Papanikolas, 1982). The militia and detective agency carefully planned the attack against the striking coal workers and their families who were residing in tents pitched near the mine. The Death Special—a car-mounted machine gun that the Baldwin police owned—was fired at the campground around 10 a.m. on April 20, 1914, killing 20 men, women, and children.

Local militia (later the National Guard) was also used to break strikes. The militia resorted to violence against the working class. Perhaps the most famous strikes were the result of the Great Railroad Uprising of 1877 (see Yellen, 1969). These strikes were part of a massive revolt by the nation's railroad workers who were being forced to take wage cuts of 10 to 20%. The uprising was crushed only with great bloodshed that left more than 100 workers dead and several hundred wounded. The most brutal police violence during the Great Railroad Uprising occurred in the Pittsburgh strike. At first the city attempted to mobilize the local militia to suppress the strike. That failed largely because many in the local militia and in the local government were sympathetic to the strikers (Walker, 1998, p. 66). Thus, the Philadelphia militia was called in at the request of the Pennsylvania Railroad. In one confrontation with thousands of Pittsburgh citizens, the militia opened fire, killing 20 people. Over the next few days, more railroad workers were killed. By the time the strike was crushed, federal troops were occupying Pittsburgh, and between 26 and 40 engineers, conductors, shop men, trackmen, and clerks were killed, while hundreds of other workers and citizens were injured.

State police departments such as the Texas Rangers were also established early in the 19th century. The Rangers were primarily created in response to the perceived threat by Mexicans and Native Americans. These early Texas Rangers were extremely violent. Historian Walter Prescott Webb described the main duty of the early Texas Ranger as ensuring that "the Indian warrior, Mexican bandit, and American desperado [were apprehended] and delivered safely within the jail door or the cemetery gate. It is recorded that he has sent many to both places" (cited in CRCJ, 1975, p. 26).

In the South, the slave patrols were replaced with new forms of public policing that were primarily established to ensure that Southern plantation owners could "recover the free labor provided by slaves prior to the Civil War" (Lynch & Groves, 1989, p. 89). Sheriffs were often paid for each arrest. During the post–Civil War era, the Black Codes placed severe restrictions on land ownership. In addition, many codes required that blacks prove they were employed. Those who couldn't were arrested and then sentenced to hard labor on plantations owned by the Southern elite. Blacks lucky enough to find employment on farms as laborers or sharecroppers often discovered that they were in debt to white landowners. When blacks did not fulfill work contracts, they were arrested (under the Black Codes) and then sentenced to hard labor (Zinn, 1980). Violence in the South by the police against blacks also increased greatly after the Civil War. It was not uncommon for police to be members of the Ku Klux Klan and participate in the lynching, beating, and burning of blacks (CRCJ, 1975; Harding, 1981).

It is clear that early American police came out in force to violently repress strikes, maintain order among the working class, ensure racial oppression, and control threatening populations. Eventually, however, the volunteer watch, fee-for-service, and militia policing systems gave way to organized salaried police forces.

POLICING AND VIOLENCE IN THE PUBLIC POLICING ERA

The fear of civil disorder precipitated the emergence of professional police (Lane, 1971; Michalowski, 1985; Silver, 1967). Unlike the private police, the professional police would be responsible for maintaining public order and controlling the dangerous classes.

According to Spitzer (1981), however, several social conditions needed to be met before the public police could become a reality. First, the centralization of police functions had to be legitimated in the eyes of the masses. In relation to the private police, the public police were not as likely to be viewed as puppets of the manufacturing elite. Moreover, popular views of private property needed to be altered. Before the emergence of the public police, theft and property destruction were considered a matter of private concern. For example, early English opponents of publicly salaried police argued that the public should not be required to pay the cost of apprehending a thief or vandal because theft and vandalism were private matters. To legitimate the idea of public police, reformers argued that property crime must be taken seriously because it threatened the general welfare.

Second, a sufficient fiscal base was needed to provide the tax base necessary to support public police (Spitzer, 1981). This tax base obviously took time to develop as capitalism began to develop. Third, the interests of individual capitalists had to give way to generalized capital interests. Early industrialists could expect to adequately train and maintain order among a locally proximate and dependent labor force (e.g., in a company town). As company towns and geographic boundaries began to disappear, however, companies could not hope to bear the cost of control over the general workforce, which needed to be healthy, trained, disciplined, and obedient. Thus, there was a collective interest in socializing the costs of maintaining human capital through various social services such as the police.

New York created the first organized and trained police force in 1845; Chicago followed in 1851, New Orleans and Cincinnati in 1852, Philadelphia in 1855, Newark and Baltimore in 1857, and Detroit in 1865 (Lynch & Groves, 1989). The ruling class appointed manufacturers and business leaders to be police commissioners and superintendents. Most early police work was general in nature and dealt with issues of general order. Police not only patrolled the city but also performed many other social welfare duties such as cleaning the streets, inspecting boilers, feeding the poor, providing shelter for the homeless, and operating emergency ambulances. When police did patrol, they often patrolled the "business districts and adjacent areas of vice and disorder but ignored most of the residential districts" (Walker, 1998; see also Schneider, 1980).

Tremendous changes in policing occurred between 1845 and 1915. For instance, police uniforms were created; more training and experience were provided; technological advancements were employed; and police forces were enlarged, organized, and bureaucratized. Just as in the early English system, the police were divorced from their class backgrounds. According to Harring (1981, p. 302), this was accomplished through four measures aimed at ensuring the "loyality of rank-and-file officers to the goals of police administrators rather than to the working class." First, police were drilled in military fashion with force instilled in "esprit de corps." Such training made the defection of an individual officer difficult. In the Pullman strike, for instance, a number of officers were suspended from the force for being sympathetic with striking workers (Harring, 1981, p. 304). In addition, officers who did not follow orders were liable to be dismissed. Second, police were provided with secure work at relatively high pay. This tactic created a class distinction between the police and the people they patrolled. Police salaries at the time were nearly double the salaries of unskilled or semiskilled laborers. The patrol officer could often move out of working-class neighborhoods into middle-class areas (Watts,

1973). Third, the use of idealized law as a force was used to properly socialize patrol officers. Harring (1981, p. 301) uses the following example to support this point:

> A brutal beating of a crowd of strikers against a Chicago street railroad company was preceded by a lofty statement about the necessity of "value free" law and order from Captain Bonfield: "If the railway company wants to run its cars it is entitled to protection and should have it. The cars shall be run if the company desires it, and people who do not wish to get hurt had better keep out of the way." The next day the Superintendent of the Police Doyle addressed the men from the steps of the police station, "Whatever your private views or mine may be, property must be defended, the law just be upheld and you are its deffenders."

Fourth, ethnic divisions unique to the United States were exploited. Early American police were likely to be members of ethnic groups that were American born, whereas the groups they controlled were likely to be recent immigrants (CRCJ, 1975).

Early police were not popular among many city residents and were often the target of violent attacks: "Gangs of young men found it great sport to taunt police officers, throw rocks at them, or worse. Drunks fought back when arrested" (Walker, 1998, p. 62). Fear of violence was so great among early New York City police that they refused to wear their copper stars for fear that they would be identified and assaulted.

Walker (1998, p. 67) notes that police were also violent and brutal. Police reporter Lincoln Steffens reported "Many a morning when I had nothing else to do I stood and saw the police bring in and kick the bandaged, bloody prisoners, not only strikers and foreigners, but thieves too, and others of the miserable friendless, troublesome poor" (cited in Walker, 1998, p. 62). One of the more famous tales of police brutality among early New York police concerns the story of Alexander "Clubber" Williams:

> Williams, on his first day on the job, picked a fight with the two toughest thugs in the neighborhood, clubbed them unconscious, and pitched them through a plate glass window of a saloon. . . . Even as an administrator, Williams continued to prowl the streets, making free with his club. He was brought up on charges before the Board of Commissioners on 358 occasions and fined 224 times, but he was never dismissed. (Reppetto, 1978, p. 49)

One former police officer employed in the New York Police Department during the start of the 20th century observed:

> For 3 years, there has been through the courts and the streets a dreary procession of citizens with broken heads and bruised bodies against a few of whom was violence needed to effect an arrest. Many of them had done nothing to deserve an arrest. In a majority of such cases, no complaint was made. If the victim complains, his charge is generally dismissed. The police are practically above the law." (Reiss, 1970, p. 274)

Police also increased their efforts at controlling strikes. The police were known for breaking up labor business meetings through their "aggressive use of the baton." One of the major technological advancements of the time was the patrol wagon and signal system (Harring, 1981). The patrol wagon was essential to controlling strikes.

> Whereas earlier methods might require hours to round up enough police officers to march in force to the scene of a strike or other demonstration, the patrol wagon system could move 10

to 20 officers to the scene in five minutes, double or triple that number in 10 to 15 minutes . . . city after city cited the system's reputation for crowd control. (Harring, 1983, p. 53)

The patrol wagon could also be used as a weapon and driven through crowds in order to disperse them. Special police were trained in strike and crowd control. The major weapon of police was typically the "wholesale clubbing of strikers."

Police were also willing to use firearms, "not just as a reaction to forces beyond their control, but as part of escalating class violence that they helped to foster" (Harring, 1983, p. 127). Most police began carrying guns without official authorization. In 1858 a New York City police officer used a personal weapon to shoot a fleeing felon. The case against the officer was presented to a grand jury, which did not indict the officer. After that police officers in New York began to arm themselves. A similar incident in Boston prompted police in that department to carry weapons (Walker, 1998).

POLICING AND VIOLENCE IN THE REFORM ERA

A myriad of diverse reform movements occurred during the first three decades of the 20th century. Some movements were the result of working-class struggles, while businesses and professionals brought other movements about. Whereas the former movements were often concerned with changing the economic and political system, the latter were aimed at stabilizing it. Along with various reforms came calls to reform the police. By 1900 the police could be considered semiautonomous from the capitalist class (Greenberg, 1976; Spitzer, 1981). Some autonomy from the capitalist class was essential if police were to be viewed as legitimate agents of social control. Progressives (i.e., those interested in political, educational, and other types of reform) in business, government, and the universities, however, were strongly critical of the police. Departments were often corrupt and ineffective—they could not provide the services needed by the community. According to advocates for reform, the police aggravated conflict through "corruption, brutality and general incompetence" (CRCJ, 1975, p. 34). In response to the calls for reform, President Herbert Hoover established the National Commission on Law Observance and Enforcement (i.e., the Wickersham Commission). Ernest Jerome Hopkins commented on the Wickersham Report in his popular 1931 book entitled *Our Lawless Police: A Study of Unlawful Enforcement of Law:*

> Citizens must suffer the effects of whatever hatred and antagonism against our public institutions may be bred by the departures of our police from constitutional justice and law. . . .
> Street brutality by policemen, loose kidnapping or false arrest, unlawful imprisonment and incommunicado imprisonment in police jails, the use of unfair pressure to get evidence and confessions, the perjury indulged in by policemen to gain convictions—these practices have greatly operated to turn the average man against his police and deprive them of his support in turn. Outrageous incidents are published, and the citizen wonders: "what if I were next?" (p. 3)

The main objective of early Progressive police reformers such as Hopkins, O.W. Wilson, and August Vollmer was to "transform police into an agency that would help to secure the loyalty of the potentially delinquent classes at the same time that it efficiently contained their disruptive behavior" (CRCJ, 1975, p. 34). Above all, police reform meant "stabilizing the existing political and economic structure" through the development of police professionalism that severed police from any community influence and through the promotion of new technologies aimed at making social control more effective (see CRCJ, 1975).

Reformers believed that the establishment of police professionalism would increase the efficiency and legitimacy of the police. One product of the reform era was better organizational design for the police. In Philadelphia, for example, the newly appointed public safety director claimed that in 1913 the police reforms in his city produced a department that was more military in appearance and higher in efficiency than any other department of the time (Walker, 1998, p. 133). Police departments began to assert greater control over patrol officers with technologies such as police radios, cars, and telephones. Police training was enhanced and minimum standards were set.

New police policies such as the Golden Rule (used by the police chief Fred Kohler in Cleveland in 1905 among others) provided for the diversion of those arrested for minor violations and also released minors to the custody of their parents rather than placing them in jail. According to Walker (1998, p. 134), the Golden Rule had a dramatic impact on arrests, which fell from 30,418 in 1907 to 10,085 in 1908. Policies on police violence were also adopted. One Toledo mayor, Samuel Jones, took away police officers' billy clubs. The International Association of Chiefs of Police, which consisted of police chiefs of most major metropolitan police agencies, unanimously voted in favor of a resolution condemning the use of police torture and beatings to obtain confessions prior to trial (Vila & Morris, 1999). During the reform era, the "police were transformed into both a defender of capital and protector of individual rights" (Lynch & Groves, 1989, p. 90). Little changed in many of the black communities, however, as Williams and Murphy (1999, p. 42) explain:

> As dramatic as this change must have appeared to the white middle-class inhabitants of America's major cities, the transition to the professional era from the political era was barely noticeable to blacks and other minorities. Relying on law rather than politics as the source of police authority had many desirable aspects for those provided full protection by the law. Once again, however, for those who lacked both political power and equal protection under the law, such a transformation could have little significance.

Although there is little question that police violence against citizens decreased as a result of the reform movement and this decrease aided in legitimizing the public police, violence during the reform era did not disappear. For instance, some of the most brutal and violent incidents occurred during this time. In the 1915 Chicago garment workers' strike, large numbers of women were clubbed by the police. In some instances police violence against strikers was so brutal that strikers actually requested protection from the police by the National Guard. For instance, in 1913 in Akron, Ohio, 20,000 workers walked out of the rubber plants on strike:

> The peaceful progress of the strike ended suddenly on March 7. Five hundred stikers were listening to speeches by Wobblies and socialists and had formed a human chain in front of the Goodrich plant when Sheriff Fergusson asked the pickets to move across the street. As the crowd began to move it was charged by Akron police officers, reinforced by 30 special deputies. The battle lasted 30 minutes. Sixty strikers and one police officer were injured. The only person arrested was an IWW organizer, who was charged with inciting a riot. . . . The

> indiscriminate nature of the police clubbing can be seen in the fact that Sheriff Fergusson
> was accidentally struck in the face by a special deputy. Vigilantes patrolled the streets in pri-
> vate cars, wore Akron police department badges, and carried clubs. At this point the strikers
> asked Governor Cox for National Guard troops to protect them from the city police and their
> vigilante allies. (Harring, 1983, p. 130)

The end of World War I brought intensified conflict and police violence in the United States. Race riots, strikes, and political dissent were pervasive. In 1919 more than 20 race riots occurred (Deakin, 1988, p. 110). The Chicago Riot, which resulted in the death of 23 blacks and 15 whites, occurred between July 27 and August 2. Witness reports suggest the riot started when a police officer refused to arrest a white murder suspect in the killing of a black youth even though several individuals reported to the police that they had observed the murder. In the South, police routinely engaged in the lynching of blacks (Mann, 1993). In the Southwest, police were reportedly involved in the deaths of numer-ous Mexican workers (Escobar, 1999). In the 1930s the Great Depression intensified class conflict and led to many instances of violent oppression by police on the working class. For instance, in 1934 San Francisco and Oakland police killed two workers and injured hundreds more. In 1937 in Chicago, the police opened fire on a peaceful labor demonstra-tion without warning, killing 10 workers.

The federal government created new police forces during the professional era of policing. The Bureau of Investigation was created in 1908 by President Theodore Roosevelt to aid in the enforcement of the Sherman Antitrust Act. In 1935 it was renamed the Federal Bureau of Investigation (FBI). After its creation, the FBI was mostly con-cerned with espionage and sedition perpetrated by labor unions (Belknap, 1977). As Lynch and Groves (1989, p. 92) note, "in a relatively short period, the Bureau's anti-labor and anti-communist movements became synonymous."

As progressive labor leaders were removed from power and other state institutional control apparatuses were put in place, striking workers became less of a threat to the eco-nomic order. According to Platt (CRCJ, 1975, p. 42), "the central concern of the police was accordingly shifted to non-union, working class Blacks and other Third World people who were less integrated into trade unions."

POLICING AND VIOLENCE DURING THE 1960S

By the start of the 1960s the United States was undergoing massive political protests that threatened the economic order. The Civil Rights Movement was concerned with equal rights—including an end to police brutality. Extensive media coverage of civil rights marches, war protests, and urban uprisings, however, created public fear. Many people be-lieved that society was coming apart. Beginning in 1964, a series of race riots occurred in nearly every large city. Police actions often precipitated the riots (see Walker, 1998, p. 21). For example, in 1965 a Los Angeles police officer arrested a young drunken driver in Watts and scuffled with the boy's mother who appeared at the scene. A crowd of onlook-ers became angry over the events that unfolded. The officer reacted by drawing a firearm and calling for backup. News of the incident spread and a massive 6-day riot ensued. In the end nearly 14,000 troops assisted approximately 1,500 Los Angeles Police Depart-ment (LAPD) officers who were fighting against 50,000 blacks. When the riot ended 34 people had been killed, approximately 900 were injured, and 4,000 were arrested. The 1964 New York riot began when a black teen was shot and killed by an off-duty white officer; the 1967 Detroit riot began when the police raided a bar in the black community.

In many instances the police are reported to have reacted to protesters and rioters with extreme brutality. In 1967 three black Detroit rioters were captured and "systematically executed by the police in the Algiers Motel" (CRCJ, 1975, p. 44). In response to these forms of police brutality, some blacks formed militant groups to protect themselves from the police and help their communities. Citizens also demanded oversight of the police through the use of citizens' review boards. Police shootings were also an important issue in the Civil Rights Movement. The fleeing-felon rule gave police the right to shoot any suspected fleeing felon even when the community was not threatened and the officer's life was not in danger. According to the Center for Research on Criminal Justice (1975, p. 44), nearly 3,000 police-caused homicides occurred between 1961 and 1970. Most people killed by police were African American. In 1970 the ratio of blacks to whites killed by police was 7 to 2 (Sherman & Cohn, 1986). This trend continued well into the mid-seventies when police-caused homicides reached an all-time high of 559 (Geller & Scott, 1992).

As a result of the radical protests in the 1960s, "law and order" became an integral part of the political agenda. Responding to widespread public fear in the wake of civil unrest, President Lyndon Johnson created the Kerner Commission to report on the cause of urban disorders. The Kerner Commission held formal hearings, heard testimony from hundreds of witnesses, and conducted more than 1,200 interviews in 23 cities. The main conclusion of the commission was that "deep hostility between police and ghetto communities is the primary cause of the disorders surveyed by the commission" (National Advisory Commission on Civil Disorders, 1968). The commission also found that the most serious public disturbances occurred in cities that had the "best organized, best trained, and most professional police in the country." The commission made several recommendations for change. The most important recommendation was the reduction of economic and racial inequality through improvements in education, housing, and occupational opportunities for blacks. Sadly, "the only commission recommendation that was vigorously pursued centered on increasing the size and fire-power of the police" (Lynch & Groves, 1989, p. 84). Special Weapons and Tactics (SWAT) units were developing in most major cities. The push for law and order led to a renewed interest in creating police forces that were well-organized strike forces equipped with military-style weapons and military command. Police began using more powerful firearms such as the riot shotgun and the .357 magnum. Some departments also began using dumdum bullets, which expand to create bigger wounds when entering the body. Corporations also aided police in developing new weapons to use in crowd control—especially against civil rights and war protesters. Rubber bullets, water cannons, and chemical gases are among the less-than-lethal weapons that were widely incorporated into the police arsenal to combat protesters.

POLICING AND VIOLENCE TODAY

The military model of the 1960s came under harsh criticism. Massive spending on more effective weapons did not reduce crime but did alienate and anger citizens. The end result was a call for police to develop closer ties to the communities that they policed. Starting in the 1970s, many departments began to develop real community relations programs. Research on policing indicated that the crime-fighting approach adopted under the military-industrial model of policing did little to reduce crime. Police departments began communicating with the community by sending representatives to speak at schools and community centers. Police departments around the country also increased training efforts. Police hiring practices changed and the police actively began recruiting college graduates. Many departments began to rewrite their standard operating procedures. One of the most notable changes in the manuals was to restrict police use of deadly force to "defense of life" situations only. By the time the Supreme Court settled the landmark case of *Tennessee v. Garner* in 1985, most departments had already restricted the use of deadly force. In that case the Court ruled that the police were allowed to use deadly force in apprehending a fleeing felon only when their life or the life of a citizen was in danger. The results of these combined efforts appear to have reduced police violence. Police shootings have steadily declined over time. The ratio of blacks to whites killed by the police had decreased to approximately 2.8 to 1 in 1978 (Sherman & Cohn, 1986).

Police violence, however, is still pervasive. In a detailed study of police violence in the United States, Paul Chevigny found that police violence occurs frequently in cities such as Los Angeles and New York. According to Chevigny (1995, p. 46), "Los Angeles city police shoot more people in proportion to the size of the force, than any other major U.S. police department." Many of these shootings are not justified. For instance, the *Los Angeles Daily News* looked at 202 on-duty shootings by officers between 1985 and 1990 and found that nearly one fourth were questionable because the victim was unarmed and eyewitnesses discounted the officers' accounts of the situation (Chevigny, 1995, p. 46).

As long as some members of society are marginalized, exploited, and oppressed, police violence will remain an inevitable part of policing. Throughout recent U.S. history, police violence has tended to be directed against individuals who are poor, unemployed, and nonwhite. By all indications, racial and class inequality is intensifying. Today more than 30 million Americans live below the Census-defined poverty level (U.S. Bureau of the Census, 1996). In addition, the gap between the rich and poor is widening. The U.S. Bureau of the Census (1998) indicates that income inequality is greater today than at any other point in history. Chandler (1998) found that despite claims of recent economic gains by most Americans, the rich have gotten richer and the poor have gotten poorer. Between 1977 and 1994 the average after-tax income of the wealthiest 1% of American families increased by 72%, even after adjusting for inflation, while the average income of the poorest 20% of American families decreased by nearly 16% (see also Wolff, 1995). Income distributions in the United States are highly skewed by race. In 1997 the median white family income was nearly twice the median income of nonwhite families. Nearly one third of all nonwhite households have no positive wealth (Wolff, 1995).

Racial segregation is also intensifying in many major metropolitan areas (Massey & Denton, 1993). As aggressive police departments continue to adopt patrol strategies to wage a "war on crime," they often portray entire minority communities as "criminal." Police violence in these communities tends to be pervasive (Independent Commission on the LAPD, 1991). The recent killing of Amadou Diallo by officers working for the New York Police Department can be seen as the result of aggressive community policing tactics (Harring & Ray, 1999). Diallo was attempting to enter his apartment when police shot him to death. The officers who killed Diallo were working for an aggressive crime control unit in the department. They fired at Diallo 41 times, hitting him 19 of those times. According to the autopsy report, the first few bullets that struck Diallo paralyzed him, causing him to fall to the ground. At that point he was shot a dozen more times. Diallo was not the person police were looking for, nor was he armed. According to the department, the shooting was simply a "mistake" (Harring & Ray, 1999, p. 4).

As class inequality intensifies and global awareness becomes more pervasive, public police will be forced to deal with more political protests. One of the largest protests in recent U.S. history occurred in Seattle, Washington, at the 1999 global meeting of the World Trade Organization (WTO). More than 40,000 protesters flooded the streets of Seattle to protest the WTO and its position on the environment, labor, human rights, peace, and debt reduction for poor nations. The Seattle police were unable to control the crowd without violence, and several citizens have reported that the police resorted to unprovoked clubbings and the unnecessary use of chemical agents ("Seattle Protest," 1999). The Seattle mayor declared a civil emergency during the protests and the governor called in the National Guard to help police clear the streets (Burgess & Pearlstein, 1999). In the end the Seattle police chief resigned over criticism concerning the role his department played in the WTO protests.

Recent incidents of police violence have also attracted a good deal of public attention and prompted protests against the police in cities such as New York; New Brunswick, New Jersey; Oakland; Los Angeles; Miami; and Chicago. One of the most brutal cases occurred in 1997 when a Haitian man, Abner Louima, was misidentified by a New York City police officer as the person who assaulted him outside a social club. The officers at the scene arrested Louima. On the way to the station house, the officers stopped at a vacant lot and beat him. After arriving at the station, the arresting officers stripped Louima in an effort to humiliate him in front of the other officers present. Next, the officers forced Louima into a restroom where they sodomized him with the handle of a toilet plunger, causing internal injuries that resulted in bleeding from the rectum. The toilet plunger handle was then forced into Louima's mouth, knocking out several of his teeth. None of the officers who witnessed the event, or heard the victim's screams for help, intervened on Louima's behalf as they were legally required to do. Nor did any officer subsequently report or investigate Louima's injuries. The internal affairs department became involved in the case only after hearing reports of the assault in the media. A nurse at the hospital where Louima was taken heard the story of Louima's torture and called the media (Harring & Ray, 1999).

A significant resurgence in private policing is occurring as we move to a global economy, characterized by monopoly capitalism. According to most police scholars, private policing has expanded because the public police have not "been able to provide adequate or desired levels of protection in the business, industrial, or residential settings" (Gaines, Kappeler, & Vaughn, 1999, p. 446; see also Bailin & Cort, 1996). Today there are approximately three times as many private police as there are public police (Bailin & Cort, 1996; Lynch & Groves, 1989). Moreover, annual expenditures on private police exceed $52 billion, whereas expenditures on public police total about $30 billion. These new private police, however, are not the violent strikebreakers that were mobilized by giant corporations against labor in the late 1800s and early 1900s. Instead, they are "simple extension of the effort to rationalize capitalist production . . . through security screening, surveillance, fingerprint analysis, and polygraph examinations geared toward the prevention of such problems of employee theft" (Spitzer, 1981, p. 333). Violence at the hands of the new private police is usually directed at individuals who threaten or are perceived to threaten company property or profits.

Thousands of private police are also taking on traditional public police roles. Reminiscent of the thief-taker system in early England, many private police serve as bounty hunters and work for bail bondsmen to protect their "investments." As one bounty hunter claims, "we're the largest private arrest organization in the world . . . we arrested 23,000 bail skippers last year" (Booth, 1997, p. A3). Perhaps the most infamous incident of bounty hunter violence occurred when two bounty hunters wearing black ski masks and body armor broke into the wrong house in Phoenix, Arizona, and shot a young couple to death while holding their children at gunpoint (Booth, 1997).

In the new technological era of production, the private police are also becoming more enmeshed in the public domain (Spitzer, 1981). The Pinkertons of today now routinely engage in the policing of farmers' fields for agribusiness giant Monsanto Corporation to determine if farmers are replanting the company's patented "Roundup Ready" seed without properly paying for it. The investigative techniques include random DNA tests of farmers' crops. Monsanto claims that farmers, who sometimes replant seeds reproduced from the previous years, are stealing the company's product and reproducing it illegally. As of 1999, Pinkerton was in the process of investigating more than 525 cases of replanted seed theft (Weiss, 1999).

Private policing, as an industry, makes huge profits. Like public police, private police are clearly class-based institutions. Their services are purchased by companies and individuals who have the financial resources to do so. Not only do private police work for large corporations, but they also work for wealthy groups of individuals. Nearly 20,000 gated communities throughout the United States, for example, hire private police to guard them (Diamond, 1999).

IN SUM

Many police, police scholars, and members of the public view police-related violence as the outcome of bad individuals, situational factors, and/or poor police training. Such a view is ahistorical in that it ignores how police violence is shaped and influenced by larger social structures. Like Spitzer (1981), I propose that variations in police violence can be referenced to variations in the stages of capitalist development (for comparisons of police violence across countries with different political and economic systems, see Chapter 9). Specifically, in this work I have examined police violence by appropriately linking it to "historical change and institutional contradiction" (Mills, 1959, p. 2). It is only through such a broad understanding of the development of police violence that we can come to imagine a society where it does not exist.

REFERENCES

BAILIN, P., & COURT, S. (1996). Private contractual security services: The U.S. market and industry. *Business Economics, 31*(2), 57–62.

BEIRNE, P., & MESSERSCHMIDT, J. (1991). *Criminology*. San Diego, CA: Harcourt Brace Jovanovich.

BELKNAP, M. (1977). The mechanics of repression: J. Edgar Hoover, the Bureau of Investigation and the radicals, 1917–1925. *Crime and Social Justice, 7*(1), 49–58.

BELLAMY, J. (1973). *Crime and public order in England in the later Middle Ages*. London: Routledge and Kegan Paul.

BERRY, M. (1994). *Black resistance, white law: A history of constitutional racism in America*. New York: Penguin Books.

BOOTH, W. (1997, September 7). Slayings in Arizona heighten calls for controls on bounty hunters. *The Washington Post,* p. A3.

BURGESS, J., & PEARLSTEIN, S. (1999, December 1). Protests delay WTO opening in Seattle, police use tear gas, mayor declares a curfew. *The Washington Post,* p. A1.

CANTERBERY, R. (1995). *The literate economist: A brief history of economics*. New York: HarperCollins.

CENTER FOR RESEARCH ON CRIMINAL JUSTICE. (1975). *The iron fist and the velvet glove: An analysis of the U.S. police*. Berkeley, CA: The Center for Research on Criminal Justice.

CHANDLER, C. (1998, April 13). A market tide that isn't lifting everybody. *The Washington Post's National Weekly Edition,* p. 18.

CHEVIGNY, P. (1995). *Edge of the knife: Police violence in the Americas*. New York: New Press.

CLARKE, J. (1998). *The lineaments of wrath: Race, violent crime, and American culture*. New Brunswick, NJ: Transaction Publishers.

CRITCHLEY, T. (1972). *A history of police in England and Wales*. Montclair, NJ: Patterson Smith.

DEAKIN, T. (1988). *Police professionalism: The renaissance of American law enforcement*. Springfield, IL: Charles C Thomas.

DIAMOND, D. (1999, January 31/February 2). Behind closed gates. *USA Weekend,* pp. 4–5.

EREIRA, A. (1981). *The people's England*. Boston: Routledge and Kegan Paul.

ESCOBAR, E. (1999). *Race, police, and the making of a political identity: Mexican Americans and the Los Angeles Police Department, 1900–1945*. Berkeley: University of California Press.

FOSTER, J. (1974). *Class struggle and the industrial revolution: Early industrial capitalism in three English towns*. London: Weidenfeld and Nicolson.

GAINES, L., KAPPELER, V., & VAUGHN, J. (1999). *Policing in America*. Cincinnati, OH: Anderson.

GELLER, W., & SCOTT, M. (1992). *Deadly force: What we know*. Washington, DC: Police Executive Research Foundation.

GREENBERG, D. (1976). On one-dimensional Marxist criminology. *Theory and Society, 3,* 610–621.

GREENSHIELDS, M. (1994). *An economy of violence in early modern France*. University Park: Pennsylvania State University Press.

HARDING, V. (1981). *There is a river: The black struggle for freedom in America*. New York: Harcourt Brace Jovanovich.

HARRING, S. (1981). Policing a class society: The expansion of the urban police in the late nineteenth and early twentieth centuries. In D. Greenberg (Ed.), *Crime and capitalism* (pp. 292–313). Palo Alto, CA: Mayfield.

HARRING, S. (1983). *Policing a class society: The experience of American cities, 1865–1915*. New Brunswick, NJ: Rutgers University Press.

HARRING, S., & RAY, G. (1999). Policing a class society: New York City in the 1990s. *Social Justice, 26*(2), 63–73.

HIRSCHEL, D., & WAKEFIELD, W. (1995). *Criminal justice in England and the United States*. Westport, CT: Praeger.

HOPKINS, J. (1931). *Our lawless police: A study of the unlawful enforcement of the law*. New York: Viking.

HOWSON, G. (1970). *Thief-taker general: The rise and fall of Jonathan Wild*. London: Hutchinson.

HSIAO, K. (1960). *Rural China; Imperial Control in the nineteenth century.* Seattle: University of Washington Press.

INDEPENDENT COMMISSION ON THE LOS ANGELES POLICE DEPARTMENT. (1991). *Report of the Independent Commission on the Los Angeles Police Department.* Los Angeles: Author.

KLOCKARS, C. (1996). A theory of excessive force and its control. In W. Geller & H. Toch (Eds.), *Police violence: Understanding and controlling police abuse of force* (pp. 1–22). New Haven, CT: Yale University Press.

LANE, R. (1971). *Policing the city: Boston, 1822–1885.* New York: Atheneum.

LEE, W. (1901/1971). *A history of police in England.* Montclair, NJ: Patterson Smith.

LYNCH, M., & GROVES, B. (1989). *A primer in radical criminology.* Albany, NY: Harrow and Heston.

MANN, C. (1993). *Unequal justice: A question of color.* Bloomington: University of Indiana Press.

MARTIN, J., & WILSON, G. (1969). *The police: A study in manpower: The evolution of the service in England and Wales, 1829–1965.* London: Heinemann Educational.

MASSEY, D., & DENTON, N. (1993). *American apartheid: Segregation and the making of the underclass.* Cambridge, MA: Harvard University Press.

MARX, K. (1976). *Das kapital* (Vol. 1). (B. Fowkes, Trans.). New York: Vintage Books. (original work published 1867)

MICHALOWSKI, R. (1985). *Order, law, and crime.* New York: Random House.

MILLER, W. (1999). *Cops and bobbies: Police authority in New York and London 1830–1870.* Columbus: Ohio State University Press.

MILLS, C. W. (1959). *The sociological imagination.* New York: Oxford University Press.

NATIONAL ADVISORY COMMISSION ON CIVIL DISORDERS. (1968). *Report of the National Advisory Commission on Civil Disorders.* Washington, DC: U.S. Government Printing Office.

PAPANIKOLAS, H. (1982). *Buried unsung: Louis Tikas and the Ludlow massacre.* Salt Lake City: University of Utah Press.

REISS, A. (1970). Police brutality . . . answers to key questions. In M. Lipsky (Ed.), *Law and order: Police encounters* (pp. 274–275). Chicago: Aldine.

REITH, C. (1952). *The blind eye of history: A study of the origins of the present police era.* London: Faber and Faber.

RELLIN, D. (1996, November 15). The strike of the century. *Scholastic Update,* pp. 18–20.

REPPETTO, T. (1978). *The blue parade.* New York: Free Press.

SCHNEIDER, J. (1980). *Detroit and the problem of public order, 1830–1880.* Lincoln, NE: Lincoln University Press.

"Seattle Protest." (1999, December 10). *The Los Angeles Times,* p. 8.

SHERMAN, L., & COHN, E. (1986, October). *Citizens killed by big city police: 1970–1984.* Unpublished manuscript. Crime Control Institute, Washington DC.

SILVER, A. (1967). The demand for order in civil society: A review of some themes in the history of urban crime, police, and riot. In D. J. Borda (Ed.), *The police: Six sociological essays* (pp. 1–25). New York: Wiley.

SPITZER, S. (1981). The political economy of policing. In D. Greenberg (Ed.), *Crime and capitalism* (pp. 314–340). Palo Alto, CA: Mayfield.

STEEDMAN, C. (1984). *Policing the Victorian community: The formation of English provincial police forces, 1856–1880.* Boston: Routledge and Paul Kegan.

TAYLOR, D. (1997). *The new police in nineteenth-century England: Crime, conflict and control.* New York: Manchester University Press and St. Martin's Press.

TOBIAS, J. J. (1979). *Crime and police in England, 1700–1900.* New York: St. Martin's Press.

UNITED STATES BUREAU OF THE CENSUS. (1996). *Income, poverty, and valuation of non-cash benefits, 1994.* Current Population Reports, Series P-60, No. 189. Washington, DC: U.S. Government Printing Office.

UNITED STATES BUREAU OF THE CENSUS. (1998). *Money income in the United States, 1997*. Current Population Reports, Series P60-200. Washington, DC: U.S. Government Printing Office.

VILA, B., & MORRIS, C. (1999). *The role of police in American society*. Westport, CT: Greenwood Press.

WALKER, S. (1998). *Popular justice: A history of American criminal justice*. New York: Oxford University Press.

WATTS, E. (1973). The police in Atlanta, 1890–1905. *Journal of Southern History, 39,* 165–183.

WEBER, M. (1958). *From Max Weber: Essays in sociology*. (H. H. Gerth & C. Wright Mills, Trans.). New York: Oxford University Press.

WEISS, R. (1978). The emergence and transformation of private detective industrial policing in the United States, 1850–1940. *Crime and Social Justice, 9*(1), 35–48.

WEISS, R. (1999, February 3). Seeds of discord, Monsanto's gene police raise alarm on farmers' rights, rural transition. *The Washington Post,* p. A1.

WILLIAMS, H., & MURPHY, P. (1999). The evolving strategy of police: A minority view. In V. Kappeler (Ed.), *The police and society* (pp. 27–50). Prospect Heights, IL: Waveland Press.

WOLFF, E. (1995). *Top heavy: A study of increasing inequality of wealth in America*. New York: Twentieth Century Fund Press.

WORDEN, R. (1996). The causes of police brutality: Theory and evidence on police use of force. In W. Geller & H. Toch (Eds.), *Police violence: Understanding and controlling police abuse of force* (pp. 23–51). New Haven, CT: Yale University Press.

YELLEN, S. (1969). *American labor struggles*. New York: Arno.

ZINN, H. (1980). *A people's history of the United States*. New York: Harper & Row.

2

Violence by and Against the Police

Jason T. Carmichael
David Jacobs

INTRODUCTION

Early one morning, four New York police officers who were seeking a rapist fired 41 shots at an unarmed West African immigrant. Amadou Diallo, who did not understand English well, quickly died from 19 bullet wounds. The officers later testified that when he was approached and told to "Stop!" and "Show your hands!" the 5-foot-6 150-pound victim instead reached into his pocket and withdrew a dark object that looked like a gun but turned out to be a wallet. A civilian witness claimed that Diallo was standing with his back to the officers when one yelled "Gun!" and all four officers started firing. Officer Kenneth Ross testified that as he got out of his unmarked patrol car, one team member was lying on the ground. Ross said he started firing because "I thought my partner had been hit." Another officer wept on the witness stand as he recalled his shock when he realized that Diallo had a wallet rather than a gun in his hand.

The officers were members of a special unit designed to seek out and stop crime that had been formed in response to Mayor Rudolph Giuliani's stress on law and order and proactive police tactics. This elite unit had already been sharply criticized for overly aggressive conduct. In the month before the Diallo killing, Street Crime Unit officers had fired on rapper ODB during a traffic stop, thinking he had a gun, but no weapon was found.

Because Diallo was black but all four officers were white, many believed that racial bias explained this shooting. In reply, Mayor Giuliani claimed that "There is a tendency of some people in our society to blame the police in broad strokes that is just as vicious a prejudice as any other prejudice" ("New York Officers Charged," 1999). Yet the mayor's minority critics remained unconvinced. After Giuliani's successful law-and-order campaign and his emphasis on aggressive policing, police misconduct charges grew by more than 45%. Black leaders claimed that the mayor's refusal to curb the police showed he was completely indifferent to such injustices.

Following bitter denunciations of the mayor and furious demonstrations, the officers' criminal trial was moved from the Bronx to upstate New York. At the start of the trial the judge told the jury that New York State law allows police officers to use deadly force if they believe their lives are in danger. In response to these instructions and highly emotional but often contradictory testimony, the racially mixed jury of four blacks and eight whites acquitted all four officers. Although the U.S. attorney's office investigated Diallo's death, additional federal charges for civil rights violations were not filed.

The relationship between the police and the public in a racially divided democratic society such as the United States has been labeled a "balanced tension" (Bittner, 1970; McLaughlin, 1990). Walker (1992) described strains between the police and minority citizens as the most persistent problem facing the police. National media stories about alleged police abuses such as the Diallo killing are all too common. Many plausible claims have been made that justice in the United States is not color-blind in large part because the police do not act appropriately toward minorities.

Given the attention to the racial aspects of the issue of equal justice, it is not surprising that minorities and whites are sharply divided in their opinions about the police. Since the advent of polls that asked questions about such issues, blacks and Hispanics have consistently given the police lower ratings than whites (Cox, 1996; Flanagan & Vaughn, 1995; Smith, Graham, & Adams, 1991; Walker, 1992). In a 1970 Harris poll, only 20% of the African American respondents believed that local police officers enforced the law equally. Sixty-two percent believed that the police were "against African Americans," 73% believed that the local police were dishonest, and 67% believed that police officers were more concerned with injuring African Americans than with preventing criminal acts (Feagin & Hahn, 1973).

More recent polls indicate that African Americans are more likely than whites to report harassment and to know someone who has been a victim of police misconduct (Bessent & Taylor, 1991; Kappeler, Sluder, & Alpert, 1994). The persistence of claims that the police treat minorities more harshly than they treat otherwise equivalent whites suggests that we may not have completely overcome the horrific conflicts about race that were such a dominant feature of our history.

This chapter reviews the literature on violence used by the police and violence used against them. We begin by spelling out the coercive techniques that officers use to deal with resistance and then discuss the legal provisions that regulate their use of force. Next, we review the social science research on the factors that contribute to the use of both nondeadly and deadly force by the police and then present a summary of the literature on the determinants of nonlethal and lethal violence used against officers. We close by discussing what seems to us to be the best way to reduce unwarranted violence by the police.

VIOLENCE USED BY THE POLICE

Modern democratic states avoid the military and employ domestic agencies to ensure domestic order. In fact, the principal activity that separates the modern police force from other civic organizations is its legal authorization to use justifiable force (Bittner, 1990). Bittner points out that the primary distinguishing characteristic of almost all police tasks is *not* a concentration on crime (in fact, attention to crime comprises only about 30% of the average officer's time on the job). Instead, the fundamental unifying characteristic of almost all police tasks is an officer's legitimate capacity to use violence to carry out the lawful directives of public officials or to maintain civic order. Yet how this force is used remains an extremely divisive issue, particularly in a racially divided society such as the United States.

The police have a wide range of weapons at their disposal to project force and control the public. Faulkner (1999) provides an action-response use of force continuum that spells out these alternatives. In addition to the side arm, the typical officer's options include the application of physical restraints by one or more officers, pepper spray, stun guns, and the baton.

Although the clublike baton has disadvantages (its use can provoke a wrestling match), in comparison to firearms, this weapon gives an officer a far more flexible set of options. The baton can be used as a passive restraint or as a club, but the target need not be a vulnerable area. Blows with various degrees of force to places other than a head can project authority without doing significant damage and without leaving enduring marks or injuries that could be subsequently embarrassing to the officer when the victim appears in court. Because alternatives such as mace, stun guns, or the baton provide such useful substitutes for firearms, we can see why guns are so infrequently used in police work.

In fact, in "legalistic departments" (Wilson, 1971) that make the greatest efforts to follow the law, officers have strong incentives to avoid any use of their side arm. Discharges directed at a citizen, particularly if someone is wounded or killed, are subject to intense departmental scrutiny. Even if an officer who uses a firearm is vindicated by the virtually automatic internal investigation that follows, he or she almost certainly will be moved to another district. Because a close familiarity with the geography and other features of an officer's immediate working environment are absolutely critical to effective police work, officers do not welcome such transfers.

Thus, an officer's firearm is a powerful weapon that imposes costs on both the officer and the person who is shot. These considerations explain why the great majority of officers who regularly patrol the streets in the most violent areas of their city have never fired a weapon at a citizen. In fact, many experts conclude that with such a wide range of force options available to control resistance, a properly trained officer should find the discharge of a firearm unnecessary throughout a long career on the street.

The Law and the Use of Force by the Police

Given the stakes involved, the federal courts have made extensive efforts to regulate the use of force by police officers. We begin this section by discussing the law on lethal violence.

The Law on Deadly Force. In *Tennessee v. Garner* (1985) the Supreme Court laid down a definitive standard when it stipulated a "balancing test" for which the state had to "balance the nature . . . of the intrusion on the individual's Fourth Amendment interests against . . . the governmental interests alleged to justify the intrusion" (the Fourth Amendment protects individuals from unlawful search and seizure). This balancing test should take into account both the need for effective policing to ensure order and the value that the state must place on the freedom and individual liberties of its citizens (Faulkner, 1999).

According to the Supreme Court, the government can take the life of an individual only when an officer has good reason to suspect that the individual's actions present immediate danger to others in close proximity. Immediate danger is defined as the possession of a weapon with an intent to use it. The Court ruled that the possession of the weapon alone is not sufficient to warrant lethal violence (*York v. City of San Pablo,* 1985). This influential decision effectively prohibited the long-standing use of deadly force to apprehend non-dangerous fleeing felony suspects.

It is significant that the *Garner* decision was based on rights found in the Fourth Amendment. A claim of excessive force brought under the Fourth Amendment requires the plaintiff to show that the force in question was unreasonable. A claim under the Eighth Amendment instead would demand proof that the use of force in question inflicted cruel and unusual punishment. If such a claim had been upheld under the provisions of the Fourteenth Amendment, plaintiffs would be required to show that the force in question violated their right to judicial proceedings designed to safeguard their legal rights. To make this legal distinction about due process vivid, Sherman (1980a) calls the unwarranted use of deadly force by police officers "executions without trial."

In examining the effects of *Garner,* Culliver and Sigler (1995) found that after this decision, the number of reported firearm discharges by police officers in Tennessee decreased dramatically. Most of this reduction took place in smaller jurisdictions because many urban departments already had implemented more stringent firearm policies prior to *Garner.* Sparger and Giacopassi (1992) also examined the influence of *Garner* in Tennessee and found that "both the overall shooting rate and the apparently discriminatory application of lethal force were reduced greatly as a result of the post-*Garner* deadly force policy" (p. 224). At the national level, Tennenbaum (1994, p. 257) reported that the *Garner* decision resulted in approximately 60 fewer killings per year by police officers, or a reduction of more than 16%. While the *Garner* decision clarified the use of deadly force, the legal guidelines that cover the use of *nondeadly* force remained unclear until 1989 when the Court attempted to control nonlethal forms of police violence.

The Law on Excessive but Nondeadly Force.   In *Graham v. Conner* (1989) the Supreme Court held that the issue of a police officer's use of excessive force during an arrest should be resolved on the basis of the Fourth Amendment's objective reasonableness standard. This standard holds that the use of force must be "judged from the perspective of a reasonable officer coping with a tense, fast evolving situation." The Court decided that the "reasonableness" of a specific officer's conduct "is not capable of precise definition" (*Graham v. Conner* 1989: 1871). While this standard remains somewhat ambiguous, at least *Graham v. Conner* (1989) gives a legal guideline that begins to show when the use of nonlethal force is or is not justifiable.

With these rulings, the Court attempted to establish principles that determine what is reasonable and what is excessive police violence. When an officer's actions go beyond what the High Court deems "reasonable," victims have several legal remedies.

Penalties for Excessive Violence.   The police are subject to civil lawsuits alleging the use of excessive force at either the state or federal level. To be successful in a federal suit, the plaintiff must prove that the officer's actions caused a deprivation of a constitutionally guaranteed right. The Supreme Court has recently begun using a section of the U.S. Code to establish proof of constitutional deprivation. Title 42 of the U.S. Code, Section 1983, entitled Civil Action for Deprivation of Civil Rights (1999), requires the plaintiff to show that the conduct in question was committed by a person acting under color of state law, and that this conduct deprived a person of rights, privileges, or immunities secured by the Constitution or by the laws of the United States. If the plaintiff is successful, the defendant is liable for monetary damages.

As a practical remedy, however, civil suits have severe disadvantages. In the rare instance when plaintiffs win judgments against the police, the resulting monetary penalties typically are paid out of municipal revenues. Such damages are rarely subtracted from departmental funds. Therefore, a department that does not sufficiently discourage inappropriate violence is unlikely to suffer budgetary penalties. Civil remedies do not have strong effects on the use of excessive force for additional reasons. In many cities, judgments against officers are viewed as a normal cost of policing (Chevigny, 1995).

The public also is protected from excessive force by criminal codes at both the state and federal levels. Although officers are authorized to use force if it can be shown that they acted reasonably, all states have legislated criminal penalties if force is inappropriate. At the federal level, victims of excessive force have legal remedies established in Federal Title 18 (Federal Rules of Criminal Procedure 18 USC 687 [1940]). Under this statute, officers are subject to criminal sanctions for unwarranted use of lethal force with a penalty of up to a $1,000 fine and imprisonment from one year to life if a death results for any person who "under the color of law, statute, ordinance, regulation or custom willfully subjects any inhabitant of any state . . . to the deprivation of any right, privileges, or immunities secured or protected by the Constitution or laws of the United States."

Aspects of the legal process, however, weaken these remedies as well. Although the criminal penalties for officers using excessive and deadly force can be severe, prosecutors rarely litigate these cases. They know that officers are unwilling to testify against other officers and that the public is unwilling to use penalties normally reserved for criminals against the police (Faulkner, 1999). When these cases are litigated, conviction is unusual (Kobler, 1975).

Internal investigations conducted by the police department are just as unlikely to find misconduct. Faulkner (1999) reported that San Diego police officers were absolved in all 190 shootings that occurred from 1985 until the end of 1990. Whether the inquiry is conducted by the department or by the courts, guilty verdicts against officers are not common.

As we have seen, the use of force by police officers is regulated by federal, state, and local laws. With these regulations in mind, we can now turn to analyses of the social conditions that encourage or reduce the use of force by the police. We begin with a discussion of nondeadly force and follow this treatment with a discussion of the conditions that make deadly force more likely.

Empirical Findings About the Police Use of Nondeadly Force

Only a few studies have examined the use of nonlethal force. This lack of empirical research is primarily due to an absence of accurate data. Hirschel, Dean, and Lumb (1994), for example, claim that violent police-citizen encounters that do not involve deadly force are not well documented by police departments. The use of all forms of force also is difficult to explore because it is unusual compared to the number of contacts the average officer on the street has with citizens.

In a study involving 1,600 police-citizen interactions in three cities, for example, Friedrich (1977) found that officers used "excessive" force in only 1.8% of these contacts. Similarly, in another analysis of 24 police departments, officers used "improper" physical force in just 1.3% of their encounters with citizens (Worden, 1995).

Both Friedrich (1977) and Worden (1995) focus primarily on excessive force, but they also examine the use of force that seems warranted. Friedrich found that officers used reasonable force in 3.3% of their contacts with citizens, whereas only 2.3% of the officers in Worden's study used reasonable force. If we add incidents that were improper or excessive to encounters involving the use of force that apparently was appropriate, Friedrich's research suggested that officers use some type of force in only about 5% of their encounters with the public, while Worden's study showed that this percentage was just 3.6%.

Other studies give similar results. Bayley and Garofalo (1989) reported that in 486 "potentially violent" police-citizen contacts, New York City police officers used some type of force in 8% of these encounters. In an analysis of police behavior in Rochester, New York, Croft (1986) found that officers used physical force in fewer than 2,400 of the 123,500 arrests that occurred during the period covered by his study. When he analyzed police behavior in Dade County, Florida, Klinger (1995) found that the force used in the majority of police-citizen contacts was nonphysical (i.e., verbal commands).

The two most common accounts for the use of force focus on either the individual characteristics of officers or the situational conditions that make violence in police-citizen contacts more likely. Sherman's (1980b) discussion continues to be among the most authoritative of all reviews.

The Personal Characteristics of Officers.   Individual officer characteristics such as age, height, race, and education have been explored often in the literature. Conventional police wisdom suggests that younger officers tend to be more aggressive and more prone to make mistakes (Sherman, 1980b). In a study of this relationship between age and performance, Cohen and Chaiken (1972) found that those officers who were the oldest at the time of their appointment were less likely to have a complaint filed against them for excessive force. The conventional police wisdom that officer height matters has not been supported, however. Minimum height standards have little to do with performance but were used in the past to screen out female applicants.

Much of the research on officer race and behavior is somewhat dated; nevertheless, there have been some interesting results. Some research suggests that differences exist in the behavior of black and white officers, but the results have not been consistent. Reiss (1972) found that black officers used unjustified force more often than whites, both in general and especially against black citizens. Yet Friedrich (1977) found only modest differences in the conduct of black and white officers after differences in patrol areas were held constant. Such adjustments are critical because black officers are far more likely to live and work in high-crime areas. As we will see, the literature on gender is more inconclusive because the duties given to female officers may not be as likely to elicit violence as the duties assigned to their male counterparts.

The supposition that college-educated officers are not as likely to use force has received only mixed support. Cascio (1977), in a study of 940 officers in Dade County, Florida, found fewer allegations against officers with more education, but Friedrich (1977) found no differences between officers with some college and those with none.

Situational Effects.   Several situational conditions have been used to explain police use of force. This research has primarily examined the characteristics of suspects. Most of this research focused on suspects' race, demeanor, and social class. Some investigators contend that officers of any race are more likely to use excessive force against blacks. Reiss (1972) found that black suspects are victims of police use of force at less than half the rate of white suspects, but we have not found other studies that support this surprising finding.

Investigations that examine the effect of a suspect's demeanor on the likelihood of police use of force have repeatedly found that those who physically or verbally challenge officers are much more likely to be subjected to unwarranted police violence (Friedrich, 1977; Reiss, 1972). Banton (1964) claimed that lower-class suspects receive comparatively harsh police treatment, and some additional research supports this claim. Friedrich (1977) found that police treat suspects from lower-class backgrounds negatively more often than they do higher-status suspects. In a reanalysis of the data used by Reiss (1972), Friedrich (1977) found that lower-class suspects comprised 100% of those subjected to excessive force, but only 68% of the suspects that police encountered had lower-class backgrounds.

Some researchers argue that when police act proactively and initiate an encounter with citizens, they will be granted less legitimacy than when they are reactive and intervene after their assistance is requested (Reiss, 1971; Sherman, 1980b). This distinction may have important effects on the use of force. When officers initiate encounters, citizens are more likely to challenge their authority (Reiss, 1971). As one might expect, the police respond antagonistically when they are challenged (Friedrich, 1977). It follows that when the police act proactively, officers (and perhaps citizens) are more likely to be injured— suggesting that violence is especially probable when officers become more assertive (Reiss, 1971).

Worden (1995, p. 57) claimed that in comparison to officers in more bureaucratic departments, officers in less rule-bound, more decentralized departments were less likely to use force even when it might have been justified. Officers from such departments tried to handle problems in other ways, or they did not take actions in the early stages of an encounter that would increase the probability of violence later.

Worden's unique and unreplicated conclusions are interesting, but they are inconsistent with all the research showing that police violence is more unusual when departments make greater efforts to regulate the use of force with bureaucratic rules. The organizational literature suggests that organizations that employ such bureaucratic methods are more likely to be centralized. Yet most of the literature on the police suggests that in contrast to Worden (1995), the comparatively centralized and more bureaucratic departments that make greater efforts to control the unwarranted use of force with rules tend to be more successful than the less bureaucratic departments that do not use such provisions.

Analyses of Citizen Complaints.   Because reliable information about excessive force that is not lethal has been difficult to obtain, some researchers have examined citizen complaints instead. Most U.S. police departments have procedures in place that allow counts of accusations about officer misconduct. Several studies have found that minority citizens, especially African Americans, are more likely to file such complaints (Pate & Fridell, 1993; Wagner, 1980).

In Los Angeles, African Americans make up only 13% of the population, but they made 41% of these complaints (Rohrlich & Merina, 1991). Lersch (1998) found that both blacks and Hispanics are more likely than whites to complain about excessive force. Pate and Fridell (1993) found that complaints by African Americans were less likely to be sustained than those made by Hispanics or by whites. Unfortunately, little agreement about the reasons for these disparities can be found.

Although findings based on the analysis of complaints may give us some insight about police-citizen relations, the use of such data has been contested. An increasing number of complaints filed with a particular agency may not necessarily reflect a deterioration in officer behavior. Instead, a growth in complaints could indicate increased citizen confidence in the complaint system (Pate & Fridell, 1993, p. 35; West, 1988, p. 113) or increased publicity about its existence.

Formal accusations about officer misconduct may be due to other factors as well. It is possible that some populations are more likely than others to complain about officers. The data on this issue probably are biased because these complaints are underrecorded by many departments and because departments may be unduly selective about whose accusations they record. Federal civil rights laws give local departments incentives to ignore minority complaints. We can summarize this section by noting that with little reliable information about the use of nondeadly force, the literature on these incidents is less than conclusive.

Nondeadly force is used by police officers in the majority of situations in which they encounter resistance, but the use of lethal violence has rightly been subjected to far more scrutiny. We next turn to a detailed examination of the conditions that determine when officers employ deadly force.

Empirical Findings About the Police Use of Deadly Force in a Few Cities

Microlevel research confined to a few departments on the use of deadly force has found several important determinants. Some researchers have studied the situational conditions that may instigate the use of deadly force by officers, while other researchers have tried to account for these outcomes by examining the individual attributes of victims or officers.

Let us begin this discussion with some broad generalities about the use of deadly force by the police. Blumberg (1993) cited Geller and Karales (1981) who identified a typical pattern:

> The most common shooting of a civilian by a police officer in urban America is one in which an on-duty, uniformed officer shoots an armed, black male between the ages of 17 and 30 at night in a public location, in connection with an armed robbery. Typically, the shooting is subsequently deemed justifiable by the police department following an internal investigation. (p. 56)

This finding presents some of the most important circumstances that lead to the largest number of deadly force incidents, but we need to conduct a more detailed examination of the evidence on such a critical issue.

Officer Characteristics.   Only a few studies have examined the relationship between individual officer characteristics and the propensity to use deadly force. Sherman and Blumberg (1981) looked at the attributes of officers in Kansas City who were involved in a shooting. They explored factors such as race, education, height, marital status, and prior military service but found that these attributes did not predict whether an officer had used deadly force.

Geller and Karales (1981) also examined the racial differences in the use of firearms and reported that black officers had a higher rate of firearm use than whites, but again, once residence and assignment area were held constant, their results were consistent with Sherman and Blumberg's (1981) conclusions about the use of nondeadly force. Racial differences in firearm use are eliminated when the place of residence and area of assignment are taken into account largely because black officers are more likely to live and work in areas with higher violent crime rates.

Sherman and Blumberg (1981) found that only officer age and length of service were strongly related to the use of deadly force. Younger officers and those with fewer years of service were more likely to be involved in a deadly shooting than older, more experienced officers. Again, however, the types of assignments given to younger, less experienced officers may account for this difference.

According to Sherman and Blumberg (1981), gender and social class were the only other characteristics that distinguished shooters from nonshooters. Female officers and officers from middle-class backgrounds were less likely than male officers and officers from other than middle-class backgrounds to use firearms. Whether these gender differences will persist is not clear. It is possible that in contrast to the assignments given to males, female officers may be given less dangerous duties that are not as likely to require violent responses.

Some authors disregard the possibility that differences in assignments matter and conclude that hiring more female and middle-class officers will reduce police violence; such recommendations are controversial. Grennen (1987) compared officer partners and found that after assignments were matched in this manner, females were just as likely as their male partners to use force. Such findings strongly suggest that hiring more females will not reduce the use of inappropriate force as long as the assignments given to male and female officers differ.

Citizen Background.   The findings about racial differences in the public's evaluations of the police discussed at the beginning of this chapter suggest that the use of violence against minorities is a primary determinant of citizen distrust of the police. Most of the researchers who conducted empirical research on the police use of deadly force conclude that it is disproportionately used against African Americans and Hispanics (Blumberg, 1981; Chevigny, 1995; Geller & Karales, 1981; Jacobs & O'Brien, 1998).

Several early studies confined to departments in a few large cities illustrate these racial disparities in the police use of deadly force. Harding and Fahey (1973) found that

75% of the victims of the police use of deadly force in Chicago were African Americans, but African Americans accounted for only 32% of the total population of that city. Jenkins and Faison (1974) reported that in New York City, 52% of those killed by police over a 3-year period were black, and 21% were Hispanic. In a 7-city study by Milton, Halleck, Lardner, and Abrecht (1977), 79% of those shot by police were black, but only 39% of the total residents of these cities were black.

Yet researchers cannot agree about the reasons for these disparities. Chevigny (1995) suggested that the disproportionate shootings of African Americans and Hispanics are due to officer perceptions that these groups are more dangerous than others. Others (e.g., Goldkamp, 1976) stress discriminatory police behavior by claiming that African Americans and Hispanics are disproportionately the victims of police violence because they are more likely to be inappropriately arrested for violent crimes. Fyfe (1981) and Blumberg (1981), however, suggested that these disparities in arrest rates reflect greater minority propensities to commit such crimes. The controversial position taken by Fyfe and Blumberg implies that minorities are more often killed by the police because they are more likely to commit the violent crimes that lead to reciprocally violent responses by officers.

It is not possible to conclude that African Americans commit a disproportionate amount of violent crimes if one looks only at arrest data because these statistics just provide information about the race of those who are apprehended. It is possible that police officers are more likely to arrest minorities than whites even though there are no differences in the criminal behavior of these groups. It is equally possible that minorities are more often arrested for such acts because they commit more than their share of violent crimes. Perhaps self-report studies or information from victimization surveys can begin to resolve this issue.

Many studies have compared the extent of delinquency among whites and blacks with self-report measures. In contrast to official arrest data, investigators who use this approach ask subjects detailed questions to elicit admissions about criminal activities. Investigations that use this method find little racial differences in criminality (Chambliss & Nagasawa, 1969; Gould, 1969; Hirschi, 1969).

Yet the validity of self-report investigations is questionable. Racial (and other) groups may differ in the accuracy of their reports. Lower-class respondents or respondents who commit more serious crimes may be less likely to trust predominantly middle-class interviewers. Self-report data are far more likely to capture the nonserious crimes that almost everyone has committed. This method, therefore, is not likely to provide definitive conclusions about racial or other differences in the commission of violent crimes.

In another more promising approach, Hindelang (1978) used national victimization survey data and restricted his analysis to some of the most dangerous violent crimes (rape, aggravated assault, and robbery). He generated racial crime rates imputed from victim reports about the race of their assailants from the yearly surveys conducted by the Census Bureau that cover large numbers of respondents. Hindelang then compared these racial crime rates to purported racial disparities in the arrest rates. He concludes that only "a small proportion of the white/black discrepancy in arrest rates is attributable to selection bias of some sort" (p. 100).

The evidence on this question is not conclusive, but the findings from the Hindelang study appear to tell us much more about the conditions that may produce police violence than conclusions based on self-report or arrest data. What evidence we have suggests that minorities are more likely to commit serious crimes at least in part because they are more likely to be poor (Hindelang, 1978). According to Krivo and Peterson (1996), after racial and ethnic differences in economic standing and impoverished neighborhoods were held constant, racial differences in the propensity to commit serious crimes largely disappeared.

Even if racial differences in the commission of violent crimes are modest when the effects of poverty have been eliminated, the likelihood that the police single out minorities is not attributable only to *completely unreasonable* racism and discrimination! Police officers must operate under conditions of extreme uncertainty, yet their failure to act even when they have incomplete information may lead to criminal acts that inflict substantial harms on the innocent. One response is to use what is called statistical discrimination to reduce these potentially dangerous uncertainties.

Police organizations are primarily reactive rather than proactive agencies (Manning, 1977; Rubenstein, 1973; Wilson, 1971) because officers cannot see through walls, cannot read minds, and are not as numerous as the number of potential lawbreakers they must attempt to control. An officer's capacity to detect criminal intent before the commission of a harmful criminal act therefore is limited (in fact, these conditions explain why most department responses to crime are first requested by citizens [Rubenstein, 1973; Wilson, 1971]). These and other potentially dangerous uncertainties make the use of a form of discrimination extremely tempting. Statistical discrimination or profiling uses differences in population means to resolve uncertainties about individuals, but the net effect of this use of statistical profiling remains discriminatory.

The conventional police wisdom is that minorities are much more likely than whites to commit serious street crimes. Although many poor whites also commit such crimes, police often "round up all of the usual (i.e., minority) suspects" first. Hence, even if mean group differences in the propensity to commit violent crimes are modest, the police try to control the real costs of their limited information by singling out minorities. This kind of statistical discrimination or racial profiling ensures that minorities will be more likely than whites to be stopped, interrogated, and arrested even if they are only slightly more likely than equivalent whites to engage in injurious criminal acts. The resulting increased potential for conflict between the police and minorities probably accounts for the substantial contrasts in the police use of force against minorities rather than whites.

Although micro studies of the conditions that produce more killings by officers give us insights about the detailed processes that contribute to these deaths, macro studies that investigate the conditions that lead to variability in lethal force rates in many jurisdictions provide more general conclusions about the conditions that lead to these deaths.

Empirical Findings About Police Killings in Multiple Jurisdictions

The statistical studies of police killings in multiple jurisdictions vary sharply in their quality. In one of the first and most innovative studies conducted using information from many large jurisdictions, Kania and Mackey (1977) used public health data to compute the number of killings committed by the police in all of the U.S. states between 1961 to 1970. To adjust for the unusual nature of these events and to develop plausible comparisons across states that differ greatly in their populations, Kania and Mackey computed the rate of police killings per million state residents over this 9-year period. There were substantial state differences in these standardized rates. Georgia, for example, with 37.97 per million residents killed by the police had the highest population standardized rate during these 9 years, while both Wisconsin and New Hampshire had rates just under 3 killings per million residents.

Unfortunately, when Kania and Mackey attempted to analyze the social determinants of these comparable deadly force rates, they ignored the presence of minorities and tried to measure the degree of economic inequality (or differences in the economic resources of the poor and the affluent) with the proportion of welfare recipients. This procedure is misleading because the most unequal (or economically stratified) states had the smallest welfare rolls, not the largest (Dye, 1969). These problems and Kania and Mackey's failure to adjust for the effects of alternative explanations make their correlational evidence suspect.

Jacobs and Britt (1979) reanalyzed Kania and Mackey's data with a procedure called multiple regression that let them examine the independent effects of alternative potential causes. This technique gives researchers the opportunity to simultaneously hold multiple determinants that may explain an outcome constant and thereby isolate the unique effects of each possible determinant after the effects of the others have been eliminated. Jacobs and Britt (1979) found that the most unequal states with the largest gaps between the incomes of the rich and the poor were most likely to have the highest number of police killings after state population differences were removed. The rate of criminal violence in the states explained these killings as well. This last result makes sense because officers should be particularly likely to use deadly force when they must control a more violent population.

States, however, are not the best unit for such an analysis. An investigation that uses data from the states must inappropriately combine the deaths that result from police behavior in many diverse police departments. Data collected from cities are more appropriate for several important reasons. Because people respond to conditions in their immediate environment, community characteristics should explain the police use of lethal force, but statistics from states will average out these community differences. Sherman (1980b) justifies cities as the best unit in such analyses when he writes, "Theoretically the community level should be given the most attention. . . . Rossi, Berk, and Edison (1974) found that in comparing city of employment and officer's personal characteristics as explanations of the use of aggressive detection tactics, 67 percent of the variance was uniquely attributable to the city" (p. 94).

Four studies of cities that used multiple regression to simultaneously hold various alternative explanations constant and isolate the independent effects of competing explanations have been published. Sherman and Langworthy (1979) and Liska and Yu (1992) measured police killings by combining data from *Vital Statistics of the United States* with two different surveys of police departments. Unfortunately, the estimates from *Vital Statistics* were about half as large as the estimates of police killings from either of the surveys used in these studies. The overlap in the merged data that were used to estimate the rate of police killings is modest in both investigations. In Sherman and Langworthy's study of just 32 cities, the correlation between the estimates from their survey and the *Vital Statistics* estimates of police killings is just 0.56; in the Liska and Yu study of 45 cities this correlation is only 0.45. The problems make the validity of these measures of city police killing rates questionable. This problem together with the modest number of cases used in these investigations and other difficulties probably explain the inconsistent findings in the two studies.

Sorensen, Marquardt, and Brock (1993) overcame some of these deficiencies by analyzing Supplemental Homicide Report data collected by the FBI from local police reports on the number of police killings. They also constructed a rate to adjust for differences in city populations, and they confined their analysis to larger cities with more than 100,000 residents. These Supplemental Homicide Report data on the police use of deadly force probably are more accurate than the public health statistics partially used by Sherman and Langworthy (1979) and Liska and Yu (1992) because local public health officials often fail to report all police-caused deaths.

There are substantial differences in the rates of the police use of deadly force in these cities (we report statistics from the Jacobs & O'Brien, 1998, study of deaths in these cities because we have immediate access to this data). The mean rate of police killings per 100,000 residents across all 170 cities was 1.99 per 100,000 residents. The five cities with the most substantial rates were Fort Lauderdale, Florida 7.41; Dallas, Texas 7.30; St. Louis, Missouri 7.17; Newark, New Jersey 7.02; and New Orleans, Louisiana 6.83; however, 31 of these 170 cities had no people killed by the police during the entire period from 1980 to 1986. Given the subsequent problems in Los Angeles with videotaped police violence that led to a severe riot, it is interesting that the Los Angeles Police Department ranked 20th with a police use of lethal force rate of 4.23 per 100,000 residents, giving this city one of the highest but not the highest rate.

Sorensen, Marquardt, and Brock (1993) found the police are more likely to use deadly force in the more economically unequal cities (where income differences between the affluent and the poor were greatest) and in cities with the highest violent crime rates. Their results showed that cities located in the South had higher police killing rates as well, but there were problems with the procedures they used. They held only a few competing explanations constant in their analysis. Their results could be spurious because they were biased by factors the researchers did not control. Furthermore, the statistical procedure they used did not produce accurate results when the outcome in question was unusual.

Although there is considerable variation in the police use of deadly force across cities, police killings are extremely rare even in the largest cities. Sherman and Cohn (1986) found that in Jacksonville, Florida (a city with one of the higher rates of police killings), an officer could expect to work 149 years before killing a citizen. An officer in Milwaukee, however, would have to spend 1,299 years on the job, while a Honolulu police officer would have to work 7,692 years before using deadly force just once! Research that uses a statistical procedure that does not handle such unusual events well probably will generate inaccurate findings.

Jacobs and O'Brien (1998) used a different statistical technique to overcome these difficulties. They isolated effects of more potential explanations, and they conducted a separate examination of the determinants of police killings of blacks. The latter analysis let them compare the factors that explained all police killings to those that explained the use of deadly force against this racial minority.

The results from the Jacobs and O'Brien study suggest that police killings stem from problematic urban conditions. As one might expect, cities with higher murder rates have more police killings of all citizens and more police killings of blacks. Jacobs and O'Brien also found that police are more likely to use lethal force in the largest cities. This result is not surprising because it is more difficult to identify offenders in most populated urban areas, so officers are more handicapped in such environments and therefore more likely to use lethal force.

Higher divorce rates produce higher total police killing rates probably because this kind of family breakdown produces more interpersonal violence among family members that officers often must control when they make domestic violence stops. The presence of female-headed black families is positively associated with the police use of deadly force against blacks as well.

In contrast to Jacobs and Britt's (1979) state-level analysis or the Sorensen, Marquardt, and Brock (1993) study of police killings in cities, Jacobs and O'Brien found no evidence that economic inequality (or greater gaps between the incomes of the rich and the poor) is related to police killings. But studies that use cities often do not find that such economic disparities are associated with criminal justice outcomes. Limiting an analysis to what happens within cities excludes many prosperous community residents who live in the adjacent suburbs. Thus, the effects of differences in community incomes probably are underestimated when researchers use data from cities and ignore the affluent residents who live in the suburban areas surrounding a city.

Jacobs and O'Brien also found that minority presence matters. More police killings occur in cities with larger percentages of black residents. Prior research has shown that cities with more blacks tend to have larger police departments (Jackson, 1989; Jacobs, 1979), but this research found that the officers in such cities were more likely to use lethal force. The standard interpretation for such findings hinges on threat effects. Following Blalock (1967), this explanation suggests that in jurisdictions where blacks are relatively numerous, white dominance is threatened. Whites respond to this menace by using social control agencies such as the police to maintain their dominant position. Findings (that persist after other explanations have been held constant) that departments are larger and that officers are more likely to use deadly force in cities with more blacks support such racial threat accounts.

Yet the primary results in the Jacobs and O'Brien study suggest that two political factors explain the use of deadly force by the police. First, more substantial differences in the incomes of blacks and whites reduce the black population's political influence and its ability to curb police violence. Probably for this reason, Jacobs and O'Brien found that greater disparities in the incomes of blacks and whites led to a greater likelihood that the police will use deadly force. Most important, this suggests that a willingness of dominant groups to interfere with harsh police methods is diminished in cities where differences in the economic resources of blacks and whites are most pronounced (we will return to this argument in our conclusion). Second, Jacobs and O'Brien found that the police in cities with a black mayor were significantly less likely to use lethal violence against blacks. Because these results suggest that racial and political factors explain the likelihood that the police will use deadly force *after the amount of criminal violence and other plausible explanations have been held constant,* both findings contradict the conventional wisdom that police killings are almost entirely due to levels of community violence that the police must control.

We can summarize this research by noting that at least two quasi-political effects help us understand city differences in the propensity of the police to use deadly force against all citizens and against minorities. First, when blacks have more political influence because the city has a black mayor, police killings of blacks will be significantly reduced. Second, deadly force will be less likely in cities where blacks have greater economic influence and greater political power than they do in most cities.

But citizens sometimes use force against officers. We now examine the conditions that lead to violence directed against the police.

FELONIOUS VIOLENCE AGAINST POLICE OFFICERS

Microlevel Research

Although most of the literature on police-citizen violence focuses on the police use of force against citizens, a modest number of studies examine the conditions that produce violence directed against the police. Some investigations study officer and citizen characteristics to see if personal attributes increase the likelihood of attacks on officers.

Nonlethal Assaults. In an effort to identify the individual characteristics of those officers who were assaulted, Meyer, Magedanz, Dahlin, and Chapman (1981) examined three types of assaults (general, robbery-related, and ambush) against police in five states (Oklahoma, New Mexico, Louisiana, Arkansas, and Texas). They found that most officers were assaulted while answering a call during a weekend evening. Assaulted officers tended to be younger and more inexperienced. Meyer et al.'s (1981) findings showed that the risk of an assault was greatest when relatively inexperienced officers responded alone to disturbance calls.

Studies of the characteristics of offenders who assault police suggested that such offenders have much in common with those who are guilty of more conventional crimes. When researchers confined their analyses to officer assailants involved in the more serious assaults, these offenders were found to be disproportionately male and nonwhite (Meyer et al., 1981).

The same researchers concluded that the majority of the assailants involved in the more serious robbery and ambush assaults (77% and 67%, respectively) are unemployed. Interestingly, these investigators found that assailants who commit the least serious assaults are more likely to be under the influence of drugs or alcohol. Fifty-five percent of these offenders used alcohol and 10.5% used drugs prior to these assaults. Such statistics suggest that the least serious assaults against officers stem from an inability to control one's actions. Offenders involved in more serious assaults, however, were not intoxicated or under the influence of other drugs. Such contrasting results suggest that in comparison to their less violent counterparts, serious assaults against the police are more likely to be premeditated and intentional.

Lethal Assaults. Research based on a few cities that examines killings of police officers provides the most detailed findings. First, a surprisingly large number of those killed were accidentally shot. In their study of police killed in one city (Chicago) between 1974 and 1978, Geller and Karales (1981) reported that nearly two fifths of those officers either shot themselves or were shot by other officers. This study also suggests that a substantial percentage (44%) of those officers who were intentionally shot by citizens were off duty at the time (Geller & Karales, 1981). This finding is important because the circumstances surrounding an officer's being killed vary by duty status. In Chicago on-duty officers are most commonly shot while responding to a "shots fired" or "person with a gun" incident (32%), whereas off-duty officers are most likely to be shot during an alleged armed robbery (33%) (Geller & Karales, 1981).

Geller and Karales (1981) reported that during a 5-year period in Chicago, 108 officers were fired on and hit by citizens, an annual average of 1.6 officers per 1,000 on the force. Of those shot, 81% (91) were wounded and 15.7% (17) were killed. More recently, Chevigny (1995) found that in New York City over a 4-year period (1990–1993), 90 officers were shot and 4 were killed. Relatively few officers are shot in the line of duty, and only a small percentage of those officers die.

Macrolevel Research Based on Many Cases

Macro Data on Nonlethal Assaults Against Officers.   Data from many reporting departments on assaults against officers and on officers killed are available. The FBI enumerates assaults against the police. An inspection of this data suggests that departments differ in the rules they use to determine whether incidents are counted, so these statistics may give a misleading picture if they are used to compare assault rates in various cities. Table 2.1 shows trends and the type of weapons used by assailants. Despite the relative inaccuracies in the enumerations of these incidents across departments, conclusions about the trends in these data probably are valid. Table 2.1 shows that fewer assaults against the police have been committed between 1989 and 1998. In 1998, 59,545 assaults were reported against officers who were on duty, an average of 13 for every 100 police officers (Federal Bureau of Investigation, 1999). Assaults resulted in personal injury in just under one third of the reported cases. The majority of the reported assaults were conducted without a weapon (82%). Assailants used a firearm or a knife in only 5% of these assaults. Consistent with the findings reported by Meyer et al. (1981) for prior years, the largest proportion of these nonlethal assaults (33%) happened while officers were responding to a disturbance call (family quarrels, bar fights, etc.). The rate of assaults on officers in 1998 was 16% higher than the rate in 1997 but 28% lower than it was in 1989 (FBI, 1999), so these changes represent minor fluctuations in a generally consistent downward trend.

National Data on Lethal Assaults Against Officers.   Police officers are more likely to be killed in the United States than in most other countries. According to the FBI (1999), no other occupational group in the United States has a higher lethal victimization rate, but the numbers of deaths have steadily diminished since the 1980s. At the national level, 61 police officers were killed in the line of duty in 1998 (FBI, 1999). This total is 13% lower than that in 1997 and 8% lower than that in 1989. Figure 2.1 shows the more recent trends in the number of felonious killings of police officers. Bailey and Peterson (1994) suggested that a primary reason for these reductions is the increasing use of body armor by officers in dangerous situations.

To discover the conditions that are most likely to lead to the use of lethal force against officers, Bailey and Peterson (1994) calculated percentages from the FBI data for the United States from 1981 to 1989. They found that the killings of officers most often

TABLE 2–1   Police Officers Assaulted, Type of Weapon, and Percentage Receiving Personal Injury, 1989–1998

Year	Total[a]	Firearm	Knife or Cutting Instrument	Other Dangerous Weapon	Personal Weapons	Number of Reporting Agencies	Population (in 1,000s)	Number of Officers[b]
1989 Total assaults	62,172	3,154	1,379	5,778	51,861	9,213	189,641	380,232
Percent injured	35.2	30.2	30.5	40.8	35.0			
1990 Total assaults	72,270	3,665	1,650	7,436	59,519	9,512	199,834	414,037
Percent injured	36.3	29.3	29.5	42.5	36.1			
1991 Total assaults	62,852	3,532	1,493	7,014	50,813	9,043	187,866	399,020
Percent injured	37.6	30.8	30.6	43.5	3.75			
1992 Total assaults	81,252	4,455	2,095	8,604	66,098	10,862	217,997	460,430
Percent injured	36.5	25.5	30.4	40.9	36.9			
1993 Total assaults	66,975	4,002	1,574	7,551	53,848	9,858	211,914	456,565
Percent injured	35.9	27.4	31.0	36.3	36.6			
1994 Total assaults	64,912	3,168	1,513	7,210	53,021	10,434	217,935	473,946
Percent injured	35.7	26.3	29.4	36.7	36.3			
1995 Total assaults	58,063	2,373	1,362	6,451	47,877	8,895	198,155	440,582
Percent injured	30.1	19.4	24.2	31.0	30.7			
1996 Total assaults	46,695	1,887	871	5,084	38,853	7,808	166,038	373,575
Percent injured	32.1	24.9	30.7	39.5	31.5			
1997 Total assaults	49,151	1,844	895	5,389	41,023	8,522	191,303	423,930
Percent injured	26.7	15.1	18.5	29.4	27.0			
1998 Total assaults	59,545	2,073	1,077	7,266	49,129	8,000	190,189	445,898
Percent injured	30.6	21.1	23.4	30.3	31.2			

[a]Prior years' assault figures have been adjusted subsequent to publication.

[b]Total number of sworn officers employed in reporting agencies.

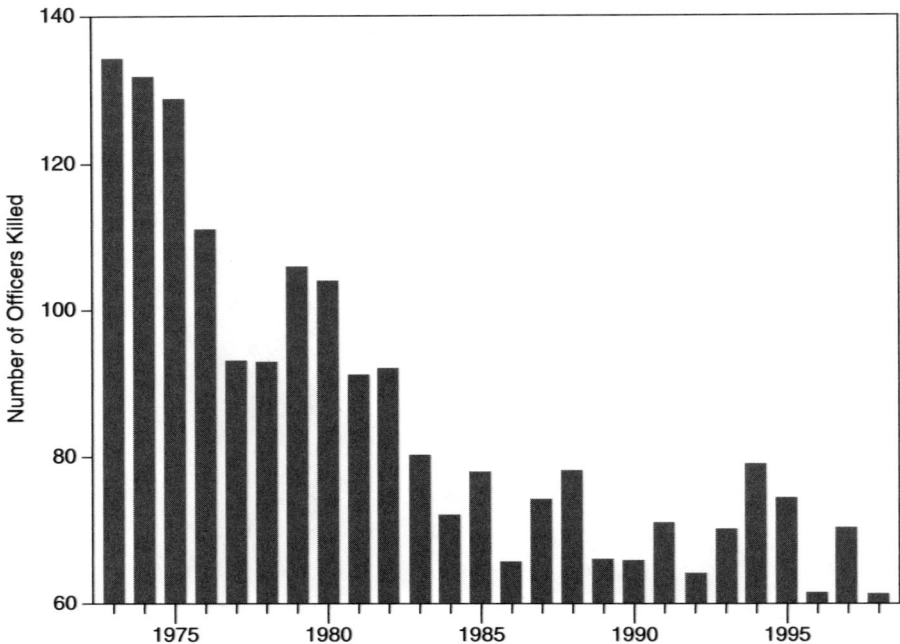

FIGURE 2.1   Number of U.S. police officers killed from 1973 to 1998.

occurred during arrests (40.9%), but disturbance calls led to an additional 16.5% of these deaths. Another 14.4% occurred during suspicious person stops. Other less lethal situations included traffic pursuits and stops (13.5% of these deaths), ambushes (8.7%), and handling prisoners (4.2%), while killings by the deranged accounted for 1.6% of all felonious lethal assaults against officers.

Additional national FBI statistics indicate that racial explanations may be important. Blacks are far more likely than whites to kill officers than their presence in the population would suggest. African Americans committed 39.6% of all police killings in the United States from 1981 to 1985. In some years (1985, for example), black offenders were responsible for a majority of these killings (and these percentages remain equivalent after 1985) even though only about 12% of the population then was black.

Attempts to Determine Causes with Multivariate Techniques.   Because it is difficult to use data from cities to analyze unusual events such as officer killings with statistical procedures such as multiple regression that let us isolate the independent effects of competing explanations, little empirical research on the determinants of officer killings across multiple jurisdictions exists. A few investigators (Cardarelli, 1968; Lester, 1978a, 1978b, 1982) report correlations that show only weak and inconclusive relationships. Because alternative, competing explanations were not held constant, such findings could be spurious.

The little credible multivariate research published that held multiple explanations constant used higher levels of aggregation than cities. Bailey and Peterson (1994) analyzed trends in yearly data to find the determinants of the rate of officers killed annually throughout the entire nation. They focused on the deterrent effects of executions, but they found negligible relationships between various measures of the certainty of capital punishment and the killings of police officers.

In another study Peterson and Bailey (1988) again used multiple regression in an attempt to isolate the factors that best explain the rates of officers killed, but in this investigation they analyzed these deaths in the 50 U.S. states. If rates of officers killed per million officers in the states are summed over multiple years, it may be possible to avoid a large number of zero scores that destroy the accuracy of relationships calculated with the statistical technique they used (Greene, 1993).

When Peterson and Bailey analyzed these state rates in a particular year, they did not find relationships that were likely to differ from chance; many states had no police officers killed in any single year, so many of these state scores were zero. When they examined these rates summed over four years so that fewer of the states had zero scores, Peterson and Bailey began to find some relationships that probably were not due to chance. After several alternative explanations had been held constant, they found that more officers would be killed in states with the highest divorce and absolute poverty rates.

Again, however, states are not an ideal unit for analysis. It is plausible that community rather than state conditions would be more likely to explain these killings because people respond to conditions in their immediate environments. Community determinants will be obscured if the researchers use data from states because the resulting state averages will hide many important community differences. An analysis that uses cities will let the researcher analyze more cases. For all of these reasons, a study that uses data from cities to examine the conditions that produce the killings of officers should provide more accurate results than attempts to explain these deaths in large units such as states.

In an unpublished investigation that analyzes the number of officers killed between 1981 and 1990 in the 165 U.S. cities with more than 100,000 residents, Jacobs and Carmichael (2001) used a statistical technique more appropriate for detecting the determinants of unusual events. The results showed that two theoretically important political effects always explained the use of lethal force against the police. Officers were more likely to be killed in cities where income differences between blacks and whites were most substantial, but felonious lethal assaults against police officers were less likely in cities with an African American mayor. Both findings suggest that the political and economic subordination of African Americans is an important explanation for the killings of police officers.

Many conventional measures of social disorganization are unrelated to these killings. Neither poverty, crowding (or the percentage of housing units with more than 1.01 persons per room), nor unemployment accounts for the number of officers killed, but the evidence about family disruptions is mixed. We find that officers are more likely to be killed in cities with higher divorce rates, but city differences in presence of female-headed families are unrelated to these lethal events.

As one might expect, the killings of police officers also are more likely in cities with the highest violent crime rates. Felonious deadly force used against police officers evidently occurs more often in larger cities as well. The use of deadly force against an officer is a hazardous endeavor that ought to be much more likely if the offender has a better chance of escaping. As the population of cities grows, the likelihood of identifying assailants should not continue to decrease at the same rate. We find support for this expectation because our results show a positive relationship between city size and officers killed, but this relationship starts to taper off after city populations go beyond a certain threshold.

Based on the national FBI data on the disproportionate number of blacks who kill police officers, racial factors proved to be the most important explanations. First, these killings are reduced in racially segregated cities perhaps due to foresight. In such segregated cities where the black underclass lives apart from majority whites, the police may be especially careful when they enter these more dangerous districts (Bailey & Peterson, 1994). Second, the number of officers killed is greater in cities with the most blacks.

Yet the most interesting results concern black economic and political subordination. The number of officers killed is greater in cities where the gap in economic resources was most pronounced between blacks and whites, but the presence of a black mayor reduces these killings. Our findings suggest that lethal violence directed against the most visible control agents of the state is most likely in cities where blacks have the least political influence.

CONTROLLING THE POLICE USE OF FORCE

Research Findings

The problem that has received the most attention, however, is the use of inappropriate force by the police. Researchers interested in curbing police violence have investigated the effects of various policies. In this section we summarize the empirical literature, but we put off making recommendations until the final part of this chapter. The available studies suggest that three changes may reduce the use of unwarranted force by the police. Perhaps modifying the relevant state and federal laws will produce a decline in police violence, but the research suggests that changes in department rules should be far more effective. Another plausible way to reduce the use of violence by officers focuses on personal characteristics and the kinds of officers departments should recruit.

Statutory Changes.   Statutory remedies have already been employed to reduce police violence. But some evaluations of the effects of state provisions on police shootings are not encouraging. Waegel (1984), for example, found that the 1973 Pennsylvania law that made the shooting of a nonviolent fleeing felon illegal did not decrease deadly force. His research indicated that after this law was enacted, nearly 20% of those killed by the police were killed in violation of the statute. Waegel concluded that in the absence of a clear message from a department's administration, subcultural values that justify violence against some citizens appear to take precedence over legal provisions (p. 137).

Bittner's (1990) work supports Waegel's findings. Particularly in the poorest parts of a city, Bittner found that officers are evaluated for keeping order, but the departments he investigated did not pay much attention to how this goal was attained. As a result, informal police norms were created that justify a greater use of force in the skid row districts of the city that Bittner studied. These and other findings suggested that in contrast to the findings about the impact of the Supreme Court's *Garner* decision in smaller jurisdictions, changes in state laws will not be effective at least partly because these statutes have not been credibly enforced (see the earlier discussion of enforcement difficulties).

Changes in Departmental Weapons Policies.   Far more researchers have examined the effects of departmental policies about the use of deadly force and found far more encouraging results. Fyfe (1979), Meyer (1980), and Geller and Scott (1992) concluded that restrictive departmental firearms policies significantly reduced the number of police shootings. Geller and Karales (1981) found that before a more stringent departmental policy was adpoted, nearly one out of four killings committed by police could have been avoided had the department's policy been limited to "defense of life." In another study Geller and Scott (1992) reported that when the Dallas department changed its shooting policy on two separate occasions during the 1980s, each change led to reductions in the number of intentional discharges.

The literature also suggests that these alterations in department policies do not seem to put officers at greater risk. Studies indicate that more restrictive departmental firearm policies do not affect officer safety (Fyfe, 1979; Geller & Scott, 1992). In fact, Sherman and Cohn (1986) reported that after the adoption of such policies, the number of police officers killed by citizens fell by two thirds. Although this decline in officer deaths may partly have been due to other causes, Sherman and Cohn's findings raise questions about the widespread police belief that restrictive firearm policies increase officer risks. In general we can conclude that alterations in departmental rules about the use of firearms probably are the most effective way to reduce police violence.

Changes in Recruitment.   Some researchers argue that officers with particular attributes may be less likely to use firearms. If this were the case, to reduce the amount of violence directed against citizens, departments could vigorously recruit officers with the appropriate characteristics. Recall from our prior discussion that comparisons of officer race, education, height, and length of service have not been encouraging. Marital status and prior military service also do not predict differences in the propensity to use force (Sherman, 1980b). According to Sherman and Blumberg (1981), Geller and Karales (1981), and Fyfe (1981), the personal attributes of officers who shot citizens were no different from those of officers who had not used deadly force, after place of residence and assignment were held constant.

There is one exception. Sherman and Blumberg (1981) found support for a claim that younger officers and those with fewer years of service were more likely to be involved in a shooting than older, more experienced officers. Yet even if these disputed findings are valid, budgetary constraints that limit departmental wage bills and officer pay (which increases with seniority) and departmental retirement policies keep younger officers on the street.

Police departments typically follow military career practices and strongly encourage retirement after only 20 or 25 years of service in part because such liberal retirement policies give potential recruits an inducement to accept the low wages common in police work. Even if Sherman and Blumberg (1981) are correct when they suggest that having older police officers on the street will be an effective way to reduce police violence, low budgets and these relatively fixed personnel practices combine to make it difficult to increase the average age of officers on the street.

WHAT CAN BE DONE?

A Brief Summary of the Relevant Research Findings

Although the great majority of the studies we have reviewed were done by criminologists, most of the findings support sociological accounts for violence used by or against police officers. In comparison to the characteristics of individual officers, research shows that local community arrangements, the organization of police departments, and the resulting formal and informal rules departments use to control their employees seem to provide the best explanations for the likelihood that officers will use inappropriate force (Fyfe, 1979; Geller & Scott, 1992; Meyer, 1980). Recall the research by Rossi et al. (1974) that indicates that city-level factors tell us far more about the behavior of officers than their personal attributes.

The studies we reviewed that analyze the police use of deadly force in multiple cities to reach general conclusions rarely contradict this claim. In fact, this aggregate research repeatedly suggests that conditions in the social environments that surround departments provide the best explanation for police behavior. Officers seem to be responding to various features of their immediate social situation that reward some actions but do not reward others. But the immediate social situation that officers find themselves embedded in is determined by the organization of the larger community that surrounds an officer's department.

Large cities in which the level of interpersonal violence makes the work of the police more difficult or cities in which racial and ethnic minorities are less capable of restraining the police because they have diminished political or economic influence have significantly greater amounts of police violence. Yet in cities with a black mayor who often has important political support from minorities and strong reasons to restrain the police, we find significantly less police violence. With these considerations in mind, we can begin to make some tentative recommendations.

A Political Remedy

Let us begin with a fundamental but unfortunate fact. In the absence of close restraints based on deliberate efforts to reduce the number of incidents of police violence, the use of unwarranted force by the police becomes far more likely (Chevigny, 1995). Put differently, excessive police violence is *probable* unless it is purposely controlled. Many reasons for this state of affairs exist.

First, remember that officers are expected to preserve order rather than enforce the law (Bittner, 1990). Explicit or implicit departmental imperatives to achieve this goal make the quick and sometimes inappropriate use of violence a tempting shortcut. Second, unpredictable but substantial personal risks are an inevitable part of police work. Third, most police behavior is not readily observed, so it is difficult to control the use of exces-

sive force. These conditions combine to give officers strong incentives to protect themselves and others by employing violence quickly, sometimes well before it is necessary.

Because inordinate force can be such a tempting remedy for the many irresolvable
problems that officers on the street must face, in cities where the threat of underclass violence is most severe, the police will be more likely to respond in kind with what sometimes will be excessive force. All of these conditions combine to produce a situation in
which unjustified police violence can be expected unless those with power are willing to
make deliberate efforts to stop it.

In a brilliant essay on the attitudes of German citizens toward what happened in the
concentration camps during the 1940s, Hughes (1962) argued that a willingness to remain
conveniently ignorant about the activities of the people he called "the dirty workers" provided a compelling explanation for much official brutality. The Germans he interviewed
did not want to know what was going on in the camps, so they remained unknowing. This
logic is applicable to not only the German public's feigned ignorance about the atrocities
they did not want to see but to other situations as well.

Perhaps you are tempted to believe that what happened in Hitler's Germany more
than 55 years ago is hardly relevant now. But consider just one of many possible contemporary examples. Those of us who are not vegetarians find it convenient to remain unedu-
cated about exactly how the animals we eat were treated. We certainly do not want to
stand nearby when they are slaughtered. In fact, a close examination of what workers do
in packing plants probably would make most of us lose our appetites for meat.

In cities where racial and economic disparities are most substantial, dominant
groups often will feel threatened by the resulting increases in the potential for underclass
violence that they fear may be directed against them. Greater differences in the economic
resources of dominant whites and underclass minorities should increase feelings of relative deprivation (or the comparisons with others that everyone uses to decide they are not
getting what they deserve). Minority perceptions that they are not being treated fairly
should increase when such disparities become more evident. It follows that unequal distributions of resources (or more substantial differences in the economic rewards that go to
the prosperous and the least prosperous) should produce both the motivation and greater
potential rewards for violent acts that take goods from the rich. In the most unequal jurisdictions, of course, the affluent also have far more property for the poor to remove.

Perhaps prosperous citizens who are more influential therefore respond to the menace of an economically deprived underclass in much the same manner as the German citizens described by Hughes. *They choose to remain conveniently ignorant about the harsh
methods their police force uses to maintain order and preserve their position!*

One conclusion that follows from this argument is that the best remedy for police
violence is political. If elected officeholders and their elite supporters make their distaste
for police brutality abundantly clear, then police administrators will face strong incentives
to change the department regulations that govern the use of force. In almost all U.S. cities
the most powerful police administrators are not protected by civil service regulations, so
they can be easily discharged. Thus, police administrators have compelling reasons to
alter department practices about the use of force if that is what municipal elites want.

The literature repeatedly indicates that such changes to department policies will dramatically reduce the amount of police brutality. But if the public tacitly supports harsh police methods by electing "law-and-order" candidates (such as Mayor Giuliani in New

York) who at least implicitly encourage the use of force to maintain order, such unfortunate outcomes should not be surprising. As long as elites and the public find that it is expedient to act like citizens in Hitler's Germany and look the other way, we can expect continued unwarranted violence by police officers.

The Diallo killing described at the beginning of this chapter provides apt but regrettable illustration of the recent increase in police brutality in New York City. Before the election of a law-and-order mayor, the New York City police department had an exemplary reputation. Its officers seemed to be much better at avoiding inappropriate violence than the police in other large cities (Chevigny, 1995). But it is difficult to believe that Mayor Giuliani's repeated stress on law and order and aggressive policing did not make the recent police shootings and assaults against citizens in New York City much more likely. In fact, some media accounts claim that both liberals and economic elites did not object to Giuliani's "law-and-order" initiatives because both groups enjoyed the appearance of civic order that the mayor's emphasis on aggressive police tactics seemed to produce.

We can conclude from all this that because unwarranted violence is such a tempting way to deal with the inescapable problems the police must handle, its use will be inevitable unless it is deliberately controlled. A close examination of the literature leads to a suspicion that in cities where excessive police violence is problematic, significant reductions in this violence will be likely only when influential citizens decide to act together to put pressure on political officials to curb these injustices.

REFERENCES

BAILEY, W., & PETERSON, R. D. (1994). Murder, capital punishment, and deterrence: A review of the evidence and an examination of police killings. *Journal of Social Issues, 50*, 33–74.

BANTON, M. (1964). *The policeman in the community.* New York: Basic Books.

BAYLEY, D. H., & GARAFALO, G. (1989). The management of violence by police officers. *Criminology, 27*, 1–25.

BESSENT, A. E., & TAYLOR, L. (1991, June 2). Police brutality: Is it no problem. *Newsday*, p. 5.

BITTNER, E. (1970). *The functions of police in modern society.* Chevy Chase, MD: National Institute of Mental Health.

BITTNER, E. (1990). The police on skid row. In E. Bittner (Ed.), *Aspects of police work* (pp. 30–62). Boston: Northeastern University Press.

BLALOCK, H. (1967). *Towards a theory of minority group relations.* New York: Capricorn Books.

BLUMBERG, M. (1981). Race and police shootings: An analysis in two cities. In James J. Fyfe (Ed.), *Contemporary issues in law enforcement* (pp. 152–166). Thousand Oaks, CA: Sage Publications.

BLUMBERG, M. (1993). Controlling police use of deadly force: Assessing two decades of progress. In R. Dunham and G. Alpert (Eds.), *Critical issues in policing: Contemporary readings* (pp. 469–492). Prospect Heights, IL: Waveland Press.

CARDARELLI, A. (1968). An analysis of police killed by criminal action: 1961–1963. *Journal of Criminal Law, Criminology, and Police Science, 59*, 447–453.

CASCIO, W. (1977). Formal education and police officer performance. *Journal of Police Science and Administration, 5*, 89–96.

CHAMBLISS, W., & NAGASAWA, R. (1969). On the validity of official statistics: A comparative study of white, black, and Japanese high school boys. *Journal of Research in Crime and Delinquency, 6,* 71–77.

CHEVIGNY, P. (1995). *Edge of the knife: Police violence in the Americas.* New York: New Press.

CIVIL ACTION FOR DEPRIVATION OF CIVIL RIGHTS 42 U.S.C. §1983 (1999).

COHEN, B., & CHAIKEN, J. (1972). *Police background characteristics and performance: Summary.* New York: Rand Institute.

COX, S. (1996). *Police: Practices, perspectives, problems.* Boston: Allyn and Bacon.

CROFT, E. B. (1986). *Police use of force: A twenty year perspective.* Paper presented at the annual meeting of the Academy of Criminal Justice Sciences, Orlando, FL.

CULLIVER, C., & SIGLER, R. (1995). Police use of deadly force in Tennessee following *Tennessee v. Garner. Journal of Contemporary Criminal Justice, 11,* 187–195.

DYE, T. (1969). Income inequality and American state politics. *American Political Science Review, 63,* 157–162.

FAULKNER, S. (1999). *Decision making and legal precedence.* Columbus: Ohio Peace Officer Training Commission.

FEAGIN, J., & HAHN, H. (1973). *Ghetto revolts: The politics of violence in American cities.* New York: Macmillan.

FEDERAL BUREAU OF INVESTIGATION. (1999). *Law enforcement officers killed and assaulted.* Washington, DC: U.S. Government Printing Office.

FLANAGAN, T. J., & VAUGHN, M. (1995). Public opinion about police abuse of force. In W. A. Geller and H. Toch (Eds.), *And justice for all: Understanding and controlling police abuse of force* (pp. 113–128). Washington, DC: Police Executive Forum.

FRIEDRICH, R. (1977). The impact of organizational, individual, and situational factors on police behavior. Unpublished doctoral dissertation, State University of New York at Albany.

FYFE, J. (1979). Administrative intervention on police shooting discretion: An empirical examination. *Journal of Criminal Justice, 7*(4), 309–323.

FYFE, J. (1981). Who shoots? A look at officer race and police shootings. *Journal of Police Science and Administration, 9*(4), 367–382.

GELLER, W., & KARALES, K. (1981). *Split-second decisions: Shootings of and by Chicago police.* Chicago: Chicago Law Enforcement Study Group.

GELLER, W., & SCOTT, M. (1992). *Deadly force: What we know.* Washington, DC: Police Executive Research Forum.

GOLDKAMP, J. (1976). Minorities as victims of police shootings: Interpretations of racial disproportionality and police use of deadly force. *Justice System Journal, 2,* 169–183.

GOULD, L. (1969). Who defines delinquency: A comparison of self-reported and officially-reported indices of delinquency for three racial groups. *Social Problems, 16,* 325–336.

GRAHAM V. CONNER. 109 S. Ct. 1865 (1989).

GREENE, W. (1993). *Econometric analysis.* New York: Macmillan.

GRENNEN, S. (1987). Findings on the role of officer gender in violent encounters with citizens. *Journal of Police Science and Administration, 15,* 78–85.

HARDING, R., & FAHEY, R. (1973). Killings by Chicago police, 1969–1970: An empirical study. *Southern California Law Review, 46*(2), 284–315.

HINDELANG, M. (1978). Race and involvement in common law personal crimes. *American Sociological Review, 43,* 93–109.

HIRSCHEL, J. D., DEAN, C. W., & LUMB, R. C. (1994). The relative contribution of domestic violence to assault and injury of police officers. *Justice Quarterly, 11,* 99–117.

HIRSCHI, T. (1969). *Causes of delinquency.* Berkeley: University of California Press.

HUGHES, E. C. (1962). Good people and dirty work. *Social Problems, 10,* 3–11.

JACKSON, P. (1989). *Minority group threat, crime, and policing: Social context and social control.* New York: Praeger.

JACOBS, D. (1979). Inequality and police strength: Conflict theory and social control in metropolitan areas. *American Sociological Review, 44,* 913–925.

JACOBS, D., & BRITT, D. (1979). Inequality and the police use of deadly force. *Social Problems, 26,* 403–412.

JACOBS, D., & CARMICHAEL, J. T. (2001). Subordination and violence against state control agents: Testing political explanations for lethal assaults against the police. Unpublished manuscript.

JACOBS, D., & O'BRIEN, R. (1998). The determinants of deadly force: A structural analysis of police violence. *American Journal of Sociology, 103,* 837–862.

JENKINS, B., & FAISON, A. (1974). *An analysis of 248 persons killed by New York City policemen.* New York: Metropolitan Research Center.

KANIA, R., & MACKEY, W. (1977). Police violence as a function of community characteristics. *Criminology, 15,* 27–48.

KAPPELER, V., SLUDER, R., & ALPERT, G. (1994). *Forces of deviance: Understanding the dark side of policing.* Prospect Heights, IL: Waveland Press.

KLINGER, D. (1995). The micro-structure of non-lethal force: Baseline data from an observational study. *Criminal Justice Review, 20,* 169–185.

KOBLER, A. (1975). Figures (and perhaps some facts) on police killings of civilians in the United States, 1965–69. *Journal of Social Issues, 31*(1), 185–191.

KRIVO, L., & PETERSON, R. (1996). Extremely disadvantaged neighborhoods and urban crime. *Social Forces, 75,* 619–650.

LERSCH, K. (1998). Predicting citizen race in allegations of misconduct against the police. *Journal of Criminal Justice, 26*(2), 87–97.

LESTER, D. (1978a). A study of civilian caused murders of police officers. *International Journal of Criminology and Penology, 6,* 373–378.

LESTER, D. (1978b). Predicting murder rates of police officers in urban areas. *Police Law Quarterly, 7,* 20–25.

LESTER, D. (1982). Civilians who kill police officers and police officers who kill civilians: A comparison of American cities. *Journal of Police Science and Administration, 10,* 384–387.

LISKA, A., & YU, J. (1992). Specifying and testing the threat hypothesis. In A. Liska (Ed.), *Social threat and social control* (pp. 53–68). Albany: State University of New York Press.

MCLAUGHLIN, E. (1990). Patterns of policing: A comparative international analysis. *Sociological Review (1992), 40*(3), 619–622.

MANNING, P. (1977). *Police work.* Cambridge, MA: MIT Press.

MEYER, M. (1980). Police shooting at minorities: The case of Los Angeles. *Annals of the American Academy of Political and Social Sciences, 452,* 89–110.

MEYER, K., MAGEDANZ, T., DAHLIN, D., & CHAPMAN, S. (1981). A comparative assessment of assault incidents: Robbery-related, ambush, and general police assaults. *Journal of Police Science and Administration, 9,* 1–13.

MILTON, C., HALLECK, J., LARDNER, J., & ABRECHT, G. (1977). *Police use of deadly force.* Washington, DC: Police Foundation.

"NEW YORK OFFICERS CHARGED WITH MURDER COUNT." (1999, April 1). *Los Angeles Times,* p. A–11.

PATE, A., & FRIDELL, L. (1993). *Police use of force—official reports, citizen complaints, and legal consequences.* Washington, DC: Police Foundation.

PETERSON, R., & BAILEY, W. (1988). Structural influences on the killing of police: A comparison with general homicides. *Justice Quarterly, 5,* 207–233.

REISS, A. (1971). *The police and the public.* New Haven, CT: Yale University Press.

REISS, A. (1972). Police brutality. In L. Radzinowicz and M. E. Wolfgang (Eds.), *The criminal in the arms of the law: Vol. 2. Crime and justice* (pp. 293–308). New York: Basic Books.

ROHRLICH, T., & MERINA, V. (1991, May 19). Racial disparities seen in complaints to LAPD. *Los Angeles Times*, p. 1.

ROSSI, P., BERK, R., & EDISON, B. (1974). *The roots of urban discontent: Public policy, municipal institutions, and the ghetto*. New York: Wiley.

RUBENSTEIN, J. (1973). *City police*. New York: Farrar, Straus and Giroux.

SHERMAN, L. (1980a). Execution without trial: Police homicide and the constitution. *Vanderbilt Law Review, 33,* 71–100.

SHERMAN, L. (1980b). Causes of police behavior. *Journal of Research in Crime and Delinquency, 17,* 69–100.

SHERMAN, L., & BLUMBERG, M. (1981). Higher education and the police use of deadly force. *Journal of Criminal Justice, 9*(4), 317–331.

SHERMAN, L., & COHN, E. (with Patrick R. Gartin, Edward E. Hamilton, and Dennis P. Rogan). (1986). *Citizens killed by big city police, 1970–84*. Washington, DC: Crime Control Institute.

SHERMAN L., & LANGWORTHY, R. (1979). Measuring homicide by police officers. *Journal of Criminal Law and Criminology, 70,* 546–560.

SMITH, D. A., GRAHAM, N., & ADAMS, B. (1991). Minorities and the police: Attitudinal and behavioral questions. In M. J. Lynch and E. B. Patterson (Eds.). *Race and criminal justice* (pp. 22–35). Albany, NY: Harrow and Heston.

SORENSEN, J., MARQUARDT, J., & BROCK, D. (1993). Factors related to killings of felons by police officers: A test of the community violence and conflict hypotheses. *Justice Quarterly, 10,* 417–440.

SPARGER, J., & GIACOPASSI, D. (1992). Memphis revisited: A reexamination of police shootings after the *Garner* decision. *Justice Quarterly, 9,* 211–225.

TENNENBAUM, A. (1994). The influence of the *Garner* decision on police use of deadly force. *Journal of Criminal Law and Criminology, 85,* 241–260.

TENNESSEE V. GARNER, 105 S. Ct. 1694 (1985).

WAEGEL, W. (1984). The use of lethal force by police: The effect of statutory change. *Crime and Delinquency, 30*(1), 121–140.

WAGNER, A. E. (1980). Citizen complaints against the police: Summary report of a national survey. *Journal of Police Science and Administration, 8,* 247–252.

WALKER, S. (1992). *The police in America: An introduction*. New York: McGraw-Hill.

WEST, P. (1988). Investigation of complaints against the police: Summary report of a national survey. *American Journal of Police, 7,* 101–121.

WILSON, J. (1971). *Varieties of police behavior*. New York: Atheneum.

WORDEN, R. (1995). The "causes" of police brutality: Theory and evidence on police use of force. In *And justice for all: A national agenda for understanding and controlling police use of force* (pp. 31–60). Washington DC: Police Executive Forum.

YORK V. CITY OF SAN PABLO. 626 F. Supp. 34 (N.D. Cal.) (1985).

3

From Report Takers to Report Makers

Understanding the Police and Violence

Robert P. McNamara

INTRODUCTION

For some time, Americans have been concerned about the abuses of authority by police officers. In a number of dramatic instances, the police have used excessive
force against suspects and have abused citizens. For example, early one morning on
February 4, 1999, a young immigrant from Guinea named Amadou Diallo was returning to his Bronx apartment when he was approached by four plainclothes New York
City police officers. According to some accounts, Mr. Diallo fit the description of a serial rapist who had assaulted some 40 women in areas around Manhattan. What happened as the officers approached Mr. Diallo is unclear. The officers contend that they
identified themselves and said that Mr. Diallo's behavior led them to believe he was
reaching for a weapon. Others present at the time disagree with this interpretation of
events. What *is* known is that the officers drew their weapons and fired a total of 41
shots, resulting in Mr. Diallo's death ("Only a minority," 1997).

In 1997 Abner Louima, a 30-year-old immigrant from Haiti, was arrested when
he tried to intervene in a fight outside a Brooklyn nightclub. When Mr. Louima arrived
at the police station, he was dragged into a restroom and sodomized by officers with
the handle of a toilet plunger, which was then forced into his mouth. Eventually, he
was taken to the hospital after having been charged with resisting arrest and disorderly
conduct. Mr. Louima was critically injured, with a perforated colon, a lacerated blad-
der, several missing teeth, and an assortment of other injuries (Puddington, 1999).

In 1996 a South Carolina state trooper assaulted a motorist while she attempted to exit her vehicle after a traffic stop. The videotape from the officer's vehicle showed that he physically and verbally abused her without justification. Incidents such as these raise many questions concerning the attitudes, values, and behavior of police officers around the country.

At the same time, ample evidence indicates that police officers experience various forms of victimization by members of the communities they serve, often with lethal consequences. In Florida, a female police officer discovered a vehicle parked in a cemetery late at night. After radioing her dispatcher of her location, she went to investigate. When the dispatcher could not raise the officer on the radio, a supervisor was sent to the location, where he found the officer shot in the back of the head with her own weapon (Craig, 1997).

According to the *Uniform Crime Reports,* which collects data on the number of officers assaulted and killed in the line of duty, since 1988, nearly 700 police officers have been killed in the line of duty, another 629 have been killed in duty-related accidents, and more than 600,000 have been assaulted (U.S. Department of Justice, Federal Bureau of Investigation [FBI], 1998). The latest figures available indicate that the numbers are decreasing somewhat. In 1998, 61 officers were killed in the line of duty, a 6% decrease from 1997. However, in 1997, 65 officers were killed in the line of duty, a 16% increase from 1996, when 56 officers were slain. Assaults on police officers have steadily increased since 1995, but the numbers varied in the late 1980s and early 1990s. In 1998, 59,545 assaults against police officers were reported across the country, with nearly 31% of them resulting in injury to the officer. More will be said on this in the section on violence against the police, but for now, how can we explain incidents in which officers are offenders? What are the reasons for the increased attacks on the police? In this chapter, explanations of both types of incidents are explored.

The first part of this chapter explores the reasons why officers can feel justified in using excessive force and describes of how officers are socialized, including an overview of the subculture of the police. One way to understand the use of violence by police officers is to suggest that officers are part of a larger group that socializes individuals to embody a set of behavioral expectations. This chapter also addresses the nature versus nurture debate in policing—are officers socialized to act a certain way, or do they already possess psychological traits that result in certain behaviors?

The second part of this chapter focuses on why individuals use violence to victimize police officers. Similar to the subcultural explanation of officers who engage in inappropriate violence, frustration-aggression and social learning theories along with the subculture of violence hypothesis help us to understand how and in what ways some members of the community justify the use of violence against the police.

VIOLENCE BY THE POLICE

Whenever incidents of brutality or other forms of misconduct by police officers occur, the explanations typically focus on cultural themes. Officers are said to be members of a police culture, which promotes solidarity, secrecy, and mistrust of outsiders. This police culture allows a variety of acts, such as those that recently occurred in New York City. Officers have traditionally been trained to believe that they must protect each other in all circumstances. They have also been trained to view the world in a particular way, seeing many threats to their safety.

Crank (1998) developed a rather unique way of understanding and explaining the police culture, particularly the dimension of solidarity. Building on the work of Coser (1956), Crank argued that the high level of integration and the strong sense of internal cohesion among police come from the conflicts the police have with a host of out-groups: the criminal population, politicians, and the general public. In other words, in responding to the grievances made against them, officers bond together against a common enemy (nonpolice), and the adversity creates strong ties of allegiance.

Part of the reason solidarity is so pervasive in policing comes from the nature of those conflicts. The dangers of police work, like combat, engender a particularly strong sense of loyalty and concern for one's comrades. Not all police work is dangerous, however, so the cohesion that is generated cannot be simply explained by the violent nature of some activities. Crank (1998) argued that an additional component must exist that, although far less dangerous in the physical sense, is sufficiently threatening to the group to result in the loyalties that are one of the hallmarks of policing. These main factors are the threats or political challenges the police face from other groups, such as the public, the courts, and the media. From these challenges, a number of themes emerge that serve to reaffirm membership in the police culture. Three of the most important themes Crank describes are *police morality, masculinity,* and *solidarity.* Solidarity introduces the notion of the police subculture and the debate over whether officers are socialized in a certain way or possess personality traits that make them more likely to become police officers.

Police Morality

To explain police morality, Crank (1998) suggested that the police see themselves as representatives of a higher morality. They view themselves as guardians whose responsibility it is to rid society of its deviants. Officers are trained not only to deal with certain individuals but also to assert police morality over a particular kind of individual—the person who complains or challenges the way the police do their work. These individuals are what Van Maanen (1978) referred to as "assholes."

The moral dimension of policing is said to be at the heart of the police culture (Caldero, 1995), and this police morality justifies all the police do to carry out their mission—even if this means abusing suspects and offenders. This is enhanced by a sense of high-mindedness that involves identifying who "deserves" harsh treatment. Thus, the police can be heavy-handed with a societal miscreant because he or she deserves to be punished and might not engage in future immoral behavior if given a bit of street justice. The problem, of course, is who determines if the person is a societal miscreant? Officers do not enter into interactions with citizens with a neutral state of mind. They have already used a variety of cues to size up the person and to determine if he or she is, in Van Maanen's term, an asshole. In fact, officers, over time, tend to begin viewing anyone they interact with as a potential or outright asshole. As a result, coercive behavior may be justified in their minds when, in fact, it is not at all appropriate. Van Maanen also argued that the process of defining people as cops or assholes is progressive. Not only are the public, politicians, lawyers, and criminals assholes, even other cops become assholes, too.

Van Maanen describes it this way: "You're at roll call and hear your buddy make the same wisecrack for the thousandth time, and you think, Jeez that guy's an asshole. One morning you look at yourself in the mirror and you realize that there's an asshole looking back at you. At this point the term asshole becomes so universal that it loses all meaning" (1978, p. 78).

Thus, police morality and high-mindedness and the police role as the protectors of morality lead to a strong sense of cohesion and, by extension, justification of the use of excessive force.

Masculinity

As a cultural theme, masculinity carries with it the ideas of appropriate behavior in policing. Masculinity dictates how police work should be done and by whom to maintain the public order. This is obviously emphasized in training: physical conditioning, fighting skills, marksmanship—skills that are part of the traditional male roles in society—along with certain traits—to be tough, to have courage, to be physical. All of these skills and traits are needed to address the dangers of police work and are thus a central theme in understanding the police culture. Even inappropriate behavior by officers is sometimes minimized if it is couched in terms of masculinity. The idea that "boys will be boys" is a tempering mechanism that, in some instances, allows officers to escape responsibility for their actions (e.g., officers who demand sexual favors from prostitutes in lieu of arrest).

Masculinity in policing is further entrenched because many officers come from working-class backgrounds in which stereotypical ideas about the roles of men and women are firmly established at an early age. Related to masculinity and the way men are socialized is the notion of bravery (Crank, 1998). In fact, one might argue that bravery is the vehicle by which masculinity is transmitted throughout the police culture. Episodes of bravery are told and retold to officers, particularly young ones, and they convey the subtle and not-so-subtle message about how police work should be done. Because these "war stories" are told repeatedly, they reify the value of masculinity in policing. More important, bravery comes in different shapes and textures. Although the most obvious form of bravery comes from the officer's willingness to put himself or herself in harm's way, bravery can also be identified in the refusal to show certain emotions, such as fear, sympathy, or compassion. In short, bravery involves the hiding of one's feelings, especially personal ones.

Solidarity

Anthony Bouza (1990) once remarked, "The sense of 'us vs. them' that develops between cops and the outside world forges a bond between cops whose strength is fabled. It is called the brotherhood in blue and it inspires a fierce and unquestioning loyalty to all cops, everywhere" (p. 74). Crank (1998) argued that loyalty is a central feature of the police culture, derived primarily from the belief that officers can rely only on each other. Along with the potential dangers of police work, officers perceive of a lack of support by the public. Officers also believe that the organization itself does not protect them: Administrators are more concerned with political gains or legal liability or are so out of touch with the realities of policing that they leave officers vulnerable and do not support them in their time of need. Collectively, these threats lead to a profound sense of loyalty among officers.

The external emblems also promote a sense of solidarity and loyalty among officers; uniforms, badges, rank, authority, and weapons are all reminders of the authority of the police. Thus, solidarity is carefully cultivated, taught formally, and reinforced informally through the first few years on the job, resulting in a sense of family that makes allowances for indiscretions or mistakes. Since the external threats are always present, an overly critical administration or a citizenry that does not understand or appreciate the dilemmas of police work leads officers to believe that in times of trouble, the only ones they can rely on are other officers.

On the surface, loyalty and solidarity are positive components to policing. A strong sense of integration and esprit de corps allows officers to be more productive and happier and to feel a sense of commitment and responsibility to others, as well as an element of safety in numbers. As we have seen repeatedly, however, this sense of loyalty and solidarity can become so distorted that the mandate of the police, to protect the public, becomes less important than protecting one's comrades when they engage in inappropriate behavior.

Where do these themes of police morality, masculinity, and solidarity come from? How do they become a part of policing? The obvious answer comes from the way officers are socialized and how they learn the expectations within the police subculture. Although these themes help us to describe the characteristics of police officers to a degree, we need to understand the context in which these themes occur. To do that we must understand how officers learn their craft.

SOCIALIZATION AND THE POLICE

The concept of socialization has been subjected to extensive analysis with the definitions of the concept varying widely. Generally speaking, we can say the term *socialization* is used to describe the ways in which people learn to conform to their society's norms, values, and roles. Many sociologists contend that people develop their own unique personalities as a result of the learning they gain from parents, siblings, relatives, teachers, and all the other people who influence them throughout their lives (Elkin & Handel, 1989). The importance of socialization then is that people learn to behave according to the expectations of their culture and transmit that way of life from one generation to the next. In this way, the culture of a society is reproduced (see Parsons & Bales, 1955; Danziger, 1971).

Socialization also occurs throughout an individual's life as he or she learns the norms of new groups in new situations. Generally speaking, there are three categories of socialization: *primary socialization,* which involves the ways in which the child becomes a part of society; *secondary socialization,* during which the influence of others outside the family becomes important; and *adult socialization,* when the person learns the expectations of adult roles and statuses in society. Adult socialization includes learning the standards set by one's occupation.

The Socialization Process in Occupations

Of the many roles that an individual is called on to perform, few surpass the importance of possessing the skills and attitudes necessary for his or her occupation. This is especially true in modern society in which occupation has a central place in the life of the vast majority of adults. In fact, occupation is challenged only by the family and the peer group as the major determinant of behavior and attitudes (Moore, 1969). To the degree that adequate socialization occurs to permit an individual to adequately perform in an occupation, his or her worldview, attitudes toward others, and general well-being are influenced.

Interestingly, occupational socialization has not elicited the kind of scholarly interest that one might expect. Academic interest in socialization has traditionally focused on infancy and childhood. Only within the past 30 years or so have researchers become keenly interested in occupational socialization, or what is sometimes referred to as the sociology of work (see Erikson &Vallas, 1995). Moreover, the topics seem to focus on the normative dimensions of occupations, that is, the rules relating to the proper conduct and attitudes of an individual in a particular job or career.

In a classic study of socialization into an occupation, Becker, Greer, Hughes, and Strauss (1961) examined the process by which medical students are socialized into their profession. At the University of Kansas Medical School, Becker et al. (1961) found that lower-class medical students, by virtue of their undergraduate education and commitment to becoming successful physicians, had clearly assimilated middle-class norms and values. Becker et al. also found that first-year medical students had idealistic reasons for becoming physicians; helping people was more important than making money. In the beginning of their profession, then, many students had a strong sense of idealism and believed that medical school would give them the opportunity to develop the skills needed to further that goal.

The process of medical training, however, caused the students to alter their views. Early on, they adapted to the expectations of medical school and developed a strong appreciation of clinical experience (working with patients rather than reading about disease and studying it in the laboratory). The students also learned to view disease and death as medical problems rather than as emotional issues. In addition, despite their idealism, the students quickly learned that they could not learn everything they needed to know to practice medicine and soon directed their efforts toward finding the most economical way of learning. Generally, this meant guessing what their faculty wanted them to know so that the material could be studied for the examinations. Thus, during the course of their medical training, idealism was replaced with a concern for getting through the program. Becker et al. observed that medical students may in fact become cynical while in school but these attitudes were often situational. As graduation approached, idealism seemed to return once the students were no longer under the intense pressure to perform. The immediate problem of completing their studies had passed. When isolated in an institutional setting, the students adjusted to immediate demands. Once released from that setting, their attitudes changed to again conform to their new surroundings.

The broader implications of Becker et al.'s work are that individuals are socialized to meet the expectations that important institutions or organizations place on them. Their attitudes, values, and beliefs become centered around fulfilling those expectations. In the case of the physician, who has a great deal of autonomy, the original ideological concerns reemerge at the end of his or her training, largely because he or she has the ability to determine what type of medicine to practice and under what circumstances. In those professions with an intense training period, less autonomy, and greater internal control by the organization, the individual is greatly influenced by the members of that organization. In other words, the greater the freedom to practice one's profession, the less socialization results. In those professions in which the individual is constrained by organizational rules and regulations, however, the other members are more influential on the thoughts and actions of the individual. This is exacerbated in professions that actively promote a sense of camaraderie and solidarity among its members, such as policing.

Resocialization

Perhaps the most significant aspect of the socialization process is that members within an organization (or, more broadly, within a society) internalize a set of norms that dictate appropriate behavior. Should this fail to occur, the organization is forced to employ corrective methods to ensure conformity. This includes rehabilitating deviants or criminals. Most people are resocialized because of a decision to join a new group. A good example of this occurs when an individual selects a particular career, such as a soldier or police officer. Here the work of Erving Goffman plays a significant part in our understanding. In his classic *Asylums,* Goffman (1961) contended that the resocialization of individuals often occurs in "total institutions," defined as places where the individual's physical and social freedom are constrained and channeled in a certain direction. Goffman described resocialization as a two-step process. First, an individual undergoes what he calls the "mortification of the self," where the attitudes, worldviews, and behavioral patterns of the individual are stripped away. Goffman (1961) states:

> The recruit comes into the establishment with a conception of himself made possible by certain stable social arrangements in his home world. Upon entrance, he is immediately stripped of the support provided by these arrangements. In the accurate language of some of our oldest total institutions, he begins a series of abasements, degradations, humiliations, and profanations of self. His self is systematically, if often unintentionally, mortified. He begins some radical shifts in his *moral career,* a career composed of the progressive changes that occur in the beliefs that he has concerning himself and significant others. The processes by which a person's self is mortified are fairly standard in total institutions; analysis of these processes can help us to see the arrangements that ordinary establishments must guarantee if members are to preserve their civilian selves. (p. 14)

This paves the way for the second step in resocialization, where a new set of attitudes, values, and beliefs are provided:

> Once the inmate is stripped of his possessions, at least some replacements must be made by the establishment, but these take the form of standard issue, uniform in character and uniformly distributed. These substitute possessions are clearly marked as really belonging to the institution and in some cases are recalled at regular intervals to be, as it were, disinfected of identifications. . . . While the process of mortification goes on, the inmate begins to receive formal and informal instruction in what will here be called the privilege system. In so far as

the inmate's attachment to his civilian self has been shaken by the stripping process of the institution, it is largely the privilege system that provides a framework for personal reorganization. (Goffman, 1961, p. 19)

For instance, in the case of the military, the new recruit or civilian is brought to a boot camp and stripped of any individual characteristics: Clothes are taken away, haircuts are given, and rules on every aspect of life in the institution are explained. During this process, the sense of self gives way, and the individual becomes a cog in a much larger machine. Only after this process is complete can the organization implement the second part of the resocialization process. Upon completion of boot camp, the recruit has a different sense of self, along with a new set of attitudes and behavior patterns.

A similar process occurs in policing. The police academy (also considered a total institution) begins the first overt process of resocialization after the selection of recruits. In addition to the skills and techniques needed to become an effective police officer, recruits are indoctrinated and exposed to the vernacular used by the police and the cultural norms dictating acceptable and unacceptable police behavior, as well as the worldview from the policing perspective. These values, attitudes, and beliefs are reinforced informally as new officers interact with more experienced ones outside the classroom. The war stories told by more seasoned officers reinforces the points made by the formal classroom lessons. Over time, recruits develop attitudes and behaviors that provide a consistent framework in which to understand the role of the police and the individual officer (Radelet, 1986).

The resocialization process continues after the academy, when the recruit is usually assigned some sort of field training. The time spent in this phase of training varies by department but can be up to six months. The field training officer (FTO) is responsible for teaching the new officer how to apply lessons from the academy to the tasks on the street. The FTO is also charting the progress (or lack thereof) of the recruit. The style of the FTO, as well as the way in which the FTO interacts with citizens, will tend to be reflected in the recruit's behavior. In this way, FTO training is a part of the resocialization process even though it may not be a conscious process (Radelet, 1986).

After FTO training, the officer remains on probation for a period of time, usually one year. During this time, a supervisor evaluates the officer in terms of progress and overall performance in the job. As described by Becker et al. (1961), most recruits will admit that part of the learning process involves knowing the unique expectations their supervisor/teacher has for them. When this is learned, the officer will modify his or her behavior to conform with that of the supervisor (Radelet, 1986). If, for instance, the officer learns that the sergeant places a great deal of emphasis on police-community relations, the officer will, in turn, have more community contacts. These learned behaviors are part of what Goffman (1961) referred to as *working* the system. More important, these behaviors are the essence of occupational socialization.

For the most part, this is a normal part of the learning process. In order to be an effective police officer, the rookie officer must first learn the tricks of the trade, and the most knowledgeable officers should impart their wisdom to their less learned colleagues. However, the potential exists for various forms of misconduct to be taught as well as the proper procedures and attitudes.

NATURE VERSUS NURTURE IN POLICING

As mentioned earlier, some researchers contend that police officers have very different personalities from people in other occupations. Others maintain that a cultural distinction separates policing from other occupations. Still others contend that officers have neither personality nor cultural differences from other occupations. In sum, what we know about the police culture and personality is dependent on how one views police behavior. No single perspective provides a complete understanding of the varieties of police behavior, but there is a long history of debate as to whether police officers have unique personalities or whether socialization and subcultures play a significant part in their behavior. What can be said with some confidence is that the roles and functions of the police set officers apart from other members of society (Radelet, 1986).

Cops Are Made

A number of researchers argue that personality is not fixed and rigid and is subject to change based on different personal experiences and socialization. The "nurture" school of thought believes that cops are made. This school of thought focuses on the role of the police in society and how professionalization, training, and socialization influence an individual's personality and behavior. Researchers operating from this paradigm study how the work environment, peers, and academy training shape and affect a police officer's personality and behavior. Many of these researchers, such as Adlam (1982), still focus attention on an individual's unique experiences and the development of individual personalities.

A somewhat different approach contends that socialization occurs, but it is more of a group experience than an individual one (Stoddard, 1968; Van Maanen, 1978). Van Maanen (1978) disagreed with the idea that police officers have certain personality characteristics, such as authoritarianism. He argued instead for a perspective based on both group socialization and professionalism. Professionalism is the process by which norms and values are internalized as an individual begins his or her new occupation. In this way, just as attorneys and physicians learn the values endemic to their profession, so, too, do police officers.

This perspective assumes that police officers learn their "social" personality through training and exposure to the demands of police work. If police officers become cynical or rigid, it follows then that it is not because of their existing personality or individual experience, but because of the demands of the job and the shared experiences of others. Some research supports this idea. For instance, Bennett (1984) found that although probationary officers' values are affected by the training process, little evidence suggested that their personalities were shaped by their peers in the department. Part of this explanation involves the legitimacy of newly hired officers, who do not become "real" police officers until they are accepted as a member in standing of the police subculture.

Other studies, such as Putti, Aryee, and Kang (1988), found that a temporal factor may be at work in the socialization of police officers. Socialization into the subculture of the police may occur at different points in the officers' careers. Little evidence exists concerning the extent of how fellow officers affect the personality of older officers, but it seems that in the beginning of their careers, the officers' occupational values are shaped during the training and probationary process.

Still another model is offered by Kappeler, Blumberg, and Potter (1993), who believe in an acculturation process whereby the beliefs and values of police work are transmitted from one generation of officers to the next. In effect, the group socializes the individual officer into ways of acceptable and unacceptable behavior. This perspective draws heavily from anthropology and introduces the concept of the police subculture more concretely.

Cops Are Born

Many researchers adopting the "nature" perspective, however, believe that personality is fixed and does not really change by choice of occupation or experience. In other words, each person has a fixed personality that does not vary during the course of his or her life (Adlam, 1982). This does not imply that personality is inviolate or does not have some degree of malleability, but generally speaking, it stays the same. As it applies to the police, most of the research in this area focuses on the personality characteristics of people who choose to become police officers. This perspective assumes that people with certain types of personalities enter policing as an occupation and behave in certain ways.

One of the most influential experts in this area is Milton Rokeach. In comparing the values of police officers in Michigan with those of a national sample of private citizens, Rokeach, Miller, and Snyder (1971) found that police officers seemed more oriented toward self-control and obedience than the average citizen, and officers were more interested in personal goals, such as "an exciting life." Officers were also less interested in larger social goals, such as "a world at peace." Rokeach et al. (1971) also found evidence that the experiences of police officers did not significantly influence their personalities. Rokeach et al. concluded that most officers probably have a unique value orientation and personality when they embark upon their careers in policing.

In a similar study, Teevan and Dolnick (1973) compared values of officers in the Cook County, Illinois, Sheriff Department with those Rokeach et al. encountered in Lansing, Michigan. The findings suggested that the values of police officers in a large urban department were also far removed from those of the general public. Some of the reasons, according to Teevan and Dolnick, were that officers are isolated within society, they are required to enforce unpopular laws, and self-imposed segregation occurs as officers think of themselves as a last bastion of middle-class morality.

Research suggests that police officers tend to be more authoritarian than civilians (e.g., Rokeach, Miller, & Snyder, 1971). In describing the authoritarian personality, Adorno (1950) characterized it in part as being aggressive, cynical, and rigid. People with these characteristics are said to have a myopic view of the world and see issues, people, and behavior as clearly defined: good or bad, right or wrong, friends or enemies. They also tend to be very conservative in their political orientation (see also Niederhoffer, 1967; Bayley & Mendelsohn, 1969). Levy (1967) proposed that certain personality traits established early in life were clues to whether a person would be more likely to find policing attractive as a profession. She states:

We find that the appointees most likely to remain in law enforcement are probably those who are more unresponsive to the environmental stresses introduced when they become officers of the law than are their fellow-appointees. These stresses include becoming a member of a "minority" (occupationally speaking) group, need to adhere to semi-military regimen, community expectation of incongruous roles and the assumption of a position of authority complete with the trappings of uniform, badge, holster, and gun, and all these imply. The officers who remain in law enforcement may well be the sons of fathers who imposed a rigid code of behavior to which their children learned to adhere, and who do not feel a strong need to defy or rebel against authority. (p. 275)

On the other hand, some researchers have pointed to a few positive aspects of the authoritarian type of personality in police officers. For instance, Carpenter and Raza (1987) found that police applicants as a group are less depressed and more assertive in making and maintaining social contacts. Moreover, they found that police officers are a more homogeneous group, which may be based on their similar interests in becoming police officers as well as sharing similar personality traits and worldviews.

Ultimately, many police officers develop an occupational or working personality, characterized by authoritarianism, suspicion, and cynicism (Alpert & Dunham, 1992; Neiderhoffer, 1967; Rubenstein, 1973; Van Maanen, 1978). Skolnick (1994) provides perhaps the best description of the police personality:

The policeman's role contains two principal variables, danger and authority, which should be interpreted in the light of a "constant" pressure to appear efficient. The element of danger seems to make the policeman especially attentive to signs indicating a potential for violence and lawbreaking. As a result, the policeman is generally a "suspicious" person. Furthermore, the character of the policeman's work makes him less desirable as a friend, since norms of friendship implicate others in his work. Accordingly, the element of danger isolates the policeman socially from that segment of the citizenry that he regards as symbolically dangerous and also from the conventional citizenry with whom he identifies. (p. 43)

An integral part of the police personality is cynicism: the notion that all people are motivated by evil and selfishness. Police cynicism develops among many officers through the nature of police work. Most police officers feel set apart from the rest of society because they have the power to regulate the lives of others. Moreover, by constantly dealing with crime and the more unsavory aspects of social life, their faith in humanity seems to diminish.

Probably the most well-known study of police personality was conducted by Arthur Neiderhoffer (1967). In *Behind the Shield,* Neiderhoffer built on the work of William Westley (1970) that most officers develop into cynics as a function of their daily routines. According to Westley, being constantly faced with keeping people in line and believing that most people intend to break the law or cause harm to them led officers to mistrust the people they were charged to protect. Neiderhoffer tested Westley's assumption by distributing a survey measuring attitudes and values to 220 New York City police officers. Among his most important findings were that police cynicism did increase with length of service; that patrol officers with college educations became quite cynical if they were denied promotion; and that military-like academy training caused recruits to become cynical about themselves, the department, and the community. As an illustration, Niederhoffer found that nearly 80% of first-day recruits believed the department was an "efficient, smoothly operating organization." Two months later, less than a third professed that belief. Similarly, half of the recruits believed that a supervisor was "very interested in the welfare of his subordinates," while two months later, those still believing so dropped to 13%. Niederhoffer (1967) states:

> Cynicism is an ideological plank deeply entrenched in the ethos of the police world, and it serves equally well for attack or defense. For many reasons police are particularly vulnerable to cynicism. When they succumb, they lose faith in people, society, and eventually in themselves. In their Hobbesian view, the world becomes a jungle in which crime, corruption, and brutality are normal features of the terrain. (p. 9)

In sum, the police personality emerges as a result of the nature of police work and of the socialization process. To deal with the social isolation that is derived from their use of authority, some of it self-imposed, officers use other members of the profession to cope with social rejection. As a result, many, perhaps most, police officers become part of a closely knit subculture that is protective and supportive of its members, while sharing similar attitudes, values, and views of the world.

THE SUBCULTURE OF POLICING

Occupational socialization creates occupational subcultures (Radelet & Carter, 1994). The idea of the police being a subculture is not new and has been well documented (Bittner, 1970; Kirkham, 1976; Rokeach, Miller, & Snyder, 1971; Westley, 1970). For our purposes, subculture may be defined as the meanings, values, and behavior patterns unique to a particular group in a given society. Entry into this subculture begins with a process of socialization whereby recruits learn the values and behavior patterns characteristic of experienced officers.

The development and maintenance of negative attitudes and values by police officers has many implications. Regoli and Poole (1979) found evidence that an officer's feelings of cynicism intensify the need to maintain respect and increase the desire to exert authority over others. This can easily lead to the increased fear and mistrust of the police by the general public. This, in turn, can create feelings of hostility and resentment on the part of the officer, creating what is sometimes known as *police paranoia* (Regoli & Poole, 1979, p. 43). Regoli and Poole also found that these negative attitudes result in conservative attitudes and a resistance to change among the officers.

As mentioned earlier, the creation of the police subculture also stems from this unique police personality. Despite the evidence, however, many researchers disagree with the notion of a police subculture. Balch (1972) in his study of the police personality states: "It looks like policemen may be rather ordinary people, not greatly unlike other middle Americans. We cannot be sure there is such a thing as a police personality, however we loosely define it" (p. 117). Similarly, Tifft (1974) argues that the attitudes of officers may be influenced by their work environment, but the idea that officers maintain uniform personality traits developed through socialization or innate drives is fallacious. Thus, he argues that the activities and responsibilities most officers engage in have a role to play in how they see the world, but in many ways this is symptomatic of many other occupations. He states: "Task related values, attitudes and behavior are occupationally derived or created out of specialized roles rather than being primarily due to the selection factors of background or personality" (p. 268).

Thus, the debate over whether or not officers possess a distinct working personality, as well as whether or not the subculture of policing is pervasive, continues. What is important to remember is that the nature of police work remains complex and the issues surrounding policing have not been completely understood. Incidents such as the Rodney King beating will, unfortunately, continue. We simply do not know the reasons why officers engage in brutality. For some, it may be due to a psychological impairment; for others, it may simply be that they are following the rules set out by the larger group in certain situations. Our task as researchers is to sufficiently understand the context in which these incidents occur and attempt to offer some insight as to why these behaviors develop and continue. To date, the answers to these questions remain elusive.

VIOLENCE AGAINST THE POLICE

In Inglewood, California, in 1993, Sergeant Donald Fry was sitting in his squad car, its engine running, making a notation in his log book when a man wearing a parka and blue jeans appeared out of the darkness. "How are you doing?" the man asked. He took another step toward the car and then pulled a semiautomatic pistol and fired at the officer. Fry grabbed at the man's hand, but he jerked free and ran as Fry managed to fire a few shots at him. Fortunately, Fry was wearing a bulletproof vest, which saved his life (Corwin, 1993).

Los Angeles police officer Bob Brannon was parked at a fast-food restaurant near Figueroa and 50th Streets one evening, when he heard what he thought was a brick being thrown at his car. He looked up and saw a man, about 20 feet away, shooting at him with a .357-caliber magnum handgun. The man fired three more shots, leaving four holes in Brannon's vehicle. A few inches higher and Brannon would have been struck by those shots (Corwin, 1993).

According to the *Uniform Crime Reports,* from 1977 to 1993, the number of violent assaults against police officers rose steadily (U.S. Department of Justice, FBI, 1998). In 1977, the first year data were kept on this topic, about 49,000 officers across the nation were assaulted, primarily with guns or knives. As Table 3.1 indicates, by 1991, that number had increased to almost 63,000. During the 1990s, assaults on police officers declined significantly. In 1995, 58,063 assaults on officers were reported nationwide, a 21% decrease from 1990. In 1996, that number was 49,695, and in 1997, 49,151 officers were assaulted. In 1998, that number rose to 59,454. Firearm-related assaults decreased between 1995 and 1998, from 2,373 to 2,073. What we are seeing then is a steady increase of officers being attacked since 1977, and since 1995, the number has fluctuated slightly.

Table 3.2 shows the trend of officers killed in the line of duty since 1990. Although the total of 616 seems relatively small over a 9-year period, with an average of 68 officers per year, what is interesting is that between 60 and 80 officers are killed each year, a fairly consistent number.

It seems that the number of officers killed in the line of duty has decreased somewhat in recent times, and it appears that the number of officers assaulted has declined as well. The data also suggest that whereas officers are frequently assaulted, only about a third sustain injuries, with most of the problems for officers occurring during arrests. Despite these decreases, policing remains a high-risk profession as offenders are willing to attack and even kill officers.

TABLE 3.1   Law Enforcement Officers Assaulted, 1990–1998

Year	Total Assaults	Percent Injured	Firearm-Related
1990	72,270	36.3	3,154
1991	62,852	37.6	3,532
1992	81,252	36.5	4,455
1993	66,975	35.9	4,002
1994	64,912	35.7	3,168
1995	58,063	30.1	2,373
1996	46,695	32.1	1,887
1997	49,151	26.7	1,844
1998	59,545	30.6	2,073

Source: Uniform Crime Reports, Table 36, Law Enforcement Officers Assaulted, Type of Weapon and Percent Receiving Personal Injury, 1989–1998.

The police have a documented and somewhat stormy history in the use of violence against the public, but substantial evidence exists that the people they are sworn to serve frequently victimize them. Some people might argue that the reason for the violence against the police, now and over the sweep of history, has to do with retaliation—the police use violence unjustly, and the citizenry responds in kind. Whereas this may be true in some instances, as a general explanation of why officers are attacked, it is incomplete. So how do we understand violence, particularly violence against the police?

TABLE 3.2   Law Enforcement Officers Killed in the Line of Duty, 1990–1998

Year	Officers Killed
1990	66
1991	71
1992	64
1993	70
1994	79
1995	74
1996	61
1997	70
1998	61
TOTAL	616

Source: Uniform Crime Reports, Table 16, Law Enforcement Officers Feloniously Killed, 1989–1998.

Theories of Violence

Clearly we need to derive some sort of explanation for violence, especially in our society. We know a little about the patterns of violence; it occurs more often in urban settings, during warmer months, and among young minority males. Because of these predictable patterns, logic suggests that social factors must be operating when people engage in violence. One explanation suggested by Marvin Wolfgang and Franco Ferracuti is that a subculture of violence exists.

The logic behind this explanation for violence is relatively simple and draws from social learning theory. People who grow up in a subculture that places high approval on violent behavior have a greater chance of learning to be violent. Wolfgang (1958) wanted to determine why the homicide rate was relatively high among young, lower-class African American males. In his classic study, Wolfgang examined homicide cases in Philadelphia from 1948 to 1952.

From his analysis, Wolfgang concluded that young, lower-class African American males connected honor, masculinity, and identity with the willingness to be violent. They see violence as the appropriate response to an insult about one's race, name and honor of one's mother, and masculinity, among other things. In situations in which most people would find the slights trivial, these young men perceived the slights as challenges to their manhood, which translated into violence. Thus, one sees in these environments potent themes of violence that influence all aspects of social life: from socialization processes to interpersonal relationships to lifestyle. Members of these environments expect that violence will be used to solve social problems. In fact, an unwillingness to use violence can lead to ostracization by one's peer group.

Violence simply becomes a part of one's daily life. Violent individuals are not bound by guilt over their actions because it is an acceptable way of problem resolution. Violence is also not immoral since it fits within the community standards that accept violence as a means of preserving personal honor. Thus, Wolfgang and Ferracuti (1967) concluded that the young men in their study were growing up in a subculture of violence that teaches them to be violent because their peers and even some adult role models consider violence appropriate for a wider range of situations than the general population.

Members of this subculture are said to spend a great deal of time presenting a sense of self that is violent, tough, and willing to use any means necessary to protect themselves and their social reputations. Of critical importance is demonstrating that one is not weak—they will not back down from a confrontation. To do so would result in a loss of status. Horowitz (1983), in her classic *Honor and the American Dream,* which focused on Chicano gangs in Chicago, discovered that many of the Hispanic men in her study spent a great deal of time cultivating and preserving their honor. As she describes it:

> Honor revolves around a person's ability to command deference in interpersonal relations . . . in an honor bound subculture that emphasizes manhood and defines violations of interpersonal etiquette in an adversarial manner, any action that challenges a person's right to deferential treatment in public—whether derogating a person, offering a favor that may be difficult to return, or demonstrating lack of respect for a female relative's sexual purity—can be interpreted as an insult and a potential threat to manhood. Honor demands that a man be able physically to back his claim to dominance and independence. (p. 81)

Katz (1989) also discussed the subcultural influences on the use of violence in his book *Seductions of Crime*. In his chapter entitled "The Ways of the Badass," Katz writes:

> To be "bad" is to be mean in a precise sense of the term. Badasses manifest the transcendent superiority of their being, specifically by insisting on the dominance of their will, that "I mean it," when the "it" itself is, in a way obvious to all, immaterial. They engage in violence not necessarily sadistically or "for its own sake" but to back up their meaning without the limiting influence of utilitarian considerations or a concern for self-preservation. At this level, the badass announces, in effect, "Not only do you not know where I'm at or where I'm coming from, but, at any moment, I may transcend the distance between us and destroy you. I'll jump you on the street, I'll 'come up side' your head, I'll 'fuck you up good'—I'll rush destructively to the center of your world, whenever I will! Where I'm coming from, you don't want to know!" (p. 81)

Thus, the subculture of violence is said by many social scientists to be one of the main reasons why minor disputes erupt so quickly—spilling a drink or accidentally bumping into another person can result in a swift and violent reaction. This is especially true when an audience instigates the conflict or urges the participants on. After all, in those circumstances, the communal values are being threatened and tested.

Related to the subculture of violence hypothesis are the social learning theories. Perhaps the best-known learning theory in the social sciences is Edwin Sutherland's *differential association*. Sutherland argued that people learn how to commit violence in the same way they learn any other type of behavior—by interacting with others. From other individuals, people learn not only the techniques of violence, how to commit it, but also the motives, attitudes, and rationalizations for violent behavior. To learn that certain situations call for violence as a problem-solving mechanism depends on the people with whom one associates. As Henslin (1990) illustrated, associate with one group and you learn a particular way of acting, associate with a different group and you learn a different way. This is the essence of differential association.

Differential association helps us to explain all forms of deviant and criminal behavior, and we can apply it to the use of violence. Critical to the process, however, is that the person must come into contact with others who have an "excess of definitions favorable to using violence over definitions unfavorable to using violence" (Henslin, 1990, p. 241). In other words, the individual must come into contact with people who find violence acceptable and engage in it themselves. But how favorable? Sutherland says that differential associations may vary in frequency, duration, priority, and intensity. That is, the most significant associations for learning violence are those that are the most frequent, endure the longest, take place earliest in life, and are the most emotional and meaningful to an individual (Siegel, 1999).

Evidence of violence as learned behavior can be found in many places. Many social scientists argue that violent habits are acquired through imitation or as a result of the reinforcement of aggressive behavior. For instance, some research exists to show that physically aggressive parents tend to have physically aggressive children. Other studies, such as Bandura (1986), demonstrate that children who observe adults displaying physical aggression will be more aggressive in their later play activities than those who are not exposed.

In general, we can say with some confidence that many researchers argue that physical punishment by parents is more likely to encourage physical violence in children than to discourage it. Nevertheless, the majority of American parents continue to believe that the use of violence (spanking) is an appropriate way of raising their children. In 1999, survey data showed that 65% of Americans approved of spanking. Social class, however, influences the use of violence. Public opinion surveys showed that about 40% of college-educated Americans disapprove of spanking, whereas only 20% of those who did not complete high school disapprove (Rosellini, 1998).

As with the nature/nurture argument in policing, not everyone agrees with the subculture of violence hypothesis. Kornblum and Julian (2000), for example, argued that the subculture of violence hypothesis is based on analyses of official police records. They demonstrated that certain subcultures have higher rates of violent crime than other groups in society. However, they argued that the stereotype of an offender being a young minority man is inaccurate because official statistics do not reflect the attitudes or ideologies of individual offenders, and this makes it difficult to discover the motives for their crimes.

Kornblum and Julian's main point, then, was that violent crime can be seductive for some offenders, who obtain a thrill from hurting others, but this is a far cry from asserting that an entire group of people place a high value on committing violent crime. Thus, they argued that because of the premise on which this argument is based (that some groups value violence simply because it is enjoyable) and the data on which the premise is justified (official statistics only document the number of instances, not the motives behind the acts) people who commit acts of violence against others seem to share "not an adherence to subcultural norms and values, but rather, a similar set of psychological traits that can be found in any social, economic, or ethnic group" (Kornblum & Julian, 2000, p. 195).

Another way of understanding and explaining violence is the frustration-aggression theory. Here, violence is simply a result of frustration of some unfulfilled need. This need produces the frustration, and it is vented in aggression. In addition, the strength of these blocked needs determine the level and extent of aggression. The frustration-aggression theory has been described as the easiest and most popular explanation of all types of violence including riots, delinquency, and crime (Berkowitz, 1993). The main problem with this theory is its failure to explain why frustration leads to aggression in some instances and not in others. Moreover, frustration-aggression can be defined so broadly that it can cover almost any conceivable situation.

Related to frustration-aggression theory is control theory. Control theory states that a person's ability and willingness to follow the societal rules, or, put another way, to restrain or control impulsive behavior, is related to his or her number and level of attachments with significant others. In the absence of emotional attachments, people are free to engage in all types of behavior without guilt or remorse because they are not accountable to others in society. Thus, significant others, who would normally control the impulses people have to act in a certain way, cannot exert any influence over them (Kornblum & Julian, 2000).

Another way to link control theory to violence stems from the frustration people feel when they attempt to develop relationships with others and fail. Evidence of this can be found in the fact that violence is significantly more prevalent among ex-convicts, alcoholics, and others who are out of the mainstream of society and estranged from family and friends (Kornblum & Julian, 2000). The validity of control theory is difficult to demonstrate, however, since many violent crimes are spontaneous. The lack of attachment to others could simply be one of many factors that leads a person to violence.

DISCUSSION

It seems obvious that every theory is limited to some degree in its ability to explain behavior, and these theories that attempt to explain violence and other forms of criminal behavior are no exception to that rule. Instead of debating the merits of frustration-aggression theory or the subculture of violence hypothesis, however, since neither provides a complete explanation of why people engage in violence, perhaps it makes more sense to extract relevant parts of each theory that explain why individuals use violence, particularly against the police.

In other words, by merging a number of ideas together, we might be able to produce a more effective explanation. Although it is true, as Kornblum (2000) asserted, that there are problems with collecting data on violent offenders and that there may be more similarities between offenders based on psychological traits than on learning theories, the traits explanation fails to account for the environmental influences that operate in some neighborhoods. Thus, the traits explanation alone does not help us to understand violence in a comprehensive way.

We can say the same thing about frustration-aggression theory. It is indeed plausible that many offenders who attack the police are doing so because of the frustration and powerlessness they feel in a particular situation. Usually when the police are called on to resolve disputes, many emotions are swirling in a rather heated atmosphere. In fact, many officers receive training on defusing volatile situations precisely because they are at risk and must attempt to resolve the problem without resorting to violence themselves.

In many situations, however, the people who attack the police are frustrated about the way their lives are going, the lack of opportunities to succeed, or the system's failure to adequately address their needs. In these types of situations, the police become the symbols of the larger society: oppressors of a group of people or even that particular person. As a result, this frustration leads to aggression based not on what the officer did, but what he or she represents: an unjust society.

At the same time, however, many neighborhoods where this type of reaction is not only considered acceptable but promoted exist. If many members of this community feel as though the police or the larger society have not given them a fair opportunity to succeed, and members have tried to effect social change in conventional ways, violence may become acceptable. In this way, frustration-aggression theory links with the subculture of violence hypothesis and differential association. In short, frustration is exhibited through violence in places where violence is acceptable and promoted. It is also observed by others and imitated since there are social rewards to be gained by it.

Media images play an important role here. Whereas the link between the media and violence has not been completely understood, there is an element of socialization that takes place. Consider the controversial lyrics from the rapper Ice T's "Cop Killer." It is fairly clear that rap music emerged as a way of lamenting life in fragmented and violent neighborhoods, but another message is being sent as well—the acceptability of violence as a vehicle of retaliation. Whether one agrees or disagrees with the message, there can be little doubt that songs such as this one can be a basis of learning about the acceptability of violence, particularly against the police.

Frustration-aggression theory and the subculture of violence can be linked in another way. The sense of frustration felt by some members of a community is more easily understood when unprovoked hostility and violence are inflicted upon a member of that community. In situations in which officers act inappropriately, the aggression that stems from this can fuel the attitudes, values, and beliefs that justify violence—violence is seen as the only way to keep the police from going too far. This is especially true if the problem has happened before.

We should note another element to the subculture of violence hypothesis. In many neighborhoods, violence is a method of preserving personal honor. As Elijah Anderson (2000) chronicled in his book *Code of the Street,* a set of rules exist that dictate public behavior in poor neighborhoods. Given that many members of these communities have little in the way of economic, social, or political power, their street reputation is often all some have to document their identity. In some groups, one way to preserve one's honor or to simply enhance one's standing in the subculture is specifically to victimize a police officer. This goes beyond simply using violence against others to targeting police officers in particular. The reason, of course, is that such acts bolster one's standing in these communities. As Anderson (2000) documented, the role models in these communities perpetuate the violence against the police. Younger members are able to learn firsthand the process by which one victimizes others as well as the justifications for doing so.

Regardless of which theory is used or whether portions of each theory are melded together into a more comprehensive explanation, the debate continues over why people engage in violence. The reasons remain elusive why police officers are victimized by individuals who are either prone to violence, learn to be violent, or never learned to be a part of a community. What must be included in this discussion, however, is the behavior of officers in dealing with the community. The acts of violence inflicted on others by the police only inflame the issue and can be a factor in explaining why officers are victimized.

CONCLUSION

As mentioned earlier, since 1988, more than 1,300 police officers have been killed, either in the line of duty or in duty-related accidents, and an additional 600,000 officers have been assaulted. What is perhaps even more revealing is that despite decreasing crime rates over the last several years, the number of assaults on officers has steadily increased since 1995, with about one third of the assaults against the police resulting in injuries to officers. Although there is reason to be somewhat optimistic about the overall decrease in crime, the fact that officers are increasingly becoming victims of lethal and nonlethal assaults is cause for concern.

Moreover, numerous examples of officers who have exceeded their authority and victimized citizens are being reported. The Louima case, as well as the Diallo incident, raises questions as to why the police use excessive force.

The simplest explanation is retaliation. Police officers can rationalize violence as a way of exacting revenge on a suspect for any number of reasons, and the same logic applies when a group attacks or kills a police officer. A better understanding as to why officers engage in violence against the public can be explained in part by the socialization that officers receive early in their careers as well as the cultural influences that exist in policing. Similarly, the reasons why officers are killed or injured by citizens also have cultural and social influences.

Whether it be the subculture of violence hypothesis, which says violence fits within community standards; social learning theory, which suggests violence is learned like any other behavior; or frustration-aggression theory, which focuses on the unmet needs of individuals, each subculture feels they are keeping within the standards set out by their larger group. This does not excuse the actions of those individuals, but it does give us reason to pause and wonder if the two groups, the police and their attackers, might have more in common than we realize.

REFERENCES

ADLAM, K. R. (1982). The police personality: Psychological consequences of becoming a police officer. *Journal of Police Science and Administration, 10*(3), 347–348.

ADORNO, T. (1950). *The authoritarian personality.* New York: Harper and Brothers.

ALPERT, G., & DUNHAM, R. (1992). *Policing urban America* (2nd ed.). Prospect Heights, IL: Waveland Press.

ANDERSON, E. (2000). *Code of the street.* New York: Norton.

BALCH, R. (1972). The police personality: Fact or fiction? *Journal of Criminal Law, Criminology and Police Science, 63,* 117.

BANDURA, A. (1986). *Social foundations of thought and action.* Upper Saddle River, NJ: Prentice Hall.

BAYLEY, D. H., & MENDELSOHN, H. (1969). *Minorities and the police: Confrontation in America* New York: Free Press.

BECKER, H., GREER, B., HUGHES, E., & STRAUSS, A. (1961). *Boys in white: Student culture in medical school.* Chicago: University of Chicago Press.

BENNETT, R. (1984). Becoming blue: A longitudinal study of police recruit occupational socialization. *Journal of Police Science and Administration, 12*(1), 47–57.

BERKOWITZ, L. (1993). *Aggression: Its causes, consequences and control.* Philadelphia: Temple University Press.

BITTNER, E. (1970). *The functions of police in modern society.* Chevy Chase, MD: National Clearinghouse for Mental Health.

BOUZA, A. (1990). *The police mystique: An insider's look at cops, crime and the criminal justice system.* New York: Plenum.

CALDERO, M. (1995). Community Oriented Policing Reform: An Evaluation and Theoretical Analysis. Unpublished doctoral dissertation, Michigan State University.

CARPENTER, B. N., & RAZA, S. M. (1987). Personality characteristics of police applicants: Comparisons across subgroups and with other populations. *Journal of Police Science and Administration, 15*(1), 10–17.

CORWIN, J. (1993, April). Police officers killed in the line of duty. *Police Chief,* pp. 23–25.

COSER, L. (1956). *The functions of social conflict.* New York: Free Press.

CRAIG, G. (1997, December 30). Violent attacks on police here defy U.S. trend. *Rochester Democrat and Chronicle,* p. 1.

CRANK, J. (1998). *Understanding police culture.* Belmont, CA: Wadsworth.

DANZIGER, K. (1971). *Socialization.* Harmondsworth, Engl.: Penguin.

ELKIN, F., & HANDEL, G. (1989). *The child and society: The process of socialization* (5th ed.). New York: Random House.

ERIKSON, K., & VALLAS, P. (Eds.). (1995). *The nature of work: Sociological perspectives.* Washington, DC: American Sociological Association.

GOFFMAN, E. (1961). *Asylums.* New York: Anchor.

HENSLIN, J. M. (1990). *Social problems* (2nd ed.). Upper Saddle River, NJ: Prentice Hall.

HOROWITZ, R. (1983). *Honor and the American dream*. New Brunswick, NJ: Rutgers University.

KAPPELER, V. E., BLUMBERG, M., & POTTER, G. W. (1993). *The mythology of crime and criminal justice*. Prospect Heights, IL: Waveland Press.

KATZ, J. (1989). *Seductions of crime*. New York: Free Press.

KIRKHAM, G. (1976). *Signal zero*. New York: Ballentine.

KORNBLUM, W., & JULIAN, J. (2000). *Social problems* (10th ed.). Upper Saddle River, NJ: Prentice Hall.

LEVY, R. (1967). Predicting police failures. *Journal of Criminal Law, Criminology, and Police Science, 58*(2), 275.

MOORE, W. (1969). Occupational socialization. In D. Goslin (Ed.), *Handbook of Socialization Theory and Research*, pp. 861–884. New York: Rand McNally.

NIEDERHOFFER, A. (1967). *Behind the shield: The police in urban society*. Garden City, NY: Doubleday.

"ONLY A MINORITY: POLICE BRUTALITY." (1997, August 23). *The Economist, 344*(8031), 19.

PARSONS, T., & BALES, R. F. (1955). *Family, socialization, and interaction process*. New York: Free Press.

PUDDINGTON, A. (1999). The war on the war on crime. *Commentary, 107*(5), 25.

PUTTI, J., ARYEE, S., & KANG, T. S. (1988). Personal values of recruits and officers in a law enforcement agency: An exploratory study. *Journal of Police Science and Administration, 16*(4), 245–249.

RADELET, L. (1986). *The police and the community* (4th ed.). New York: Macmillan.

RADELET, L. A., & CARTER, D. L. (1994). *The police and the community* (5th ed.). New York: Macmillan.

REGOLI, R., & E. POOLE. (1979). Measurement of police cynicism: A factor scaling approach. *Journal of Criminal Justice, 7,* 37–52.

ROKEACH, M., MILLER, M., & SNYDER, H. (1971). The value gap between police and policed. *Journal of Social Issues, 27,* 155–171.

ROSELLINI, L. (1998, April 13). When to spank. *U.S. News & World Report*, p. 52.

RUBENSTEIN, J. (1973). *City police*. New York: Farrar, Straus and Giroux.

SIEGEL, L. (1999). *Criminology* (5th ed.). New York: West.

SKOLNICK, J. (1994). *Justice without trial: Law enforcement in a democratic society* (5th ed.). New York: John Wiley and Sons.

STODDARD, E. R. (1968). The informal code of police deviancy: A group approach to blue-collar crime. *Journal of Criminal Law, Criminology, and Police Science, 59*(2), 201–203.

SUTHERLAND, E. (1947). *Principles of criminology* (4th ed.). Chicago: J. B. Lippincott.

TEEVAN, J., & DOLNICK, B. (1973). The values of the police: A reconsideration and interpretation. *Journal of Police Science and Administration, 1,* 366–369.

TIFFT, L. (1974). The cop personality reconsidered. *Journal of Police Science and Administration, 2,* 268.

U.S. DEPARTMENT OF JUSTICE, FEDERAL BUREAU OF INVESTIGATION. (1998). *Uniform Crime Reports*. Washington, DC: U.S. Government Printing Office.

VAN MAANEN, J. (1978). On becoming a policeman. In P. Manning and J. Van Maanen (Eds.), *Policing: A view from the street*. Santa Monica, CA: Goodyear.

WESTLEY, W. (1970). *Violence and the police: A sociological study of law, custom, and morality*. Cambridge, MA: MIT Press.

WOLFGANG, M. (1958). *Patterns of criminal homicide*. Philadelphia: University of Pennsylvania Press.

WOLFGANG, M., & FERRACUTI, F. (1952). *Patterns of criminal homicide*. Philadelphia: University of Pennsylvania Press.

WOLFGANG, M., & FERRACUTI, F. (1967). *The subculture of violence: Toward an integrated theory of criminology*. London: Tavistock.

4

Situational Determinants of Police Violence

Ronald Burns
Charles Crawford

INTRODUCTION

Perhaps the most controversial issue in policing is officer use of force. Recently, several instances of unnecessary and/or deadly force by police have drawn intense media coverage and public attention. For example, many citizens across the nation re-call the chilling account of the death of West African immigrant Amadou Diallo. On February 4, 1999, Diallo was struck by 19 of 41 bullets fired at him by four white New York City police officers. Diallo, unarmed at the time of the incident, was standing in the vestibule of his apartment building when the officers approached him. The officers, members of the department's Street Crime Unit, testified that Diallo was acting suspi-ciously and did not respond to their commands when they approached him. They stated that the lighting in the vestibule was dim and they thought that the wallet Diallo was holding in his hand was a gun. They also stated that they thought he was firing at them. With bullets ricocheting around the vestibule, the officers believed they were in a firefight.

"Prosecutors brought six alternative charges against each of the cops; none of them stuck—neither of the counts of murder, nor the two of manslaughter; not homi-cide, not reckless endangerment," according to Chua-Eoan (2000, p. 24). However, the case was responsible for bringing the issue of police practices to national attention once again. Cries of a corrupt police department and an unfair judicial system arose from minority communities around the country. Similar accusations were simultane-ously heard in Los Angeles, as whistle-blowing officer Rafael Perez documented vari-ous civil rights violations committed by members of the Los Angeles Police Department's CRASH (Community Resources Against Street Hoodlums) unit.

73

Manning (1980, p. 136) states, "It is clear that violence is one means of maintaining social order. But because notions such as 'order' are multiple in meaning, are situational and changing, and are subject to different evaluations, it is very difficult to provide a clear definition of the relationship between order and violence." Manning's comment and these incidents highlight the inherent difficulties involved in understanding police violence, especially our comprehension of the fine line officers must walk in controlling crime and recognizing civil liberties. Unfortunately, the nature of policing is such that mistakes will be made and corrupt police officers will slip through the cracks of the recruitment and selection processes, as well as departmental oversight. Because of the powers allocated to police officers (specifically as they relate to the use of violence), the consequences of police mistakes and corruption can be devastating, particularly when fatal.

Toch (1990) found that nonlethal violence involving injury frequently occurs during police-citizen encounters. He explains,

> This kind of violence is hard to control, because it is hard to establish and is difficult to define. Its physical cost is minor, compared to its corrupting and corrosive influence, which is subsurface. In fact, its visibility is generally minimal. Although police assaults involve thousands of daily confrontations, these incidents rarely make news." (p. 225)

In order to fully comprehend police violence, one must also consider deadly force, as well as the acts of violence (both deadly and nondeadly) committed against police officers. Yet, understanding the causes of police violence can be quite difficult, given the varied situations typically experienced by police officers. Considering the vast array of criminological theories that attempt to explain why people commit crime and the numerous theoretical approaches that examine human behavior as it relates to violence, one can clearly see why researchers have been unable to pinpoint why some police officers are more susceptible to and/or likely to use violence.

The focus of this chapter is situational police violence, or understanding the structural characteristics that influence the likelihood of police using violence, as well as their susceptibility to violent acts. Situational factors include suspect characteristics that may influence police-citizen encounters (e.g., suspect demeanor, suspect possession of a weapon, suspect race) as well as the characteristics of the settings in which police and citizens interact (e.g., the presence of bystanders, the encounter occurring in a hazardous site, the number of officers present). Whereas one could make the argument that macrolevel factors (e.g., poverty levels and the social classes in the areas in which police-citizen encounters occur) should be recognized as situational factors, we discuss situational police violence as it relates to the immediate situation in which the encounter occurs. By no means do we discount macrolevel explanations of police behavior (specifically, police violence) as credible; however, we contend that they would best fit into a different category of explanations regarding police practices (e.g., what Sherman, 1980, would call "community explanations," or what Brooks, 1997, would term "neighborhood variables"). Extensive coverage of how macrolevel factors influence police violence was provided in Chapter 2 of this text.

A substantial portion of this chapter reviews the research literature regarding situational police violence. We believe that presenting the literature provides readers with a general understanding of the current state of knowledge regarding situational police violence, as well as how these issues have been addressed from an empirical standpoint (including the inherent difficulties involved in measuring police violence). We begin with a general overview of police use of force, and then focus on situational factors that have been identified as being related to police violence. We discuss (1) the ability of situational factors to explain police violence, (2) the research surrounding the situational factors that appear to influence an officer's likelihood of using or falling victim to violence, and (3) several real-life accounts in which a city is being forced to further consider situational factors as they relate to police practices.

Currently, a substantially larger portion of the research literature addresses violent acts (both those influenced by situational factors, and those influenced by factors other than situational cues) committed by police officers, as opposed to acts committed against officers. Thus, a sizeable portion of our coverage of the topic is focused in this direction. We have included, however, several research findings regarding the impact of situational factors upon violence against police. Fortunately, current research efforts are being directed toward further understanding the situational factors affecting violence against officers.

POLICE USE OF FORCE

It is difficult to get an accurate measure of the number of incidents involving police use of force. As Fridell and Pate (1997) pointed out, researchers have tried a variety of methods to measure these incidents including survey research, observation methods, and analyses of departmental records. Perhaps the most widely accepted estimate of police use of deadly force comes from Geller and Scott's 1992 text *Deadly Force: What We Know*. The authors estimated that roughly 3,600 deadly force incidents that involve citizens occur every year. The use of deadly force in policing is rare, however, and is only one option an officer may choose. Sherman, Cohen, Gartin, Hamilton, and Rogan (1986) showed that police in all cities kill rarely and that the number of citizens killed by the police has been on a steady decline. Increasingly, departments are collecting and maintaining detailed data on officer use of deadly force that does not result in a fatality. The collection of information on less than lethal force, however, is not as advanced as that for deadly force (e.g., Garner, Schade, Hepburn, & Buchanan, 1995).

Sherman (1980) classified explanations of police behavior, specifically, detection, arrest, service, and violence, into five levels of analysis, including (1) organizational explanations, (2) community explanations, (3) legal explanations, (4) individual officer explanations, and (5) situational explanations. Whereas each play a significant role in explaining police behavior, the focus of the present chapter is largely restricted to situational explanations. A brief description of the other levels of analysis, however, helps set the stage for a lengthy discussion of situational police violence.

Sherman (1980) discussed the impact of organizational factors in explaining police behavior within the context of several areas. Particularly, he observed intraorganizational approaches (specifically, hypotheses surrounding the impact of the division of labor, the nature of supervision, and strategies of patrol work) and interorganizational approaches (specifically, the hypotheses concerned with the poorly specified concept of "professionalism"). Sherman concluded that greater research was needed with regard to the impact of organizational factors in explaining police behavior. Unfortunately, little has changed since Sherman's 1980 account, as recent research sponsored by the National Institute of Justice (NIJ) suggested that "The impact of differences in police organizations, including administrative policies, hiring, training, discipline, and use of technology, or excessive force is unknown" (NIJ, 1999, p. ix), adding that "we need to know, for example, which organizational characteristics are most consequential, which characteristics take on added significance in various environments, and which characteristics are redundant or derivative of other characteristics" (Adams, 1999, p. 11). The report concluded by highlighting the critical need for research in this area.

Sherman's (1980) discussion of community explanations as contributors to police behavior focused specifically on the influence of several aspects of the polity, economy, and demography of American cities. Sherman again noted that research was lacking in this area. However, he argued that this area, theoretically, should provide the greatest explanation of police behavior. He believed that it ought to be so powerful as to shape or override the influence of the other levels of explanation. He cited a 1974 study by Rossi, Berk, and Eidson that suggested that in "comparing city of employment and officers' personal characteristics as explanations of the use of aggressive detection tactics, 67 percent of the explained variance was uniquely attributable to the city" (pp. 148–149). Despite Sherman's beliefs regarding the strength of community factors in explaining police behavior and his call for additional research, many of the recent studies on police violence have been observations of the influences of individual officers and situational factors. We concur with Sherman's suggestion that greater research is needed in this area.

Arguably, several of the aspects constituting Sherman's (1980) legal explanations of police behavior could be categorized differently. For example, the seriousness of the offense might be considered a situational factor, as could the increased likelihood of officers making an arrest when they have personally witnessed an offense. One cannot deny, however, that Supreme Court and legislative decisions may, and sometimes do, alter the manner in which officers behave. Despite these influences, much of the research addressing police behavior has focused on other factors, including situational, organizational, and individual officer variables.

In general, individual officer variables (e.g., experience as an officer, age, race, gender, education, height) are not strong predictors of police behavior, and particularly, police use of force. Although additional verification is needed, the aforementioned NIJ study suggested with modest confidence that "Use of force appears to be unrelated to an officer's personal characteristics, such as age, gender, and ethnicity" (NIJ, 1999, p. viii). Whereas early research suggested that black officers were overrepresented in police shootings (although this finding was later explained through the officer deployment practices of the department under study; Fyfe, 1978, p. ix), and occasional findings suggest that some individual traits may play a role (e.g., Garner, Buchanan, Schade, and Hepburn's [1996] suggestion that male officers are more likely to use force with male suspects, a finding that includes an individual officer variable *and* a suspect variable, and Alpert and Dunham's [1999] suggestion that officers are more likely to use force against suspects of their own race), it is situational factors that play the largest role in explaining police violence.

SITUATIONAL FACTORS IN POLICING

As noted in the 1999 New York case involving Amadou Diallo, many situational factors influence police use of force, and for that matter, police violence in general. Historically, we have seen acts that could simply be classified as "police practices" become "racially motivated police practices," or "ego-motivated police practices." Yet, analyses of such behaviors often result in many unanswered questions. For example, how do we know that the actions were anything other than typical police practices (e.g., can we make determinations regarding motivation)? Or, if we can determine the motivation or explanations for particular incidents, can we argue that such practices, or behaviors, are reflective of all, or most, police personnel? Were these acts the result of poor recruitment, selection, and/or training efforts, or are they attributable to recently developed personality and/or character flaws? Faced with these and numerous other unanswered questions regarding violent police-citizen encounters, researchers have attempted to better understand the situational factors related to police violence with the intention of furthering our knowledge of police violence in general. Although they cannot fully explain police violence, situational factors have added a great deal to our understanding of police practices.

Researchers have documented the "paradoxes of police work" (e.g., Perez, 1997), which suggest that the nature of policing dictates that police officers are often faced with numerous conflicting tasks, sometimes leaving them in a no-win situation. For example, officers who use too much force (at least in the eyes of bystanders) are seen as bullies; those who use too little force endanger their own safety and possibly the safety of others. Faced with the need to make a split-second decision, officers do not always have the time to assess or evaluate the situation. Smith and Visher (1981, p. 168) noted that because police often make arrests quickly, officers are forced to "act on the basis of *salient situational characteristics* (emphasis added)," which prevents "a careful weighing of information."

It is hoped that their training, character, and instincts provide officers with the ability to act appropriately. Most officers do respond appropriately when their assistance is required, but not everyone may interpret their behavior as appropriate, and may subsequently attribute their actions to a particular situational factor(s) that influenced their response (e.g., see the Rodney King and Amadou Diallo incidents). We must also bear in mind the instances when officers make incorrect decisions, whether purposefully or not.

Unfortunately, assessing police behavior (either accurately and inaccurately) can lead to public distrust of policing and possibly even public disorder. For example, Fyfe (1988) cited the fatal shootings of young African American boys in New York City and Tampa as the cause of urban disorder in those areas, and the National Advisory Commission on Civil Disorders (1968) attributed several incidents involving white officers shooting black suspects as a cause of many of the urban disorders throughout the 1960s. Uchida (1997) cited direct police intervention as the cause of riots in Harlem, Watts, Newark, and Detroit (see Conyers, 1981, for an insightful account of police violence and riots). Although these instances plagued inner cities decades ago, it appears little has changed. In Blumberg's (1997, pp. 521–522) discussion of the increased research attention on police use of deadly force and suspect race, he notes that

controversial shootings involving African Americans have continued to periodically create mistrust between police departments and the citizens they serve. Birmingham, Dallas, Houston, Los Angeles, St. Petersburg, Miami and New York are among the cities that have experienced shootings which resulted in a storm of controversy, polarized the community and even led to violence in some cases.

Similar, more recent happenings can be found in New York (e.g., Chua-Eoan, 2000) and Los Angeles (e.g., Cohen, 2000).

In discussing the role of police, Fyfe (1997) observed that officers must deal with citizens and their situations (typically problems) under varied, and sometimes difficult, conditions. He added that these conditions are generally unique to policing, and often are urgent, involuntary, and public, which ultimately increases the likelihood of violence. The nature of such situations and conditions differ with each police encounter, and how officers react to the potential violence has been the topic of much research, public discussion, and police training. Thus, in addition to observing the relationship between officer characteristics (e.g., officer race, gender, experience) and organizational attributes (e.g., the organization of the department), recent attention has focused on the effects, if any, of the structural environment, nature of the interaction, and characteristics of suspects on police behavior.

These and various other situational factors have been used to explain police behavior, including police discretion and more specifically police use of force. Several studies have suggested that situational factors are powerful determinants of police officer decisions to arrest (e.g., Bittner, 1967; Cumming, Cumming, & Edell, 1965). Yet, the question remains: What, specifically, is meant by "situational factors," and how do they relate to police violence?

Sherman (1980) noted that situational explanations of police behavior suggest that "the structural attributes of police-citizen encounters will determine their outcomes regardless of the characteristics of the officers involved" (p. 77). He added that the manner in which police enter an encounter, the characteristics and behaviors of the suspect and complainant, and the visibility of the encounters are the primary situational factors that have been observed to impact police behavior. Similarly, Berk and Loseke (1981) argued that situational explanations of officer behavior in police-citizen encounters address the influence of the structural characteristics apparent in the immediate situation: the nature of the problem, the attributes and actions of the citizens, and contextual variables. Friedrich (1980, p. 84) noted that "The situational approach seeks to account for police use of force by relating it to the specific characteristics of the situations in which police encounter citizens."

For the purposes of our discussion, "situational factors" refer to the characteristics and behavior of the suspect(s) involved in the encounter, the structural characteristics found in the immediate vicinity of the incident, and the nature of the incident at hand. By no means is ours a comprehensive definition of situational factors affecting police behavior/violence; however, it does serve our purposes.

In an insightful account of the factors influencing police discretion, Brooks (1997, p. 158) noted that most research in the area has addressed the relationship between situational variables (otherwise defined as "characteristics of the encounter between citizen[s] and the police") and their impact on police discretionary behavior. Accordingly, several researchers recognized the ability of situational factors to explain police behavior, including Worden (1989, p. 669) who states:

> An impressive body of research findings testifies to the influence of situational factors on police behavior. The likelihood of formal action is related to the severity of the offense, the visibility of the encounter (i.e., whether it transpires in a public or private setting, and whether

bystanders are present), characteristics of the suspect (sex, race, age, social class, demeanor, and sobriety), characteristics of the victim (sex, race, and dispositional preference), and the relationship between the parties. Although early bivariate analyses could not reveal whether these variables have independent effects on behavior, more recent multivariate analyses demonstrate that many of these relationships hold even when other variables are controlled.

Similar studies, addressed later in the chapter, focus on individual situational variables and provide additional evidence of the ability of situational factors to assist in explaining police behavior, specifically, police violence.

Not all researchers are convinced, however, that situational factors play a significant role in explaining police behavior. Despite his earlier quote supporting such explanations, Worden (1989) suggested that one limitation of situational explanations regarding police behavior is the presumption that police behavior exists in a vacuum, that police duties are clearly defined and their behavior remains consistent with each situation. Similarly, Friedrich (1980) noted that, with few exceptions, situational explanations of police use of force were not supported by the data, further adding that situational characteristics as a whole have unimpressive explanatory power. Accordingly, Blumberg (1981) noted no differences in the situational characteristics of police shootings in Kansas City and Atlanta, regardless of race.

Nevertheless, several situational variables do appear to be related to police violence, while others provide mixed results. Some variables seem more powerful than others; thus, we address the research regarding several of the more "potent" situational factors as they relate to police violence. Although not a comprehensive account of all situational variables, nor of all of the research surrounding these factors, the following studies appear representative of the existent literature. The initial section of our review addresses suspect characteristics and behaviors, while the latter part focuses on the structural attributes of the settings in which the encounters occur and other situational factors that do not directly reflect upon the suspect.

We must caution the reader regarding the consistency of these findings, however. Our presentation of the findings regarding police violence is a compilation of existing research. We concur with Geller and Karales (1981, pp. 74, 76; as cited in Blumberg, 1997) that the studies conducted by various researchers are often not comparable to one another. We recognize problems concerning (1) varying definitions of deadly force, nonlethal force, or violence in general, (2) inconsistencies in the definitions of variables and/or their measurement, (3) inconsistencies regarding time periods and/or differences between police forces, and (4) the limitations found in the various research studies.

Manning (1980, p. 136) states, "The police represent the power and authority of the state and thus must be violent." Yet, questions remain regarding the influences on police violence, particularly as they relate to the impact of the suspect in violent police-citizen encounters.

Suspect Factors

Worden (1996, p. 37) suggested that both bivariate and multivariate analyses indicated that the use of both reasonable and improper force is more likely to occur in encounters involving violent crimes, black citizens, males, those over age eighteen, those who appear drunk or mentally disturbed, and those who demonstrate a hostile or antagonistic demeanor. These disturbing findings suggest that particular variables appear to be related to police behavior, and more specifically to police violence. Thus, a large body of research has addressed the impact that suspects, or citizens, have on police behavior, specifically, police violence. Suspect factors can basically be divided into two distinct categories: (1) individual suspect traits, or personal/physical characteristics (e.g., race, age, gender), and (2) suspect behavior (e.g., resistance or aggressiveness, demeanor, sobriety, possession of weapons). Whereas most of the research on police violence addresses acts committed by police officers, an increasing body of research has focused on violent acts *against* officers. We address both aspects of police violence, with an emphasis (due to the disproportionate amount of research) on violence by police officers.

Suspect Characteristics

Similar to the amount of research surrounding the relationship between individual officer characteristics and police violence, a vast body of research observes the impact of individual *suspect* characteristics on police violence. Although it is understandable that police behavior may become increasingly punitive in response to situational factors related to suspect behavior, it is unfortunate that police behavior is, arguably, altered by particular characteristics of some suspects. For example, an individual's race, age, or gender should not increase his or her susceptibility to police violence. Nevertheless, we have seen numerous instances in which these factors have altered police behavior, and too often the behavior has come at the infringement of civil liberties. A closer look at the research surrounding individual suspect characteristics sheds greater light on the situation.

Conflict theories assert that policing primarily serves the interests of the dominant group(s) within society (Collins, 1975; Lenski, 1966; Quinney, 1974; Takagi, 1974), which would suggest that a substantial portion of the minority population in our society is not being properly served by the police. As such, racism is one of the most widely debated topics within the policing and criminal justice literature. Aside from the historical accounts of the mistreatment of minorities by police officers (e.g., Mann, 1993; Walker, Spohn, & Delone, 2000), one merely needs to watch the evening news or read the latest news magazine to view current accounts of racial profiling, thus emphasizing the claims of racism in the criminal justice system.

It is widely accepted among researchers that the rate of African Americans shot or killed by police far exceeds the rate for whites (e.g., Blumberg, 1981; Fyfe, 1981; Harring, Platt, Speiglman, & Takagi, 1977; Meyer, 1980; Robin, 1963), and that African Americans are shot or killed by police disproportionately to their representation in the general public (e.g., Blumberg, 1981; Fyfe, 1981b; Meyer, 1980; Robin, 1963; Takagi, 1974). However, it is unclear why this is the case. Goldkamp (1976) suggested that there are basically two arguments regarding the disproportionality: (1) disproportionate minority arrest rates for violent crimes and (2) racial discrimination by the police. Several researchers subscribe to the belief that the disproportionality can be accounted for by the high rates of African Americans who are arrested for crimes of violence (e.g., Blumberg, 1981; Fyfe, 1981b), whereas others suggest that police discretion, or "differential policing," largely explains the disproportionality (e.g., Blauner, 1972; Takagi, 1974). Doerner (1998, p. 213) noted that there are some who recognize the racial imbalance as a reflection of "social inequality, economic deprivation, and all other disadvantages" associated with being in the minority.

Those who subscribe to the latter approach believe that suspect race is, and has been, a major determinant of police violence. For example, Takagi (1974, p. 30) argued that "the police have one trigger-finger for whites and another for blacks," and Arthur and Case (1994, p. 168) noted that "Police use of violence on minorities and the marginalized segments of American society has always reinforced the notion that the police are discriminatory in their deployment practices and use of force." Similar concerns can be noted from Blauner (1972, pp. 97–98), who suggested that "of all the established institutions, police departments probably include the highest proportion of individual racists," adding that "the police enforce repressive aspects of middle-class values against the distinctive ethnic orientations of Afro-Americans and other minority subcultures." In his research study, Worden (1996, p. 37) stated that "officers are more likely to use even reasonable force against blacks which might suggest that officers are, on average, more likely to adopt a punitive or coercive approach to black suspects than they are to white suspects." Black (1980) came to a similar conclusion. LaGrange (1998, pp. 396–397) summarizes the situation:

> The unequal distribution of deadly force provides critics of the police with powerful ammunition. Police shootings have the appearance of being prejudicial and discriminatory. Although few critics charge the police with *ageism* or *sexism* for their disproportionate shootings of "young" "males," charges of *racism* abound. One outraged scholar contends that "police have one trigger finger for whites and another for blacks. Adding credibility to the charges of racism are three additional factors. First, too often and for too long throughout our history the police have been racists. Second, an undeniable yet undocumentable proportion of shootings by police officers today are racially motivated. And third, activist organizations such as the NAACP and the ACLU mount effective media campaigns in the aftermath of police shootings that appear to be racially motivated.

Regardless of how one views the relationship between police violence and race, one cannot deny that the recent accounts of racial profiling (e.g., Kennedy, 1999) by departments nationwide suggest that situational factors indeed play a substantial role in police practices.

Bayley (1998), in discussing the factors that he believed will most profoundly shape the future of American policing, suggested that a real threat of group violence exists, resulting from the inequities of race, class, and ethnicity. Such social unrest will undoubtedly lead to the demise of community-oriented policing, he contended, and will result in the intensification of quasi-military police practices. He argued, and we concur, that now is the time to prepare for such turbulence.

In addition to the extensive research that has addressed the relationship between suspect race and police violence, the relationship between suspect age and police violence has received attention. In general, the results appear to be inconclusive. For example, some research suggests that young suspects are more likely to be the recipients of deadly force by police (e.g., Friedrich [1980], who noted that those 18 to 25 years old are most likely to receive deadly force), whereas other research indicates that suspect age is not an important predictor of police behavior in general (Klinger, 1996; Smith, 1984; Smith & Davidson, 1984; Smith & Visher, 1981; Visher, 1983). Earlier studies consistently suggested that the majority of the people shot or killed by police are under age 30 (Kobler, 1975; Robin, 1963), but more recent research found that suspects under the age of 30 are less likely than their elders to have restraints used against them and more likely to have tactics or nonlethal weapons used against them (Crawford & Burns, 1998). LaGrange (1998) suggested that, by overwhelming odds, young black males between the ages of 18 and 30 are the most frequent targets of police shootings. However, he also observed that this finding is not out of proportion with this group's representation in violent crime, nor with their residence in high-crime neighborhoods. Others found conflicting results when comparing the age of shooting victims with the age of arrestees (e.g., Fyfe, 1978, p. xv). Similar to the situation regarding the relationship between suspect race and police violence, it appears that, in general, "the jury is still out" regarding the existence of an identifiable relationship between suspect age and police violence.

The final individual suspect characteristic we address is gender, which appears to have an impact on police use of force. Some argue that historically, the "chivalry factor," a cultural stereotype that depicted women as helpless or childlike compared to men (Schmalleger, 1999), played a role in how police officers treated females (e.g., Anderson, 1976; Moulds, 1980). Accordingly, in his review of the research concerning causes of police behavior, Sherman (1980, p. 82) noted that "there is little doubt that police discriminated in favor of women at the time the available data on the question were collected." Earlier studies found that based on their presence in the arrest population, women were less likely than males to be shot or killed by police (Fyfe, 1978; Robin, 1963). Reiss (1972, p. 305) cited only 2 women out of the 37 victims of excessive force in one particular study, whereas females comprised 17% of the suspects the police encountered. More recently, Worden (1996, p. 40) noted that the results of the studies included in his research indicate that the use of force is affected by race as well as gender, and Crawford and Burns (1998, p. 55) found that male suspects were more likely than female suspects to have some type of force used against them and were less likely to receive verbal commands from an officer.

Although not specifically addressing police violence, Brooks (1997) cited a host of researchers who suggest that, despite the noted gender differences in police treatment of suspects and complainants found in early research, the problem is not as apparent as it once appeared (Klinger, 1996; Krohn, Curry, & Nelson-Krueger, 1983; Smith, 1984; Smith & Visher, 1980; Smith & Visher, 1981; Visher, 1983). Brooks (1997, p. 159) observed that "recent research has found that either no gender differences occur or that they are less prominent than previously thought." As females are increasingly represented in crime and the criminal justice system, it will be interesting to observe/measure the changes (if any) in this relationship.

In addition to analyses regarding the impact of suspect traits upon officer behavior, a great deal of research has addressed the relationship between suspect behavior and officer response. Police officers commonly understand that the first 10 seconds of a police-citizen encounter will determine the outcome. This commonsense notion reveals how important suspect demeanor and the subsequent officer response can be. Situational factors relating to suspect behavior (e.g., possession of weapons, apparent influence of alcohol or drugs, anger) help explain many violent police-citizen encounters. As such, numerous actions by suspects are recognized as being related to police violence.

Suspect Behavior

Recently, police officers in Philadelphia encountered difficulty while apprehending a suspect driving a stolen car. After wrestling and exchanging gunfire with the suspect (one officer and the suspect sustained bullet wounds), several police cars chased the suspect (who had commandeered an unoccupied police vehicle) and eventually cornered him, forcing him to surrender. At this point, helicopter footage of the incident began, with viewers able to see roughly 12 men (most in police uniform with their firearms drawn) surrounding the vehicle. Upon exiting the vehicle, the suspect was thrown to the ground, and numerous officers kicked and beat him.

To defuse the resulting public claims of unnecessary police use of force, police brutality, and corrupt officers, Philadelphia's mayor, John Street, emphasized that the beating that took place after the suspect was apprehended was merely one act in a sequence of events. He reminded the public, "As inflammatory as this tape might be, we have to keep in mind that the police were in the process of apprehending a criminal suspect who had resisted a number of attempts to arrest him and who had shot a police officer" (Clines, 2000; it was later determined that the suspect had not shot the officer). Similarly, the Philadelphia police chief, John Timoney, stated there would be no "witch-hunt" in this case; in other words, there would be no rush to judgment regarding the appropriateness of the officers' behaviors (Rubinkam, 2000). These officials are to be commended for their ability to refrain from basing their decisions on only "part of the picture."

This recent account highlights the relationship between suspect behavior and police violence. For instance, the incident includes violence used by, and against, officers. In addition, the simple fact that what appears as unnecessary force by numerous officers (caught on videotape) is going to be investigated leads one to believe that their behavior is going to be considered within its situational context. City officials are going to consider the entire sequence of events, not simply what was seen in the video. The situational context in this particular case includes, among other things, the suspect's resistance of arrest, his apparent possession of a deadly weapon, and his attempts to flee from an officer. Were the officers justified in their behavior? The video footage would suggest that they were not. However, an investigation that encompasses all that occurred may find that the officers' behavior was appropriate.

Based on the available research, the suspect behavior that may be the strongest predictor of police violence is whether or not the suspect is aggressive or resists arrest. For instance, Robin (1963, as cited in Toch, 1990) suggested that the behavior of violent men, both officers and civilians, explains their continual, and sometimes predictable, involvement in violent acts. He suggested that they are often involved in and become entangled in violent situations through the same means, regardless of the settings and partners. Toch (1990) argued that violent suspects often become entangled with violent officers. He believed that battles regarding self-esteem and respect emerge during encounters between these two types of individuals, often resulting in violence. Because violence can emerge when violent men encounter violent, as well as nonviolent, men, the potential for police violence (both justified and nonjustified) arises when a violent officer has evaded departmental oversight and/or a violent citizen has evaded social control.

Police officers typically seek respect by the public partly because of their role in society and partly because of human nature. In discussing the relationship between suspect behavior and police violence, Westley (1970) noted that police violence often results from taunts, simply because of the respect officers seek from the public. Chevigny (1969) believed that police behavior is largely shaped by the need to redress disrespect, and failure to do so weakens their authority. In accordance, Toch (1990, p. 228) stated:

> Perceived defiance of authority can take many forms. Some, such as wrestling the officer for his nightstick, are extreme, while others (such as refusing to move) are minor. A spectator who criticizes an officer at work may be viewed as an agitator; a person who quotes the Bill of Rights may be seen—in context—as a cop hater. Some challenges are verbal, and others are gestures.

Toch (1990, p. 229) added that most assaults on officers are the result of a suspect's resentment at having been "tampered with on unconvincing grounds."

As such, suspect resistance, or use of force, appears to be a strong predictor of police violence (as evidenced in the aforementioned discussion of the recent incident in Philadelphia). Several researchers have documented this relationship, including Garner et al. (1996), who found suspect use of force to be the best predictor of police use of force, and Crawford and Burns (1998), who, using different statistical procedures to analyze the data collected by Garner et al., found that officers were more likely to use restraints, chemical agents, and tactics/nonlethal weapons on angry or aggressive suspects.

Perhaps the strongest argument regarding the relationship between suspect resistance and police violence comes from Adams (1999) who stated with "substantial confidence" that use of force typically occurs when police are attempting to make an arrest and the suspect is resisting. His suggestion is based on numerous empirical evaluations of police use of force incidents (e.g., Alpert & Dunham, 1999; Bayley & Garofalo, 1989; Garner et al., 1996).

The relationship between suspect demeanor, or attitude, and police behavior has also been widely discussed in the research literature. Both citizens and officers have particular expectations that they believe should be met with each encounter. Deviations from these expectations could result in the officers and/or citizens reacting violently.

Most research suggests that disrespectful or uncooperative citizens are more likely to be treated punitively by the police (Black, 1980; Chevigny, 1969; Crawford & Burns, 1998; Ericson, 1982; Friedrich, 1980; Kavanagh, 1997; Manning, 1980; Piliavin & Briar, 1964; Sherman, 1980; Smith, 1987; Smith & Visher, 1981; Toch, 1969; Visher, 1983; Westley, 1970). However, Klinger (1994, 1996) raised questions concerning the adequate measurement of demeanor and the failure of previous research to adequately control for the suspect's behavior during the *entire* encounter. Following Klinger, Kavanagh (1997, p. 26) addressed the issue by stating that "Although some researchers have assumed that arrestee disrespect provokes a violent 'face saving' response from the police officer, it is also possible that, in some cases, the arrestee disrespect is part of an early stage of arrestee violence brought on by other causes, such as arrestee anger, frustration, or even police officer disrespect of the arrestee." In response to Klinger's claims, Worden and Shepard (1996) revisited the situation and determined that improper measurement of demeanor did not hamper previous research findings, although Lundman (1994) noted that the effects of demeanor depended on how the concept was measured.

Some research indicates that the use of alcohol lowers inhibitions and increases the likelihood of aggression (e.g., Bureau of Justice Statistics, 1988a; Roth, 1994). One study showed that about half of all prison inmates reported that they were drinking alcohol immediately prior to the crime for which they were serving time (Bureau of Justice Statistics, 1988a). The same study also showed that alcohol use was found most often among those incarcerated for assault as opposed to property crimes or drug offenses, and that male prison inmates reported that prior to imprisonment they were three times as likely as other men to consume an ounce or more of alcohol each day. Similarly, a survey of state prison inmates noted that 43% had been involved in daily drug use in the month prior to their current offense, while 19% were using a "major drug" on a daily or near-daily basis (Bureau of Justice Statistics, 1988a).

We are not suggesting that alcohol or drugs are directly responsible for the actions of violent criminals, but that drugs and alcohol apparently play a role in the lives of a substantial portion of these people. These findings should come as no surprise to the reader, given the documented relationship between drugs (including alcohol) and crime (e.g., Bureau of Justice Statistics, 1988b; Gropper, 1985). Much to their chagrin, officers have the task of handling abusive drunks and drug users. Apparently, the use of force becomes a primary tool in such instances. Friedrich (1980) noted that the use of force appears to relate to the citizen's use of alcohol, whereas Mednick, Pollock, Volavka, and Gabrielli (1982) found that, among other things, the influences of certain drugs and midrange alcohol intoxication are related to increased levels of violence in general.

Crawford and Burns (1998) found that officers were more likely to use restraints and tactics/nonlethal weapons on suspects impaired by drugs, and in their study, Garner et al. (1996) found that a suspect's impairment by alcohol was a consistent predictor of police use of force and that drug impairment predicted some types of force. Similarly, Kavanagh (1997) found arrestee intoxication to be significantly related to resisting arrest.

Although Adams (1999, p. viii) called for additional research in the area, he suggested that "use of force is more likely to occur when police are dealing with persons under the influence of alcohol or drugs or with mentally ill individuals." Citing research from the President's Commission on Law Enforcement and Administration of Justice (Reiss, 1967) and Garner et al. (1996), Adams believes with modest confidence that use of force is more likely to occur when suspects are mentally ill or intoxicated, findings supported by Worden (1996). However, some research results indicate otherwise, including the work of Alpert and Dunham (1999), who argue that drug impairment of the suspects in their study was unrelated to police use of force or subsequent injury.

In Magarita's (1980, p. 64) analysis of the myths and motives surrounding police officer deaths, she concluded that most killings of police officers "are not manifestations of mental illness, but rather indicate clear calculations made by both professional and amateur criminals who use violence against police only to avoid apprehension and to escape from the scene of some illegal activity." Her research was based on a study of murders of officers in New York City. Perhaps one of the most effective approaches to avoid police violence is additional officer training in identifying and handling intoxicated and/or mentally unstable individuals.

Suspects possessing a weapon, committing a serious crime, and attempting to flee are other situational factors pertaining to suspect behavior that appear to be related to police violence. Although not as well researched as the previously discussed situational factors, research findings regarding these variables nevertheless assist in understanding police violence.

Suspects in possession of a weapon are not necessarily going to harm an officer. Nevertheless, weapon possession should put officers on alert regarding the increased danger they face. Crawford and Burns (1998) found that officers were more likely to use restraints, chemical agents, and firearms on suspects who possessed a weapon. Similarly, in his study of officer discretion in the use of force, Hayden (1981) found that the suspect's weapon was of prime concern for officers in their decision to use deadly force. Simple understanding of the police officer's role in society would lead one to believe that violence, at some level, will likely result if a suspect possesses a weapon.

Guns appear to be the weapon most often used in lethal violent acts against police officers. After analyzing FBI data, Fridell and Pate (1997) reported that 92% of the killings of police officers were committed with firearms. In her study of officer deaths in New York City, Margarita (1980) also reported that roughly 90% of the assailants used guns against the police.

Police are more likely to use force when they encounter a suspect who has committed, or is committing, a violent offense. For example, Garner et al. (1996) found that arrest for a violent offense was a consistent predictor of police use of force. Accordingly, the finding that a harsher disposition emerges when police encounter a more serious offense is generally supported in the literature (e.g., Ericson, 1982; Friedrich, 1980; Piliavin & Briar, 1964; Smith, 1984; Smith & Visher, 1981; Visher, 1983; Wilson, 1968). In his research, Kavanagh (1997) found a relationship between officers charging a suspect with a serious crime and arrest resistance, whereas Hayden (1981, p. 106) found "evidence which suggests that most police focus their decision-making processes (as they relate to the use of deadly force) on the crime committed by the individual initiating their response as opposed to the physical characteristics possessed by that individual."

Toch (1990, p. 231) examined the impact of fear in relation to police violence, particularly in "preventive" violence. He considers a "youngster who flees because police spell danger may be gunned down by an officer who feels threatened by the youngster's running. Such occasions are doubly tragic, because the two parties are victims of reciprocal errors." Recent research found that officers were more likely to use restraints, tactics/nonlethal weapons, and firearms on suspects attempting to flee (Crawford & Burns, 1998). It is hoped that future research will further address this situation, with the ultimate goal of eliminating, or at least reducing, the likelihood of errors committed by both parties.

The importance of understanding the suspect's/citizen's role in police encounters has reached beyond the policing and research worlds as organizations begin to offer suggestions to citizens on how to conduct themselves during a police encounter. The American Civil Liberties Union (ACLU) offers, free of charge, a "bust card," which provides information on one's constitutional rights during a police stop or interrogation. Information provided on this card reminds cardholders to avoid threatening, or arguing with, a police officer. The card suggests ways to handle an encounter that is perceived to be illegal, noting that the detainee should not offer any explanations for his or her behavior. The card also reminds suspects to remember as many details as possible about the encounter with the police and to record, in writing, the details as soon as possible. The bust card is available for download at the ACLU's web site at http://www.aclu.org/.

Structural and Other Situational Factors

Aside from the personal and behavioral characteristics of suspects, several additional situational factors appear to influence the likelihood of police violence. We could categorize these factors as "structural factors" because they typically relate to the immediate surroundings or structures found in police-citizen encounters. However, such a categorization may not aptly encapsulate all aspects of these remaining situational factors. For example, the method by which an officer enters an encounter may not be directly attributable to the structure of the scene. Yet, other factors about certain encounters, such as their originating as domestic calls, occurring at night, and occurring in the presence of bystanders (e.g., in public), could be considered structural factors. Nevertheless, a number of nonsuspect-related situational factors exist that influence police performance, particularly as it relates to police violence. These factors largely assist in explaining the unpredictable, exciting, interesting, and sometimes dangerous nature of policing. Accordingly, these factors are widely addressed in police training curricula, as well as in the policing literature.

The method by which officers enter a situation appears to have ramifications regarding the outcome of the situation (Scharf & Binder, 1983). In discussing the unique aspects of policing, Fyfe (1997, p. 537) noted that "Many of those who come to police attention do not seek it, but become unwilling clients through the intervention of third parties or of officers themselves." When police proactively enter into citizen encounters (without being warranted), they will be granted less legitimacy than when they enter reactively. Such a situation appears to affect officer behavior. Proactive encounters, which occur less frequently than reactive encounters (Reiss, 1971), comprise as little as 13% of all citizen contacts and are most often concerned with legally petty offenses (Black, 1971). They appear to differ substantially from reactive encounters, as citizens are typically more antagonistic to the police in proactive encounters (Reiss, 1971), thus encouraging officers to become more punitive. Smith and Visher (1981) offered that officers maintain a greater range of options in handling proactive encounters since such instances are less visible to the department and cannot be found in department records.

Research has also addressed officer danger as it relates to the manner in which officers enter into situations. For example, Reiss (1971) speculated that resisting arrest was more common in officer-initiated arrest situations because in such instances it is more difficult for the officer to establish the legitimacy of his or her presence. More recent research (Kavanagh, 1997) supported Reiss's contention by suggesting that officer-initiated arrests are related to resisting arrest. Friedrich (1980), however, suggested that the relationship between resisting arrest and officer-initiated contact may be spurious; arrestee resentment over the petty reasons for the police intervention may be the underlying causes for resisting arrest, as opposed to the manner of police involvement. We could also argue that officers displaying a more proactive and aggressive patrol style subsequently provoke arrestee resentment and arrest resistance.

Aside from arrest resistance, the likelihood of officer injury and death does appear to be affected by how officers enter a situation. For instance, Reiss (1971) noted that violence, and hence officer injury, is more likely to result from proactive encounters. In their research regarding officer killings, Fridell and Pate (1995, cited in Fridell & Pate, 1997) reported that roughly one third (34%) of the officers were dispatched to the incident in which they were killed, whereas a similar percentage (31%) proactively initiated the contact and 20% were on assignment (e.g., serving a warrant, questioning a witness) at the time of their deaths. Another 8% were ambushed (e.g., assailants seeking out particular officers). The latter finding is supported by Toch (1990), who noted that snipings or premeditated ambushes are responsible for roughly 10% of all killings of police officers.

The nature of policing suggests that officers could easily find themselves in the uncompromising position of simultaneously protecting or restricting the public, maintaining their own personal safety, and subduing a violent suspect. The need to balance these tasks is typically done through proper use of authority and accurate assessment of the situation. Fyfe notes the always important task of crowd control during heated police-citizen encounters. He suggests that

> A consequence of the public setting of police work is that officers must be attentive not only to the immediate problems of the clients they have been summoned to treat, but also to third-party reactions to their efforts. If they are to avoid criticism and even interference from bystanders, police officers summoned to restrain emotionally disturbed or drug-crazed persons on the street must do so in a way that is demonstrably proper and humane. (1997, p. 537)

He adds that

> Officers must also be acutely aware that the presence of an audience of bystanders may affect their clients' behavior. In some cases the embarrassment of having one's problems aired in public may cause—or increase—irrational behavior on the part of the client. (1997, p. 538)

When responding/reacting to an incident, proper assessment and control of the situation could potentially play a substantial role in reducing the likelihood of violence. As such, officers should be properly trained in this area, and continued training should be provided to all officers.

Several researchers assessed the relationship between the presence of bystanders, or visibility of the encounter, and police-citizen violence. For example, in their study, Garner et al. (1996) found the presence of bystanders to be a consistent predictor of police use of force, and Westley (1970) concluded that the presence of bystanders was related to police-citizen violence. Similar results were observed by Friedrich (1980) and Smith and Visher (1981, p. 168) who stated that "The presence of an audience may threaten police control of the situation and prompt formal action to re-establish authority." Crawford and Burns (1998) found that officers were more likely to use restraints on suspects when witnesses were present and more likely to use restraints and tactics/nonlethal weapons when the arrest was being made at night (lending support to the notion that visibility affects officer behavior). Similarly, Kavanagh (1997) found "other arrestees present" to be significantly related to resisting arrest. Finally, in his research regarding officer discretion in the use of deadly force, Hayden (1981) found that the presence of bystanders was of prime concern for officers in their decision to use such force.

Reiss (1972) found that excessive police use of force most often occurs in private places, although bystanders who witnessed the excessive force (e.g., strangers or acquaintances, friends or enemies, concerned or not concerned) rarely reported it. This finding led Reiss to suggest that the *quality* of bystanders is important during police-citizen encounters. In addition to highlighting the relationship between police procedures and the likelihood of violence, these findings emphasize the necessity of proper police training.

Research has also addressed visibility of police-citizen encounters and its relationship to the dangers of policing. For instance, in their research on police killings, Fridell and Pate (1995, cited in Fridell & Pate, 1997) reported that about one half of the officers killed were roadside at the time of their deaths and another one fourth were outside (although not roadside). They reported that most of the killings of officers that took place inside occurred in residences, as opposed to commercial establishments (Fridell & Pate, 1995, cited in Fridell & Pate, 1997), lending support to the claims of officer danger when responding to domestic disputes (see the discussion of domestic violence). FBI data analyzed by Fridell and Pate (1997) showed that roughly half of the felonious police deaths occurred during officer shifts between the hours of 8 P.M. and 4 A.M., with the hours of 8 P.M. to midnight being most dangerous to officers. They showed that the fewest police deaths occurred between 4 A.M. and noon. At face value, these findings suggest that hours with the least visibility are most dangerous for police officers.

The presence of other officers may also influence the occurrence of police violence. Earlier research suggests that an officer is more cautious and less threatening when alone than when accompanied by other officers (e.g., Banton, 1964; Friedrich, 1980; Wilson, 1963). This finding seems logical considering an officer's inherent concern for personal safety and the underpinnings of the "strength in numbers" concept. Accordingly, Hayden (1981) found that the availability of officer backup was of prime concern for officers in their decision to use lethal force. Additional research in this area should be used to revise department policies with the ultimate intention of reducing police violence.

The final situational variable to be discussed is the relationship between police violence and domestic disturbances. Traditionally, police officers responded slowly to domestic violence calls, with the hope that the situation would defuse by the time they arrived (Lundman, 1980). Aside from concerns regarding the documented dangers involved in responding to domestic disputes, police officers, like many civilians, are embarrassed and uncertain when intervening in family disputes, especially considering the lack of clarity regarding their legal authority to enter an individual's home and make an arrest (Langworthy & Travis, 1999). These situations are difficult for officers for several other reasons, including the increased likelihood of intense emotions and suspect intoxication, as well as the long-standing American belief that "what goes on behind closed doors is nobody's business." Nevertheless officers must contend with these situations, utilizing almost all of their policing skills, especially mediation.

Research suggests that as intimacy between complainant and suspect increases, police are less likely to take official action (e.g., Black, 1971; Smith & Visher, 1981). Brooks (1997, p. 160) noted, "It may be that police believe that taking official action against a suspect who is in a relationship with the complainant may cause future problems, or they may feel that it is not part of police responsibility."

Despite Margarita's (1980, p. 63) statement that "contrary to public opinion, police are not often killed during domestic disturbances," responding to domestic disturbances remains recognized as one of the most dangerous tasks of a patrol officer, and is a primary concern for society in general. According to Lyman (1999, p. 156), such acts of violence are "by far the most prevalent form of violence confronting contemporary society, and patrol officers must frequently respond to such occurrences." One estimate regarding the extent of domestic violence suggests that it is responsible for 1 out of every 4 homicides and serious assaults (involving both officers and civilians) in the United States (Bureau of Justice Statistics, 1994). Fridell and Pate (1997) reported that officers killed while intervening in *ongoing crimes* were most frequently intervening in domestic disturbances (24%). According to FBI data (1990), from 1980 to 1989, 56 officers were killed responding to family disturbances. Despite claims that responding to domestic violence calls is not necessarily dangerous for police officers, such situations clearly put officers at risk. Thus, proper training and revised department policies concerning responses to domestic violence calls have become primary issues in many departments across the country.

Police officers encounter varying situations, actors, and conditions with each interaction with the public. They must be prepared to properly respond to a plethora of possible reactions from those involved. Although the majority of their encounters are harmless, it takes only one incident for an officer to lose his or her life. Similarly, it takes only one incident for a suspect to be victimized by improper police procedure, regardless if an officer's action is intentional or accidental. Thus, the proper recruitment, selection, and training of police officers play a significant role in determining whether a department is continually the top story on the news each night, constantly faces litigation, or suffers other detrimental repercussions. Officers cannot be expected to make proper decisions in *every* situation (i.e., "nobody is perfect"), but the likelihood of them suffering harm, or of them harming others, can be greatly reduced if the proper personnel are adequately recruited, selected, and trained in how to respond to the wide array of situations officers face.

The aforementioned findings suggest that situational variables indeed affect levels of violence in the lives of police officers. As noted, some factors appear to be more strongly related to violence by, and against, officers, and only further research will lead us to a more complete understanding of this important aspect of policing. Existing research on the situational variables affecting police violence adds a great deal to our understanding of the behaviors and lives of police officers, but there remains a great deal to learn. A clear need exists for additional qualitative studies of police violence, although such methodologies are not always feasible given the nature of policing. A notable lack of research also exists regarding use of force against police officers. It is hoped that our efforts to further research police violence will continue to be facilitated by departments that are willing to expose their behavior to public scrutiny. On a promising note, we address two recent developments that should largely assist in our future efforts to measure police violence (specifically, police use of force). These recent developments provide ample evidence that much remains to be learned about police violence.

THE APPLICATION OF FORCE

To gain a greater understanding of the situations and complexities of the encounters between police and citizens, researchers as well as numerous police departments have begun to look at the use of force as a continuum. Too often, past research utilized dichotomous analyses of police force, including measurements of force/no force and deadly/nondeadly force. Based on the limitations of such studies, recent research (e.g., Crawford & Burns,

1998; Garner et al., 1996) finds that the continuum perspective provides a more accurate assessment of the force used at arrest.

The continuum of force typically consists of six steps: officer presence, verbal commands, restraints, chemical agents, tactical weapons, and firearms. There are other variations of these six that reflect different training standards and suggest acceptable responses from officers involved in various situations. For example, a control continuum designed by Calibre Press for its street survival seminar includes some common response options and permits ranking the intensity of the response and allowing for adaptation based on the officer's department and skill level.

Previous research suggests that a continuum of force exists in police-suspect encounters (e.g., Americans for Effective Law Enforcement, 1988; Connor, 1991; Desmedt, 1984; Garner et al., 1996; Schultz, 1990; Sykes & Brent, 1980). For example, Garner et al. (1996) defined the continuum as the notion of multiple categories of progressively increasing suspect resistance matched to progressively increasing officer responses. This notion of a continuum is not merely descriptive; it is intentionally used to specify the highest level of appropriate response for a given level of suspect resistance. Officers are not committed to this continuum; they may justifiably disengage from a confrontation or leap over a stage on the continuum to gain compliance.

The continuum perspective has proved to be a useful tool for predicting and understanding how and why officers increase the level of force against a suspect. As such, analyses of situational factors within the context of the continuum of force add to our understanding of police violence. Although the continuum perspective is receiving increased research and training acceptance, it is not the only measure available to understand the use of force by police as a proportional response to suspect resistance.

Alpert and Dunham (1997) recognize the work of Garner et al. as the most detailed study on police use of force in the last few decades. However, they developed a similar measure that greatly adds to the study of police use of force. The force factor has been posited by Alpert and Dunham (1997) as a measure that focuses on the level of force used by the police relative to the suspect's amount of resistance. Thus, the force factor is unique in that it captures the amount of force used in an encounter by both the arresting officer and the suspect.

To calculate the force factor, one must measure the suspect's level of resistance and the officer's level of force on the same scale. The scale ranges from 1 to 4, with 1 being "no force" and 4 being "forcibly subduing suspect." Suspects and officers are assigned scores for their actions, and suspect resistance is then subtracted from the officer's score. For example, no resistance from the suspect and no force from the officer would equal 0 [1 (no force) −1 (no resistance)].

One notable benefit of the force factor is that it allows meaningful comparisons in the use of force across departments. For instance, Alpert and Dunham noted several significant findings in their use of the force factor while studying police use of force in departments in Miami, Florida, and Eugene and Springfield, Oregon. They found that overall, Miami Metro-Dade was skewed to the negative side, indicating that "on average the level of force used was slightly lower than the level of resistance" (1997, p. 18). Interestingly, in Oregon the distribution was skewed toward the positive side, suggesting that police use of force was slightly higher than the level of resistance offered. Further investigation revealed that the departments differ slightly in their training procedures. Metro-

Dade trained their officers to choose a level of force slightly lower than the level of resistance, whereas Eugene and Springfield trained their officers to choose a level of force slightly higher than the resistance offered. As the authors pointed out, these training variations are slight, yet the force factor was able to distinguish the difference in application.

The research by Alpert and Dunham (1997) also suggested that consideration and recognition of officer and suspect characteristics and, more important for this discussion, situational factors enhance our understanding of the use of force. Perhaps the most significant contribution of their research (and of the research conducted by Garner et al., 1996) is their development of an innovative method to measure police use of force. Nevertheless, Alpert and Dunham believe more work remains to be done to enhance the effectiveness of the force factor. They note that with any quantitative method there may be further need for refinement, suggesting the possibility of a "ceiling effect" that could affect the results. For example, a greater tendency for a positive score emerges when no or little resistance exists. The authors believe that, once refined, the force factor may become more widely accepted and standardized and will allow for interdepartmental comparisons of force at time of arrest.

THE REALITY OF THE USE OF FORCE

Up until this point, the discussion of the use of force has been academic and research-oriented. However, we realize that the reality of the use of force can be far different from an abstract concept of a continuum or a remote quantitative measure of a force factor. Although these measures are very useful as training guides and for establishing/guiding a standard operation for a department, the decisions officers make in the field are fast and furious, with numerous complicating and competing situational factors that must immediately be addressed. In their text, *Policing in America,* Bartollas and Hahn (1999) provided an insightful account of the dilemmas officers face when using force.

In order to get a better appreciation of the difficulties some officers face on a regular basis, we ask our readers to imagine they are facing an encounter with a noncompliant suspect who attacks suddenly! A surge of fear and adrenaline rages in your body; you have flashing thoughts of survival. Add to this a din of noise and a crowd forming and closing in. You search for friendly faces or other officers to assist; there are none. You have a split-second decision to make and choose a course of action one step above the suspect's use of force. Questions begin to flood your mind as the adrenaline is still raging through your body. Was the action legal? Was the suspect hurt? Was your choice tactically feasible and appropriate? Was it justifiable according to department policy? How does this encounter fit into the community history and standards? In other words, are the race and ethnicity of the suspect and officer (you) going to be an issue?

Our point is to illustrate that the use of force does not happen in a laboratory, but on the street with many complexities that researchers may not be able to capture and those outside of the encounter and policing may not be able to understand. Although many departments, as well as a number of training experts, use the continuum as a starting point in training, officers are not required to strictly adhere to this approach. In fact, it may be extremely dangerous for an officer to wait to increase the use of force based on the suspect's actions. The reader must keep in mind that most unruly suspects do not consider policies or continuums nor do they adhere to the rule of law. Police officers are human and realize the same fears and stress that any of us would experience in a dangerous situation facing a suspect intent on escaping apprehension or obtaining revenge.

Jerome Skolnick (1994) wrote at length on the working personality of police officers and what he terms the "symbolic assailant." Skolnick was trying to understand the police officer's world, and he found that police work often requires officers to become preoccupied with potential violence. Through their preoccupation, Skolnick argued, police officers begin to develop perceptual shorthand to identify certain kinds of people as symbolic assailants (e.g., a person who uses speech, dress, and gestures that the police have come to recognize as a prelude to violence). The police are trained to be suspicious and aware of potential danger. This personality-shaping preoccupation is something that cannot be quantified and may be a reason why some officers are willing to escalate the use of force on the continuum more quickly than others.

Many citizens inaccurately perceive all police officers as being in control of their emotions and somewhat akin to an automaton in enforcing the law and handling dangerous suspects. As Skolnick pointed out in his research, many officers may not be willing to discuss the danger and fear of the job, but it is always present with them:

> Police officers themselves do not necessarily emphasize the peril associated with their work when questioned directly and may even have well developed strategies of denial. The element of danger is so integral to an officer's work that explicit recognition might induce emotional barriers to work performance. (1994, p. 46)

Skolnick further pointed out that it is not necessary for an officer to personally suffer some form of violence to undergo this preoccupation; routine police work, including the stressful and continuous hazards and threats, largely shapes the officer's working personality. To highlight some of the inherent difficulties officers face in the course of their job, as well as the significance of several of the aforementioned situational factors, we examine two recent incidents involving officers and noncompliant suspects. These incidents, both involving the use of coercive (less than lethal) force, help illustrate the complexities of applying the continuum in the field. We could have chosen numerous examples involving deadly force. However, research has shown that deadly force incidents are statistically rare in policing. Geller and Scott (1992) illustrated this fact by looking at the number of years an officer would statistically have to work to kill a suspect. The number of years ranged from a high of 7,692 in Honolulu to a low of 193 years in Portland, Oregon. We present two more representative examples of encounters in policing and hope they provide more insight into the profession. Perhaps more important, they also depict the impact that situational variables have on police violence.

In one medium-size Midwestern city of less than 100,000, two cases involving the use of force and accusations of racial discrimination occurred. The first incident involved two African American teenaged sisters who began fighting. Two white officers were in the neighborhood responding to a burglary complaint when they heard the fight. The officers entered the residence through an unlocked door and saw the girls struggling. The officers say they made every effort to separate the girls, starting with verbal commands, and then attempted to physically pull them apart. Unsuccessful in their attempts to physically separate the sisters, the officers elevated their use of force to chemical agents and utilized their pepper spray. Both sisters were sprayed at about the same time that their grandmother entered the residence and asked the officers for permission to care for her granddaughters. The officers claimed the girls continued to struggle and shout profanities, at which time they were given another blast of pepper spray.

Eventually, the girls were arrested and spent the night in jail. Both the suspects and their grandmother believed that the use of pepper spray was unwarranted as well as excessive and that the officers were out of control. They have since filed a complaint against the officers, and the grandmother, who said that she is not one to claim racism, insists that the department needs to face some tough questions about the disproportionate use of pepper spray on minorities. At first glance it may appear that the officers used excessive force in this incident, as they escalated too quickly through the continuum. The officers, however, believed that, based on the total circumstances, their behavior was acceptable. Going from verbal commands to an alleged attempt at pulling the girls apart, to utilizing their pepper spray and subsequently having to justify their actions despite the fact that their primary intention was to quell a family quarrel—this is the reality of police work.

Brief conversations with several officers from the department involved in this case provided additional insight. The consensus among the officers was that it was the individual officers' choice regarding the handling of the situation. Some officers said that they would have attempted to wrestle the girls apart, even though such actions would leave them vulnerable to attack and could lead to increased violence against the girls. For example, suppose one of the girls struck the officer who was attempting to separate them. The necessary use of force could then escalate beyond tactics and involve the use of a nightstick. Such a situation would have likely led to a more controversial case, particularly if one of the girls had been seriously hurt. Ultimately, the police department tried to reassure the public that the officers in this encounter were acting well within the guidelines of the department policy.

Pepper spray is often used to avoid more serious confrontations and to provide officers with another option in subduing noncompliant suspects. Police training tactics from 15 to 20 years ago did not include the option of chemical agents; strikes and compliance holds such as lateral vascular neck restraint (the Lindell system chokehold) were more likely to be employed. Such tactics resulted in many more injuries to suspects. The reality of the application of force is that it may be necessary to escalate the use of force to prevent more serious injuries. This important aspect of policing may be difficult for the general public to understand.

A more complicated and sensitive case also happened in the same Midwestern city. This case provides several important discussion points and lessons involving the use of force in the field. An African American couple were heading home after work during the afternoon when they passed a sheriff's department vehicle. The deputy made a U-turn and followed the couple. Upon pulling the couple over, the deputy asked for the driver's license and registration. The couple asked why they were stopped, and the deputy replied that he believed that they were speeding. This is where the case takes a decided turn. The deputy radioed in to check the records of the driver, and the report came back that he had a suspended license. The deputy returned to the stopped vehicle to place the driver under arrest. The driver began to argue as he exited the vehicle, denying that he had a suspended driver's license. (If he had obtained his "bust card" from the ACLU, he might have decided to behave differently.)

A subsequent investigation discovered that the driver's license was *not* suspended. He had numerous suspensions in the past, making his record confusing to the dispatcher as to its current status. The dispatcher misinterpreted the status of the driver's license and told the deputy it was suspended. In sum, we have a minority suspect who appears to have committed an arrestable offense and a citizen who sees a white officer attempting to arrest him for something he knows he did not do.

Under the state law of this Midwestern city, a citizen has the right to resist an unlawful arrest, even up to the use of deadly force. This may seem a peculiar law, and many would agree it would not be a good idea to test it. Playing devil's advocate, however, what about cases such as Abner Louima's? What would you do if an officer threatened to take you to a police station and do something as horrible as sodomize you with a wooden stick? Would you consider resisting arrest?

Returning to our story, a scuffle ensued between the officer and the citizen. At this point the stories vary somewhat, although the suspect does end up in handcuffs and being slammed against the car. The suspect received a sprained arm. During the confrontation, the suspect's wife began yelling at the officer to stop fighting with her husband. As the officer placed the driver in his patrol car, he then turned to confront the driver's wife. She claims the deputy pushed her and injured her arm and acted as if he was "on some kind of drug." As the driver witnessed this, he became enraged and began kicking at the window of the deputy's vehicle. The deputy was about to mace the suspect when another officer intervened and calmed the driver down. The driver's wife was placed under arrest as well, and both were taken to jail. Another officer informed the department about the incident, in particular, about the officer's possible mistreatment of the suspects and possible use of unnecessary force.

On the surface, this case may not seem very complicated; nevertheless, the following questions (and others) remain. Was the stop racially motivated? Did the officer need to place the suspect under arrest? Could more information have been gathered before deciding on arrest? Did the suspect's demeanor play a role? These are complex questions that the department and the community were asking months after the incident.

To add to the complications involved in this case, we would be remiss if we did not share other details surrounding this incident. The day prior to this traffic stop, a local police officer was shot four times (three in the stomach and one grazing his ear) while he was attempting to serve a warrant. The officer was able to return fire and killed the suspect before collapsing outside. This shootout troubled the officers in the area and received a great deal of press coverage.

Additional information surrounding the arresting officer's background surfaced, leading some to believe that his behavior was prompted by a prior experience. The general public did not know that the deputy on the traffic stop had been shot during his career and had only recently returned to work with 80% use of his arm. We can only speculate what was going through the deputy's mind as he read about another officer being shot, and then faced a noncompliant and combative suspect on a traffic stop the very next day. Both the suspect and officer were well within their rights: The suspect could resist what he perceived as an unlawful arrest, and the deputy had an arrestable offense and the authority to use force to defend himself. The situation could have resulted in tragedy on both sides. The county sheriff issued an official apology to the couple, and to the dismay of many officers, the arresting deputy was suspended for what many of his fellow officers viewed as doing his job.

This example illustrates the complexities of policing in America. In general, numerous factors in the surrounding context must be considered in our attempts to understand police behavior—including human emotions. These issues may be difficult, if not impossible, to quantify in a continuum or a force factor, yet they are extremely important if we are to gain a greater understanding of how and why coercive force is used in policing.

With the great deal of uncertainty found in police practices, it may seem surprising to some that more officers are not injured, or that more officers do not unnecessarily and/or more quickly accelerate up through the continuum of force. We can speculate that based on the increased research focus in this area, and the continued use of video cameras in police patrol cars, a promising future lies ahead. The research will assuredly permit us to better understand police use of force, and video cameras will not only protect officers against fraudulent claims of violence but also assist in regulating officer behavior. The footage they provide is a welcome addition to police training curricula.

So what does the future of situational policing violence hold? Basing his discussion on the historical record, Bayley (1998) argues that the growth of destructiveness in criminal violence is going to profoundly shape the face of American policing. He does not believe that people will become more violent or bloody-minded; however, he suggests that technological advances will facilitate large-scale violence. Thus, it is important that departments be prepared for what could be considered "techno-violence," as departments around the country continue to alter their crime-fighting approaches from a reactive to a proactive posture. Such a development will undoubtedly lead to, among other things, the need for additional research, policy making, and training. It will also lead to additional situational variables with which officers will have to contend.

Thus, the battle between the "good guys" and the "bad guys" continues. It is hoped that the future will not bring about new forms of violence but instead a better comprehension of the traditional behaviors of these "good" and "bad" guys, as well as a greater understanding of why they are battling. Such information will provide a significant step in our understanding of crime and justice in general.

REFERENCES

ADAMS, K. (1999). What we know about police use of force. In National Institute of Justice, *Use of force by police* (NCJ 176330, pp. 1–14). Washington DC: U.S. Department of Justice.

ALPERT, G., & DUNHAM, R. (1997). *The force factor: Measuring police use of force relative to suspect resistance*. Washington, DC: Police Executive Research Forum.

ALPERT, G., & DUNHAM, R. (1999). The force factor: Measuring and assessing police use of force and suspect resistance. In National Institute of Justice, *Use of force by police* (NCJ 176330, pp. 45–60). Washington DC: U.S. Department of Justice.

AMERICANS FOR EFFECTIVE LAW ENFORCEMENT. (1988). *Use of force tactics and non-lethal weaponry*. Prospect Heights, IL: Waveland Press.

ANDERSON, E. (1976). The chivalrous treatment of the female offender in the arms of the criminal justice system: A review of the literature. *Social Problems, 23,* 350–357.

ARTHUR, J., & CASE, C. (1994). Race, class and support for police use of force. *Crime, Law and Social Change, 21,* 167–182.

BANTON, M. (1964). *The policeman in the community*. New York: Basic Books.

BARTOLLAS, C., & HANH, L. (1999). *Policing in America*. Boston: Allyn and Bacon.

BAYLEY, D. (1998, November/December). Policing in America: Social science and public policy in America. *Society,* 16–19.

BAYLEY, D., & GAROFALO, J. (1989). The management of violence by police patrol officers. *Criminology, 27*(1), 1–27.

BERK, S., & LOSEKE, D. (1981). Handling family violence: Situational determinants of police arrest in domestic disturbances. *Law and Society Review, 15*(2), 317–346.

BITTNER, E. (1967). The police on skid row: A study of peace keeping. *American Sociological Review, 32,* 699–715.

BLACK, D. (1971). The social organization of arrest. *Stanford Law Review, 23,* 1087–1111.

BLACK, D. (1980). *The manners and customs of the police.* New York: Academic Press.

BLAUNER, R. (1972). *Racial oppression in America.* New York: Harper and Row.

BLUMBERG, M. (1981). Race and police shootings: An analysis in two cities. In J. Fyfe (Ed.), *Contemporary issues in law enforcement.* Beverly Hills, CA: Sage.

BLUMBERG, M. (1997). Controlling police use of deadly force: Assessing two decades of progress. In R. Dunham & G. Alpert (Eds.), *Critical issues in policing: Contemporary readings* (3rd ed., pp. 507–530). Prospect Heights, IL: Waveland Press.

BROOKS, L. (1997). Police discretionary behavior: A study of style. In R. Dunham & G. Alpert (Eds.), *Critical issues in policing: Contemporary readings* (3rd ed., pp. 149–166). Prospect Heights, IL: Waveland Press.

BUREAU OF JUSTICE STATISTICS. (1994). Violence between intimates, National Crime Victimization Survey, selected findings. (NCJ-149259). Washington, DC: U.S. Department of Justice.

BUREAU OF JUSTICE STATISTICS. (1988a). *Report to the nation on crime and justice,* 2nd ed. Washington, DC: Department of Justice.

BUREAU OF JUSTICE STATISTICS. (1988b). Drug use and crime: State prison inmate survey, 1986. *BJS special report.* Washington, DC: Bureau of Justice Statistics.

CHEVIGNY, P. (1969). *Police power: Police abuses in New York City.* New York: Vintage Books.

CHUA-EOAN, H. (2000, March 6). Black and blue. *Time,* pp. 24–28.

CLINES, F. (2000, July 14). Images of beating by police flood Philadelphia. *New York Times,* p. 15A.

COHEN, A. (2000, March 6). Gangsta cops. *Time,* pp. 30–34.

COLLINS, R. (1975). *Conflict sociology.* New York: Academic Press.

CONNOR, G. (1991, March). Use of force continuum: Phase II. *Law and Order,* pp. 30–32.

CONYERS, J. JR. (1981, January/February). Police violence and riots. *The Black Scholar,* pp. 2–5.

CRAWFORD, C., & BURNS, R. (1998). Predictors of the police use of force: The application of a continuum perspective in Phoenix. *Police Quarterly, 1*(4), 41–63.

CUMMING, E., CUMMING, I., & EDELL, L. (1965). Policemen as philosopher, guide and friend. *Social Problems, 12,* 276–286.

DESMEDT, J. (1984). Use of force paradigm for law enforcement. *Journal of Police Science and Administration, 12,* 170–176.

DOERNER, W. (1998). *Introduction to law enforcement: An insider's view.* Boston: Butterworth-Heinemann.

ERICSON, R. (1982). *Reproducing order: A study of police patrol work.* Toronto: University of Toronto Press.

FEDERAL BUREAU OF INVESTIGATION. (1990). *Uniform Crime Reports: Law enforcement officers killed and assaulted, 1989.* Washington, DC: U.S. Government Printing Office.

FRIDELL, L., & PATE, A. (1995). *Death on patrol: Felonious homicides of American police officers.* Washington, DC: Uniform Crime Reports Section, Federal Bureau of Investigation, U.S. Department of Justice.

FRIDELL, L., & PATE, A. (1997). Death on patrol: Killings of American law enforcement officers. In R. Dunham & G. Alpert (Eds.), *Critical issues in policing: Contemporary readings* (3rd ed., pp. 580–608). Prospect Heights, IL: Waveland Press.

FRIEDRICH, R. (1980, November). Police use of force: Individuals, situations, and organizations. *Annals of the American Academy of Political and Social Science, 452,* 82–97.

FYFE, J. (1978). Shots fired: An examination of New York City police firearms discharges. Unpublished doctoral dissertation, State University of New York at Albany.

FYFE, J. (1981a). Race and extreme police-citizen violence. In R. McNeely & C. Pope (Eds.), *Race, crime and criminal justice* (pp. 89–108). Beverly Hills, CA: Sage.

FYFE, J. (1981b). Toward a typology of police shootings. In J. Fyfe (Ed.), *Contemporary issues in law enforcement* (pp. 136–151). Beverly Hills, CA: Sage.

FYFE, J. (1988). Police use of deadly force: Research and reform. *Justice Quarterly, 5*(2), 165–205.

FYFE, J. (1997). The split-second syndrome and other determinants of police violence. In R. Dunham & G. Alpert (Eds.), *Critical issues in policing: Contemporary readings* (3rd ed., pp. 531–546). Prospect Heights, IL: Waveland Press.

GARNER, J., BUCHANAN, J., SCHADE, T., & HEPBURN, J. (1996). Understanding the use of force by and against the police. In *National Institute of Justice: Research in brief* (NCJ 158614). Washington, DC: U.S. Department of Justice.

GARNER, J., SCHADE, T., HEPBURN, J., & BUCHANAN, J. (1995). Measuring the continuum of force used by and against the police. *Criminal Justice Review, 20*(2), 146–168.

GELLER, W., & KARALES, K. (1981). Shootings of and by Chicago police. Chicago: Chicago Law Enforcement Study Group.

GELLER, W., & SCOTT, M. (1992). *Deadly force: What we know*. Washington, DC: Police Executive Research Forum.

GOLDKAMP, J. (1976). Minorities as victims of police shootings: Interpretations of racial disproportionality and police use of deadly force. *Justice System Journal, 2,* 169–183.

GROPPER, B. (1985). Probing the links between drugs and crime. In *National Institute of Justice: Research in brief.* (NCJ 158614). Washington, DC: U.S. Department of Justice.

HARRING, S., PLATT, T., SPEIGLMAN, R., & TAKAGI, P. (1977). The management of police killings. *Crime and Social Justice, 8,* 34-43

HAYDEN, G. (1981). Police discretion in the use of deadly force: An empirical study of information usage in deadly force decisionmaking. *Journal of Police Science and Administration, 9*(1), 102–107.

KAVANAGH, J. (1997). The occurrence of resisting arrest in arrest encounters: A study of police-citizen violence. *Criminal Justice Review, 22,* 16–33.

KENNEDY, R. (1999). Suspect policy. *The New Republic, 20,* 30–35.

KLINGER, D. (1994). Demeanor or crime? Why "hostile" citizens are more likely to be arrested. *Criminology, 32,* 475–493.

KLINGER, D. (1996). More on demeanor and arrest in Dade County. *Criminology, 34,* 61–82.

KOBLER, A. (1975). Figures (and perhaps some facts) on police killing of citizens in the United States. *Journal of Social Issues, 31,* 185–191.

KROHN, M., CURRY, J., & NELSON-KRUEGER, S. (1983). Is chivalry dead? An analysis of changes in police dispositions of males and females. *Criminology, 21,* 395–416.

LaGRANGE, R. 1998. *Policing American society* (2nd ed.). Chicago: Nelson-Hall.

LANGWORTHY, R., & TRAVIS, L. (1999). *Policing in America: A balance of forces* (2nd ed.). Upper Saddle River, NJ: Prentice Hall.

LENSKI, G. (1966). *Power and privilege*. New York: McGraw-Hill.

LUNDMAN, R. (1980). *Police and policing: An introduction*. New York: Holt, Rinehart & Winston.

LUNDMAN, R. (1994). Demeanor or crime? The midwest city police-citizen encounter study. *Criminology, 32*(4), 631–656.

LYMAN, M. (1999). *The police: An introduction*. Upper Saddle River, NJ: Prentice Hall.

MANN, C. (1993). *Unequal justice: A question of color*. Bloomington and Indianapolis: Indiana University Press.

MANNING, P. (1980, November). Violence and the police role. *Annals of the American Academy of Political and Social Science, 452,* 135–144.

MARGARITA, M. (1980, November). Killing the police: Myths and motives. *Annals of the American Academy of Political and Social Science, 452,* 63–71.

MEDNICK, S., POLLOCK, V., VOLAVKA, J., & GABRIELLI, W., JR. (1982). Biology and violence. In M. Wolfgang & N. Weiner (Eds.), *Criminal violence* (pp. 21–80). Thousand Oaks, CA: Sage.

MEYER, M. (1980). Police shootings of minorities: The case of Los Angeles. *Annals of the American Academy of Political and Social Science, 452,* 98–110.

MOULDS, E. (1980). Chivalry and paternalism: Disparities of treatment in the criminal justice system. In S. Datesman & F. Scapitti (Eds.), *Women, crime and justice* (pp. 275–299). New York: Oxford University Press.

NATIONAL ADVISORY COMMISSION ON CIVIL DISORDERS. (1968). *Report of the National Advisory Commission on Civil Disorders.* New York: Dutton.

NATIONAL INSTITUTE OF JUSTICE. (1999). Executive summary. *Use of force by police: Overview of national and local data.* (NCJ 176330). Washington, DC: U.S. Department of Justice.

PEREZ, D. (1997). *The paradoxes of police work: Walking the thin blue line.* Incline Village, NV: Copperhouse.

PILIAVIN, J., & BRIAR, S. (1964). Police encounters with juveniles. *American Journal of Sociology, 70,* 206–214.

QUINNEY, R. (1974). A critical theory of the criminal law. In R. Quinney (Ed.), *Criminal justice in America.* Boston: Little, Brown.

REISS, A. (1967). *Studies on crime and law enforcement in a major metropolitan area.* President's Commission on Law Enforcement and Administration of Justice, Field Survey No. 3. Washington, DC: U.S. Government Printing Office.

REISS, A. (1971). *The police and the public.* New Haven, CT: Yale University Press.

REISS, A. (1972). Police brutality. In L. Radzinowicz & M. Wolfgang (Eds.), *The criminal in the arms of the law* (pp. 293–308). New York: Basic Books.

ROBIN, G. (1963, May/June). Justifiable homicide by police. *Journal of Criminal Law, Criminology, and Police Science,* 225–231.

ROSSI, P., BERK, R., & EIDSON, B. (1974). *The roots of urban discontent: Public policy, municipal institutions, and the ghetto.* New York: Wiley.

ROTH, J. (1994). Psychoactive substances and violence. In *National Institute of Justice: Research in brief.* (NCJ 158614). Washington, DC: U.S. Department of Justice.

RUBINKAM, M. (2000, July 15). Philadelphia police chief seeks "no rush to judgment." *Fort Worth Star-Telegram,* p. 4A.

SCHARF, P., & BINDER, A. (1983). *The badge and the bullet: Police use of deadly force.* New York: Praeger.

SCHMALLEGER, F. (1999). *Criminal justice today* (5th ed.). Upper Saddle River, NJ: Prentice Hall.

SCHULTZ, D. (1990). *Police unarmed defense tactics.* Placerville, CA: Custom.

SHERMAN, L. (1980). Causes of police behavior: The current state of quantitative research. *Journal of Research in Crime and Delinquency, 17,* 69–100.

SHERMAN, L., COHEN, E., GARTIN, P., HAMILTON, E., & ROGAN, D. (1986). *Citizens killed by big-city police, 1970–1984.* Washington, DC: Crime Control Institute.

SKOLNICK, J. (1994). *Justice without trial: Law enforcement in a democratic society.* New York: Macmillan.

SMITH, D. (1984). The organizational aspects of legal control. *Criminology, 22,* 19–38.

SMITH, D. (1987). Police response to interpersonal violence: Defining the parameters of legal control. *Social Forces, 65,* 767–782.

SMITH, D., & DAVIDSON, L. (1984). Equity and discretionary justice: The influence of race on police arrest decisions. *Journal of Criminal Law, 75,* 234–249.

SMITH, D., & VISHER, C. (1980). Sex and involvement in deviance/crime: A quantitative review of the empirical literature. *American Sociological Review, 45,* 691–701.

SMITH, D., & VISHER, C. (1981). Street-level justice: Situational determinants of police arrest decisions. *Social Problems, 31,* 167–177.

SYKES, R., & BRENT, E. (1980). The regulation of interaction by police: A systems view of taking charge. *Criminology, 18*(2), 182–197.

TAKAGI, P. (1974). A garrison state in a "democratic" society. *Crime and Social Justice: A Journal of Radical Criminology, 5,* 27–33.

TOCH, H. (1969). *Violent men: An inquiry into the psychology of violence.* Chicago: Aldine.

TOCH, H. (1990). The shape of police violence. In N. Weiner, M. Zahh, & R. Sagi (Eds.), *Violence: Patterns, causes, public policy* (pp. 223–231). Orlando, FL: Harcourt Brace.

UCHIDA, C. (1997). The development of the American police. In R. Dunham & G. Alpert (Eds.), *Critical issues in policing: Contemporary readings* (3rd ed., pp. 18–35). Prospect Heights, IL: Waveland Press.

VISHER, C. (1983). Gender, police arrest decisions, and notions of chivalry. *Criminology, 21,* 5–28.

WALKER, S., SPOHN, C., & DELONE, M. (2000). *The color of justice: Race, ethnicity, and crime in America* (2nd ed.). Belmont, CA: Wadsworth.

WESTLEY, W. (1970). *Violence and the police: A sociological study of law, custom, and morality.* Boston: MIT Press.

WILSON, J. (1968). *Varieties of police behavior.* Cambridge, MA: Harvard University Press.

WILSON, O. (1963, May). One man patrol cars. *The Police Chief,* pp. 18–24.

WORDEN, R. (1989). Situational and attitudinal explanations of police behavior: A theoretical reappraisal and empirical assessment. *Law and Society Review, 23,* 667–711.

WORDEN, R. (1996). The causes of police brutality: Theory and evidence on police use of force. In W. Geller & H. Toch (Eds.), *Police violence: Understanding and controlling police abuse of force* (pp. 23–51). New Haven, CT: Yale University Press.

WORDEN, R. & SHEPARD, R. (1996). Demeanor, crime, and police behavior: A reexamination of the police services study data. *Criminology, 34,* 83–105.

5

Police Use of Deadly Force

Where We Should Be Looking

Steven E. Reifert

I can remember it like it was yesterday—a hot July night, relative humidity about 300%, and calls holding from the day shift. I'm new to the department but not new to police work. Still, though, that feeling of not doing anything wrong to avoid being labeled a rookie or a "boot" was omnipresent. It was going to be one of those weird calls, it came in as a B&E in progress, but the theft was some meat from a freezer and the victim was still there inside the house. Oh yeah, the other part was that the suspect grabbed her breast on the way out while she was breast-feeding her baby. Kind of sets the stage while I'm enroute to the house where the victim is waiting. A backup officer is also dispatched to assist because of the nature of the call.

When I arrive, I first come in contact with the suspect (having been described by the victim when I was given the dispatch) standing in a side yard. I contact him and immediately realize he is high on something. My first thought is crack cocaine. About that time the victim steps out and says, "That's the one," as the suspect picks up a package of frozen meat off the front lawn. Anyone familiar with police calls and criminal investigations knows they simply do not happen like this. Something's wrong and I think its because the suspect is high on something.

As my backup and I close in, the suspect is now threatening us, calling us on. As a side note, we were still carrying the old wooden nightsticks that we always left in the car, and our mace was the older type of spray that only served to anger people when we sprayed them and was usually not even carried. Apparently my partner believed we were going to arrest this guy—I still wasn't sure because of the physical state of the suspect—and went to tackle the suspect. The fight was on!

Both of us were new to the department but had been officers at other departments. We tried the physical restraints and hand strikes to subdue this guy but nothing was working. He felt no pain at all. Strikes to the limbs and chest did nothing. Suddenly, we were falling down an embankment into a parked car and I felt the presence of another person, a second suspect (I learned later), who was coming to help his friend get away from the police. I pulled off the second guy and looked around and saw the first suspect on top of my partner choking him. I could see my partner reaching for his gun, but because we had rolled down an embankment into a parked car, he was at such an angle that he could not reach his side arm. I had thrown the second guy off over the car, and he was recovering from falling over backwards.

Many things raced through my mind at that time. The suspect looked as if he was going to kill my partner, who was actually going to try to shoot this guy. I was wondering if I should shoot this guy, but all the while realizing he was feeling no pain but was nonetheless unarmed. How do I stop him when nothing is working? To this day I remember pulling my gun and thinking, "My God, I'll be fired and go to jail for shooting this guy." Weird thoughts go through your head when it looks as if you might actually shoot someone. We were very close and no doubt if I had shot I would have killed him; we were at point-blank range.

I reached around, pulled out my handcuffs, wrapped them around his neck, and squeezed. I held on until he started choking and got off my partner. But then, all of a sudden, I thought, "You better let go, you're going to kill this unarmed man." I let off the cuffs, and the fight was on again. Fortunately for us, other units arrived and subdued the suspect.

I'm summarizing in little more than a page an incident that gave me nightmares for weeks. The written prose does not give justice to the horror of the incident, because tactically we had failed and morally we had almost taken a life. Incidentally, I saw the suspect some four hours later in our jail, and he had not an idea why he was there. He had been on a crack cocaine binge for days and was just coming down.

INTRODUCTION

What does this incident have to do with this chapter? Well, I ask people to consider why I didn't shoot. Believe me, after reading my report, even our Internal Affairs officer asked me why I didn't shoot. I was justified at the outset, believing I had no initial alternatives, and the suspect was killing my partner. My partner did go to the hospital but was released with no injuries. Comments from the street ranged from "Good job" to "You should have shot the bastard." After all, he was trying to kill another officer, and culturally, we take care of each other. Why didn't I shoot? Today, I answer and reaffirm to myself that I did the right thing. The suspect, by the way, is in prison right now for various offenses such as breaking and entering (B&E), rape, and more. Still the question looms: Why didn't I shoot? Was it the fear of being fired or the fear of being sued? The fear of civil litigation is driven home, ad nauseam, in all the police academies. If you do this, you may get sued, or if you don't do this, you may get sued. The fear of civil liability is omnipresent today in police work. Do not think for a second that the above incident is an isolated occurrence. It happens daily in America. Some officer has to decide whether to shoot or not. More often than not, we decide not to shoot. The question remains though: Why don't we shoot when we can, or think we can, based on our training and guidelines set forth by policy and directives?

The answers are not clear, and the movement within the police field toward how to handle deadly force issues is not clear. The past two decades have sent two different messages to the police. On the one hand, the courts have tightened the use of police deadly force through cases such as *Tennessee v. Garner* (1985) that have put constraints on police concerning when, where, and how they use deadly force. The use of vehicles in high-speed pursuits has just recently been reviewed, with movement to caution police regarding their methods and use of force. On the other hand, and contrary to the courts' decisions, the police have steadily built up their arsenal of new and improved weaponry. Special Weapons and Tactics (SWAT) teams have grown by leaps and bounds. Police carry MP-5 automatic 9-mm submachine guns and other sophisticated weaponry. The courts say "limit police discretion," while at the same time the police field gives us high-tech weaponry and says "here, use these" (Kraska, 1996).

> Kalamazoo, Michigan, January 2000—Two officers on patrol respond to a person breaking into cars near a residence. Officers respond to the address given but inadvertently and unbeknownst to them walk past the suspect and the vehicles he is breaking into. They backtrack and one officer shines his flashlight under a car and sees someone lying under the car. Both officers, together now, give commands to the individual to get out from under the car. The individual rolls to the opposite side and tries to get away. The officers reposition and give commands for the individual to stop. The individual starts to get up, pulls a handgun from his waistband, and points it at the officers as he starts to run away. Both officers draw their guns; one fires two shots, the other does not fire. The suspect is not hit and is caught a short time later hiding under some other cars in the area. The officers were about 10 feet apart from each other. Both saw the gun and both drew their guns. One fired, one did not.

> Kalamazoo, Michigan, May 2000—Officers are in foot pursuit of someone reportedly having a gun. The suspect flees after officers corner him in a backyard. He flees by jumping the fence before officers can get to him. After several blocks, one officer gives chase after he sees the suspect go into a backyard with a high fence. As he approaches the suspect who is now trying to jump the fence, the suspect turns and pulls a handgun from his waistband and points it directly at the officer's chest. They are at that time, according to the officer, 15–20 feet apart. The officer maintains his running speed and goes shoulder long into the suspect, knocking both to the ground. The gun is knocked clear, but the suspect lunges for the gun and grabs it. The officer tackles him and holds on until other officers arrive. The officer sustains a severely dislocated shoulder with the potential for permanent debilitation.

In the first incident, one officer decided to shoot, while the other did not. One determines the need to use deadly force, while the other does not. In the second scenario, the officer chooses not to shoot as the suspect points a gun at him at close range. In any situation, why does one officer shoot and the other does not? Why does an officer facing a handgun at short range choose to use physical force rather than shoot another human being?

My intention in writing this chapter is to question the existing literature dealing with police use of deadly force. To do so, I use the three scenarios to point out what information is available and what information and theoretical basis is lacking. Police use deadly force, we know that. But why do some officers use it, while others do not? What constraints hinder an officer, or what is it that causes the reluctance, as some authors call it, of officers to use deadly force? Should we be more concerned with the fact that police use deadly force or more concerned with why they do and do not use deadly force? I offer a slightly different outlook on this topic. I offer my insights not as an outsider looking in but rather as an insider looking out. My standpoint emanates from that of a police officer working for more than 20 years in the field. I was given a machine gun at the age of 19 and told to go guard aircraft in the U.S. Air Force. My career since has been filled with patrol work, undercover narcotics work, crime prevention, and community policing roles. Academically, I worked nights achieving small goals: first a bachelor's, then a master's, and finally my doctoral work in sociology. I make no excuses nor waver from my stance. It is based both on formal education and hard knocks on the street.

USING FORCE

Police use force to do their job and this force sometimes is deadly. Officers, in the performance of their jobs, kill people. Legally they have the right to use such force to protect the lives of others or themselves. Generally, the use of deadly force is used, or allowed to be used, to stop an immediate action in which someone's life is at stake and immediate cessation of that act would prevent the loss or severe dismemberment of any individual. The case of *Tennessee v. Garner* (1985) made illegal the act of shooting a fleeing felon and put constraints on the police to shoot only in life-threatening situations. Several departments do allow the use of deadly force for the apprehension of felons in such cases as homicide, rape, and extreme aggravated assault (Alpert & Dunham, 1997; Roberg, Crank, & Kuykendall, 2000).

The term *deadly force* is often included with other categories in data collected on police use of force. This does not seem to give the appropriate priority to that category. In other words, we can gloss over police use of deadly force when we study it in such a way. We lose the importance of the topic by not looking at it separately. I believe we should look at all categories of the use of force by police and break out the use of deadly force as a separate category.

Another complicating issue to consider when observing police use of deadly force is intent. Most often we define police use of deadly force as an intentional act in which the officer inflicts death or great bodily injury (Roberg et al., 2000). The officer intends to cause the harm. What clouds the issue are the incidental or accidental deaths or great bodily harm that police inflict when they did not intend to cause death or grave injury. Such things as choke holds or high-speed pursuits in which an accident occurs and someone dies or is seriously hurt are often considered police use of deadly force (Fyfe, 1983, as cited in Roberg et al., 2000). I focus, however, on the intentional acts of the police to use deadly force. The issue at hand is why the officer decided to use, or not to use, deadly force.

Three issues are of consideration when discussing the use of deadly force and the resistance thereto. The first is the reliability of the information on police use of deadly force. Where do we get our information on the police use of force, and in particular the use of deadly force, or even, as I will show, the attempted use of force that is not recorded? The second is the push to overcome any resistance to using deadly force. In other words, we should train our officers to overcome any natural resistance to killing another human being. This would also encompass the after-the-fact consequential factors that arise after an officer takes someone's life. These would include disability relief and so on. A third issue, and one I believe of importance here, is the lack of information and research regarding the inability or intentional resistance to using deadly force. As my earlier scenarios illustrate, officers can be side by side, each facing the same threat, and one may choose to fire his or her weapon, while the other may choose not to fire.

HOW WE MEASURE POLICE USE OF DEADLY FORCE

The measurement of police use of force, in particular the use of deadly force, has long been a source of controversy between researchers and practitioners. Long before the passage of the 1994 Crime Bill, researchers called for expanded collection of data on the police use of force (see, for example, Alpert & Fridell, 1992; Fyfe, 1988; Geller & Scott, 1991). A method to collect detailed data on police use of force and deadly force was sought. General information on police actions was needed both for policy making and further research. It begged the question, though, how do we capture this type of information? Where do we turn to get information on police use of force? Do we get reliable information reported by the police? Would the police cooperate in such data collection? Studies on police and their subculture would argue that there is a deep-seated cultural resistance to reporting matters pertaining to the use of force and to any implication that excessive use of force may be involved on the part of the police (Crank, 1998; Crank & Caldero, 2000; Kappeler, Sluder, & Alpert, 1998; Waegel, 1984).

For the past several years, the National Institute of Justice (NIJ) has provided reports on police use of force. These reports provide information relative to police-citizen encounters throughout the country. They deal with face-to-face encounters with the police and the amount of force used by the officers to complete their tasks. One of the first publications submitted by the NIJ to Congress (submitted in April 1996) was entitled "National Collection on Police Use of Force," a collection of research and information on this issue. The report points out one of the first difficulties in collecting data on use of deadly force by the police. The Federal Bureau of Investigation (FBI), through its Uniform Crime Report (UCR) reporting requirements, collects data on homicides and reports it in a supplementary report. On the same page, the NIJ report points out that other researchers have found "inconsistencies between the numbers reported by the FBI and numbers reported in other data collection efforts" (NIJ, 1996, p. 21). These other sources are usually in the form of medical reports, county health reports, or coroners' reports that record the deaths per county, summarized through the states (Sherman & Langworthy, 1979).

The methodological limitations are immense when we attempt to gain information pertaining to police use of deadly force. Geller and Scott (1991) wrote early in the 1990s about the limitations involved in collecting data on police use of force or police use of deadly force. Among other things, they argued, most sample sizes are too small, and the information about police shootings is maintained by police agencies, medical examiners, or coroners' offices, with the information recorded and kept for reasons other than research. Most of the focus on police use of deadly force is to determine justifiability rather than provide some realm of information as to when, where, and why. Police are required to report homicides to the FBI via the UCR reporting requirements and the supplemental homicide report; likewise, deaths are recorded through the medical authority in a particular county. Thus, we have somewhat accurate records pertaining to actual deaths attributed to police use of deadly force. The other type of information pertaining to use of deadly force is either unavailable or not recorded, for example, if researchers are interested in use of deadly force that did not result in death or situations in which the officer could have used deadly force but chose a different option.

If we wish to uncover and look closely at police shooting incidents, where would we find the information? Several earlier studies attempted to use observational methods (Fyfe, 1989; Scharf & Binder, 1983; Waegel, 1984) but were unable to produce sufficient information for worthwhile analysis. Beginning in 1996, the National Institute of Justice attempted to use surveys to record police-citizen contact and the use of force encountered by citizens with the police. This method was useful in shedding light on police encounters and the use of force as reported by citizens but fell short of providing information on the use of deadly force. As a self-report survey concerning encounters with police, it had the same weaknesses we see in all surveys of this nature, including fabrication, exaggerations, diminutions, and other limitations.

Still other roadblocks impede the collection of information pertaining to police use of deadly force. Officers in certain departments must report the "pulling of their side arm" when in public view, excluding visits to firing ranges. The information is not for public dissemination but rather administrative use to ward off criticism from the public and allow the administration to know when a side arm has been brandished. This collection of information is for internal use and is rarely, if ever, disclosed to the public and, generally, only upon request. The public use of this information would most likely discourage the reporting of such incidents, especially when it is a one-on-one situation. Since this type of information could be used for disciplinary action, fellow officers would probably be discouraged from reporting such events. It would perhaps be covered up by the officer for fear of second-guessing their actions.

Where does the police subculture fit into the reporting of police use of deadly force? When we define use of deadly force, must we also include the attempted or threatened use of deadly force by the police? If we follow the notion that a police subculture exists (see, for example, Crank, 1998; Crank & Caldero, 2000; Kappeler et al., 1998) by which officers establish mechanisms to perpetuate their occupation, then we must accept that police might not report or might intentionally cover up the use or attempted police use of deadly force:

> Police officers must be prepared to use force . . . and those who are unable to put themselves in harm's way without giving way to fear are shunned. . . . The linkage between force and culture is often viewed negatively, as a collusion among officers to keep quiet about abuses of force. According to this idea, the need to cover up abuses of force requires that officers cover for each other, and spawns a culture of secrecy impenetrable to administrative oversight. (Crank, 2000, pp. 64–65)

The notion of an occupational subculture (Souyral, 1992) that perpetuates itself by self-protection forces officers to deviate and fail to report certain instances of attempted use of deadly force and/or to alter or change occurrences during an actual deadly force encounter.

Kappeler et al. (1998) referred to such activities as "learning to deviate." They argued that the police use motives and justifications to deviate from reporting, and thus covering up, use of force, including the use of deadly force. Motives to use deadly force and the actual use of force are acceptable because of the "we/they" scenarios encountered daily by the police. Force used by an offender against the police or other member of society is viewed as wrong, whereas force used by police to do their job is viewed as acceptable because it is virtuous and seen as a necessary evil. It's a part of the job and needed to keep society safe. Justification comes from society's confirmation of the police use of force as an acceptable means used to keep offenders and perpetrators away from law-abiding citizens. Applying Sykes and Matza's (1957) neutralization of crime and delinquency approach to police behavior, these justifications include police denial of responsibility, denial of injury, denial of a victim, condemning those who simply don't understand police work, and appealing to a higher loyalty. Denial of responsibility means that it is never the officer's fault. The officers shot a person because the individual made them. No innocent person was hurt and the person shot deserved it because he or she was a dreg on society. These techniques may be reinforced by the thought that citizens who are not familiar with police work on the streets cannot understand the need to protect fellow officers. Such talk and belief perpetuate the covering up of information on police use of deadly force.

Perhaps we have to turn to our local newspapers for the collection and review of data on police use of deadly force. Only there do we find out about and read about police actions. Local newspaper coverage of the earlier scenario in which one officer shot and the other did not was buried on page three in the local newspaper. The story simply indicated that officers had shot at someone trying to break into cars. The scenario that I was involved in was never in the local newspaper, and the third scenario made the newspaper, although it simply noted that a person was arrested after the police chased him. The weakness, of course, to this method is that it is local in its attempts to gather information and the incidents we are interested in may or may not be printed. Gathering and capturing data concerning police use of deadly force from such sources can be valuable but, again, difficult to retrieve. The only good thing about this is that once the information is found, police records can be requested to corroborate the information.

Geller and Scott (1991) indicated that the two major sources of information pertaining to police shootings are the FBI's supplementary homicide reports and the National Center on Health Statistics' annual report, the latter simply recording only deaths. Other studies report battery rates by the police, shootings of civilians by police, shootings of police, and police shooting police. None of these get at what is behind the use of deadly force. They simply try to give us a feel or a number upon which to base the police use of deadly force.

It seems to me that we, both inside the profession and out, would want to know more about this phenomenon. The weaknesses persist. It is time for academe to step up and call for the collection of relevant data and research on such issues as "why one officer shot and why one did not." The task seems monumental, but it is something we must consider and embrace to help the profession and help the public further understand the nature of police use of deadly force.

TEACHING US TO KILL

Admittedly, police training has evolved tremendously over the past two decades. All states have established an accreditation process and have mandated certain qualifications and standards for officers (Roberg et al., 2000; see also Gaines, Kappeler, & Vaughn, 1999). In this vein, the training that officers receive on using deadly force has increased. As a member of the profession, I can remember lining up outside at the outdoor pistol range, standing back with a .38-caliber revolver, and shooting at a stationary paper target some 25 yards downrange. This training was limited and did not reflect the reality of police work nor deadly encounters.

Things have changed over the years. Research has led us to understand that most confrontations happen within 7 yards and that the targets or threats are generally moving. We realize we may or may not be standing, sitting, or running when faced with a deadly force decision. With this realization, the past two decades have seen the switch from revolvers to semiautomatics and changes in firearms training to incorporate night shooting, strobes, and distractions from both the target and the officers coupled with multiple shooting positions (Alpert & Dunham, 1997). Realistic targets are used and officers are trained to stop the threat, not necessarily to kill the aggressor.

Legal changes such as the ruling from *Tennessee v. Garner* (1985) have forced police officers to train differently. We now include such issues as ability, opportunity, and jeopardy in our firearms training. The emphasis is on protecting oneself and others as a justifiable use of a firearm. Warning shots, fleeing-felon shots, and the like are strictly prohibited. These had been common among officers prior to the changes in the mid-1980s. Of course, these are positive changes and have enabled the police, as a profession, to reap the rewards of more effective training on deadly force issues.

Recently, Nancy Marion reviewed a police academy and the training they provided their new police recruits. She found that firearms training was part of the "skills" portion of the academy and was "the most necessary and popular area of training. . . . For many it is the highlight of the academy" (Marion, 1998, as cited in Roberg et al., 2000, p. 380). She noted that the training for new recruits received at the academy was adequate but noticed shortcomings in dealing with victims and the elderly. She also noted the perpetuation of a "we/they attitude" by the instructors in relation to the public.

Another change in training with regard to police use of firearms involves the use of simulation machines. These machines run an officer through a scenario to see if they shoot or don't shoot. Videos assist in the portrayal of the "shoot/don't shoot" scenarios. The emphasis is to train officers as to when they should shoot and when they should not: "Shoot a threat, do not shoot an innocent citizen." These training aids assist the police in quickly recognizing a threat and taking some sort of action, preferable to shooting. Many departments invest in such training aids, thinking they will train officers and soothe the public by showing that the departments have a distinct interest in training officers when to use and not use deadly force. Alpert and Dunham (1997) wrote of the negative experience of the Miami Police Department when using simulators. The essence was to either shoot or not to shoot and employed no alternative to using a firearm. There was no emphasis on alternative training, on how to escape or avoid the deadly confrontation before one was put in a deadly force situation. The newer simulation machines or, more appropriately, computers have integrated alternatives to using firearms. Preconfrontational situations can be programmed in so the officers face multiple changing situations under training conditions. Officers are encouraged to seek cover to avoid the use of deadly force by using less-lethal weapons and interviewing techniques. It is no longer "shoot/don't shoot" but use all available alternatives prior to placing yourself in a deadly force situation.

We can, and do, train people to use firearms to defend themselves or defend others. Technically, we can train someone to use a gun to shoot at a target, role-play in computer-generated situations, and appropriately react to a perceived threat under training conditions. The question then is what happens on the street? Have we overcome a social barrier to killing when we turn new recruits out on the street based on the training they received at the academy? Does the recurring training police receive through in-service training prepare them to kill if the situation arises?

We recruit police officers from within our own communities and society in general. In other words, police come from our society; they are socialized the same and they live the same, side by side with the rest of the members of society (Alpert & Dunham, 1997; Crank & Caldero, 2000; Dunham & Alpert, 1997; Gaines et al., 1999; Roberg et al., 2000). They are human and susceptible to the same feelings, concerns, and stresses that all of us in society feel. However, we do ask the police to do something that the rest of society believes is taboo, and that is to kill. We ask them to step up in dangerous situations and possibly kill someone. It goes against the grain. We ask them to do something that is shunned in society.

Grossman (1996) maintained that a resistance to kill exists in our society. It is seen in police officers as well as in soldiers we ask to fight for our country. We can provide the technical training to squeeze the trigger and align our sights to react to a perceived shooting situation, but can we ensure someone will pull the trigger to take a life? Facing the same threat, different individuals will react differently. I refer, again, to the scenario in which both officers are facing the same credible threat and one shoots while the other does not.

Grossman (1996) relied heavily on S.L.A. Marshall and his work from Word War II, when the general realized that only 15 to 20% of the men on the line were firing their weapons and actually trying to kill someone. Marshall realized that "the average and healthy individual . . . has such an inner and usually realized resistance towards killing a fellow man that he will not of his own volition take life if it is possible to turn away from that responsibility. . . . At the vital point . . . the solider becomes a conscientious objector" (Grossman, 1996, p. 29). The soliders feared killing or being forced to kill more than they feared being harmed or killed.

Grossman argued that this resistance, this fear of killing, has been cloaked in silence for millennia. No one before Marshall addressed the issue. No one spoke of the inability, or sheer resistance to kill, until Marshall realized what was occurring on the battlefield. According to Grossman, "There does indeed seem to be a conspiracy of silence on this subject. . . . But there is no secret master plan responsible for the lack of attention given to this subject" (p. 35). Grossman wrote of "a massive unconscious cover-up," using psychologist-philosopher Peter Marin's term, "in which society hides itself from the true nature of combat that was occurring" (pp. 34–35). Humans throughout history have chosen to avoid, distort, and contort the facts of war and killing so as to avoid the implications of taking a life.

Grossman asks the question, "Where does this resistance to killing one's fellow man come from? Is it learned, instinctive, rational, environmental, hereditary, cultural, or social? Or a combination thereof?" (1996, p. 37). The search for this answer continues, coupled with guesses, hypotheses, and theories attempting to explain our aversion to killing. The answer remains hidden from us. Grossman states,

> We may never understand the nature of this force in man that causes him to strongly resist killing his fellow man, but we can give praise for it to whatever force we hold responsible for our existence. And although military leaders responsible for winning a war may be distressed by it, as a race we can view it with pride. There can be no doubt that this resistance to killing one's fellow man is there and that it exists as a result of a powerful combination of instinctive, rational, environmental, hereditary, cultural and social factors. It is there, it is strong, and it gives us cause to believe that there may just be hope for mankind after all. (1996, p. 39)

Grossman was also quick to point out that academe, psychologists, and psychiatrists, in general, ignored this aversion to killing, but the U.S. military forces did not. Whereas the psychiatric profession labeled it "combat fatigue, acute combat reaction," and other seemingly innocuous labels, the military saw it as trouble. The gist of the military is to kill others to achieve the objective. To achieve objectives, such as taking a hill in Vietnam, our side had to kill other human beings on their side. The U.S. military quickly changed its training tactics and overcame the resistance seen in World War II, when 15 to 20% of the men failed to shoot; in Vietnam almost 95% of the soldiers were shooting their weapons to kill.

The military took it upon itself to establish a triad of conditioning to overcome this resistance to killing. They used "desensitization, conditioning and denial defense mechanisms" (Grossman, 1996, p. 251). Desensitization utilizes a dehumanizing effect: A person is reprogrammed to believe that the other person is not human, is different, and does not have the same human feelings. The enemy is evil and different and does not feel human emotions.

Grossman stressed that the most effective method that the military has used, however, is classical Pavlovian conditioning and Skinnerian operant conditioning—Pavlovian in that we reward for a certain type of behavior and Skinnerian in that we alter images through behavioral engineering. The rewards come after quick and successful shooting, and the operant conditioning comes from the way the soldiers train. Much the same as police training changed from paper shooting at motionless targets to moving targets at varied ranges, so too did the military change the way they shoot. According to Grossman,

> Instead of laying prone on a grassy field calmly shooting at a bull's-eye target, the modern soldier spends many hours standing in a foxhole, with full combat equipment draped about his body. . . . At periodic intervals one or two olive-drab, man-shaped targets at varying ranges will pop up . . . and the soldier must instantly aim and shoot at the target. (1996, p. 253)

The emphasis is on a quick shot at a human-shaped target or "snap shooting," with no thinking involved and no association to the target being a person. The penalty for not snap shooting is ridicule by one's peers and retraining in the form of more snap shooting (Grossman, 1996).

So what does this have to do with police firearms training? Do we want our officers trained like the military so that we snap shoot at our targets? Perhaps we do. As noted earlier, we have changed our firearms training to more closely resemble what is experienced on the street. We have computer simulators that run us through scenarios to shoot or don't shoot, with options for alternative means of force, but what are we training for? Are we training for practical shooting situations, or is this military-like operant conditioning to overcome the natural resistance to shoot?

In its October 1999 bulletin, "Reluctance to Use Deadly Force: Causes, Consequences, and Cures," the FBI, a leader in police training, argued that police should overcome the resistance to kill (Williams, 1999). Williams, citing Grossman exclusively throughout the article, writes, "taking their cue from the military, law enforcement agencies have developed training methods to ensure that their officers will employ deadly force when the need arises" (1999, p. 1). Williams writes about the Pavlovian and Skinnerian conditioning in the military and law enforcement agencies, transposing this conditioning to the police. Williams opines, "this conditioning takes place early in police training. Though not officially sanctioned to do so, instructors at the academy often describe criminal offenders in derogatory terms," and thereby "the impressionable officers become desensitized and conditioned" (p. 2). Marion (Roberg et al., 2000, pp. 380–381) wrote of the sexist and "we/they" attitudes portrayed by some instructors at some academies; Williams believes the conditioning received by police reinforces these attitudes. The changes in firearms instruction to match street-level threats and the change to computer-simulated firearms training all add to the conditioning toward killing. Just as Grossman argued for changes in military-style shooting, Williams wrote:

> After a period of intense firearms training that includes multiple, varied range exercises, in conjunction with the positive reinforcement of instructor approval, peer acceptance, and passing grades, recruits respond to threats with desired action. Once recruits decide that a threat meets the criteria established by agency policy and the law, only one response exists. Officers set aside their moral objections in favor of conditioned response. (1999, pp. 2–3)

Clearly, Williams is arguing that we should train the police, like the military, to react to certain situations by shooting, or by killing: "Successful conditioning trains officers to overcome their aversion to injuring or using deadly force against other people" (1999, p. 2).

Williams calls for a disciplined approach to conditioning officers regarding the use of deadly force:

> Discipline controls officers' behavior in their use of deadly force against a perceived threshold threat. Officers internalize the discipline from training in general and firearms range in particular, incorporating it into their evaluations of threats. Thus, a disciplined approach to firearms training ensures that officers assess the suspect's actions prior to employing the conditioned response. (p. 3)

My response is: Hogwash! First, Williams tells us to use operant conditioning to overcome our aversion to killing, then tells us to use a disciplined approach to this conditioning. Which is it? Should we kill or not? Williams is saying strongly to use conditioning to overcome our resistance to killing, but if it's too strong and it "contradicts the values of today's community policing environment" (p. 3), then use a disciplined approach. Williams seems to want it both ways. I find him contradictory; do not tell us in the field, or on the streets, to train by conditioning our officers to shoot, providing little other options, but in the same article, tell us a disciplined approach should overcome any problems with inappropriate shoots, or the officer's failure to shoot.

I have a problem with Williams's argument and overall article. First, I do not believe, nor would I believe, that our communities would want our police trained to react like the military to threatening situations. Give us the skills; I do not argue to the contrary here. We need exposure to different scenarios and different threats. Teach us how to deal with these threats along with alternatives to killing someone.

How would Williams explain my three scenarios? In my case, perhaps it was the disciplined approach that stopped me from shooting the offender choking my partner. At first, all I could think was that the person was unarmed and my training says we do not shoot an unarmed person. Second, I thought of the repercussions for shooting this person—the threat of lawsuits and other scrutiny that was drilled into our heads during training: "Go ahead and shoot, but if you're wrong, this could happen or that could happen to you." Consciously I'm thinking about the repercussions of shooting someone from a legal standpoint, but I'm sure some unconscious reluctance was at work. By the time I had reached this "shoot/don't shoot" situation, I had received both the military-style training and the police-style training. I had not received the rigorous infantry-style training to kill but had received my share of firearms training, both U.S. Air Force and police in-service training. I chose not to shoot.

What about the scenario involving the two officers both squared off with an offender wielding a gun? Our training indicates that if a person points a gun at us, we can shoot him or her. It is a real perceived threat that clearly calls for a shoot. One officer shoots, the other does not. What is going on here? As a side note, both officers had the same basic training at an academy, followed by in-service training at their department. Both would have met Williams's operant conditioning training and would have been on an equal plane.

In the third scenario, I later interviewed the officer who was injured by tackling a suspect. He believed when he saw the gun coming out of the suspect's waistband that he was "going to take a round." He thought he had two choices, take a round in his vest or slow his approach and draw his gun and fire. Thinking he may not have enough time to draw his gun, he chose to tackle the suspect. The result was that he was injured and the suspect was not. The suspect did not fire, nor did the officer. A deadly force situation was resolved with no one being killed.

In each case, the officers involved were not rookies. Personally, I had been in police work for more than 11 years at the time. The two officers who squared off with the suspect with the handgun each had more than 5 years of experience. The last officer had more than 12 years of experience. So the rookie argument does not hold. The argument that the officers did not shoot because they did not have the experience does not apply.

I think Williams falls short of what is needed in police training. We are not training mindless people to be conditioned to react by shooting someone. There is and should be a large difference in the way we train the military and the way we train our police officers. Williams acknowledges that "the consequences of that conditioning (operant and behavioral) can make officers insensitive to the needs and rights of the citizens they serve"

(1999, p. 4). It is beyond insensitivity and goes to the argument of who we have policing our streets.

Alpert and Dunham (1997) point out that new training is on the horizon. They call it restraint training, which involves instituting scenario-based training into deadly force situations. The key is teaching alternatives and restraint in these situations. They write, "Restraint training has the potential to provide officers with techniques to resolve high-risk, potentially violent situations without violence" (1997, p. 230). They also admit that we do not know what causes the differences in officer responses in these high-risk encounters on the street. What is behind the officer's reactions in training and then nonreaction in the field? Are the police acting one way in training, based on peer pressure and the need for acceptance and praise from the trainer and organization, and acting another way on the streets?

How *do* we explain my scenarios? If it is not operant and behavioral conditioning that makes us respond the way we do, then what is it? Accepting the fact that we all have an inherent aversion to killing someone—barring the sociopaths in society and I hope they are not police officers—can we explain the reluctance to shoot or use deadly force by other means? Have we truly attempted to get at the heart of this issue?

EXPLANATIONS OF SHOOTING SITUATIONS

Dwyer, Graesser, Hopkinson, and Lupfer (1990) addressed the issue of police use of deadly force by implying that script theory offers an explanation for why police use or do not use deadly force. Prior to *Tennessee v. Garner* (1985), officers had two options for which to justify the use of deadly force. The first involved using deadly force to address an imminent (deadly) threat to themselves or others, or in other words, to save lives. The second justifiable use of deadly force concerned the fleeing-felon rule. Deadly force was authorized based on an officer's belief that a suspect had committed a felony and was fleeing from the police. Operating under the rules prior to *Garner,* officers "were not forced into a split-second decision as to whether their lives were in jeopardy. If they were not quite certain that they were faced with imminent harm when they shot a suspect, their actions were still consistent with the 'fleeing felon' alternative" (Dwyer et al., 1990, p. 295). Thus, based on the fleeing-felon rule, officers could justify their actions even if the threat was not imminent, which ultimately and unfortunately allowed for the after-the-fact justification of shootings—shootings that by today's standards were inappropriate and illegal.

Script theory is based on a cognitive process whereby an officer follows certain learned scripts stored in his or her psyche. Abelson (1981, as cited in Dwyer et al., 1990) states that it is "a cognitive structure or framework that, when activated, organizes a person's comprehension of stereotypic situations, allowing the person to have expectations and to make inferences about [the] potential outcome of a set of events" (p. 296). These scripts contain certain properties and elements. When these properties or elements occur, or are perceived as occurring, a script is activated that allows a person to make these inferences about how the event will turn out and adapt his or her behavior to ensure the event does turn out as hoped.

Three conditions are necessary for scripted behavior to be invoked. First, the person must have a stable cognitive representation of the particular script, followed by an evoking context for the script, and third, the person must physically enter the script (Dwyer, 1990). This leads to script recognition and the four related requirements, which include:

> First, the likelihood of recognizing the correct script (in other words accuracy) increases as a function of the amount of overlap between the perceived features of the situation and the content of the script. Second, this overlap (and resulting accuracy) increases as a function of either the number of perceived features of the number of information units in the script. . . . Third, accuracy improves to the extent that the perceived features and script information units are distinctive. Fourth, ambiguity occurs to the extent that more than one script is activated as potential interpretations of an experience. (Dwyer, 1990, p. 296)

The fourth characteristic can and does lead to the notion that scripting can be inaccurate based on the number of scripts one confronts at any one time. Multiple scripts can provide multiple and conflicting outcomes and reactions from the person.

Dwyer et al. (1990) argued that two categories of scripts are related to police use of deadly force. One is called the social-situational script and the other the deadly force script. The social-situational scripts are built up over time. An officer has many of these scripts saved in his or her cognitive memory. Officers rely on these scripts for interpreting activities surrounding criminal events. The situations differ from event to event and script to script, but the content of each has relevance to decisions and scripts in deadly force situations. The deadly force script reflects the training and decision-making strategies the officer has with regard to deadly force situations. These include when to draw one's weapon, when to fire, and so on. Officers can keep separate deadly force scripts or combine them with social-situational scripts. For an officer, a single script may be one he or she is willing to act upon: "If a person draws a weapon, and if that weapon is pointed at me, and if I can respond, then I will shoot." The officer may decide that his or her use of a deadly force script solely involves saving a life: "I will shoot only to defend another. I'm willing to take a risk, but I will not risk another's life."

Dwyer et al. (1990) raised several questions: What scripts do officers follow in deadly force situations? Where do they originate? What determines whether a script will be stored? What situational factors evoke the use of scripts? What if we use an incorrect script? These questions are perplexing, and if we knew the answers, we could better prepare our officers for dealing with deadly force situations.

Dwyer et al.'s 1990 study, in effect, was to test whether script theory was a valid measure or explanation for police use of deadly force. Their study provided 60 scenarios to both supervisory and nonsupervisory officers. These scenarios were prepared based on actual officer situations and involved deadly force situations. The results of the questionnaires and the responses were examined with multiple regression analysis. Based on their results, four strong predictors emerged of the use of deadly force or of shooting likelihood. These included "suspect has weapon, suspect intends to harm, suspect is committing a felony, and suspect is leaving a building" (p. 300). Dwyer et al.'s results indicated that these four predictors explained almost 50% of the variance. For nonsupervisory officers these four combined explained 51%, and for supervisory officers it was 50% of the variance. These are indicators of a strong relationship.

In their discussion, Dwyer et al. (1990) attributed these results to two particular theories. The first was script theory as "script theory emphasizes the importance of goals, plans, and actions in knowledge organization" (p. 300). The second explanation was that officers responded based on their expertise. Officers are experts in police work and in law enforcement, and therefore base their responses to the vignettes on their training experience and expected outcome.

Mentioned often in the research literature on police use of deadly force is the Binder and Scharf (1980) and Scharf and Binder (1983) model, in which a four-phase model for police-citizen encounters was conceptualized. This model has its roots in sequential decision theory in that each decision in a police-citizen encounter is contingent upon prior choices. Reiss (1980) said that:

> Decision theory based on sequential choice models focuses both upon the options or alternatives attached to each decision and how each decision affects subsequent ones. To manage sequential choices requires information about choices and their options and about opportunities to control the choices as they are made sequentially. (pp. 127–128)

Binder and Scharf (1980, 1983) conceptualized the four phases police officers go through in deadly confrontations with citizens. These phases are anticipation, entry and initial contact, information exchange, and final frame. In each of the four phases, attention is given to the alternative beliefs and behaviors of the officer and opponent and to the situational factors that hamper choices (Fridell & Binder, 1992). Anticipation is the first phase and deals with an officer either receiving a call from dispatch or observing an incident. Either way, it sets the stage for follow-up actions by the officer. During the entry and initial contact phase, the officer first encounters the situation and begins to react with choices and behavior. This phase confirms or refutes the initial anticipation phase. The officer starts reacting to the situation and can call for backup, take cover, draw his or her weapon, and so on. According to Scharf and Binder (1983), two factors weigh heavily on determining the outcome of the encounter: "the degree to which an officer positions himself to control the situation—that is, expand his options and limit those of the opponent—and his ability to weigh effectively his direct impressions against what he has learned earlier about the opponent" (p. 124).

The information exchange phase includes verbal exchanges, nonverbal cues, and a combination of all that is occurring that either warns, or calms, the officer. The content and duration weigh heavily in this phase and can speed up or slow down the move to the next phase. The final frame includes the moments just prior to the shooting. It is the result of the factors witnessed or experienced in the prior phases. The final-frame phase is the culmination of the previous phases that causes or ceases the shoot situation.

Many realize that deadly force encounters do not necessarily go through each of these phases. An officer may come upon a scene and bypass the anticipation phase or not have time for an information exchange. The point of the model is to indicate some of the steps officers may go through prior to the shoot situation. It does not discount the split-second shoots, but provides for a conceptualization prior to that moment. According to Fridell and Binder, "The Binder/Scharf model implies that final-frame decisions to shoot or not to shoot are dependent upon the interaction among earlier decisions, earlier actions, and situational factors" (1992, p. 387).

Fridell and Binder's (1992) study attempted to test the theory as set out previously by Binder and Scharf and focused on the four phases described earlier. Realizing that previous studies had focused only on shoot situations rather than potential shoot situations, they expanded their efforts to deal with violent encounters in which the police would have reasonably been expected to shoot. The study collected information about police-citizen encounters that involved shooting or nonshooting situations from four cities through follow-up interviews with the police concerning their decisions to shoot or not shoot.

As a quick note, I found two limitations to the data used by Fridell and Binder (1992) with regard to their study. First, the information collected was from a period, 1977–1980, that is prior to *Tennessee v. Garner* (1985) when police response to these situations drastically changed. Second, the data used were based on interviews of the officers. Interview information always runs the risk of fabrication and distortion, as it involves the perception of a single person, in this case, the officer. Fridell and Binder (1992) address this by stating:

> There remains, of course, the possibility of deliberate distortion or confabulation. However, there would seem no reason to expect officers to falsify their recollections in regard to the approach variables of central importance to this study. Nor is there any reason to expect systematic differences in recall and reporting accuracy between shooters and nonshooters.
> (p. 390)

I disagree, but not to the point of discounting their study. Police, who are constantly challenged both by the administrations for which they work, the courts for their work on the street, and the media for their actions in volatile situations, are constantly on guard for possible retribution and discipline for their actions in shooting situations. Police are constantly surveyed, questioned, and prodded for information regarding their actions on the street. As a result, they remain guarded about the information they provide. I am not discounting this study, but I think Fridell and Binder inaccurately assume the police will not protect themselves from discipline or other potential action against them in a shoot situation. Police learn quickly how to answer questions about deadly force situations, and this factor must be considered, not summarily dismissed.

Nonetheless, the results of the Fridell and Binder (1992) study did provide some insightful information. Of particular interest was the fact that more nonshooters faced opponents with guns than shooters. In sum, Fridell and Binder noted two important findings regarding deadly force situations. First, "deadly force situations, more than averted shooting situations, are characterized by ambiguity and surprise" (p. 397). They found that the deadly force situations in which a shooting occurred likely involved an officer who had little information on which to base his or her actions. The emotional state of the opponent could not be determined and the officer had apparently not perceived the situation as a deadly encounter. Second, the exchange of information phase seems to be the critical phase in determining the outcome of the situation. The response to the officer's commands, or lack thereof, can escalate the situation and deadly force may be the result. Fridell and Binder call for further investigations to see where the intersection lies between the suspect's characteristics and the officer's characteristics and the context of the situation to determine the use of deadly force. They assume that the four phases are determined by the various characteristics of the players involved and the context of the confrontation.

Blumberg (1997), in "Controlling Police Use of Deadly Force: Assessing Two Decades of Progress," pointed out that we must be cautious about studies of police use of deadly force. Blumberg took his advice from a 1981 study by Geller and Karales, indicating the difficulty in using data from different research studies on deadly force situations. Geller and Karales cautioned that these studies, for various reasons, are not comparable. Blumberg suggested four problems exist when comparing these studies. First, there are varying definitions of the use of deadly force. Is the term *deadly force* applied only when someone dies, or is it attempted use of deadly force or a deadly force situation if deadly force was averted? Second, the ambiguity of variable definitions adds to the difficulty in comparing studies. What is an armed confrontation? For example, is an incident involving a vehicle an armed confrontation if the driver tries to run over an officer? Third, and one I questioned earlier, is the time frame. From my perspective, the rules changed significantly with *Tennessee v. Garner* (1985), forcing officers to justify their actions on life-threatening behavior regardless of the commission of a felony. Finally, there are the inherent limitations in the incidents themselves that researchers examine. These include things such as off-duty shootings, accidental shootings, and situations arising outside the officer's jurisdiction.

Blumberg (1997) also pointed out that most studies focus on the split-second syndrome, as if the totality of the incident is based on the split-second decision to shoot. The Fridell and Binder (1992) study was an important link to the Binder and Scharf model and showed that attention to the preceding events and the characteristics of the officer and opponent have an impact on the outcome of the situation. As their study pointed out, more nonshooters faced opponents with a gun than shooters. There seems to be support for a sequential-transactional theoretical model especially when explaining situations in which an officer does not shoot. According to Fridell and Binder's (1992) study, when the officer is taken by surprise or faces ambiguity of the situation, shooting is more likely to occur. At least initially, it appears that officers can avoid a shooting situation if there is some realm of control and the officers can assess the situation before the situation escalates.

It seems plausible that we can use the Binder/Scharf model and script theory to explain each of my three scenarios. In my case, clearly I had some anticipation about potential problems because the call just did not sound right. My entry and initial contact provided some valuable information in that I discovered the opponent was apparently high on crack cocaine. The information exchange phase did not go well as we ended up in a physical confrontation. As we wrestled around on the ground and I got thrown off, the situation escalated into a deadly force situation, but my predetermined scripts entered in and would not allow me to shoot. My scripts told me to choke the suspect with my handcuffs (a result of training received in the Air Force), instead of shooting the suspect. Regarding the scenario in which one officer shot and the other did not, one must ask: Was one officer able to process through the phases faster and shoot, or vice versa? Did the aversion to kill stop the officer from shooting, or did a script he relied on stop him from shooting? Did the officer who fired follow a predetermined script that said "opponent is armed—shoot"?

What about the third scenario in which the officer told me he was going to take a round in the vest because he was so close to the opponent that he was not sure he could shoot? To me, this represents a clearly played-out script by the officer. Thinking he was too close, he figured he would continue on his path of injury, get shot, but stop the suspect. He told me he knew that many officers were in the area because of the nature of the pursuit (a foot pursuit) and that if he could just tackle him, the other officers would arrive. This scenario represents a clear processing of the Binder/Scharf model coupled with thought-out scripts that replayed themselves through his mind as he attempted to deal with the opponent. The officer's knowledge of the area and what was occurring allowed him to call on stored knowledge to react to the threat, even though he was faced with getting shot.

Although other studies exist that attempt to explain what is going on in deadly force situations, most do not capture the perception and feelings I encountered prior to and during deadly force situations. Arguably, we are not there yet. How are we explaining the actions of the officers side by side with one shooting and the other not shooting? Could there be something else going on?

CULTURAL EXPLANATIONS

Much has been written about the police culture (see, for example, Crank & Caldero, 2000; Gaines et al., 1999; Kappeler et al., 1998; Manning, 1997; Roberg et al., 2000; Waegel, 1979, 1984). Is there a police subculture that perpetuates deception, corruption, and the "we/they" syndrome? Is there a code of silence between officers that allows for excessive force and for the justification of deadly force on perpetrators? What does the literature provide on this matter?

Building on Westley's (1953) earlier work regarding the existence and impact of the police subculture, Waegel (1984) set the stage in the early 1980s for the discussion of a police subculture and the allowance for the use of deadly force. He examined how the police, in fact, have rules for who they can shoot and how to justify it. Waegel (1984) argued that perhaps police work is so stressful that it leads to killings, or that

> another explanation, rooted in the sociology of occupations, emphasizes the influence of the work environment on attitudes, values, and behavior. . . . The occupational environment of the police generates a collective emphasis on secrecy, an attempt to coerce respect from the public, and a legitimation of almost any means to accomplish an important arrest. In the everyday activities of policing, these values take precedence over legal responsibilities. Thus, in certain areas of police work—for example, the apprehension of an armed felon or the handling of a sex offender—the police justify excessive physical force as good, proper and useful. (p. 145)

Waegel's basis for these statements came from his participant-observation study involving 10 months of ride-alongs with officers and a review of 459 police-related shootings. Waegel discussed the legal ability of the police to use deadly force and its significance in relation to the development of the code of silence pertaining to the use of deadly force. He argued that because police can use deadly force, they thereby created this code of silence to protect that right. Understanding that the review process for shootings is vague and escapable, officers fashion their justification to meet the review standards. The standard for the shoot, then, is the review process, not the legal requirements. According to Waegel, police understand this process and thereby establish, subculturally, the guidelines for using deadly force. Police employ "techniques of neutralization" (p. 147) to escape penalties for improper deadly force incidents: "The occupational subculture of the police contains beliefs and understandings about using firearms against citizens. Legal norms formally governing the use of deadly force may be rendered situationally ineffective through reference to shared understandings about justification for infractions" (p. 147).

Furthering Waegel's narrow view of what's going on, he called on several cliches to indicate what he thinks is occurring. The cliches include "I'd rather be judged by twelve than carried out by six," or "What's another dead animal," or "Some of these guys want to hand out justice on the streets." Accordingly, it is the perpetuation of the police subculture that allows officers to shoot and kill someone and later justify it through some sociological occupational subculture explanation. This highly cynical look at police use of deadly force does present some questions.

First, it is difficult for one in the profession, such as myself, to read Waegel's sinister account of police using deadly force. Most of the officers around me do not use and have not used their guns to shoot a perpetrator. Fortunately, this is an extremely rare occurrence. There is, however, a kernel of truth to Waegel's handling of police shootings and excessive force incidents. Most often the police can and do manipulate the reports so as to put blame more on the suspect for escalating an incident than the police. Oftentimes the situation can be escalated by an officer, which forces the incident into a deadly force encounter. For example, my scenario was escalated by my backup officer who tackled the opponent. Certainly, the report read that the suspect resisted and was tackled; however, had he waited a couple more minutes, we would have had more troops there to quell the situation.

Second, policing, as a profession, has progressed by leaps and bounds since Waegel's (1984) study. I am not claiming that deception and rewording of incidents does not still occur, but for the most part, the profession has evolved either forcibly by statutory and regulatory forces or by changes in selection and education requirements. The profession includes higher-caliber, more educated personnel than in the 1980s. I have seen the evolution myself. The use of psychological tests and complex written tests to select candidates indicates a change in attitude toward recruitment.

Key to this notion of selection of fit officers is the cultural aspect of socialization or predisposition. Socialization theory espouses that police are socialized to secrecy; a code of silence exists, and officers must subscribe to certain police values, for example, how to act and talk like the police. To a certain degree this is true. But this theory also argues that corrupt officers learned their behavior through police socialization. They learned it from the job. The predispositional theory argues that if we lie, cheat, and steal as cops, we were already predisposed to act in such a way. Corrupt police do not necessarily learn this behavior on the job but rather were predisposed to this type of behavior. This theory suggests that "the behavior of a police officer is primarily explained by the characteristics, values, and attitudes that the individual had before he or she was employed" (Roberg et al., 2000, p. 267). Several studies support this contention (as cited in Roberg et al., 2000). As such, there are eight central principles to the predispositional theory for police, which include the following:

1. Police have distinctively different values from other groups in American society.
2. Police values are highly similar to the values of the groups from which they are recruited.
3. Police values also are determined by particular characteristics of their personality, which sets police officers apart from the groups from which they are recruited.
4. Police values are unaffected by occupational socialization.

5. The values carried by police officers are stable over time.

6. Regardless of racial or ethnic differences, police officers hold similar values.

7. Education has little impact on values held by police officers.

8. The police socialization process has little effect on the values of individual officers. (Roberg et al., 2000, pp. 267–268)

In *Police Ethics: The Corruption of Noble Cause,* Crank and Caldero (2000) discussed this issue and agreed that certain values were already in place, little changed over time, and screening processes ensure that the standards of values and behaviors consistent with police officers are already in place. As pointed out by Roberg et al. (2000, p. 268), "Police work selectively accents some of these values; for example, working-class values are reflected and intensified in the strong loyalties officers have for one another."

What do we make then of the code of silence? The literature is replete with information on the code, perpetuated by both police socialization and the need to protect each other on the street. Typically, the discussion of the code of silence refers to corruption within the police ranks and the officers' attempt to hide prohibited behavior. Waegel, however, had made an interesting distinction in pointing out that the code of silence may be used to either excuse or justify the use of deadly force. Crank (1998) writes of the "code of secrecy," or code of silence, as protecting the officer from those who simply do not know what an officer encounters on the street.

> Secrecy serves several purposes: it protects line officers from organizational oversight, it insulates them from the inspection of citizens who will not understand police situational use of violence, treatment of assholes, and frequent violation of procedural guidelines. . . . Secrecy is central to the police culture; those who violate principles of secrecy may encounter ostracism, loss of friends, and a shortage of back-up. (p. 224)

I have a final note on the cultural aspects of police work concerning lying and the usefulness of lying. Deception can be used in police work not for personal gain but to avoid censure and discipline. In his classic *Police Work: The Social Organization of Policing,* Manning (1977) discussed internal lying. Manning (1997), who gathered information through participant-observation with both American police and British police, observed four situations in which internal lying occurred within police work. The first was an arrest and charging situation, whereby the arresting officer and supervisor negotiated the correct charge. The process of "formulating a lie and its corollary" or "covering your ass" (p. 163) was observed in this encounter. The second type, and of most importance, is the lie under the threat of discipline. The third type of lie is by using silence. One simply does not report an occurrence and thereby avoids scrutiny. The fourth type of lying involves lying to fellow officers. We can observe these lies as insignificant trivialities, or we can observe them as a description of the police in general. Manning (1997, p. 165) notes:

> These examples of police lying are significant if they are a feature of a large number of police organizations. It would appear that insofar as the structural and social-psychological features of police organizations in Anglo-American society are generic, then so is lying. Since the police are representatives of the moral order in everyday life, their lying is endemic in police operations, it is not an isolated commentary on the moral status of the police officers as individuals, or of police organizations; it is a commentary on all these and on the society in which the activity is rooted.

Lying is not an endemic or cultural aspect of police work but an overall reflection on society. People lie to save their jobs and lie to get their jobs. If we follow this argument, then it follows that some officers will be liars and thieves regardless of the position they hold. It is hoped that this is a small proportion of the police out there, but it is a matter of course. Could we then have lying going on to cover up a deadly force situation? The answer is clearly, yes. Is there pressure among police to become involved in deadly force shootings based on a secretive police subculture? If we follow Waegel, then perhaps we believe there is. If we believe and follow the predispositional theory, then officers who justify shooting and killing someone without justification, or wrongfully killing someone, do not belong in the profession to begin with.

The question remains, though, is there cultural pressure among officers to use deadly force? Perhaps there is pressure to deliver unnecessary violence toward some citizenry. There may be pressure to deliver street justice by the police. At the forefront of this argument is the example of the Rodney King incident. Kappeler et al. (1998) wrote of the incident and the dark side of the police culture. They asked, was it aberrant police conduct or a subculture of violence within the Los Angeles Police Department (LAPD)? Chief Daryl Gates was quick to call the incident an aberration. Skolnick and Fyfe (1993, as cited in Kappeler et al., 1998, p. 138) stated: "Two cops can go berserk, but twenty cops embody a subculture of policing." Follow-up investigations by a commission empaneled to examine the violence brought out by this incident uncovered a pattern of excessive force used by the LAPD. Knowing that excessive force was being used by officers, the administration at the LAPD did little to stop or thwart this activity. Laurence M. Powell testified before the commission and noted that he was admonished for failing to use his nightstick enough; he was told he should be more aggressive when doling out blows if the situation calls for it. Kappeler et al. (1998) argued that "[Stacey C.] Koon, [Laurence M.] Powell, [Timothy] Wind and [Theodore J. (Ted)] Briseno spent much of their working lives in this subculture of prejudice and violence. They learned how to police the 'City of Angels' based on beliefs, values and attitudes embraced by this environment" (p. 141). The use of excessive physical violence does not necessarily lead to the improper use of deadly force, but seems to me to be a good indicator that somewhere along the lines deadly force was used when not justified. Other atrocities followed, including intentional lying in police reports and to the media with regard to Mr. King's physical state and to drug use. The whole incident revealed a police subculture of lying, excessive force, and a downtrodden approach to the community that the LAPD served. Perhaps there is something to the police subcultural attitude toward the people that the police safeguard.

Are there subcultural underpinnings associated with my three scenarios? How do we know? If there is a conspiracy of silence among the police, then can we really get to the truth of the matter? I can speak for the incident I was involved in. Rest assured, no one knew that my backup officer moved before I was ready for him to. That sort of information is kept between us. Does this support the police subculture? Yes, it does. But what were the attitudes toward the person we arrested? Remember the rhetoric mentioned earlier, the "You should have shot the bastard" comments. Does this perpetuate the close-in ranks of the thin blue line? The scenario involving the two officers has the undertones of the police culture as well. I know that the officer who did not shoot was questioned more by his peers than the officer who shot. In the eyes of the officers, clearly it was a shoot situation, but why did one of our fellow officers not fire?

SUMMARY

There are many aspects to police use of deadly force. We know police are put in danger-ous situations in which deadly force may have to be employed. My listing and usage of the research literature is not by any means exhaustive. What I have chosen to use seems appropriate based on my experience on the street.

First and foremost, police, like the citizenry they protect, have an aversion to kill. Grossman (1996) spelled out this argument, and I believe it based on my experience. I have seen it firsthand and have been overpowered myself by the resistance to shoot or kill anyone. Does this make me a weak or ineffective officer? Certainly not! My police cul-ture, however, would perhaps argue that it is a sign of weakness. I hope, however, that the profession has grown past that sort of stigma and cultural dogma. The resistance to kill is deep-seated and beyond perhaps our ability to overcome. Fortunately, for the average po-lice officer, he or she is unlikely to be placed in a situation in which deadly force is neces-sary. Unfortunately, there are officers out there in large metropolitan areas who have been involved in several shooting incidents.

Where does the profession stand on this issue? If we follow Williams (1999), we are training to overcome our resistance. We are using the military model, operant condition-ing, to overcome this resistance and are becoming increasingly able to kill someone. Williams argues that we need to train this way for the officer's safety. However, recall the studies that showed that even officers facing a gun were not necessarily likely to shoot (Fridell & Binder, 1992). It was surprise attacks and the ambiguity of the situation that prompted officers to shoot. The officers were not able to quickly process the needed infor-mation to avoid the shooting situation. From the Binder/Scharf model, the officers were caught off guard and were either short on the anticipation phase or short on the entry/ini-tial contact phase. From a script theory perspective, the incidents were so quick the offi-cers were not able to process through their available predetermined scripts designed for a deadly force situation. My other difficulty with Williams's stance is the apparent "back-stroking" he does in the article. He provides all this insight into the needed conditioning of the police to overcome the weakness or aversion to killing someone, and then attempts to tame what he is saying by telling us to take a disciplined approach. What is a disci-plined approach to operant conditioning? I would argue there is none. It seems to me to be an all-or-nothing proposition.

As a side note, I wonder if this type of behavioral, operant, nonthinking type of training has been beneficial to the profession. Alpert and Dunham (1997) called for in-creased restraint training. I have heard it called de-escalation training, akin to verbal judo, in which the suspect is brought down (de-escalated), thereby avoiding the use of deadly force. When we review instances in which officers shoot multiple times at a single person because one officer shot first, we see we must review this nonthinking-type training and incorporate more humanistic intervention-style tactics.

Is there a cultural aspect to using deadly force? Is it socialization or predisposition? It appears to be both. There is a certain socialization that occurs in police work. The code of silence, protecting one's partner, the thin blue line, and other police vernacular can con-jure up images of the police and their apparent silence to outside questioning. The belief that "they don't understand because they are not one of us" permeates the ranks of police. Held fast by union strength and solidarity among officers, the silence runs deep. One of the earliest memories I have of this on the streets involves a senior officer telling me, "whatever you think of the other officer, it doesn't matter. Out here it's us and them and you do what you have to protect your partners." I do follow Crank (1998) in his argument that most deeply rooted values held by officers are already instilled in them prior to taking the job. Values such as honesty and a strong work ethic are already there but merely accentuated by the job. As Crank (1998) said, a strong work ethic can lead to this protectionist attitude the police have for themselves and their partners. Some people bring ingrained dishonest tendencies to the job with them. They are the small percentage of the police force that brings discredit to us all. When Kappeler et al. (1998) wrote about the "forces of deviance" in police work, they were addressing the small percentage of cops that somehow made it in and are taking advantage of the trust bestowed upon them. Their text should not be read as representative of the police in general.

There is a cultural tug to incorporate or justify our work, including the use of deadly force, to fit the guidelines laid out by legal restraints (constraints, if one views it that way) and the courts. Remember my backup officer who escalated too soon. Where would one read about that? Nowhere. Manning (1997) argued it is a part of the social organization of police work. Lying goes on in police work and sets certain guidelines on whom the police may lie to and when. Therein lies a problem and Skolnick (1996) lays out the basis of the problem. We allow and often encourage deceitful tactics in police work. We allow the police to lie to suspects during investigations, we allow them to lie while undercover, and we allow them to lie while interrogating someone, but we tell them not to lie in court or to administrators or supervisors. We fashion our reports to fit the needed outcomes, not that we are lying or fabricating, but we learn quickly in the profession what type of report keeps us out of court.

CONCLUSION

In 1985, William Geller wrote in the *Journal of Police Science and Administration,* "Officer Restraint in the Use of Deadly Force: The Next Frontier in Police Shooting Research," which was noted as the next needed step in studying police use of deadly force. Even in 1985, Geller wrote, "as for the miniscule literature concerning averted police shootings, none of it draws on systematic evidence of these encounters" (p. 157). Geller then went on to discuss the Binder/Scharf (1980, 1983) model as a potential flow of events officers go through prior to the shoot. Geller pointed to the weaknesses in the available information pertaining to officers shooting or not shooting. He mentioned the lack of information I alluded to earlier but presented some possible research methods and possible data sources. What I find particularly interesting and in keeping with this chapter is his focus on those officers who do not shoot in a high-risk situation rather than on those officers who do shoot. Do not misunderstand me—both aspects are important, but we always focus more attention on the shooter than the successful abstainer. The point is, and put well by Geller, "although the research being called for is designed to bring us closer to the development of effective techniques for controlling *unnecessary* (italics in the original) police uses of deadly force (the "failures"), researchers might do well to cast their inquiry not as a study of officer use or misuse of deadly force but as a study of officer restraint" (1985, p. 161). Geller made a convincing argument in his article, but what has taken place since its publication? Is it lack of research, lack of police cooperation, or a combination of both?

If we follow Williams's (1999) argument, maybe we do not want to study that part of police deadly force. If we recognize that police have a set of values and beliefs brought with them to the job and believe there is a subculture perpetuating the status quo of the work, we then have to accept the fact that we need to train in other areas. I do not believe the profession as a whole wants to follow, nor should follow, a regimented training program dictated by behavioral operant conditioning to shoot or don't shoot. There is just too much going on in a volatile situation to not have other options. Geller (1985) felt that the Binder/Scharf model was a potential answer to understanding what led up to a police shooting, but the Fridell and Binder (1992) study said it was surprise attacks and the uncertainty of the situation that often lead to a police shooting. Should our training focus on eliminating the potential for surprise encounters and on gaining control of a situation before confrontation? Well, we're already there. Officers learn tactics on how to approach people, how to approach buildings, how to approach vehicles, how to stand when talking to someone, how to prevent anyone coming up from behind, and how to avoid letting anyone get too close. We are trained very well to avoid surprise, but unfortunately things go bad on the street and we have no control of a situation and enter into volatile confrontations by surprise. We deal with people and we sometimes have no control.

I had an interesting conversation with several students about doing police work. Their concern was that if they go to college in one state and then choose to work in another state, they have to go to different training academies. One student was attending college, started to attend courses for the police academy, and realized it was useless in her state. They asked, why can't we train all recruits in the same manner so that certification will apply in all states? The answer to that would perhaps take another chapter, but my response to them was that maybe the profession, starting at the academic level, should focus on the things that all police officers do. Sure, we uphold the law, but more basic is that we deal with people, write reports, carry a gun, and drive a car to get there. Break it down even further and we deal with people, a lot. We are constantly interacting with people for various reasons. Where is the training for that? Geller and Scott (1991) called for more human relations training and violence reduction training. Marion (1998) stated that she found that firearms training in academies were the most "popular area of training" (p. 380), but what of the other areas? Students had no training in police ethics and little training in special populations (mostly focused on gangs). The victims of crime were not dealt with, and domestic violence training was received but it mainly focused on officer safety. Officers had a good portion of diversity training, but Marion opined that they did not take it seriously. Once again little training in dealing with victims, the elderly, or ethics was provided. In addition, the instructors tended to incorporate a "we/they" attitude toward the citizenry we serve. Most academies are run similarly and are concerned with the technical training, which is good, but the trade-off is the lack of emphasis on interpersonal skills, communication skills, and diversity issues.

The issue remains; there appears to be no effort, on either side, academe or policing, to focus on the nonshooters. It appears that in both professions there has been a lack of a concentrated effort to uncover this phenomenon. When we attempt to measure what is occurring, we can count those who are killed, but we cannot count the shots not fired. Culturally, there may be a lack of reporting and capturing of this type of data by the police. In other words, the police are resistant to talk about or indicate or report, "shoot/don't shoot" situations for fear of being second-guessed. Current police training focuses more on the mechanics than the interpersonal/human interaction training needed to avoid surprise confrontational encounters.

We must now enjoin both the police profession and academe to work together on this often neglected area. We need to negotiate the collecting of more information from the police. Currently, it is simply not there to examine. We need to devise these measurements in a way that does not threaten the police and their occupational culture. We need to expand the literature and information pertaining to the don't shoot situations rather than simply focusing on the shoot situations. We need to partner more on this important issue because the police profession needs it and the public perception of the police needs it.

REFERENCES

ABELSON, R. (1981). Psychological status of the script concept. *American Psychologist, 36,* 715–729.

ALPERT, G., & DUNHAM, R. (1997). *Policing urban America.* Prospect Heights, IL: Waveland Press.

ALPERT, G., & FRIDELL, L. (1992). *Police vehicles and firearms: Instruments of deadly force.* Prospect Heights, IL: Waveland Press.

BINDER, A., & SCHARF, P. (1980). The violent police-citizen encounter. *Annals of the American Academy of Political and Social Sciences, 452,* 111–121.

BLUMBERG, M. (1997). Controlling police use of deadly force: Assessing two decades of progress. In R. Dunham & G. Alpert (Eds.), *Critical issues in policing, contemporary readings* (3rd ed.). Prospect Heights, IL: Waveland Press.

CRANK, J., & CALDERO, M. (2000). *Police ethics: The corruption of noble cause.* Cincinnati, OH: Anderson.

CRANK, J. (1998). *Understanding police culture.* Cincinnati, OH: Anderson.

DUNHAM, R., & ALPERT, G. (1997). *Critical issues in policing: Contemporary readings* (3rd ed.). Prospect Heights, IL: Waveland Press.

DWYER, W., GRAESSER, A., HOPKINSON, P., & LUPFER, M. (1990). Application of script theory to police officer's use of deadly force. *Journal of Police Science and Administration, 17*(4), 295–301.

FRIDELL, L., & BINDER, A. (1992). Police officer decision making in potentially violent confrontations. *Journal of Criminal Justice, 20,* 385–399.

FYFE, J. (1983). Enforcement workshop: Los Angeles Controversy. *Criminal Law Bulletin,* pp. 1961–1967.

FYFE, J. (1988). Police use of deadly force: Research and reform. *Justice Quarterly, 5*(2), 165–201.

FYFE, J. (1989, May). Police/citizen violence reduction project. *FBI Law Enforcement Bulletin, 58*(5).

GAINES, L., KAPPELER, V., & VAUGHN, J. (1999). *Policing in America* (3rd ed.). Cincinnati, OH: Anderson.

GELLER, W., & KARALES, K. (1981). Split second decisions: Shooting of and by Chicago police: A report of the Chicago Law Enforcement Study Group.

GELLER, W. (1985). Officer restraint in the use of deadly force: The next frontier in police shooting research. *Journal of Police Science and Administration, 13*(2), 153–171.

GELLER, W., & SCOTT, M. (1991). Deadly force: What we know. In C. Klockars & S. Mastrofski (Eds.), *Thinking about police: Contemporary readings* (2nd ed.). New York: McGraw-Hill.

GROSSMAN, D. (1996). *On killing: The psychological cost of learning to kill in war and society*. Boston: Little, Brown.

KAPPELER, V., SLUDER, R., & ALPERT, G. (1998). *Forces of deviance: Understanding the dark side of policing* (2nd ed.). Prospect Heights, IL: Waveland Press.

KRASKA, P. (1996). Enjoying militarism: Political/personal dilemmas in studying U.S. police paramilitary units. *Justice Quarterly, 13*(3), 405–429.

MANNING, P. (1977). *Police work: The social organization of policing*. Cambridge, MA: MIT Press.

MANNING, P. (1997). *Police work: The social organization of policing* (2nd ed.). Prospect Heights, IL: Waveland Press.

MARION, N. (1998). Police academy training: Are we teaching recruits what they need to know? *Policing: An International Journal of Police Strategies and Management, 21*(1), 54–79.

NATIONAL INSTITUTE OF JUSTICE. (1996, April). National data collection on police use of force. Washington DC: U.S. Government Printing Office.

REISS, A. (1980). Controlling police use of deadly force. *Annals of the American Academy of Political and Social Sciences, 452,* 122–134.

ROBERG, R., CRANK, J., & KUYKENDALL, J. (2000). *Police and society* (2nd ed.) Los Angeles: Roxbury.

RUBINSTEIN, J. (1973). *City police*. New York: Farrar, Straus and Giroux.

SCHARF, P., & BINDER, A. (1983). *The badge and the bullet: Police use of deadly force*. New York: Praeger.

SHERMAN, L., & LANGWORTHY, R. (1979). Measuring homicide by police officers. *Journal of Criminal Law and Criminology, 70*(4), 546–560.

SKOLNICK, J. (1996). Deception by police. In M. Braswell, B. McCarthy, B. McCarthy, & W. Gillespie (Eds.), *Justice, crime and ethics* (2nd ed.). Cincinnati, OH: Anderson.

SKOLNICK, J., & FYFE, J. (1993). *Above the law: Police and the excessive use of force*. New York: Maxwell Macmillan International.

SOURYAL, S. (1992). *Ethics in criminal justice: In search of the truth*. Cincinnati, OH: Anderson.

SYKES, G., & MATZA, D. (1957). Techniques of neutralization: A theory of delinquency. *American Sociological Review, 22,* 664–670.

TENNESSEE V. GARNER, 475 U.S. 1, 105 S. Ct. 1694, 85 L. Ed 2d 1 (1985).

WAEGEL, W. (1979). Case routinization in criminal investigation work. Dissertion, University of Delaware.

WAEGEL, W. (1984). How police justify the use of deadly force. *Social Problems, 32*(2), 144–155.

WESTLEY, W. (1953). Violence and the police. *American Journal of Sociology, 49,* 34–41.

WILLIAMS, G. (October, 1999). Reluctance to use deadly force: Causes, consequences, and cures. *FBI Law Enforcement Bulletin*. Washington, DC: U.S. Government Printing Office.

6

Training and Police Violence

Kenneth W. Flynn

> A man can seldom—very, very seldom—fight a winning fight against training: the odds are too heavy.
>
> —*Mark Twain*

INTRODUCTION

Police practices, particularly officer use of force, are of increasing concern to many interested in policing and the behavior of police officers. Several incidents of misconduct involving forceful or violent conduct by officers have received national attention, bringing enormous pressure to bear on police departments and police administrators. Most were shocked at the violent encounter between several Los Angeles Police Department officers and Rodney King that was videotaped following a vehicle pursuit and shown around the world. Regardless of one's opinion about what really occurred that night on the Los Angeles streets, the incident left much of the world aghast. The credibility of that department and the entire policing profession were called into question.

Matters of criminal and civil liability are of grave concern to police officers and their departments, as well as to government bodies when force is used. The potential negative consequences of the use of force, especially when force is used inappropriately, require that police departments ensure that officers are properly trained. Whether an officer is responding alone in the middle of the night to resolve a violent disturbance or perhaps a number of officers are attempting to control a large televised protest, training is essential to the safe, effective, and legal conclusion of police-citizen encounters.

Many in our society cannot differentiate between violence and the use of force by police officers. Some also consider *any* use of force by police officers to be violence, and usually unnecessary and unjustified. For purposes of this chapter, police use of force and police violence are considered synonymous terms. However, the present chapter is not designed to define terms. Instead, it is focused on a frequently misunderstood part of a difficult occupation. Definitions of these terms will show police use of force can be legal and illegal, justified and unjustified. Police officers will not like the comparison between use of force measures and violence, but they should understand that many people they serve consider them the same.

During nearly 20 years in law enforcement, I have worked as a patrol officer, patrol supervisor, detective, and commander of detectives. I have been questioned by Internal Affairs and later served as an Internal Affairs investigator. I am also a citizen, exposed to the power of the police, and know the foreboding feeling that occurs when confronted with police authority. Professionally and personally, I know how much impact the police officer and his or her actions can have on the life of an individual.

The present chapter addresses both police use of force and the necessary police training in the use of force. Included is a discussion of education and police training, use of force training, training standards, training and civil liability, methods of training, and the relationship between training and an officer's decision to use force. The chapter concludes with an overall examination of police use of force and police training.

EDUCATION AND TRAINING

The twofold goal of *educating* and *training* police officers cannot be overemphasized. Simply put, education is the sharing of knowledge or being instructed or taught. Training is the practical instruction in how to use that knowledge. In part, training involves officers applying knowledge gained in the classroom. It is hoped that it provides officers with the necessary skills to act and react properly on the streets.

You have not actually *learned* something until it has changed or influenced you. You have really learned a skill or procedure when it becomes second nature and you respond accordingly, without thinking about your reaction. For instance, training in proper use of the police baton is found in many manuals. However, officers will find it difficult to use a baton in a confrontational situation without hands-on training (or continued practice). In fact, the baton could become a liability, even causing the officer injury. A common warning among officers is that at least one handgun is involved in every contact an officer has with the public. Of course, that weapon belongs to the officer. Along those lines, the officer must not forget that any weapon—whether it be a baton or pepper spray—carried by that officer can be used against him or her in a confrontation.

Again, much classroom teaching concerns the proper methods of controlling a subject through various holds, often called open-hand control. When an officer has truly learned this, he or she finds that when the need arises, he or she may have a suspect in a certain type of control hold without having thought about it. This is particularly important with regard to the officer's safety in dealing with hostile subjects.

In the modern beginnings of policing, an individual (usually male) was hired as a police officer, handed a badge and a weapon, and sent out to patrol the streets and answer citizen calls for service. Formal training, if any, came weeks or months later in the form of brief training classes. Informal training consisted of several days of riding with an experienced officer, sort of an on-the-job training process, after which the officer was a duly qualified solo patrol officer. The following statement reflects the mind-set passed down to rookie officers from their veteran peers in years past:

> When you hit a suspect, hit him hard.
> When you tell someone something, tell him only once, because once is enough.
> Do not trust anyone—not even your wife. (Sullivan, 1971)

Peers, particularly those who are experienced veterans of the force, provide the greatest source of influence on an officer's behavior. Considering the potential impact of such influences, it is not difficult to understand why, under stress or in conflict, an officer sometimes responds violently. Some officers enter all police-citizen encounters with the belief that they cannot trust anyone except a fellow officer; everyone else is a threat to their safety.

Historically, policing was recognized in many circles as a blue-collar occupation, as opposed to a profession. Fortunately, modern-day officers reflect society's diverse makeup, and, among other improvements, are better trained. For example, in 1993 the U.S. Department of Justice reported that 97% of all local police departments had a formal education requirement for new officers, whereas new recruits were required to complete formal training in 90% of all local police departments (which employed 99% of all local police officers). On average, local police departments require 640 training hours of new recruits, including 425 classroom hours and 215 field training hours (U.S. Department of Justice, 1997). Similarly, a study conducted by the Police Executive Research Forum (Carter, Sapp, & Stephens, 1989) found that the average level of education among officers nationwide was roughly 14 years of schooling. Nevertheless, the question remains: What is the basic purpose of training?

Training is designed to change an officer's behavior, provide alternative solutions to problems or confrontations, and, it is hoped, persuade an officer to assume the values and ideals of the department. Conser and Russell defined education as "that which one has learned. Learning can be defined as a process that changes a person's knowledge, behavior, or attitude. It refers to changes that are determined primarily by the individual's interaction with his or her environment" (2000, p. 351). The authors also suggested that "The common link between education and training is the process of teaching or instruction, which includes a broad range of activities" (p. 323).

A thorough recruiting process, which includes a sound psychological examination to eliminate applicants unsuited for a policing career, should provide a training program or police academy with high-quality trainees who have the potential to become professional police officers. It is an understatement to say that individuals with a psychological proclivity for abuse must be eliminated during the selection process. Psychological exams, assessment centers, and interviews are designed for that purpose.

As in the past, police officers today reflect the culture of the department that employs them. Standards that officers are expected to follow are primarily established by the chief of the department. The officers are exposed to the standards through various means, including formalized departmental training, codified rules and policy, and behavioral standards learned through disciplinary action. Strong leaders set the tone for officers to follow. A large part of the socialization into the culture of their department takes place during training. Officers learn proper techniques, such as those required to secure an arrest and/or properly use a baton, but more important, the ideals and standards of the department become a part of them. It is not that the rookie officer is assimilated by the department, but often he or she accepts the values and ideals of the department, and those already serving in it, as his or her own. This is much more significant than training an officer through forced discipline or coercion to follow orders or rules. When the officer understands the spirit or purpose of the rules, he or she has no problem adhering to them.

A funny story tells of a mother trying to keep her little boy seated during church. After being told several times to sit down and not stand in the pew, the exasperated child sits down and states, "I may be sitting down on the outside, but I'm standing up on the inside." Officers who obey the rules only under threat of disciplinary action are much like that little boy. Officers who accept the standards of their police department, and model their behavior accordingly, are likely to be more professional, treat the public better, and have far fewer disciplinary problems.

The beginning of the training process usually occurs at a police academy, during which the new officer is indoctrinated into the culture of the police department and begins the transition from the civilian life to the life of a sworn police officer. As mentioned earlier, local police departments, on average, require 425 classroom hours (U.S. Department of Justice, 1997). This usually takes place prior to field training, although this may not always be the case. During the classroom training, the new officer becomes familiar with the policies and procedures of his or her police department. These policies and procedures normally dictate use of force guidelines, approved weapons, rules for vehicle pursuits, and almost everything else that will guide the officer in his or her day-to-day practices. The officer also receives in-depth training in relevant state laws and local ordinances. In larger municipalities, a police legal advisor or a representative from the city attorney's office serves as the instructor for legal issues and penal code. The new officer must also be taught safe and proper methods of traffic stops, weapons handling and retention, offense and accident investigation, and many other important issues.

Training officers comes at some expense. As such, police departments are faced with the possibility of training officers only to see them leave and join a different department. The original employer has incurred the costs of training plus the expense involved in hiring another person to take the departed officer's place. To address this issue, some departments will hire only officers who are already trained. Although this approach often works well, there are times when departments may overlook questionable practices in an officer's history for the sake of economy. Such unfortunate practices render negligent departments extremely vulnerable with regard to liability issues.

To address the problem of investing in officer training only to have officers leave the department, Swanson, Territo, and Taylor (1998, p. 290) suggested that

> A growing number of jurisdictions have reduced repetitive costs through the use of training contracts, which may be used for both entry-level and specialized or advanced courses. The total cost of providing the training, including an officer's compensation and the course tuition, is calculated. These costs are identified in a contract between the jurisdiction and the officer, in which as a condition of attending the course, the officer agrees that if he or she voluntarily leaves before a specified term, he or she will repay a corresponding amount.

Such contracts help assure that police departments recognize at least some of the benefits of having invested in a particular officer (for further discussion of departments requiring officers to agree to such contracts, see Robertson, 1996).

USE OF FORCE TRAINING

No one is born a police officer, just as no one is born qualified for any occupation. The skills necessary to handle people and situations take years to master and involve a combination of knowledge and experience. The new officer can, and in fact must, be guided in the proper physical, mental, and moral concepts to succeed in a career in policing. Few occupations offer such a mix of experiences and challenges or expose its practitioners to such risk. Policing is a discipline in its own right and requires training and commitment to gain competence.

Training is an educational process that begins with police academy training, followed by field training with an experienced officer, and is complemented by annual in-service classes. In short, training is an ongoing learning experience that continues throughout an officer's career. It is therefore essential that police departments have qualified academy instructors and competent field training officers to guide and instruct new officers. Many, perhaps even most, potentially volatile police/citizen encounters are quelled by the presence and words of an officer, which is the lowest level of the use of force. An officer's attitude, body language, and demeanor convey a world of information that cannot be communicated through words alone. An officer must learn to apply what was gleaned in the classroom to make the technical become practical.

Many years ago a commercial claimed that a certain brand of tires proved themselves where "the rubber meets the road." Training is much the same. Theory taught in the academy and reinforced through field training is applied when the officer demonstrates himself or herself as a professional police officer in the situations he or she experiences.

The use of force, including deadly force, requires a substantial amount of training. This includes teaching officers of their right to defend themselves and demonstrating the correct way to do so. In many ways, the use of force is a skill all its own that requires a specialized curriculum, skilled instructors, and practical training. During use of force training, an officer should learn the proper use of departmentally sanctioned weapons and use of force techniques. These include various hands-on methods of physically controlling a person (e.g., open-hand control), chemical sprays (e.g., pepper spray, mace), police baton, and firearms. These weapons require both classroom instruction and hands-on training and practice to develop the necessary skills required to ensure a safe resolution whenever possible.

Proper training in the various uses of force teaches officers different ways to protect themselves and reduce (or prevent) injury to those involved. Thus, it is important to consider the various alternatives to what most people consider the common use of force by police. What is seen most often on television is an officer striking someone with fists or a police baton, or forcefully taking a subject to the ground. Although these can be proper methods of force, when necessary, training can provide an officer with other options. One method, often referred to as "verbal judo," involves officers using words, as opposed to force, in "hot" situations. Verbal judo involves sparring with words. It is an attempt to use discussion or conversation to quell a disturbance, distract a subject, or change an individual's demeanor. In fact, much of successful police work is found in the verbal and psychological skills developed through formal training and hands-on experience.

Many people do not recognize verbal commands as a type of force. Similarly, many do not recognize the mere presence of a uniformed, armed officer as a type of force. Verbal skills fall into the most basic, nonaggressive level that can prevent further force or help justify the use of more force. If an officer's verbal skills cannot control or resolve a situation, physical force may be the next step. Frequently, the mere presence of a uniformed officer encourages people to change their behavior.

Words sometimes have different meanings to different people. Until this point, several terms have been used quite loosely. As such, a closer examination of what is meant by the terms "force" and "violence" is necessary. These definitions will, it is hoped, provide the reader with a better understanding of terms representing issues that are of significant importance to policing.

Kania and Mackey defined force as the exertion of power to compel or restrain the behavior of others (1977, p. 29). As mentioned earlier, force can be classified several ways in policing. According to Fridell and Pate (1997), the use of force in policing can be deadly or less than lethal, justifiable or excessive, as well as actions that could have been avoided. The Fort Worth Police Department (FWPD) General Orders Manual defines force as

> the compulsion or restraint exerted upon or against a person for the purpose of compelling a person to comply with an officer's direction; or, overcoming resistance by a suspect during arrest or detention; or defending any person or yourself from an aggressive action by a suspect which represents a threat of physical injury or death. (2000, pp. 300–314)

The Fort Worth Police Department Defensive Tactics Manual defines the noun usage of the word *force* as "strength or energy brought to bear; cause of motion or change; or active power" (2000, p. 4). The verb usage of the word *force* is defined as

> to do violence; to compel by physical, moral or intellectual means; to make or cause through natural or logical necessity; to achieve or win by strength in struggle or violence; an aggressive act admitted by any person which does not amount to assault and is necessary to accomplish an objective. (p. 4)

Reasonable or necessary force is defined as "the minimum amount of lawful aggression sufficient to achieve a legitimate law enforcement objective" (p. 4).

Researchers have uncovered a multitude of factors and causes of violence, so it should come as no surprise that there are many different definitions of violence. Raymond Flannery offers a straightforward definition of violence as "the intentional use of force to injure or abuse another" (1998, p. 20). Although straightforward, the definition is not all-inclusive as violence is a complicated act. Extending beyond simple definitions, violence can be both legal and illegal. In policing, it can be necessary and unnecessary.

In the context of these definitions, an officer can be trained to use force lawfully. The overriding purpose of training police officers is to teach them to effectively and safely do their jobs within the confines of legally appropriate behavior. This involves officers acknowledging that physical force will occasionally be necessary and that proper training increases the likelihood that many situations can be addressed with the minimum amount of force.

Training enables officers to act professionally regardless of their personal feelings. It is impossible to face confrontations, verbal or physical, without stirring natural human emotions such as fight or flight, or fear or anger. Training can help discipline and control these emotional responses. Control of these emotions helps prevent injury to officers and citizens, may reduce liability to police departments, and helps avoid the destruction of promising careers. Although training standards vary among states and jurisdictions, I briefly examine the training standards for police officers in Texas as an example.

TRAINING STANDARDS

The Texas Commission on Law Enforcement Officer Standards and Education (TECLOSE) is an organization responsible for regulating and tracking the professional training standards of Texas police officers. TECLOSE maintains updated records on mandated training courses provided to officers throughout the state. TECLOSE requires a minimum of 560 hours of academy training for police recruits. One hundred four of those hours must address the following areas of training (TECLOSE, www.texas.gov/agency/407.html):

- 8 hours on the laws relating to the use of force
- 16 hours on the concepts of the use of force
- 40 hours on the strategies of defense—mechanics of arrest
- 40 hours on the strategies of defense—firearms

The Fort Worth Police Training Academy currently requires 640 hours of training for police recruits. Approximately 197 of those hours are dedicated to the use of force topics. Many of the additional hours beyond those required by TECLOSE are spent on areas in which the use of force directly impacts the public: mechanics of arrest and firearms training. On completion of those 640 hours, recruits spend another 40 hours in officer survival training, which directly relates to use of force tactics. These 680 training hours are followed by 14 weeks of field training with an experienced training officer. Use of force tactics are reviewed and reinforced during this time.

TRAINING AND CIVIL LIABILITY

More than 10 years ago, the U.S. Supreme Court (in *City of Canton v. Harris,* 1989, pp. 1204–1205) restricted the use of inadequate training as the basis for Section 1983 actions. The Court ruled that a person's civil rights have been violated when "the failure to train amounts to deliberate indifference to the rights of persons with whom the police come in contact" and the indifference subsequently becomes part of the officer's routine. As such, plaintiffs must demonstrate that the officer received inadequate training, which, in turn, was closely related to the damages incurred (for elaboration of this issue, see Schachner, 1991).

In *Police Supervision,* Glensor, Peak, and Gaines (1999, p. 93) stated that

> Our nation's growing social, economic, and legal problems challenge the police to acquire and maintain the knowledge, skills, and abilities necessary to cope with an ever-changing world. Proper training also provides a vital link to employee performance and accountability and may protect the agency from unnecessary litigation.

Police training must keep pace with changes in society, particularly as they pertain to police-related issues. For example, officers should be informed and/or kept abreast of the newest illegal drugs on the streets, new or altered weapons, the latest self-defense techniques, and suspicious individuals or groups whose actions might require police intervention.

All training should be well documented, as police departments frequently have to respond to challenges regarding an officer's behavior. A common tactic in civil lawsuits is to link an officer's behavior to a lack of department-sponsored training, in attempts to find an agency responsible. Also, it is common for an officer to allege he or she was not properly trained if his or her actions are called into question. Such attempts and allegations necessitate examination of the quantity and quality of the training, including assessments regarding the qualifications of the instructors.

Swanson et al. (1998) suggested that negligent supervision and negligent training were the two areas that have been the greatest sources of litigation under Section 1983 in recent years. They noted the enormous increase in the past two decades regarding the number of lawsuits filed against police departments for wrongful deaths. The vast majority of these lawsuits did not involve injuries to innocent bystanders, but instead addressed whether or not the suspect should have been shot. Swanson et al. (1998, p. 409) noted:

> Unfortunately, in the past, police officer training has too often focused on the issue of how to shoot and not when to shoot. Many times when a problem does arise relating to the use of deadly force, it is not that the officer failed to qualify at the police pistol range or that the weapon malfunctioned, but that the officer made an error in judgment.

The authors further add that police administrators must question whether the wrongful shooting was the result of human error or of the department's failure to provide proper guidelines to the officer.

Swanson et al. (1998) noted that officers should become familiar with their department's use of deadly force policies during recruit training, through their work with a field training officer, and during roll call and in-service training (arguably, these are ideal opportunities for officers to become familiar with *all* departmental policies, but because of the inherent seriousness and consequences involved with its use, deadly force issues should receive priority treatment). Several issues must be addressed if it is determined that a wrongful shooting was the result of a department failing to provide proper guidelines. First, we must consider whether or not the officer had access to or was familiar with the policies. Second, we must consider the adequacy of the policy. Swanson et al. (1998, p. 410) suggested that an adequate policy regarding the use of deadly force should address the following topics: defense of life and fleeing felons; juveniles; shooting at or from vehicles; warning shots; shooting to destroy animals; secondary guns; off-duty weapons; and registration of weapons. Troubleshooting can be a police administrator's most valuable skill when it comes to police use of force and the potential for litigation.

METHODS OF TRAINING

It goes without saying that training is inherently based on principles of learning. Conser and Russell (2000) listed Benjamin Bloom's three levels of learning, otherwise known as learning domains, which include cognitive, psychomotor, and affective learning. Cognitive learning involves acquiring knowledge; more specifically, it encompasses understanding and learning skills. At this level the new officer learns, among other things, the laws he or she will enforce, department policy, the mechanics involved in the use of force, report writing, and accident investigation. This usually takes place in the classroom portion of the police academy.

How is an officer taught to appropriately use force? A combination of classroom study (education), practical application such as role-playing, practice exercises, hands-on defensive tactics (training), and field training conducted by experienced officers appears to be the most effective approach. It is helpful to expose police recruits to role-playing situations that emphasize what was taught in the classroom. These role-playing events include physical confrontations, domestic violence situations, shoot/don't shoot exercises, mock traffic stops with angry motorists or fleeing suspects, and other realistic, high-stress scenarios. Police officers, civilian employees, and citizens assist the training academy by assuming the roles of various characters.

These episodes familiarize new officers with what they will confront on the street and prepare them for how they, personally, may react under such stressful conditions. For example, a realistic domestic violence scenario—complete with an angry, violent spouse and an injured, crying partner—will help prepare the novice officer for what he or she may have to deal with on a regular basis. It may also expose the rookie officer to personal feelings and reactions, such as fear and/or anger, which for some may be a new experience. The officer learns how to use force and how to prepare to defend against the use of force when threatened by the abuser (of particular importance is being prepared to respond to threats made by victims). Officers may also find out how quickly threats to one's safety can become personal issues and how professional their response to such threats might be.

The psychomotor domain consists of motor skills and the ability to perform the defensive tactics taught in police training, including engaging in safe pursuits and/or defusing volatile situations. These skills must become second nature for the officer, for the purposes of his or her own safety and for the safety of citizens. This area is where the "how to" builds on knowledge previously learned.

The affective domain includes perhaps the most visible, and thus most significant, aspect of police practices. Affective learning impacts an officer's emotions, values, response to cultural differences, and his or her view of the value of particular individuals. This learning occurs in the police academy, field training, and throughout the remainder of his or her career. This type of learning is largely influenced by peers and friends and occurs at all times and all levels of an individual's life.

THE DECISION TO USE FORCE AND THE PROPER USE OF FORCE

It is important to consider factors that affect an officer's decision to use force and how he or she determines how much force to use. A comparison of the age, sex, size, physical training and skill, and conditioning of the officer and the offender is critical. For example, a suspect who is intoxicated or high is more difficult to handle, but a large, muscular officer would have difficulty justifying using more than a minimum of physical force against a petite, nonathletic female or a very small male, even with resistance on the suspect's part. On the other hand, a small female officer could easily justify escalating up to intermediate force (pepper spray, police baton) if confronted with a large, violent suspect. In fact, some cases involving the use of deadly force have been deemed justified in such situations when the officer could articulate that his or her life was at risk (e.g., the shooting of Amadou Diallo by New York City police officers). One officer versus multiple offenders is another circumstance in which an officer can justifiably escalate up the use of force continuum.

Chapter 4 of this text addressed these and other situational factors related to police officer use of force. It is necessary, however, to highlight the variability of police-citizen encounters, which can require split-second, accurate decision making by the officers. Officer decision-making skills are shaped during the training period.

Recent court decisions have supported police officers' need to use force. In several cases the actions of the officer(s) were questioned, even by other officers. The courts often rule in the officer's favor, however, even in gray areas of judgment, except when misconduct and brutality are clear. These decisions may stem from jurors' unease in handing down verdicts that question an officer's judgment. Jurors may recognize that decisions against officers may ultimately weaken their discretionary use of power and hamper their ability to act forcefully and decisively.

An officer will almost certainly find it necessary to use force against another individual at some point during a career in policing. The level of force varies from the basic methods of controlling unruly persons, open-hand controls, chemical or pepper sprays, or police baton to the undesirable (and fortunately rare) use of deadly force that may lead to serious injury or death. Another certainty is that an officer will be the victim of some type of violence, ranging from a simple assault from a suspect attempting to avoid arrest to being seriously wounded or killed in the line of duty. Proper training is critical in every police encounter for officers to avoid or reduce injury, or even to survive if seriously injured. Officers must understand, particularly early in their career, that *they will encounter people who will try to hurt them*. It is often difficult for a citizen, or an inexperienced officer, to comprehend this; however, it is an important lesson in the training process. It is taught in the police academy and reinforced by training officers.

Another vital aspect of police training involves teaching officers that controlled, proper use of force can not only prevent or reduce injury to the police officer but can also protect citizens. The basic reason a police officer uses force is to gain and maintain control (FWPD Defensive Tactics Manual, 2000, p. 5). Few things are worse for an officer than allowing a situation to escalate out of control. As much as possible, an officer must maintain control of the situations he or she encounters, for his or her benefit and to assist and protect others. Even suspects who wish the officer harm are safer and subjected to less injury when force is used correctly. This is one of the realities of a dangerous occupation.

Yet, if not properly addressed, the continuous need to gain control may cause an officer to become suspicious and critical of everyone and become a cynic at heart. This attitude separates officers from those they protect and may cause them to become hardened, which, in turn, can influence the way they treat the public (and their own families). Fortunately, community-based programs, as they exist within modern approaches to community policing, are often designed to help officers keep a healthy balance of trust and skepticism. Chapter 8 of this text discusses the relationship between community policing and police violence.

WHAT IS THE USE OF FORCE?

A significant problem when discussing the use of force or violence by police is achieving a realistic view of the issue. As such, we must ask ourselves: "What is the use of force?" and "What constitutes violence?" Is it possible for police officers to police the community without occasionally having to resort to force? Do citizens want a police force lacking the power to use force or violence, if and when it is necessary? Virtually all citizens want the officer to respond with power and decisive action when they call the police for assistance; that is, as long as police powers are directed against the one causing the disturbance. In the simplest terms, any action taken by an individual against another, especially if against his or her will, is the use of force. Simply handcuffing an individual, and thereby temporarily limiting his or her freedom, can be construed as the use of force. No one likes to be arrested and/or handcuffed and temporarily lose his or her freedom. Those who resist arrest or fight the police do not appreciate the officer's response to those acts.

The degree of force used by officers depends on a number of factors that create the dynamics of a police-citizen encounter. The emotions, attitudes, values, and expectations of the officer and the citizen combine to determine if force will be necessary, how much force will be used, and whether force is appropriately applied. All of these contributing factors can, and must, be controlled on the part of the professional police officer. Training, if it is to be effective in controlling the use of force, needs to focus on how to gain compliance without resorting to physical coercion.

Use of force typically occurs when police officers are trying to make an arrest and the suspect is resisting. Some research indicates that police are most likely to use force when pursuing a suspect (e.g., Crawford & Burns, 1998) and attempting to exercise their arrest powers (Adams, 1999). Furthermore, suspect resistance increases the likelihood that police will use force (e.g., Crawford & Burns, 1998; Kavanagh, 1997; Smith & Visher, 1981). These findings appear intuitively sound given the mandate that police have regarding use of force. Police may use force when it is necessary to enforce the law or to protect themselves or others from harm (Garner & Maxwell, 1999).

IS THE USE OF FORCE A PROBLEM?

Is the use of force really an issue? Do police officers really abuse their power and authority, and if so, why? Undoubtedly, occasions in which force is abused occur. For example, the sexual assault (with the assistance of a wooden stick) of Abner Louima by several New York City police officers drew great public attention and disgust. Yet, despite our disgust, we must recognize these infrequent events as opportunities to further understand why they occur. William A. Westley offered one possible explanation of why an unethical incident such as this takes place (as cited in Saunders, 1970, p. 52):

> The policeman uses violence illegally because such usage is seen as just, acceptable, and, at times, expected by his colleague group and because it constitutes an effective means for solving problems in obtaining status and self-esteem which policemen as policemen have in common.

It is the responsibility of the head of the police department and his or her command staff to ensure that standards are set high enough that no officer believes illegal violence or misconduct is just or acceptable. Recently, serious allegations of misconduct by members of the Los Angeles Police Department, Rampart Area, were investigated. Bernard Parks, chief of the LAPD, stated in his executive summary of the report of the Board of Inquiry into the Rampart Area Corruption Incident (2000, p. 2):

> The men and women who chose to involve themselves in this disgraceful activity will be dealt with. But, we as an organization must recognize that, while they individually and collectively provided the motivation, we as an organization provided the opportunity. Our failure to carefully review reports, our failure to examine events closely to identify patterns, our failure to provide effective oversight and auditing created the opportunity for this cancer to grow.

Captain Ross Swope of the Metropolitan Police Department, Washington, D.C., stated, in the preface to the Rampart study, "The major cause in the lack of integrity in American police officers is mediocrity" (Parks, 2000, p. 1). Captain Swope added that this mediocrity arises from the failure to hold officers responsible and accountable. It remains the responsibility of command personnel to set a high standard of ethics and provide a good example to the troops. It is also their responsibility to initiate disciplinary action, including criminal prosecution, when necessary, and to protect the integrity of the police department by maintaining the high standards demanded by the public. The need for such accountability demonstrates the importance of continued training and departmental review (Parks, 2000).

Minor abuse of the use of force is just as unacceptable as outright brutality, but such acts seldom attract the attention of the public. I am convinced, both by research and personal experience, that the overwhelming majority of police officers perform their jobs admirably, follow a strict code of conduct based on high ideals, adhere to the law and department policy, and treat their fellow human beings with respect. It is unfortunate that a small percentage of unethical acts of police abuse of power attracts widespread societal (in particular, the media's) attention, and, despite the millions of positive police-citizen encounters that go unrecognized, casts a negative shadow over the police profession.

In 1996 the Bureau of Justice Statistics completed a pilot test of the Police-Public Contact Survey (Greenfield, Langan, & Smith, 1995). The survey shed light on the frequency of police-citizen encounters. Among the survey findings, it was found that roughly 44.6 million persons had face-to-face contacts with police officers in the previous 12 months, with men, whites, and those in their twenties most likely to come in contact with the police. The same study suggested that

> About 1 percent of people reporting contacts with police indicated that officers used force or threatened force. In the majority of those instances, respondents said that their own actions, such as threatening police or resisting arrest, may have provoked officers. (p. 16)

Despite such infrequent force-related contacts, officers must be properly trained.

Many complaints lodged against police officers concern actions that a citizen believes involved an officer's inappropriate, even illegal, use of force. After internal review, a majority of these police actions are found to have been appropriate and necessary. For example, in the last 5 years a small number of the excessive complaints against officers of the Fort Worth Police Department were sustained (proven misconduct). In 1998, out of 24 allegations of excessive force, 2 were sustained (allegation proven by fact), 9 were not sustained, 9 were unfounded (determined not to have occurred), and 4 were exonerated (conduct was justified). It is interesting to note that those 24 excessive force complaints constituted a small percentage (16.2%) of the 148 total citizen complaints received by the department that year. Similarly, in 1999, out of 19 allegations of excessive force, 3 were sustained, 4 were not sustained, 9 were unfounded, and 3 were exonerated. The 19 excessive force complaints were a small portion (15.6%) of the 122 total citizen complaints in 1999.

A recent National Institute of Justice (NIJ) study suggested that force, both excessive or otherwise, is not used in most arrests, and that force typically involves less severe forms of tactics and weapon use when it is applied. The study suggested that the findings

> provide a context for understanding excessive force, which we know can involve low-level acts of force (such as verbal threats or cursing against compliant suspects) as well as the acts of force that result in physical injury or death of civilians. Arrests that involve no force, however, cannot involve excessive force and arrests that involve low levels of force are less likely to involve excessive force. (Garner & Maxwell, 1999, p. 30)

The research further suggested that "Use of weapons is infrequent; in 97.9 percent of all adult custody arrests, police did not use a weapon. In 99.3 percent of all such arrests, suspects did not use a weapon" (p. 30), and that "the most frequent weapon used by the police was some form of a chemical agent, mostly oleoresin capsicum; it was used in 88 or 1.2 percent of the arrests" (p. 30).

What conclusion might be drawn from these data? The overwhelming majority of police arrests occur without the use of any type of weapon, and if a weapon was used, it most likely was a spray that only temporarily disables or distracts. What implications does this finding have for police officer training? Perhaps such infrequent acts (and subsequent complaints) involving the use of force suggests that we should continue the current approach to training officers. Or, perhaps, due to the infrequent need to use force, we should alter the approach to training by more closely focusing on other, more frequently occurring aspects of the profession. Further research in this area needs to address this concern.

Aside from considering the total number of complaints filed against officers, another means of assessing the public's view of police practices, particularly those involving the use of force, is to review the number of complaints against police compared to the number of police-citizen encounters. For example, in 1999 the Fort Worth Police Department made more than 41,000 arrests for felony and misdemeanor offenses. During that same year the Internal Affairs Division received 339 allegations of misconduct against FWPD officers. One hundred seventeen of these allegations were internal investigations into the actions of officers, initiated and conducted by their supervisors. Only 122 of the total number of complaints were actually lodged by citizens, including allegations made by prisoners against the arresting officer, and of those 122, only 19 involved excessive force or rough handling. Also in 1999, the police department recorded 282,715 responses to citizens' calls for service or citizen requests. To this number add traffic stops and officer-initiated activity. Even if one assumes that some citizens do not report alleged misconduct, the number of complaints compared to the number of police responses leads to the conclusion that abuse of force is not a significant problem.

However, these findings in no way justify any abuse of the use of force by an officer. One case of brutality or misuse of force is inexcusable and cannot be tolerated. If the Rodney King incident was the only case of abuse in the history of American policing, the reputation of all police departments and the trust of the public still would not have been spared. One fact always remains true: No matter how wrong the actions of a citizen, or how viciously he or she attacks an officer, a police officer is permitted to use only the force necessary to restrain or arrest the individual or prevent further escalation of violence. This lesson is ingrained in an officer's mind from the day he or she enters the academy until the day he or she leaves policing.

ABUSES OF THE USE OF FORCE

Fortunately, few instances of police brutality occur when compared to the number of situations in which officers have to use force. In fact, it has been my experience that officers show remarkable restraint, often taking more physical abuse than is necessary. This may occur for several reasons; some officers do not like to use force, some consider minor abuse as part of the job, and some officers are so concerned about department investigations or civil liability that they avoid using force whenever possible because they fear making mistakes. Occurring more frequently than police brutality (yet equally wrong) are "minor" acts of misconduct related to the use of force. These acts are difficult to prove in disciplinary investigations. Examples of such misconduct are rough treatment of a resistant prisoner once he or she is restrained, twisting a prisoner's arm behind his or her back a bit more forcefully than necessary, or overtightening the handcuffs of a verbally abusive arrestee. These incidents generally arise from anger, frustration, or even fear on the part of the officer. Misconduct of this nature may not cause injury or leave evidence of an assault that is distinguishable from other telltale signs of the encounter with the police. It is common to find scratches, handcuff bruising, and other minor marks on prisoners who are not totally compliant, and the arresting officer avoids attention. However, these acts of abuse are certainly inappropriate and weaken the community's faith in the police. Proper training should limit such misbehavior, although human nature sometimes outweighs even the best training.

EXCESSIVE FORCE

Police officer use of force cannot be thoroughly reviewed without examining the issue of excessive force. A definition of excessive force is difficult. However, Doerner (1998, p. 225) offered a general definition of the term in suggesting that it is "any reaction that goes beyond the boundaries of what most officers consider to be normal violence." Of course, some incidents are blatantly inappropriate. In many other incidents the determination lies between the officer's expression of fear for his or her safety and the complainant's allegation of wrongful treatment. Few people struck with a police baton admit to bringing it on themselves. Police officers are generally given considerable latitude and discretion to respond as they judge necessary at the time, according to their interpretation of the situation. Of course, their judgment is subject to administrative, civil, and even criminal review. Innumerable variables aid in determining if too much force is used. It can be determined only on a case-by-case basis, and even then opinions will vary. The recent shooting of Amadou Diallo by four New York City police officers is an example. At face value, it is very difficult to justify shooting at an unarmed man 41 times. However, a jury apparently recognized the importance of police officers needing to protect themselves when feeling threatened.

We can train officers as to how they should handle particular situations and hope that they respond appropriately, particularly when the stakes are raised and force is involved. Accordingly, we must remember that no two situations are exactly alike, and what may appear to the public, at face value, as inappropriate behavior may be considered to be within the confines of procedural law. Difficulties in preparing officers for the plethora of situations they will encounter is but one of the numerous challenging tasks faced by police trainers.

In its study on the use of force, the NIJ noted problems in the criteria used to make determinations of excessive force. Such uncertainty ultimately leads to varied opinions as to what, specifically, constitutes excessive force. The NIJ added, "Judges apply legal standards; police administrators apply professional standards; and citizens apply 'common sense' standards" (Adams, 1999, p. 62). The study concluded that

> Judges typically render judgments in the context of an adversarial trial process that, in principle, is designed to lay bare all relevant information. Administrative review of police conduct generally takes place behind closed doors by trained professionals who have to temper objective reasoning (e.g., "going by the book") with subjective understanding (e.g., "putting themselves in another officer's shoes"). Regarding the thoroughness of internal police investigations, there is a professional "push" to be exhaustive and demanding and a collegial "pull" to be political and practical. (p. 62)

Police officers will most likely be concerned with the professional standards they are held to by police administrators following an incident in which an officer uses a considerable amount of force. The individual officer will also be concerned with the standards applied by any court judging his or her behavior, whether criminal or civil charges are brought to bear. Generally, the standard the public employs for judgment is based on emotion and is easily influenced by factors such as the media, personal antipolice bias, community values, and a sense of right and wrong and fair play. This alone can seriously damage a police department's relationship with citizens, which, in turn, brings political pressure to bear on police administrators. No police department can successfully accomplish its mission without the faith and support of the public and the local governing body. Therefore, the only redeeming course of action for a police department employing an officer guilty of excessive force is to administer swift, decisive discipline, an important step in restoring the confidence of the public in the police department.

At no time is it more important for an officer to gain and maintain control of a police-citizen encounter than during a conflict or confrontation. *The appropriate use of force is what enables the officer to maintain control of volatile and hostile situations.* Police are most commonly called on to restore order, which is accomplished by assuming control. The FWPD Defensive Tactics Manual (2000, p. 5) states,

> Control is that degree of influence the officer must exert over the violator to take him or her safely into custody. The objective of using control is to elicit cooperation from the violator. Yet, control is a two-way street. An officer must be in complete self-control to be able to

control a violator. Self-control alone will be one of the greatest assets in dealing with a law violator. Self-control is achieved through training and practice both on and off the job.

As noted, training extends beyond the academy and beyond the occupation. As human beings we should constantly search for means to better ourselves; improving our self-control is but one way.

THE USE OF FORCE CONTINUUM

The propensity for control during any situation in which officers must use force should be weighed against the probability for damage. Officers are required to use only the minimum amount of force necessary to make an arrest. The force used should be no more than what a reasonable officer would use under the total circumstances of the situation, and it must adhere to department policy and the law (FWPD Defensive Tactics Manual, 2000, p. 7). In other words, an officer's use of force options increases or decreases according to the need or threat. During an encounter requiring the use of force, an officer must assess potential dangers and be ready to respond to the actions of a suspect or arrestee. An essential part of the training for FWPD officers in the proper use of force involves the use of force continuum. The use of force continuum is an escalating/deescalating use of force scale used to teach officers how to defend themselves and safely make arrests and how much legal force can be used in response to another's actions:

> The Use of Force Continuum is a delineation of the various force options available to officers. The actions of the officer are predicated by the actions of the violator, and the officer must continually adjust their level of force in response to the level of resistance by the violator. For these reasons, it may be necessary to the officer to skip one or more levels in the continuum, and the officer must also move to a lower force level when the resistance of the violator decreases. Even when the use of greater force is justified, officers should also continue to issue loud verbal commands in an effort to gain voluntary compliance from the violator. (FWPD Defensive Tactics Manual, 2000, p. 7)

The FWPD General Orders Manual (2000, pp. 300–314) lists the five levels of the use of force (italicized comments by author):

1. **Level 1: Officer Presence**—Defined as identification of authority.
   Often the mere presence of an officer is sufficient to quell a disturbance and restore order. This may be due to some innate respect for the badge and what it stands for, or simply that the violator knows what is likely to follow should he or she continue to be a nuisance. In many cases the presence of an officer (without additional force) is sufficient to assume control of a situation.

2. **Level 2: Verbal Commands**—Defined as commands of direction or arrest.
   Officers are taught to issue firm orders regarding their expectations for the suspect(s) and those involved. In fact, officers are taught to continue these verbal commands, even if the commands are not obeyed and force is used. If the commands serve no other purpose, they are often overheard by others and serve as evidence that an officer gave a resistant person options other than a violent confrontation.

3. **Level 3: Open-Hand Control and Restraint**—Such techniques are designed for gaining control and do not have a high potential of injury. These techniques can range from escort holds, wrist and joint locks, "come along" techniques, takedowns, multiple officer takedowns, resistant subject handcuffing, and distraction techniques involving strikes with personal weapons (hands, elbows, knees, feet, and so on).

   This level of force is often misunderstood and can generate citizen complaints. These techniques often appear more forceful than they really are. They can be painful, especially when resisted, but usually do not inflict serious injury. Citizens frequently see an officer respond on this level, failing to understand that the officer was merely reacting to the actions of the violator. An officer cannot be expected to be so passive that he, she, or innocent bystanders are injured. At the same time, an officer is expected to handle confrontations wisely and fairly. Following the guidelines of the use of force continuum helps an officer fulfill these expectations. These techniques not only help prevent injury to the officer but also help prevent escalation of the encounter, thus requiring a response higher up the continuum.

4. **Level 4: Intermediate Force**—Best illustrated when the officer meets an actively resisting subject who represents a physical threat to the safety of the officer or who attempts to use force against the officer or another but does not yet represent a life-endangering threat.

   Police action at this level can obviously be construed as a violent action. However, this does not condemn the response as illegal or improper. Responses at this point in the use of force continuum involve an officer's reaction to what basically amounts to an attack on the officer, or severe acts of resistance by the violator when other methods of controlling the conflict have failed. The officer is now taking dramatic action to gain control of a situation that, if allowed to further deteriorate, may injure the officer, innocent bystanders, and/or the violator, or allow escape.

5. **Level 5: Deadly Force**—Defined as lethal force actions.

   This is self-explanatory. If a violent encounter reaches this point, an officer is defending himself, herself, or another. This is basically survival-level police action. The need for deadly force may arise without warning and without progression through the other steps of the use of force continuum, such as being fired on by the driver of the vehicle at the outset of a traffic stop.

The objective of police officers using force is to gain control, and any and all measures applied should give the officer the advantage in order to control the situation. As stated in the FWPD Defensive Tactics Manual (2000, p. 7), "Ineffective control results when the level of force is less than the violator's level of resistance. Excessive control results when the level of force is greater than that justified by the violator's level of resistance." Proper police training should provide officers with the tools to understand when and how they should move up the continuum and when and how they should not. Proper training should also not only stress *when* and *how* movement should occur but also *why* it should happen.

Is police use of force or police violence a significant problem in American policing? Are accurate data available to determine how often force is appropriately and inappropriately used, or have several unfortunate incidents, supported by vocal antipolice groups, made the proverbial mountain out of a molehill? The NIJ (Travis & Chaiken, 1999, p. iii) concluded that

> Research consistently demonstrates that a small percentage of police-public interactions involve use of force. Various data sources, including police use-of-force reports, civilian complaints, victim surveys, and observational methods, confirm this basic finding. For example, the 1996 pilot test of the PPCS found that about 1 percent of people reporting contacts with police said that officers used or threatened force.

Regardless of one's interpretation of how much force is too much, these numbers suggest that police violence constitutes a minute (albeit important) percentage of an officer's duties. Yet, effective and thorough training is required to reduce the potential dangers inherent in the small percentage of incidents involving violence.

CONCLUSION

It is expected that police officer training will greatly improve in the near future. Although there are many reasons for this improvement, two of the driving forces are advances in technology and greater professionalism. Computer-based education is rapidly being adopted into police training. Swanson et al. (1998) noted that computer-assisted instruction programs have recently received positive evaluations of their effectiveness with regard to general police training. Essentially, three types of computer-assisted instruction programs are currently being used in law enforcement training. The first is a tutorial program that differs from traditional tutorial practices in that a computer replaces the instructor. Users (officers) interact with the computer, as opposed to an instructor, which enables them to train at their leisure. Feedback is provided by the computer, much like the feedback received from an instructor; however, users may spend a longer period of time reviewing particular material simply because they are not at the mercy of an instructor who may not be so generous with his or her time.

The second type of computer-assisted instructional program involves a computer and an instructor. "Drill and practice," as Swanson et al. (1998) referred to it, consists of instruction by a course teacher followed by trainees answering questions on a computer. Feedback is provided following each input, with users progressing to additional questions following a correct response, and users having to answer review questions pertaining to the studied material for incorrect responses.

The final type of computer-assisted instructional program is more advanced than tutorial programs and "drill and practice." Similar to "drill and practice," simulation computer-assisted instructional programs are used in conjunction with an instructor. These programs are more advanced than the others as they offer trainees the opportunity to train or practice in simulated real-life situations, created by audio and visual technology. Swanson et al. (1998, p. 538) noted that "In each presented 'game' or situation, the student must make decisions and judgments based on a variety of behavioral instincts and/or intellectual skills." They added that these programs are designed to assist all levels of law enforcement from personnel selection and promotion to top administrative testing and development. They can be used "in any area in which individuals must learn specific values and rationales from behavioral science and apply them to a dynamic and ever-changing environment" (Swanson et al., 1998, p. 538).

Force is a tool to be judiciously used by the police officer. Its proper use can be a determinate factor in the success of an arrest, quelling a disturbance, or safely controlling any individual. It is an essential tool, or a necessary evil, in an occupation that encounters people at their best and their worst. An officer's statutory right to use force must never be abused. Police abuse of power must not be tolerated. Instead, it must be dealt with swiftly. The proper use of force will, it is hoped, become a part of an officer's career experience, as does making an offense report or completing a traffic citation. Training is by far the best means of acquiring competent skill in this area. Police departments must provide the training necessary to use force effectively and also commit to the supervision of an officer's use of force.

Although most would like to see a reduction in the police use of force, we must remind ourselves that force is sometimes necessary to protect the officer and citizen's lives. Proper training is important, as an officer can lose proficiency in the necessary skills to correctly use force. This occurs from insufficient or inconsistent training, which includes the lack of hands-on, practical exercises. Continuing in-service training courses in the use of force during an officer's career is essential to maintaining competence and sound judgment in the application of force.

REFERENCES

ADAMS, K. (1999). A research agenda on police use of force. In National Institute of Justice, *Use of force by police* (NCJ 176330, pp. 61–73). Washington, DC: U.S. Department of Justice.

CARTER, D., SAPP, A., & STEPHENS, D. (1989). *The state of police education: Policy directions for the 21st century.* Washington, DC: Police Executive Research Forum.

CITY OF CANTON V. HARRIS, 389 U.S. 378, 103 L. Ed. 412, 109 S. Ct. 1197 (1989).

CONSER, J., & RUSSELL, G. (2000). *Law enforcement in the United States.* Gaithersburg, MD: Aspen.

CRAWFORD, C., & BURNS, R. (1998). Predictors of the police use of force: The application of a continuum perspective in Phoenix. *Police Quarterly, 1*(4), 41–63.

DOERNER, W. (1998). *Introduction to law enforcement: An insider's view.* Boston: Butterworth-Heinemann.

FLANNERY, R. (1998). *Violence in America.* New York: Continuum Publishing.

FRIDELL, L., & PATE, A. (1997). Use of force: A matter of control. In M. L. Dantzker (ed.), *Contemporary Policing: Personnel, Issues and Trends* (pp. 217–256). Boston: Butterworth-Heinemann.

FORT WORTH POLICE DEPARTMENT DEFENSIVE TACTICS MANUAL. (2000). Fort Worth, TX: Fort Worth Police Department.

FORT WORTH POLICE DEPARTMENT GENERAL ORDERS MANUAL. (2000). Fort Worth, TX: Fort Worth Police Department.

GARNER, J., & MAXWELL, C. (1999). Measuring the amount of force used by and against the police in six jurisdictions. In National Institute of Justice, *Use of force by police* (NCJ 176330, pp. 25–44). Washington, DC: U.S. Department of Justice.

GLENSOR, R., PEAK, K., & GAINES, L. (1999). *Police supervision.* Boston: McGraw-Hill.

GREENFELD, L., LANGAN, P., & SMITH, S. (1999). Revising and fielding the police-public contact survey. In National Institute of Justice, *Use of force by police* (NCJ 176330, pp. 15–18). Washington, DC: U.S. Department of Justice.

KANIA, R., & MACKEY, W. (1977). Police violence as a function of community characteristics. *Criminology, 15*(1), 27–48.

KAVANAGH, J. (1997). The occurrence of resisting arrest in arrest encounters: A study of police-citizen violence. *Criminal Justice Review, 22,* 16–33.

PARKS, B. (2000). *Board of Inquiry into the Rampart Area Corruption Incident: Public Report.* Los Angeles: Los Angeles Police Department.

ROBERTSON, B. (1996, February 23). Detroit to end free ride: Cops will have to stay in department or pay training. *Detroit Free Press,* p. 1A.

SAUNDERS, C. (1970). *Upgrading the American police.* Washington, DC: The Brookings Institution.

SCHACHNER, M. (1991, May 27). Written policies best defense against police liability exposures. *Business Insurance,* p. 3.

SMITH, D. A., & VISHER, C. (1981). Street-level justice: Situational determinants of police arrest decisions. *Social Problems, 31,* 167–177.

SULLIVAN, J. (1971). *Introduction to police science.* New York: McGraw-Hill.

SWANSON, C., TERRITO, L., & TAYLOR, R. (1998). *Police administration: Structures, processes, and behavior.* Upper Saddle River, NJ: Prentice Hall.

TEXAS COMMISSION ON LAW ENFORCEMENT OFFICER STANDARDS AND EDUCATION. Available at: (*http://www.texas.gov/agency/407.html*).

TRAVIS, J., & CHAIKEN, J. (1999). Foreword. In National Institute of Justice, *Use of force by police*, (NCJ 176330, pp. iii–iv). Washington, DC: U.S. Department of Justice.

U.S. DEPARTMENT OF JUSTICE. (1997). LEMAS reports. In R. Dunham & G. Alpert (Eds.), *Critical issues in policing: Contemporary readings* (3rd ed., pp. 36–73). Prospect Heights, IL: Waveland Press.

7

Police Pursuits

Just One Form of Violence

Matt Welch

❖

INTRODUCTION

Answer: Moses, Bonnie and Clyde, and O. J. Simpson.
Question: Name four people pursued by the authorities of their time.

In the beginning there were no cars, but that does not mean that there were no pursuits. Ramses and his army of men in chariots pursued Moses and his people. Later, Bonnie and Clyde were probably the most infamous objects of police pursuits when police vehicle pursuits were more of a novelty than a common occurrence. Today, television and helicopters enable the public to view and review current police pursuits. A web site even offers a paging service to alert citizens of live police pursuits in southern California. The types of police pursuits vary and the inherent violence that can result from these pursuits varies as well. Pardon the pun, but join me in the pursuit of these pursuits.

Pursuit. The word has many ramifications and meanings. Alpert and Dunham (1997, p. 235) suggested that a working definition of pursuit involves "a multi-stage process by which an officer initiates a traffic or felony stop and a suspect refuses to stop and a continued attempt to apprehend the suspect by the police officer." Homant and Kennedy (1994, p. 428) provided a more simplistic definition: "driving at a high rate of speed in order to overtake a vehicle whose driver is knowingly attempting to elude a law enforcement officer." Whether police pursuits involve cars, horses, boats, motorcycles, helicopters, or bicycles, risk plays a large role. This risk extends beyond the safety of the officer to include the suspect(s) and innocent bystanders or victims.

The present chapter examines the relationship between police pursuits and police violence. In order to better understand the police pursuit, we must understand the various types of pursuits and the different modes. Also, no examination of police pursuits would be complete without an account of the frequency of police pursuits, the policies and liability surrounding the pursuits, and officers' responses to pursuits. The chapter closes with an account of solutions that may assist in preventing police pursuits and the accompanying inherent dangers.

THREE TYPES OF PURSUITS

There are three types of pursuits in policing: pursuit of time, pursuit of a compliant subject, and pursuit of a noncompliant subject. The pursuit of time occurs when officers responding to a high-priority call are authorized by their department regulations to use emergency lights and sirens. Examples include an officer distress call, robbery in progress, and burglary in progress, just to name a few. In these cases, the officer is authorized to speed over the posted limit and proceed contrary to traffic control devices if it is safe to do so. Unlike the chases seen on television, the officer has only one vehicle actively involved, instead of two. Pursuit of time still has all of the potential hazards of a traditional pursuit (other traffic, weather, road hazards, the police vehicle limitations, and your own driving limitations) minus the suspect vehicle element.

Your radar detector just went off, and you see the flashing red and blue lights in your rearview mirror. Your heart begins to pound, your palms sweat, and for only a split second you think of not stopping. But knowing the limits of your minivan, you decide to comply and stop for the officer. I have just described a compliant subject pursuit. When an officer decides to stop someone for a traffic violation or other offense, often he or she has to turn around or cross traffic to catch the suspect. This might require rapid acceleration and exceeding the speed limit to pursue and catch the violator, especially in freeway situations. Although not traditionally thought of as pursuits, compliant subject pursuits do involve the pursuit of time and a subject. What makes these pursuits less dangerous than either of the other two is time. Compliant subject pursuits seldom take more than a few minutes, which explains the reduced likelihood for damage, as supported by findings from the Pursuit Management Task Force (1998), which found that more than 50% of all pursuit collisions occurred during the first 2 minutes of a pursuit, whereas more than 70% of all collisions occurred before the sixth minute of a pursuit.

It is 7 P.M. and you are settled back in your recliner for yet another "real" police show. Tonight's fare includes a domestic disturbance, a drunk driver, and, of course, a police pursuit. The noncompliant subject pursuit is your typical TV pursuit of good guy versus bad guy. Often these pursuits involve cutting across fields, mowing over trash cans in an alley, and crashing into a convenience store. Movies take police pursuits a step further into sensationalism and away from reality. On the big screen, often the participants trade gunfire, ram each other, hit innocent pedestrians, and never stop (for insightful discussions of media and popular culture depiction of police practices and, more generally, the criminal justice system, see Bailey & Hale, 1998; Kappeler, Blumberg, & Potter, 2000; and Surette, 1998). Missing in these examples of pursuits are the serious issues of justification, scrutiny, context, litigation, and consequences.

In addition to the types of pursuits, the modes of pursuit deserve discussion as well. Police practices have largely kept pace with technological advances. Police administrators constantly search for more effective means by which officers can go about their duties. Some of the greatest developments in police technology are found in the various methods of police pursuit.

MODES OF PURSUITS

The term "police pursuit" often conjures up images of car chases. This is the typical police chase, but other types with potential hazards unique to the type of pursuit may be involved. The various modes enable officers to more effectively pursue not only those on the roadways but also suspects who may be in places inaccessible to patrol cars.

Air Pursuits

Most large metropolitan police and urban, county, and state and federal law enforcement agencies, including the Coast Guard, use either fixed-wing aircraft and/or helicopters to aid in the apprehension of suspects. This mode of transportation may not seem particularly dangerous, especially regarding pursuits. Consider, however, an officer in a light helicopter following armed suspects who are shooting, or U.S. customs agents flying their aircraft, without any identifying lights, in pursuit of smugglers flying to an isolated landing strip also in aircraft without any lighting. This scenario happened one night while I was working in rural Colorado. Our police radio crackled with the sound of federal authority as customs agents requested ground support as they chased smugglers into our local airport. The suspects were bringing in illegal artifacts as well as marijuana. With less than 10 minutes to get to the airport 12 miles away, the chances of our department getting to the scene in time were slim to none. I arrived on the scene 3 minutes after the suspects landed. The customs agents landed 1 minute later in their Cessna Citation jet. With automatic rifles in hand, they searched the area to no avail. Eventually the suspects were apprehended, tried, and convicted in federal court. These officers, agents, and pilots have a unique mission and experience many nontraditional hazards with their pursuits.

Boat Pursuits

The Coast Guard in pursuit of drug smugglers comes first to mind when one thinks of boat pursuits. However, many seaport cities have their own harbor patrol, most large lakes have either state or municipal patrol of waterways, and some resort communities have some type of police presence in watercraft; all will engage in pursuits although most will not be as glamorous as those seen on the television show *Baywatch*. Crowded waterways and drunk-driver boaters present a real dilemma for any officer. What are an officer's options if a reported drunk boater is creating a danger for the boating and swimming public and decides to flee? If the officer decides to chase, the chance of injury exists, and on large lakes, the suspect is limited only by the amount of fuel he or she has on hand. There are no roads or predictable routes he or she might take, unlike in traditional pursuits. Should the officer wrestle the suspect in the water if he or she resists? What if the suspect drowns? These are just some of the issues faced with regard to water pursuits.

Motorcycle Pursuits

"Ponch, this is Jon. Can you break your lunch date and help me out? I'm in high-speed pursuit of some Hell's Angels for violating the laws of the good state of California!" Anyone who has seen the television series *CHiPS* will remember that every episode contained at least one pursuit. Oftentimes a motorcycle rider, other than the two main stars, would have a high-speed fall. Although this is certainly not the norm in real life, simply riding a motorcycle is itself more dangerous than driving a car, without the additional dangers involved in actually chasing another vehicle. Motorcycles enable officers, however, to access some locations that patrol cars cannot, proving to be an invaluable resource under certain conditions.

Other Modes

What other types of pursuit are there? There are ATV (all-terrain vehicles) pursuits on beach patrol (as well as other off-road areas), bicycle pursuits, mounted (horse) pursuits, and foot pursuits. These four other types are listed together as they are either rare in occurrence or do not have as much potential for hurting innocent bystanders or the parties involved. Nevertheless, *all* forms of pursuit involve accelerated risks, and officers should be properly trained and prepared to engage in such acts. Pursuit practices that may be appropriate in some situations may result in unacceptably high levels of danger in others.

Having discussed some of the types and modes of pursuits, I now delve deeper into police pursuits and explore why they occur. Increased recognition regarding the potential for violence in police pursuits will likely result in greater efforts to reduce the dangers.

ISSUES

Why are police pursuits an issue? The answer is *life, money,* and *lawyers.* Life is the predominant issue. Alpert and Anderson (1986) suggested that during pursuits, both the suspect's and officer's vehicles become dangerous weapons, arguably the single most dangerous weapon. Pursuits can cost the life of the officer, the offender, and/or innocent bystanders. These deaths and injuries are often violent and typically find their way onto the front pages of newspapers. The media often focus on the injuries or deaths of the offender and third-party victims, but consider these facts concerning police officers: Nine police officers died in 1998 during pursuits and 89 died from 1988–1997 (Federal Bureau of Investigation [FBI], 2000). Compare these numbers to the number of officers who died from arrest situations, 16 for 1998 and 250 from 1988–1997. These statistics dramatically indicate that although the pursuit is hazardous for police officers as well as the public, it pales in comparison to arrest situations. The bottom line is that pursuits, though hazardous, are not one of the most dangerous parts of the job for police officers. Nevertheless, one officer death is one too many.

Arguably, there are two constant formulas in pursuits:

Pursuits plus success = confrontation (potential for injury and death)
Pursuits plus accidents = injury or loss of life, property damage, financial loss

Loss of life, particularly among innocent citizens, is a hot topic in today's society. Consider this headline: *Arlington Man, 69, Killed in Crash: Driver of Stolen Car Is at Large After Police Chase That Caused Fatal Wreck.* Or this one: *Police Search for Suspect After Chase Kills Innocent Driver.* Both headlines, the first from print media and the second from television newscasts, address the same fatal crash. In both cases, note that the police chase is said to have caused the crash, not the fact that a felon who was fleeing struck an innocent citizen. This kind of mindset (e.g., one that automatically assumes government responsibility for the actions of another) is typical of our society that tends to displace rather than accept responsibility. Did the police contribute to the cause of this particular accident? Yes. Does the felon in the stolen car who was fleeing the police also bear some responsibility? Of course, and the brunt of it, but who is the easier target to go after, the lone offender or Big Brother?

The answer, of course, is Big Brother. One reason for this is the "deep pockets theory." The government, compared to individuals, has more resources and thus the most to lose. For example, a typical Texas minimum liability insurance policy for an individual is $20,000 for one person and $40,000 per accident. Compare that to a government- or corporate-owned vehicle that has a large policy or is self-insured. Who has the most to lose? Who would an attorney representing an injured party prefer to attack, especially when their fee is percentage-based?

Many courts do hold the police partly responsible as the causation factor in crashes. In a September 5, 1990, Associated Press report, an Austin, Texas, jury found the Austin Police Department and the Texas Department of Public Safety each accountable for 15% of the damages simply because jurors believed that the officers should have abandoned the chase of a 13-year-old boy in a stolen truck. Both agencies agreed to review their pursuit policies following the verdict (Associated Press, 1990). In reference to a Mesquite, Texas, case that involved the killing of a man, the Texas Supreme Court ruled that police could be held liable in pursuits. Supreme Court Justice C. L. Ray said that police must balance the public risk when deciding whether to give chase: "Public safety should not be thrown to the winds in the heat of the chase." In a dissenting view, Justice Eugene Cook wrote, "The majority has changed 100 years of established law and has made the police officers in this state liable for the negligent conduct of drug dealers, drunken drivers and other felons" (Associated Press, 1991).

Swanson, Territo, and Taylor (1998, p. 413) suggested that "negligence litigation focuses on the alleged failure of an officer to exercise reasonable care under the circumstances." Similar to the difficulties involved in defining the terms "reasonable suspicion" and "probable cause," the term "reasonable care," however, can mean different things to different people. Although this definition is still quite vague, reasonable care can be recognized as care that a reasonable, ethical, and moral officer would use in the same situation. As such, uncertainty remains regarding when some pursuits are appropriate and when they are not.

Citing California Highway Patrol statistics from 1991 on car pursuits, James Lasley, a criminal justice professor at California State University, Fullerton, calculated that odds are one in five that someone will be hurt every time police pursue a suspect: "The odds of Russian roulette are better than that" (Associated Press, 1992). In this ever-increasingly litigious society, more and more police agencies' pursuit policies are under fire and facing lawsuits. As such, a closer examination of liability in relation to police pursuits is required.

Swanson et al. (1998, p. 414) argued that "Liability must be based on proof that police conduct in breaching a duty owed was the proximate cause of a pursuit-related accident." They added that proximate cause can, at times, be difficult to prove, for example, when the fleeing suspect collides with an innocent victim. The bottom line is that officers and departments are responsible for any injury, losses, and/or accidents that occur when a pursuing officer is negligent of, or disregards, foreseeable danger.

According to Special Agent Daniel Schofield of the FBI Academy, the basis of most pursuit-related liability is negligence, and the litigation focuses on whether the police acted prudently and reasonably under the circumstances. He lists the following "General Principles of Liability Applicable to Police Pursuits":

> The legal theory underlying most pursuit-related lawsuits is that the police were *negligent* in conducting a pursuit. To do this, four elements must be proved:
> 1. The officer owed the injured party a duty not to engage in certain conduct.
> 2. The officer's actions violated that duty.
> 3. The officer's negligent conduct was the proximate cause of the accident.
> 4. The suing party suffered actual and provable damages. (1988)

In other words, an officer's primary duty is to protect. If the officer can be proved negligent in his or her actions *and* the plaintiff actually had damages, *then* the plaintiff has a good lawsuit.

Dantzker (2000) noted a lack of a discernible pattern with regard to court decisions concerning police pursuits, adding that

> In some instances the courts have placed liability on the police for injury occurring from a pursuit when the police apparently should have recognized the obvious potential for danger and continued the pursuit anyway. In other instances the courts have found that the police are not liable and are not violating an individual's rights when injury or death results from the pursuit. (p. 79)

Despite the court's ambivalence, some believe that police policy should not be based on the need to protect oneself against litigation but should dictate appropriate police practices. Blankenship and Moneymaker (1991, pp. 57–58) argued that "the main reason for adopting and enforcing a stringent pursuit policy should not be based solely on the desire to avoid litigation. Instead, all police activities should be motivated by the utility of their actions."

In attempts to highlight the particular areas of concern regarding liability and police pursuits, Swanson et al. (1998, pp. 416–417) offered discussion of certain factors that most often determine the extent of pursuit-related liability. These factors include the following:

- *The purpose of the pursuit.* What are the risks involved? What is the nature and seriousness of the offense? Is there a need for immediate apprehension?
- *Driving conditions.* A general assessment of the officer's equipment, the weather, roadway and traffic conditions, and the capabilities of the drivers involved in the chase.

- *The use of warning devices.* The use of visual and audible warning devices is mandated in most pursuit situations and increases the likelihood that other vehicles and pedestrians are aware of the dangerousness of the situation.
- *Excessive speed.* Excessive speed is determined by the purpose of the pursuit, driving conditions, and the ability of the police driver to handle the vehicle.
- *Disobeying traffic laws.* Officers in pursuit are statutorily obligated to use extreme care when disobeying traffic laws. These dangerous situations should be avoided because of the high potential for liability for resulting accidents.
- *Roadblocks.* It is recommended that roadblocks only be used when authorized by a supervisor and only as a last resort to apprehend a dangerous offender.
- *Discontinuation of the pursuit.* A pursuit should be terminated when the hazards of continuing outweigh the benefits and purpose of the chase.

These factors clearly deserve consideration with regard to liability issues. They must also be considered with regard to the safety of officers, the suspect, and the general public.

A CLOSER LOOK AT THE NUMBERS

Despite the dangers and costs involved in police pursuits, empirical assessments of such police practices remain limited, and what does exist sometimes suffers from methodological limitations. For example, Alpert and Fridell (1992) are among the many researchers who believe that the amount of research regarding police pursuits pales in comparison to the extensive research regarding police use of firearms. Kenney and Alpert (1997) went so far as to suggest that the quantity and quality of our knowledge surrounding police pursuits is at least 10 years behind the research surrounding police use of force. Crew, Fridell, and Pursell (1995) observed that little research has addressed the costs and benefits of pursuing various types of offenders, adding that what is available suffers from methodological problems such as data reliability and/or concentration on one particular jurisdiction. Similarly, in his discussion of the myths and realities of police pursuits and officer attitudes, Falcone (1994) noted the limitations in strictly relying on quantitative data when attempting to better understand such police practices. Kenney and Alpert (1997), in discussing the absence of quality national data regarding police pursuits, argued that reliance on the information included in the Fatal Accident Reporting Systems (as noted in the National Highway Traffic Safety Administration's reports) involves notable limitations, although actions are being taken to address the problems. In a somewhat discouraging summation of the available national data concerning police pursuits, Alpert and Madden (1994, p. 24) wrote, "Unfortunately, there are no national statistics and the number and type of pursuits that occur in the United States is unknown. Similarly, the outcome of these pursuits is unknown and the costs and benefits of these pursuits have not been calculated." In general, it appears that we have addressed only the "tip of the iceberg" with regard to our understanding of police pursuits.

Despite these limitations, several studies have addressed the frequency, dangerousness, and results of police pursuits. Still, one must refrain from making substantial generalizations based on these and other results. Although the researchers who have measured police pursuits are to be commended for their efforts as such information is badly needed, the aforementioned limitations suggest that we have far to go before we more comprehensively understand police pursuits.

Aside from the aforementioned FBI statistics regarding officer deaths from police pursuits, several others have attempted to assess the dangers involved with such actions. Although the FBI (2000) findings and results from the California Highway Patrol (1983) study reveal that pursuits generally do not result in injury or death (despite the information typically presented in the media), others recognize that the problem is significant and deserves further attention. For example, Alpert and Dunham (1988) found that at least one death occurred in 0.7% of all chases in the Miami area, and Alpert and Fridell (1992) found that a death occurred in 0.2% of all police pursuits in Minnesota.

Although the chances are much lower that a pursuit will result in a death or injury than it will produce property damage, the dangerousness of police pursuits cannot be overstated. Kennedy, Homant, and Kennedy (1992) found that 2% (or possibly less) of all pursuits result in death (or roughly 300–500 deaths per year, as noted by Homant and Kennedy, 1994). These researchers calculated that roughly 35% of police pursuits result in at least some property damage, but a different study found that in Minnesota, roughly 44% of all pursuits involved some type of property damage, with damages more likely to occur to the suspect's, rather than the officer's, vehicle (Crew et al., 1995).

Researchers have also addressed the initiation of pursuits. In his national survey of 436 police departments, Alpert (1997b) found that most pursuits originate with traffic stops, but a large percentage of pursuits also resulted from the commission of felonies. Several researchers have suggested that pursuits initiated by the commission of a felony and those originating because the driver was under the influence were most likely to result in damages (Alpert & Anderson, 1986; Alpert & Dunham, 1988; Crew et al., 1995).

We cannot completely understand police pursuits unless we determine exactly who evades the police, and why they do it. Whereas a clear demographic profile of the driver who flees from the police does not exist, results from several studies overwhelmingly suggest that this driver is male (Alpert & Dunham, 1990; Dunham, Alpert, Kenney, & Cromwell, 1998) and in his early to mid-twenties (e.g., in their study in South Florida, Alpert and Dunham, 1990, found a mean age of 23.5 years, and in their study of three different locations, Dunham et al., 1998, found a mean age of 26.2 years). It appears that further research is required regarding the racial profile of noncompliant suspects, as Alpert and Dunham (1990) found that black drivers were more likely than white drivers to evade the police, but Dunham et al. (1998) found the opposite to be true. It is likely that the differing racial composition of these areas could have influenced these contrasting results.

In their research regarding the offender's perspective on police pursuits, Dunham et al. (1998) found that suspects most often fled because they were driving a stolen vehicle (32%); others (27%) stated that they evaded the police because they were exiting a crime scene or avoiding an arrest. Interestingly, 21% claimed that they were fearful of being beaten by the police, and a similar amount reported evading the police because they were under the influence of drugs or alcohol. Further research is also needed regarding the reasons why offenders refuse to adhere to police commands.

As noted earlier, courts have become involved in determining responsibility for the damages, injuries, deaths, and other liabilities caused as the result of a police pursuit. The possibility of facing liability for harms caused by pursuits has pressured many police departments to create, or update, their pursuit policies. The influences of these court decisions on police agencies have not yet been determined (Dantzker, 2000), as we remain unsure how they have affected department considerations regarding the quality of information contained in the pursuit policies, the focuses of the policies (e.g., tactical versus decision-making approaches), and/or the emphases placed on enforcing the policies. Dantzker (2000, p. 79) suggested that "There is some concern that curtailing police pursuits may cause more people to flee from the police; however, unnecessary injury or death stemming from pursuits is not acceptable." Appropriately so, he highlighted the need for police pursuit policies.

RULES OF THE ROAD: PURSUIT POLICIES

> I would no more take pursuit away from police than take their firearms away. But you don't shoot every common criminal. And you don't chase every potential law violator.
>
> *Geoffrey Alpert*
> *University of South Carolina*

Numerous researchers have documented the potential and recognized dangers involved in police pursuits. According to Dantzker (2000, p. 78), "Injuries to and deaths of officers, suspects, and innocent bystanders have forced state legislatures and police departments to reevaluate and write or rewrite pursuit policies." To combat the outcry from the media, innocent victims, and hungry attorneys, modifications to pursuit policies have been made in most police departments, especially larger ones. In the small, rural Colorado sheriff's department in which I began my career in policing, the rules for pursuits were virtually nonexistent. We had no written pursuit policy. I was told verbally that it was acceptable to shoot at the fleeing vehicle as long as the suspect had committed a felony. We were also instructed that ramming the other vehicle was permissible, as long as your patrol vehicle was not damaged in the process. When I worked at this department in the early to mid-1980s, our policies, or lack thereof, were representative of the other departments located in the area. Compare those liberal policies to the policies in the department for which I currently work:

- Pursuits cannot involve ramming or shooting at fleeing vehicles.
- Pursuits cannot involve more than two patrol vehicles and one supervisor except in extenuating circumstances.
- The reason for the pursuit must be articulated verbally over the air to the on-duty supervisor.
- Most misdemeanor pursuits must be discontinued after a short distance.
- When the helicopter is available, all pursuits are to be videotaped.
- Postpursuit reports are made for departmental review.

This workable, middle-of-the-road approach allows officers to do their job, is a deterrent to the serious criminal element, and ensures that the public is not unnecessarily exposed to harm. Such differences between the policies found in the two departments in which I have worked support Alpert and Dunham's (1997, p. 236) observation that "Departmental regu-

lations concerning pursuits vary from vague to detailed." Swanson et al. (1998, p. 417) believe, "Where feasible, a comprehensive (pursuit) policy statement should give content to
terms such as *reasonable* and *reckless* and provide officers with more particularized guid-
ance. A policy should be tailored to a department's operational needs, geographical pecu-
liarities, and training capabilities."

In discussing the need to balance competing interests related to police pursuits, the
International Association of Chiefs of Police suggests that

> The policy issue confronting law enforcement and municipal administrators is a familiar one
> of balancing conflicting interests: on one side there is the need to apprehend known offend-
> ers. On the other side, there is the safety of law enforcement officers, of fleeing drivers and
> their passengers, and of innocent bystanders. . . . The model policy is relatively restrictive,
> particularly in prohibiting pursuits where the offense in question would not warrant an arrest.
> Most traffic violations therefore, would not meet these pursuit requirements. It is recognized
> that many law enforcement officers and administrators may find this prohibition difficult to
> accept and implement particularly where a more permissive policy has been traditionally
> accepted.
> But in this critical area of pursuit driving, law enforcement administrators must be
> prepared to make difficult decisions based on the cost and benefits of these types of pursuits
> to the public they serve. (International Association of Chiefs of Police, 1990, pp. 1–2)

This passage helps demonstrate the significance of police pursuits and some of the many
issues police administrators face in dealing with the issue.

Although there will always be debate concerning proper pursuit procedures, Geoffrey Alpert, in his article " The Management of Police Pursuit Driving," presented what
appears to be an effective, workable outline for pursuit policies (Table 7–1). Alpert's outline provides police administrators with a respectable model against which they can compare their own policies. It will undoubtedly assist those departments in need of an
updated, effective approach to police pursuits.

Recognizing that simply having a strong policy is not enough to ensure proper police pursuits, Alpert continued by outlining several ways to lessen the risk of pursuits:

1. A clear and understandable policy delineating departmental requirements within
   the context of state laws and the police mission;
2. Specific training to the policy, using examples of risk assessment;
3. A detached supervisor, trained in risk assessment, who takes control over the pursuit, who assumes its supervision and who will terminate it when it becomes too
   risky; and
4. Accountability, by requiring officers to complete pursuit critiques and having the
   forms reviewed individually to determine if the pursuit driving was within policy
   and collectively to provide information to trainers and policymakers; additionally,
   officers must receive feedback on the appropriateness of their pursuit driving.
   (1997a, pp. 560–561)

In his national survey of police agencies, Alpert (1997b) found that although 91% had
written policies addressing police pursuits, many department policies had not been updated since they were developed in the 1970s. More encouraging findings exist in a Bureau of Justice Statistics (1992) report that suggested that 99% of police agencies with
more than 100 officers reported having a pursuit policy.

TABLE 7–1   Considerations for a Pursuit Policy

1. When to Continue (Initiate) a Pursuit (e.g., officers must consider, among other things, safety issues, environmental conditions, seriousness of the offense)
2. Police Units Authorized to Participate and Their Roles (e.g., available resources, plans)
3. Supervisory Roles and Responsibilities (e.g., accountability issues, interjurisdictional issues, communications, termination of pursuit, determining plan/limitations)
4. Multijurisdictional Pursuit Issues (e.g., policy controls, detemining the lead agency)
5. Driving Tactics (e.g., speed, passing vehicles)
6. Permissible and Impermissible Exceptional Tactics (e.g., justification for exceptional tactics, including roadblocks, ramming, boxing in, use of firearms)
7. Air Support (e.g., roles played, communication, impacts)
8. Termination (e.g., when and how to end a pursuit, factors that prohibit continuation of pursuit, other units' response when pursuit terminated)
9. Capture of Suspect (e.g., who makes the arrest, medical support, interjurisdictional considerations)
10. Reporting and Postpursuit Analysis (e.g., completing pursuit reporting form, accountability, review process, sanctions for policy violations)

Source: Adapted from Alpert, 1997, pp. 559–560.

Alpert and Dunham (1997) noted that states generally rely on the Uniform Vehicle Code that provides officers with particular exemptions to traffic laws when they are faced with emergency situations. The Code (as cited in Alpert & Dunham, 1997, p. 237) states that "provisions shall not relieve the driver of an authorized emergency vehicle from the duty to drive with due regard for the safety of all persons, nor shall such provisions protect the driver from the consequences of his reckless disregard for the safety of others." Alpert and Dunham (1997) believe that simply adopting this policy is not enough, as many states neglect to explain exactly what is meant and/or how officers should abide by such a policy.

Aside from the aforementioned factors influencing an officer's decision to pursue a noncompliant suspect (including his or her adherence to the limitations placed on them by state statutes, court decisions, and department pursuit policies), Alpert and Madden (1994) argued that an officer should consider the public's understanding and support of police pursuits. In a period in which many police departments around the country are attempting to reclaim the support of their citizens, popular opinion regarding the appropriateness of police pursuit arguably could play a significant role in breaking down the "we versus they" barrier. In their research, Homant and Kennedy (1994) found that a sample of registered voters thought that most police officers used good judgment during pursuits, but a slight majority reported that they believed that additional restrictions should be placed on officers during pursuits.

The court, in *Nelson v. City of Chester, Illinois,* held that "the city's breach of its duty to properly train its police officers in high-speed pursuit might be found to be the proximate cause of the pursued driver's death, notwithstanding the contributing negligence of the pursued driver" (Swanson et al., 1998, p. 414). Because of the inherent dangers involved in police pursuits, police agencies are under increased pressure to limit officer discretion (Homant & Kennedy, 1994). Yet, Homant, Kennedy, and Howton (1993) noted that despite police policies documenting the factors to be considered in engaging in a police pursuit (with departments generally going so far as to attribute relative weights to the various factors), "the ultimate decision to initiate pursuit usually lies within the discretion of the patrol officer" (p. 293). Furthermore, in his discussion of the limitations of police pursuit policies and more generally, our understanding of police pursuits, Falcone (1994, p. 143) argued that "Many of the attitudes, values, and beliefs that underpin the articles of faith to which officers and their organizations cling are rooted not in empirically based data but, rather, in commonly held articles of faith that have not been empirically evaluated." Put simply, although pursuit policies remain a necessity, they do not necessarily provide a surefire method of preventing dangerous police pursuits. Simple development or possession of a policy on police pursuits does not directly correlate with appropriate officer behavior.

According to Alpert and Madden (1994), historically officers were charged with apprehending the suspect at all costs (in accordance with my experience in Colorado), but the past three decades have seen significant changes in the historically liberal (dangerous?) approach to police pursuits. In the 1970s, defensive driving skills were taught to officers in response to a concern over patrol car accidents and officer injuries. The focus in the 1980s was more directed toward the safety of the general public (i.e., innocent bystanders) and the avoidance of pursuit-related accidents, and away from "catching the suspect at all costs." As for the most recent developments in police pursuits, Alpert and Madden (1994, p. 23) noted that

> In the 1990s, the law enforcement community has responded to the problems by enhancing efforts to balance public safety and the need to enforce laws by an increase in leadership and the integration of policies, training, supervision and accountability. Perhaps the most critical change in the 1990s, has been the development and implementation of decision-making training skills to augment defensive driving skills.

As we begin the next century, one wonders what changes lie ahead with regard to police pursuits. Based on a recent, high-profile incident in Philadelphia, one could argue that an additional concern faces police administrators and trainers. Specifically, they will likely be faced with addressing the excessive force sometimes used by officers once they apprehend noncompliant suspects.

OFFICER RESPONSE TO PURSUITS

> When you have a bad guy in your sights, it's so hard to let him go. . . . It goes against your grain.
> *Sheriff William Hackel*
> *Macomb County, Michigan*

One recent big police pursuit story involves a videotaped account of roughly 12 Philadelphia police officers who are accused of kicking and beating a suspect who had disregarded their commands and led them on an extended chase through the streets of Philadelphia. The suspect, Thomas Jones, was spotted in a stolen car in the northern part of the city when the chase began. According to witnesses, Jones then crashed the car and fled on foot before police tackled him. While scuffling with officers, Jones grabbed an officer's gun and began shooting. He then jumped into a nearby empty patrol car. One officer was shot in the hand during the shoot-out that followed. Eventually Jones ended the chase when he was cornered. The videotape depicts numerous officers approaching the suspect's commandeered vehicle with their guns drawn. On seizing the suspect, they instantly surrounded him and dragged him to the ground amidst a flurry of punches and kicks from various officers.

Despite claims of police brutality from interest groups such as the National Association for the Advancement of Colored People (NAACP), Philadelphia Police Commissioner John Timoney stated that there is not going to be any rush to judgment in this case and that we must consider the totality of the circumstances. He said, "As inflammatory as this tape might be, we have to keep in mind that the police were in the process of apprehending a criminal suspect who had resisted a number of attempts to arrest him and who had shot a police officer" (Clines, 2000, p. 19A).

Whereas it will be interesting to see how the courts and society react to this case, we must keep in mind that not all pursuits are as volatile as this. We must also keep in mind that this may not be an isolated event. It is possible that such pursuits are not atypical, although the attention to this particular incident (and one could argue, the attention devoted to the Rodney King incident) is due in large part to the existence of video footage. Who knows how often such pursuits occur? Regardless, it remains that once again a large portion of society witnessed several officers using what appeared to be unnecessary force on conclusion of a pursuit. Thus, the question remains: "Why did the police behave as such?"

What causes pursuits and the accidents that are often the end result? Some might attribute a portion of the causes to male machismo. Policing is a male-dominated occupation, and pursuit offenders are usually male as well. Although pursuits are mostly mental, it is still a challenge. A challenge to the authority of the police officer is often perceived as "contempt of cop" (Alpert, 1997a). To the general public, common causes and the outcome of pursuits can be a result of myth or misinformation. Sheldon F. Greenberg (1999, pp. 179–186) in *Controversial Issues in Policing* explored the most common myths about pursuits:

- The vast majority of pursuits go bad.
- Prohibiting pursuits will send a signal to offenders to flee.
- Officers pursue out of anger or an adrenaline rush rather than a rational thought process or in accord with policy.
- Officers cannot or will not discontinue a pursuit. (p. 180)

In the same publication, Michael McCampbell asserted that lack of training is the primary reason for problems with police pursuits. He found that driver training for entry-level personnel averages less than 14 hours with only about 3 hours of additional training for in-service personnel, which McCampbell (among others) does not feel is enough.

McCampbell also reported that pursuits for any offense (including traffic violations) are permissible in nearly half of all police agencies (1999).

Another cause for police pursuits may be the thrill of the chase. In the immortal words of Tom Cruise in the movie *Top Gun,* "I feel the need . . . the need for speed." One cannot deny that young males, including some police officers, have a certain propensity to push the adrenaline envelope. I can remember, with vivid detail, watching the movie *The French Connection* and its unofficial sequel, *The Seven-Ups,* and their wild car chases. In Hollywood, these fun, exciting, "keep you on the edge of your seat" movies do not deal with real-life issues such as innocent bystanders and vicarious liability. Excitement and adrenaline rush are two things that we actually have little control over.

Alpert and Dunham (1997) suggested that the excitement, rush of adrenaline, and danger involved in police pursuits could cause an officer to "get caught up in the heat of the chase and disregard many safety considerations" (p. 233). Accordingly, Alpert, Kenney, and Dunham (1997) suggested that even though most officers behave professionally, such an adrenaline rush could result in officers becoming anxious at the conclusion of a pursuit and they may "pull the suspect out of the vent window" while taking the suspect into custody (p. 371) (arguably, this explains the recent police incident in Philadelphia). Kenney and Alpert's (1997) study found that force sometimes accompanies police pursuits, as 25% of the departments they sampled reported having to use force, in addition to the pursuit itself, to apprehend a suspect.

The infamous Rodney King video captured the conclusion of a vehicle police pursuit. In this highly publicized case, arguably, the police were wrong in their use of force, and King was the victim of police street justice. One could explain some of the officers' behaviors as either a result of their high levels of adrenaline from the pursuit or their reactions to the stress involved with policing in general. Perhaps Swanson et al. (1998, p. 417) were referring to officer driving skills when they noted that "The natural tendency for many police drivers is to become emotionally involved and therefore lose some perspective during a pursuit." It is possible that the loss of perspective resultant from a pursuit is carried beyond the actual chase.

Selye's (1956) explanation of the "fight or flight" mechanism helps to explain a police officer's biomedical reaction to the stresses of police pursuits. Experts suggest that the emotionalism and psychology associated with pursuits dictates that an uninvolved supervisor should assume supervision of the pursuit (Swanson et al., 1998). It is believed that this person's distance from the situation permits him or her to objectively assess the situation and help the officer(s) react appropriately.

It may be easy to second-guess afterward a person's decision to pursue or not pursue, but one cannot deny what is human nature. In their article for *Law and Order,* Bobby Westmoreland and Billy Haddock (1989, pp. 116–117) explain how fight or flight comes into play:

> Centuries of conditioning have "programmed" the human body to escape from danger, or to stand and fight. Other mammals and birds have this same mechanism, which serves them well when faced with imminent danger. However, human civilization requires higher levels of responses that may be impaired when under extreme stress.
>
> A police officer driving "code 3" is in a very stressful situation and his fight-or-flight mechanism is automatically triggered. He suddenly has several factors affecting him physically:

1. His immediate surroundings; traffic, people, weather, his own vehicle (red lights and siren), etc;

2. Apprehension about the emergency call and how he should approach the situation;

3. His own body's fight-or-flight mechanism. . . .

Considering the complexity of policing in modern society, stress control methods must be learned and practiced in order to mediate the stress response. What once served as a survival instinct could now add to the existing hazards of police work unless managed effectively.

Officer stress likely assists in explaining the results from Dunham et al.'s (1998) study suggesting that a large percentage (57%) of respondents had been physically assaulted at the conclusion of their chase (however, only a small percentage officially reported the beatings).

In lay terms, when you step onto a hot sidewalk while barefoot, you instinctively pull your foot back, but with practice you can learn to walk on a hot surface, much like those who can walk on hot coals. Practice, however, is but one solution to the problems and dangers inherent in police pursuits. As such, we must turn our attention to possible solutions to police pursuits.

SOLUTIONS

In *Smith v. City of West Point* (as cited in Swanson et al., 1998, p. 413), the court addressed police pursuit practices by suggesting that the police "are under no duty to allow motorized suspects a leisurely escape." However, as we all know, sometimes permitting a leisurely escape is better than a harmful pursuit. Police pursuits are a complex issue. Numerous inherent factors and issues with pursuits, policing, and violence come into play, and no matter what course you follow, you will always have detractors and critics. To quote an old saying, "you are damned if you do and damned if you don't." Although an ostrich may be okay with its head buried in the sand, the purveyors of pursuit policies cannot afford this, literally and figuratively speaking.

In defining a solution, we must first examine the problems associated with police pursuits, which include

- Apprehension of criminals (violent, nonviolent, felony, and misdemeanor)
- Injury and loss of life
- Legal ramifications

Officers must duly consider each of these issues when deciding to initiate, continue, or end a pursuit. Some decisions are easier than others, but officers are constantly accountable for their choices and actions. Observing the inherent problems associated with police pursuits enables a look toward solutions. As such, we can place the solutions in three categories: policy, training, and technology.

Provided earlier were examples of policies and approaches designed to restrict pursuits and to minimize the danger to everyone involved, while protecting municipalities from unnecessary litigation and exposure. Any city, county, or state police agency that does not have a comprehensive pursuit policy in place is remiss in its duty to protect its citizens both physically and financially. What is missing is a federal pursuit policy model that could be considered the gold standard for other agencies to follow. Whereas local control and states' rights are a hot issue with regard to numerous issues, a standardized federal pursuit policy model would give local and state agencies the option of adopting what would likely be a more universally accepted standard, perhaps one that would be most effective. For example, this policy would be a culmination of efforts from experts from around the country, including a cross section of law enforcement, risk management, and driving experts. This policy would likely provide the greatest benefit to the smaller agencies that typically do not have the resources to educate their top policymakers in proper protocol. Arguably, the federal government is in an ideal position to tackle this task. Let us hope that it does not take a horrific incident to instigate action.

Training has been the stepchild of pursuit policies. It is both easier and cheaper to make and enforce pursuit policies, but good quality training entails time and money. The National Survey of Police Pursuits and the Use of Force (Kenney & Alpert, 1997) found that entry-level training for pursuit driving among agencies averages less than 14 hours, and only about 3 hours of additional training are provided to in-service personnel. Training is another place in which a federal model could be of assistance. Many states and local agencies have adequate minimum standards, but others, as indicated in Kenney and Alpert's survey, appear to be sorely lacking. If the *average* length of training of those surveyed is less than 14 hours, it is entirely possible that some may have no pursuit training at all.

In addition, it is not only the quantity of training that matters, but quality is important as well. Alpert's (1997b) nationwide study of police pursuits suggested that although about 60% of police departments offer entry-level driver training at their respective academies, most of the training addresses the mechanics of defensive/pursuit driving instead of focusing on understanding why or when officers should engage in pursuit. Similarly, Alpert and Madden (1994) argued that "Many police trainers have had to rely on their own perceptions and beliefs for information to present to their officers. As a result, police officers have received information about pursuit which has been based more on emotion than reason." Perhaps, for the safety of everyone involved, it is time we provide better pursuit training for all officers.

Personally speaking, the two departments at which I have worked and taught driver training both far exceeded the 14-hour average. In my former department, although we were sorely lacking in a comprehensive policy, we did have adequate pursuit training for new officers. Our training included both legal background and proper pursuit techniques combined with hands-on track experience. In my current department, all new officers receive 40 hours of tactical driving instruction. The curriculum is from Texas A&M University and is very comprehensive (see Table 7–2).

Although there are many quality driving schools, this Texas A&M–approved curriculum and the state instructors teach our driving instructors the proper methodology and application of their driving techniques. This information is then passed along to patrol officers. There are other solutions, however, besides training, to address the issues surrounding police pursuits.

Regardless of whether damages were incurred, injuries occurred, or lives were lost, the conclusion of a pursuit should not signal the end of the situation. In other words, as Swanson et al. (1998, p. 418) suggested,

TABLE 7–2   Sample Tactical Driving Instruction Curriculum

EMERGENCY DRIVING

- Legal Aspects of Emergency Driving
- Vehicle Dynamics and Physical Forces
- Principles of Automobile Control

DRIVING EXERCISES

- Precision Maneuvering
- Serpentine
- Controlled Braking
- Evasive Lane Change
- Backing
- Obstacle Course
- Skid Pad
- Highway Response Course
- Night Driving

Law enforcement organizations should provide for an ongoing process of evaluation and documentation of pursuit-related incidents. All pursuits, including those successfully terminated without accident, should be routinely critiqued to determine whether departmental policy was followed and the extent to which any policy modification, training enhancement, or other remedial action is warranted.

Each pursuit should be recognized as an opportunity to learn more about police practices in general.

Several high- and low-tech methods enable police departments to minimize vehicle pursuits. First is the use of freeway traffic units. My current department employs police package Chevy Camaros for use by freeway traffic units. These cars are capable of rapid acceleration and high speeds and provide us with a psychological edge, as some offenders will decide not to flee, knowing their vehicle cannot outrun the Camaro. In accordance with Swanson et al.'s (1998, p. 417) statement concerning the dangers and liability issues involved with officers "required to drive different vehicles with unique handling characteristics under various road and weather conditions," these vehicles require officers to receive additional pursuit training simply because of the increased horsepower.

Helicopters are another valuable tool to minimize pursuits. When the police helicopter is physically above the violator, the patrol car can back off somewhat to avoid pushing the violator to extremes. Often in misdemeanor cases when patrol cars are called off the pursuit, the helicopter will continue to follow and lead officers to the suspect's final destination. The helicopter can also videotape pursuits to be sure they comply with department policy. Although helicopters can be a bit expensive to operate on a full-time basis, they are an invaluable resource during police pursuits.

Videotape recorders mounted in patrol cars are a valuable tool for both prosecutors and department administrators. With video, jurors can see for themselves the behaviors and actions of both the violator(s) and officer(s). Most video cameras in patrol cars are equipped to begin recording whenever an officer activates his or her emergency lights. The remote microphone attached to the officer is also activated. The officer, well aware that he or she is being recorded by both audio and video, is much more likely to adhere to department policies and can use these tapes to refute allegations of excessive force after a stop and/or to disprove claims of racial bias in initiating the stop. Videotape recorders also assist police trainers as actual footage can be used in the classroom for trainee and instructor evaluation.

Several companies now manufacture a device that permits officers to place spikes across the roadway to puncture the tires of the violator and force him or her to discontinue evading police pursuit. These spikes are portable and are located on a base that folds to place in the trunk of a car. When a pursuit is initiated, the officers with the spikes will try to anticipate the route of the violator and proceed to a destination ahead of the pursuit. On approach of the violator, the pursuing officers are advised to slow down to avoid getting their own tires punctured. This has proven to be an efficient and cost-effective method of stopping pursuits in a timely and safe manner. Officers must be sure, however, to avoid puncturing the tires of nonsuspects who may be heading in the same direction as the suspect. Caution must be used with this promising approach to ending police pursuits.

What does the future hold? Currently being tested is a new device that will disrupt the electronic ignition of the violator's vehicle and turn the vehicle off. If this method is used, new cars will be factory-equipped with the proper electronics to enable the police to activate their corresponding device to disable the car. Computer driving simulators, like flight simulators, could also be a great tool. A realistic simulator would give departments the opportunity to put scenarios in play that could greatly complement the actual driving course. On a driving track, you cannot simulate a child running from behind a parked car or a suspect shooting at you. These are but a few of the numerous advances being tested at this time (see Chapter 10 for a discussion of the future of police violence). It is hoped that increasing attention to police practices can be combined with technological advances to further protect not only police officers but everyone in society.

CONCLUSION

Death resulting from a police pursuit inevitably receives intense media coverage and societal scrutiny. Usually articles are written regarding police pursuit policies, the officer's past record with his or her department, the offender's past and current alleged crimes, and information about the victim(s). Many articles or sound bites do not detail the tragedy that surrounds what is lost when an innocent person is killed, nor do they examine the totality of the circumstances.

Although Jackie Gleason and Burt Reynolds were fun to watch during *Smokey and the Bandit,* real pursuits and accidents have consequences. I remember a pursuit-related accident that involved a member of my department. Some of the details are still not known to this day as to how the person pursued got away. The officer lost control of his patrol vehicle and hit a concrete barrier that was supposed to stop vehicles from driving off an embankment. Below was a construction site for a new section of the interstate freeway. The vehicle went through the concrete barrier and fell, nose down, 50 feet until it came to a rest. You cannot realize the finality of these horrific crashes until you see what is left of the car. Finality is also a grim reminder at funerals. At this officer's funeral, the hundreds of police officers lining the way for the family, the bagpipes playing in the distance, the 21-gun salute, the missing-man helicopter flyover, and the folded flag given to the grieving widow were all vivid reminders of the violent finality of this officer's death.

Police pursuits are in some ways like a high-wire act. Everything must be in balance or we fall and, inevitably, someone pays the price. It is hoped that with the recent attention devoted to the issues (both positive and negative information) by policymakers, researchers, media personnel, and society in general, we can eliminate, as much as possible, the dangers associated with this important and dangerous, yet arguably overlooked, aspect of police operations.

REFERENCES

ALPERT, G. (1997a). The management of police pursuit driving. In R. Dunham & G. Alpert (Eds.), *Critical issues in policing* (3rd ed., pp. 547–564). Prospect Heights, IL: Waveland Press.

ALPERT, G. (1997b). *Police pursuit: Policies and training*. Washington, DC: National Institute of Justice.

ALPERT, G., & ANDERSON, P. (1986). The most deadly force: police pursuits. *Justice Quarterly, 1*, 1–14.

ALPERT, G., & DUNHAM, R. (1988). Research on police pursuits. *American Journal of Police, 7*, 123–131.

ALPERT, G., & DUNHAM, R. (1990). *Police pursuit driving: Controlling responses to emergency situations*. Westport, CT: Greenwood Press.

ALPERT, G., & DUNHAM, R. (1997). *Policing urban America* (3rd ed.). Prospect Heights, IL: Waveland Press.

ALPERT, G., & FRIDELL, L. (1992). *Police vehicles and firearms*. Prospect Heights, IL: Waveland Press.

ALPERT, G., & MADDEN, T. (1994). Police pursuit driving: An empirical analysis of critical decisions. *American Journal of Police, 13*(4), 23–45.

ALPERT, G., KENNEY, D., & DUNHAM, R. (1997). Police pursuits and the use of force: Recognizing and managing 'the pucker factor"—a research note. *Justice Quarterly, 14*(2), 371–385.

ASSOCIATED PRESS. (1990, September 5). Family, driver win $1.3 million in fatal crash. *Houston Chronicle*.

ASSOCIATED PRESS. (1991, January 1). Police ruled liable in chase accident. *Houston Chronicle*, p. 19.

ASSOCIATED PRESS. (1992, December 13). "Thrill of the chase" puts innocent at risk. *Houston Chronicle*, p. 2.

BAILEY, F., & HALE, D. (1998). *Popular culture, crime and justice*. Belmont, CA: West/Wadsworth.

BUREAU OF JUSTICE STATISTICS. (1992). *State and local police departments—1990*. Washington, DC: Author.

CALIFORNIA HIGHWAY PATROL. (1983). *Pursuit study*. Sacramento, CA: Author.

CLINES, F. X. (2000, July 14). Philadelphia image suffers before GOP convention. *Fort Worth Star-Telegram*, pp. 1A, 19A.

CREW, R., FRIDELL, L., & PURSELL, K. (1995). Probabilities and odds in hot pursuit: A benefit-cost analysis. *Journal of Criminal Justice, 23*(5), 417–424.

DANTZKER, M. L. (2000). *Understanding today's police* (2nd ed.). Upper Saddle River, NJ: Prentice Hall.

DUNHAM, R., ALPERT, G., KENNY, G., & CROMWELL, P. (1998). High-speed pursuit: The offenders' perspective. *Criminal Justice and Behavior, 25*(1), 30–45.

FALCONE, D. (1994). Police pursuits and officer attitudes: Myths and realities. *American Journal of Police, 13*(1), 143–155.

FEDERAL BUREAU OF INVESTIGATION. (2000). [On-line]. Available: www.fbi.gov.

GREENBERG, S. (1999). Is it time for police agencies to eliminate pursuits? No. In J. Sewell (Ed.), *Controversial issues in policing* (pp. 179–186). Boston: Allyn and Bacon.

HOMANT, R., & KENNEDY, D. (1994). Citizen preferences and perceptions concerning police pursuit policies. *Journal of Criminal Justice, 22*(5), 425–435.

HOMANT, R., KENNEDY, D., & HOWTON, J. (1993). Sensation seeking as a factor in police pursuit. *Criminal Justice and Behavior, 20*(3), 293–305.

INTERNATIONAL ASSOCIATION OF CHIEFS OF POLICE. (1990). *National law enforcement driver training reference guide.* Washington, DC: D. Green Publishers.

KAPPELER, V., BLUMBERG, M., & POTTER, G. (2000). *The mythology of crime and criminal justice* (3rd ed.). Prospect Heights, IL: Waveland Press.

KENNEDY, D., HOMANT, R., & KENNEDY, J. (1992). A comparative analysis of law enforcement vehicle pursuit policies. *Justice Quarterly, 9*, 227–246.

KENNEY, D., & ALPERT, G. (1997). A national survey of pursuits and the use of police force: data from law enforcement agencies. *Journal of Criminal Justice, 25*(4): 315–323.

MCCAMPBELL, M. (1999). Is it time for police agencies to eliminate pursuits? Yes. In J. Sewell (Ed.), *Controversial Issues in Policing* (pp. 173–177). Boston: Allyn and Bacon.

PURSUIT MANAGEMENT TASK FORCE. (1998). *Pursuit management task force: A summary of the PMST's report on police pursuit practices and the role of technology.* Washington, DC: Department of Justice.

SCHOFIELD, D. (1988, May). Legal issues of pursuit driving. *FBI Law Enforcement Bulletin,* 23–30.

SELYE, H. (1956). *The stress of life.* New York: McGraw-Hill.

SURETTE, R. (1998). *Media, crime, and criminal justice* (2nd ed.). Belmont, CA: West/Wadsworth.

SWANSON, C., TERRITO, L., & TAYLOR, R. (1998). *Police administration: Structures, processes, and behavior.* Upper Saddle River, NJ: Prentice Hall.

UNIFORM VEHICLE CODE. (1966). Section 11-106.

WESTMORELAND, B., & HADDOCK, B. (1989, November). Psychological and physiological stress effects. *Law and Order,* 116–117.

8

Community Policing
and Police Violence

Rhonda K. DeLong

❖

INTRODUCTION

Rodney King, Abner Louima, Amadou Diallo—names that haunt our memories, and names that will forever be negatively linked with police officers throughout the country. The acts of police violence associated with these three individuals rocked our nation and in the case of Rodney King caused one of the worst civil disturbances in recent history. These tragic events have, sadly, come to define policing for many people. The community has been affected, as has each officer who wears a uniform and is called to protect and serve. With the peace of our nation's cities and the strained relationship between the police and the public at stake, understanding police violence is of the utmost importance. As such, we cannot overlook a possible remedy in the form of community policing.

What causes police officers to react violently in some situations? Is it the personality of the officer, the nature of police work, or other influential variables affecting the way in which officers use their power and authority? Is the job so filled with daily violence that reacting violently is the only option seen as viable? This chapter addresses these questions by examining the recruitment, selection, and training methods of police departments and the possible impact of the community policing philosophy on police violence.

The first part of the chapter defines police violence and examines how officers respond to real and perceived challenges to their authority. Following this discussion, the chapter examines police use of force and use of force models that serve as the foundation for department policy and procedure. Next, the chapter addresses the process of police officer recruitment, selection, and training, along with operational styles and their influences on this process. A discussion of the impact of the community policing philosophy and its potential to reduce and prevent violence (with an emphasis on how the media can affect citizen fear and perceptions of crime, and the need to recognize and address juvenile and gang violence) wraps up the chapter.

The philosophy of community policing can have a profound impact on all aspects of policing from selection to training, and most relevant to this chapter, police violence. The importance of the community policing philosophy cannot be understated. Once officers and administrators have a clear understanding of community policing, and allow it to influence their decisions, police violence (which, for the purposes of this chapter, is recognized as acts of violence committed by and against police officers) can be substantially reduced.

WHAT IS POLICE VIOLENCE?

Fridell and Pate (1997) noted that laws must be *enforced,* often against the will of the lawbreaker. Bringing sanctions against a violator sometimes requires the use of force or violence. Police officers are given the authority to use coercive force when appropriate. They are also given discretionary powers to decide which method will best accomplish their intended goal in any given situation, from traffic stops to shoot-outs. The daily world of an officer is filled with human tragedy, and constantly dealing with negative issues surely has an effect on officers. But does this in any way justify the use of violence toward citizens? Certainly not, but understanding why such acts of police violence occur can assist in finding answers to correct the problem.

Several complicating issues must be considered in any discussion of police use of force. For instance, we must recognize that police patrols disproportionately have contact with minority communities, both in terms of crime-fighting efforts and making arrests. It is no surprise that the police use of force adds to the racial tension that exists in some minority communities (this topic and related issues are further addressed later in the chapter). We also need to define police use of force.

Defining police use of force has been a point of great scholarly debate. For example, Kania and Mackey (1977, p. 29) define force as the exertion of power to compel or restrain the behavior of others. Force can also be classified in terms of its appropriate use. For instance, deadly force is force used with the intent to cause death or great bodily harm, and less-than-lethal force is force used with the intent to cause injury but not death. In summing up the difficulties surrounding interpretations of excessive force, Carter and Radelet (1999, p. 287) suggested that

> In situations where excessive force charges are leveled against the police, there is frequently a communication problem created by definition differences. These situations are further complicated by emotional outbursts on both sides, by charges and countercharges, and by media stories that often accentuate the negative. It is difficult to bring reason to bear on the matter and to get at the question of exactly what is being contested. Police officers sometimes make the point that the public is quick to accuse an officer of excessive force, but not so concerned when the officer is attacked, insulted or killed.

Carter and Radelet's account highlights the difficulties in simply defining the term and subsequently recognizing it within the context of police practices. A further breakdown of the use of force could address the appropriateness of its use (i.e., whether it is justifiable or excessive).

It has been suggested that excessive use of police force is often primarily responsible for stirring up emotions concerning the police-citizen relationship (Carter, 1984). According to Cheh (1995, p. 234), the use of force becomes excessive when it is used out of proportion to its need. James Fyfe (1987) further illustrates the complexities of the use of force and its categorizations by suggesting that even justifiable use of force can still be excessive or unwarranted. Essentially, there can be a legal use of force that could have been avoided. Fyfe (1987) gave the example of a well-meaning officer who perhaps lacks the skills to de-escalate a potential conflict with a suspect and simply resorts to using force that may have been avoided. These definitions have implications for both training and disciplinary actions, as departments use various definitions to decide what is necessary or excessive.

Carter and Radelet (1999) believed we tend to think of violence as a one-dimensional problem, but violence can come in many forms, and the motivation behind each form can vary as well. For example, a situation involving a suspect who physically assaults a police officer attempting to make an arrest is different from the worker who physically assaults a coworker. According to James Gilligan, "All violence is an attempt to achieve justice, or what the violent person perceives as justice . . . thus the attempt to achieve and maintain justice, or to undo and prevent injustice, is the one and only universal cause of violence" (1992, pp. 11–12). How does this relate to policing? The central links are justice, coupled with the power and control given to police officers. An officer may perceive a situation as threatening, choosing to use force to control the individual involved. If the person does not comply with the verbal commands of the officer, the officer may choose to react violently because of the person's disregard and disrespect for his or her authority.

William Westley (1970) examined this phenomenon and found that officers felt illegal force was acceptable and necessary to obtain citizen respect or to make a good arrest. The expectation of respect from citizens and the consequences when officers do not receive it has been studied extensively. Researchers such as Black and Reiss (1967), Toch (1985), and Sykes and Clark (1975) found that violence from the police is frequently a response to perceived challenges to their authority and right to control the situation. Essentially, officers expect deference to their status and power, and citizen behaviors that fall outside of this expectation are met with corrective methods, which can include violence.

This demand for respect has led to violent conflicts in society and has troubled many minority communities. This "contempt of cop" phenomenon is sometimes associated with the conclusion of a high-speed pursuit when the officer's anger and adrenaline are at their peak (see Chapter 7 for a thorough discussion of the relationship between police pursuits and police violence). The pursued driver is at risk to become another statistic of police violence because of his or her evasive actions while fleeing the officer. But this issue of "contempt of cop" is not solely associated with pursuits. As Westley's (1970) research illustrated, sometimes officers feel that force is necessary to ensure an arrest, for example, using excessive force to gain information that can be used to put a suspect behind bars. Of course, actions such as these are in direct violation of any department policy and constitutional protections, so a dilemma exists for some officers. Klockars (1980) refers to this as the "Dirty Harry problem."

According to Klockars (1980), in this moral dilemma the ends justify the means if three criteria are met: The endings are in fact positive, the dirty means will result in a positive ending, and the dirty means are the only way to achieve a positive end. Essentially, the officer may believe that reacting with violence is appropriate in order to achieve justice according to his or her perception of the situation. The attempt to "achieve and maintain justice" is operationalized in an act of violence by the officer toward the citizen. Some officers may believe that it is their right to use violence to achieve justice simply because of the authority and discretionary power they are granted. Carter and Radelet (1999, p. 354) argued that

> Physical and verbal abuse are the grounds for most of the allegations in citizen complaints against the police. Many incidents involve street confrontations, often in situations in which the police are accused of apprehending a subject for disorderly conduct, then going on quickly to providing "street justice."

The police socialization process is also an area of concern for understanding the use of force and violence in policing. The first step of the socialization process in policing occurs at the academy, where new officers learn to think, act, and speak like police officers, in addition to learning the skills of policing. The cultural values and norms of the occupation are also passed along. According to Radelet and Carter (1994), these factors interact and are reinforced by other officers, leading to the development of behaviors and attitudes consistent with police officers. This process, according to Radelet and Carter (1994), is both necessary and natural—neither good nor bad. New officers must learn these skills and how to deal with and relate to the internal structure of the police department as well as the public they serve.

Jerome Skolnick spent a considerable amount of time studying what he identifies as the "working personality of police officers." This "working personality" is created by two principal variables: *danger* and *authority*. Furthermore, the element of danger may lead to isolation and a concern with those the officer regards as sybolically dangerous (Skolnick, 1975, pp. 41–43). The perception of danger coupled with an officer's legal right to use force may create in some officers a tendency to act first and ask questions later. Skolnick observed that the police officer's attitude is similar to that of a combat soldier. A "we vs. they" attitude begins to develop, life is seen as combat, and people are defined as either good or bad. The actions that flow from such attitudes could vary from a push onto the hood of the patrol car to the use of pepper spray to the drawing of one's weapon. The officer's perceptions influence the way in which he or she handles any encounter with a citizen.

Police violence is typically defined according to the experiences and perceptions of the individuals involved. For an officer, violence may mean an inappropriate severe physical assault against another. On the other hand, a minority citizen who does not trust the police may view violence as any type of verbal or physical assault against him or her.

Because of the difficulty in our understanding if, and how much, force is necessary, police officers faced with threatening suspects often find themselves in a no-win situation. If the officer proceeds to use force, he or she may antagonize the suspect to respond with force and/or may be viewed (either by the suspect or witnesses) as instigating the violent encounter. On the other hand, the officer who does not seize control of the situation is frowned on by fellow officers and the department, and is subject to insults and jeers from the suspect and any witnesses. The nonresponding officer also exposes himself or herself and any bystanders to greater levels of danger. This is one reason why the issue of community policing is central to the prevention of police violence. This philosophy seeks to build trust among officers and the public. Everyone benefits from a relationship in which citizens understand the police and police understand citizens. Otherwise, without trust, violence will continue to be the end result of many confrontations between the police and the public.

VIOLENCE AND THE USE OF FORCE

The United States is a violent country, and people depend on the police to provide protection. Often lost in our society's reliance on the police is recognition of the dangers officers face on a regular basis. Although most of the research we have regarding officer use of force concerns practices of departments subscribing to the traditional approach to policing, we must consider police officer use of force as we progress through the community era of policing. Unfortunately, a void exists in the research literature regarding the impact of community policing on police violence.

Logically, we think that the potential for violence by and against officers should diminish as the police and community come closer together. As the barrier between the public and the police erodes, violence is likely to dissipate. We have yet, however, to document the adoption of the community policing approach as having a substantial impact on police violence. It is hoped that the impressive body of research currently under development will provide some evidence of the impact, or lack thereof, of community policing efforts in relation to violence by and against police officers. Regardless of the individual department's approach, the fact remains that officers are sometimes called on to use force and are susceptible to physical attacks by citizens.

Police officers are given the authority and right to use force whenever necessary. In fact, police officers in the United States are given a great deal of discretion in the use of deadly force, which has resulted in an enormous amount of research on the topic. Force-related research findings have provided a basis for administrators to make decisions that serve both the community and law enforcement officers. Much of the early research on the police use of force relied on coroner's reports or newspaper accounts. These early studies were problematic because coroner's reports tended to exclude suspects who were wounded, and newspapers' coverage of shootings was limited to those that were deemed important by the editorial policy (Blumberg, 1997).

Despite the considerable amount of research in this area, caution should be taken when trying to draw conclusions from different studies examining the use of deadly force. Geller and Karales (1981) pointed out that studies conducted by different researchers are often not comparable to one another. Among other reasons, there are varying definitions of what constitutes deadly, or excessive, force. Some studies examine only fatalities, whereas others include nonfatal shootings. As expected, fatal shootings are very different from nonfatal hits and harmless discharges (Blumberg, 1997).

Another complicating factor in understanding the use of force often lies in defining the term *necessary*. Department policies are detailed in their description of what constitutes the appropriate use of force. On the street, however, it may be a matter of survival, and recalling specific portions of a policy may not be part of the officer's response. When is force *necessary?* This question cannot be easily answered. Each situation an officer encounters is unique, as is each individual. Police officers are trained to deal with a variety of situations; they are given discretionary power and the tools to maintain and gain control of a situation and/or an individual. Properly trained officers, psychologically healthy officers, and critically thinking officers who can problem-solve are better prepared than those who are quick tempered and have difficulty controlling their response to "contempt of cop." Officers do not appreciate being disrespected by citizens, largely because of officers' perception of their authority and status. Officers expect compliance, and when citizens do not comply, officers may respond with physical force.

Positive public opinion of police officers is essential for effective community policing. Unfortunately, as Miller and Hess (1994) reported, a large segment of society considers police brutality a problem. Officer use of force has, on occasion, negatively impacted citizen perceptions of policing, as evidenced in the riots that broke out in several cities during the 1970s as a result of officers unnecessarily using force against minority suspects (Conyers, 1981). Many would argue that not much has changed since the 1970s, as evidenced in minority claims of misuse of power levied against officers from the New York Police Department (e.g., Abner Louima and Amadou Diallo) and the Los Angeles Police Department (e.g., Rodney King) during the 1990s. Radelet and Carter (1994) discovered that current minority complaints against the police include substandard or poor police protection, minority expectation that the police will not treat them fairly, numerous incidents of verbal abuse and harassment, police use of excessive force, discrimination in police personnel administration, stereotyping of minorities as criminals, and substandard or poor service to minorities. Although it goes without stating that most police departments and most officers do not engage in discriminatory practices, several high-profile incidents have provoked many minority citizens to recall the not-so-distant past when police departments had a greater percentage of racist and corrupt officers.

Community policing can help ease the tensions between the police and minority groups, who have historically believed that the police do not give minority needs and concerns the attention they deserve (Trojanowicz, Kappeler, Gaines, & Bucqueroux, 1998). For instance, by empowering minority citizens (as opposed to alienating them, which often occurs with traditional policing) and recognizing their complaints, police departments can help bridge the gap between the public (particularly, minority groups) and the police. By altering the manner in which all police officers interact with minority communities, minority citizen perceptions of the police are likely to change for the better, and more minority citizens may be willing to assist the police in crime prevention and crime-fighting efforts.

In their study concerning public attitudes toward police use of excessive force, Arthur and Case (1994) found that white respondents were substantially more likely than black respondents to approve of officers striking adult males under varied circumstances. More generally, they found that those with more power, status, and advantages were more likely than less privileged groups to support the police. Miller and Hess (1994) argued that different perceptions of police brutality are attributed, in part, to the differing tasks required of police officers in various communities. They cited the enforcement efforts directed at common criminals, as opposed to white-collar criminals (see Friedrichs, 1996;

Lynch, Michalowski, and Groves, 2000; and Reiman, 2001 for elaboration of this issue), as a prominent factor in shaping the perceptions of various groups in society.

The findings by Arthur and Case are likely the result of minority groups generally having negative attitudes of police officers. These attitudes are attributable in part to numerous high-profile incidents involving misuse of police power directed toward minorities. These findings should send up a red flag to police administrators who may be interested in bridging the gap between the public and the police by making their department more oriented toward community policing.

Part of bridging the gap involves ensuring that citizens are provided nonthreatening access to voice complaints (regardless of whether the complaints are force-related or not). Carter and Radelet (1999, p. 536) stated, "Police agencies today, taken generally, are doing a better job than was the case ten or fifteen years ago in the statistics and records of citizen complaints. Computers have helped. So have community pressures." The authors also suggested that despite the positive changes, "the attitude of the police about complaints is still in large measure defensive" (p. 356), which they attribute in part to human nature and to the threat inherent in any complaint. Police departments must overcome the historical difficulties of letting emotions interfere with complaint taking. Increasing the professionalism of the department, ensuring that all citizens are treated fairly, and building better police-community relations should be their primary intentions.

The basis for many department policies on use of force is the Federal Law Enforcement Training Center (FLETC) Use of Force Model. This model supports the "practice of *progressive* application of force," which implies the appropriate selection of force options in response to the level of compliance from the individual to be controlled (Graves & Connor, 1992, p. 56, emphasis in original). Still, this model relies on an officer's perception of the level of noncompliance by the individual, reinforcing the importance of selecting only psychologically stable, well-trained, educated, problem-solving individuals as police officers.

The subject is cooperating with the officer and responding to his or her verbal commands in level one of the model. In level two, the subject is passively resisting the officer's requests. The officer responds by increasing the level of force. Appropriate techniques in this level (contact controls) include the use of threats if the subject does not comply; no physical contact occurs at this level. In level three, the subject becomes defiant and actively resists the officer's requests/commands. The subject may retreat to his or her vehicle, walk away, or pull away from the officer if touched. The officer then responds with a "compliance technique" that is equal to, or slightly above, the force being used by the subject (e.g., wrist lock, arm lock). This enables the officer to gain control. Level four becomes more serious as the subject becomes physically assaultive and may cause injury to the officer. The officer will likely respond with some type of defensive tactic, which may include a baton, chemical spray, or take-down technique. In the final level (five), the subject is extremely assaultive, using a weapon in an attempt to cause serious bodily injury to the officer. At this point, deadly/lethal force may be used if the officer feels that his or her life is in imminent danger.

An officer must consider several issues prior to using deadly force against an individual. Three questions are important in such a situation: (1) Does the person have the *ability* to cause serious bodily harm or death? (2) Does the person have the *opportunity* to cause serious bodily harm or death? and (3) Has the person placed the officer or others in *jeopardy* of serious physical injury or death? An armed bank robber running from the scene of the crime does not meet these three standards; however, all three would be met and deadly force would be justified if the armed robber turned and pointed a gun at the officer.

Official policies on tactics and the use of force frequently refer to a "continuum of force." The basic principle behind the continuum perspective is the progressively increasing force in response to increasing levels of resistance from a suspect. The continuum perspective has training implications, as the National Institute of Justice (NIJ) in 1996 provided a basic force continuum, which is used as the foundation for many police departments' use of force policies (NIJ, 1996, p. 5).

Continuum of Force

Suspects	Police
0. No response	0. No response
1. Psychological intimidation	1. Police presence
2. Verbal noncompliance	2. Verbal commands
3. Passive resistance	3. Control and restraint
4. Defensive resistance	4. Chemical agents
5. Active aggression	5. Tactics and weapons
6. Firearms/Deadly force	6. Firearms/Deadly force

The mere presence of a uniformed officer can de-escalate and resolve the majority of potentially volatile police-citizens encounters. If the presence of the officer is not sufficient, the officer should proceed to the next level, dictated by the actions of the person with whom he or she is interacting. For example, an officer will increase the level of force from a verbal command to touching the individual to assist compliance if the person refuses to place his or her hands behind their head when requested to do so. If, at this time, the person pulls away, the officer again increases the level of force to "soft hand controls," which facilitates suspect compliance. If the suspect continues to resist and strikes the officer, increased force is warranted to gain control of the individual.

Officer use of force may consist of the use of pepper spray, take-down methods, or a strike behind the knee with an ASP baton. If an officer is faced with a life-threatening situation, the force level may reach the ultimate level, which is deadly force. Although each of these are legitimate uses of force by the officer, citizens may perceive them as unacceptable. Because perceptions vary, it is important to educate the public on the proper use of force by officers as well as the type of situations they must encounter on a daily basis. Citizen police academies are one way to educate the public on policing.

Citizen police academies can help bridge the gap that exists between the police and public, giving citizens a better understanding of the hows and whys of police behavior. They also assist in promoting the philosophy of community policing by involving the citizens in the police process. Citizens are able to interact with officers in an environment free from the intensity of the street, and officers are trained to deal with citizens with less suspicion, which, in turn, provides an opportunity to develop a more positive relationship. The recruitment and selection of officers who are able to communicate and interact with citizens is also a vital element in operationalizing the community policing philosophy.

RECRUITMENT, SELECTION, AND TRAINING

One of the most critical steps in controlling and preventing police violence and promoting the community policing philosophy is what I call RST (recruitment, selection, and training). Researchers have been trying to predict and understand the characteristics of officers who are likely to use force, particularly excessive force. Grant and Grant (1995) stated that no studies effectively assess the link between screening mechanisms and the use or misuse of force. Nonetheless, improper recruitment and selection of officers can create an environment of distrust between the officer and the citizen and may result in increased use of force. Candidates who are overly aggressive and have difficulty interacting with the public are usually passed over, but a department desperate to fill a position may overlook such tendencies thinking they can "train out" personality problems.

The New York State Commission on Criminal Justice and the Use of Force (1987) reported that the early identification of violence-prone individuals is difficult. Recognizing and isolating violence-related characteristics is problematic, and using psychological tests to predict violent behavior is challenging. Perhaps the best method may be examining past violent behavior by conducting a thorough background check.

One particular personnel issue that deserves significant attention with regard to the relationship between community policing and violence involves the historical practice of police departments granting preference to individuals with military experience. There are inherent problems with this practice. First, the military emphasizes armed control of situations. Training methods emphasize combat rather than service. These individuals may have a perception of policing based only on their military experience. Second, female candidates will often be overlooked by focusing on hiring those with military experience. Although more and more women are joining the military, men still outnumber them.

Recruitment and Selection

Proper recruitment is essential for effective policing. Selection of appropriate candidates is equally vital. The police officer selection process is lengthy, which, it is hoped, ensures that the best candidates are chosen. Departments should target candidates without personality issues that will negatively affect their performance on the street. Individuals with ego control problems, who maintain an authoritative personality and need to have power and control over others, do not belong in a uniform. If these individuals are given a badge and a gun, instances of unethical police violence will continue.

Instead of recruiting and selecting individuals with a military background, selecting individuals who are college educated helps bring a variety of positive attributes to policing. Carter and Sapp (1992) are among those who see the need for better-educated officers in accordance with the emergence of community-oriented policing and problem solving. College should prepare individuals to think critically and assist them in developing problem-solving skills, which are vital to today's police officer. Beyond this, college-educated officers are, arguably, better prepared to deal with diversity issues and are generally better communicators than those who did not attend college. Glensor, Peak, and Gaines (1999) suggested that the knowledge and skills required of officers to be effective decision makers, service providers, communicators, and problem solvers makes college education even more important.

Carter, Sapp, and Stevens (1992) have argued that one of the fundamental questions that has risen from the discussion on higher education for police is does college education make a better police officer? The authors believe that the research indicates that officers with a college education are less authoritarian and cynical. In addition, it appears that a college education makes an officer a more effective decision maker, a better service provider, a better communicator, and more responsive to the police mission.

Furthermore, given the emerging area of community policing, police departments may find themselves under pressure to provide greater services to the public. So the issue of college education becomes even more critical as the knowledge and skills officers may need appear to be tailored specifically to a college education.

They also suggested, however, that educated officers are more likely to leave police work and have a tendency to question orders and request reassignments with greater frequency (Carter et al., 1989). In accordance with these findings, earlier research by O'Rourke had found that

1. Many good officers do not have degrees.
2. Many poor officers do have degrees.
3. Degree requirements will negatively affect minority recruitment.
4. Degreed officers will become bored with the job.
5. Degreed officers will expect special treatment.
6. College-educated officers cause animosity within the ranks.
7. Officers without college can develop necessary people skills through in-service and on-the-job training.
8. Police departments cannot competitively recruit college graduates. (1971, p. 12)

One major concern with O'Rourke's study concerns the time period in which it was conducted. Policing has changed considerably since that time, and more departments require at least some college before officers can apply. Although it is true that many good officers do not have degrees, my opinion is that the best officers are those who have a combination of experience and education. Part of the problem with police violence, I believe, is the age at which individuals begin their police careers. Most departments set the minimum age for application at 21 years. In order to select more mature candidates, at least those who have more life experience, I would require a minimum age of 25 years. In my many years of policing and teaching, I know that some individuals are very mature at 21, but I still believe strongly that someone given the authority to take another's freedom, and possibly his or her life, must possess the knowledge and experience to make appropriate policing decisions.

O'Rourke also stated that college-educated officers will expect special treatment and may cause animosity in the ranks. This may have been true in the 1970s, but with an increasing number of individuals receiving their degrees, and more departments requiring degrees, these findings are no longer applicable. He also stated that officers without degrees can obtain the necessary skills to deal with people through in-service and on-the-job training. This may be true to an extent, but this type of training does not typically give the officer the opportunity to interact with a culturally diverse population as would likely be found in a college classroom. Also, I believe that the college classroom offers a better environment to develop problem-solving and critical thinking skills.

I do agree with O'Rourke's findings that degreed officers may become bored with the job and that police departments cannot competitively recruit degreed individuals. Unless an officer is satisfied with street patrol for a career, many may become frustrated and bored with the limited opportunities for advancement, especially in smaller departments. This is also true for officers who do not hold a degree.

Recruitment of degreed individuals is a real problem, even today. College students often list low salaries as a primary reason not to become a police officer. In personal research conducted at a midwestern university, a majority of the students listed poor pay as an important consideration in their career choice. Couple this with the working conditions of police officers, and many students did not find policing an attractive career choice.

In reviewing Carter et al.'s findings, it seems quite obvious that a college education is advantageous to officers. Some of the most important findings focused on interpersonal skills, ability to communicate, and responsiveness. These attributes serve as barriers to inappropriate use of force by police officers. Individuals who have the ability to communicate will be less likely to resort to use of physical force because they have confidence in their communication skills.

An officer may be a good communicator, or he or she may be an intimidator. An officer adopts his or her own operational style. Community policing emphasizes a style built on communication and relationship building, with the officer viewed more as a public servant than a soldier trained to do battle with the enemy. Several operational styles have been identified and are addressed in the following section.

Operational Style

A department that operates under a quasi-military style of management, and views its officers as soldiers rather than public servants, may be more likely to have its personnel engage in excessive force. The overall philosophy of this type of department may encourage an "us vs. them" mentality, which helps foster violence. Departments that emphasize strict military discipline over creative problem solving may also encourage a more aggressive response to community problems and, in turn, increase the chances of a violent reaction to those problems. Officers who are not encouraged to develop critical thinking skills may find themselves using physical force as their primary problem-solving tool. A militaristic attitude within a department typically does not promote critical thinking and problem solving on the part of its officers.

Broderick (1987) defined four operational styles of police officers: *enforcers, idealists, realists,* and *optimists.* Enforcers support the idea that their major function is to maintain order and keep society safe. They accomplish this by arresting criminals. Their focus is on law enforcement, and they tend to be cynical and dissatisfied with their jobs. Enforcers also stereotype people and are distrustful. Idealists are similar to enforcers. They are often cynical and believe that the community is against them. They believe that their primary role is to keep the peace and preserve social order while protecting the public. Realists are resentful and dissatisfied. They think that the goals and objectives of policing cannot be achieved. Realists focus on building relationships with other officers and strengthening loyalty among themselves. Finally, optimists see their role more as public servants. These officers are people-oriented, and their attitude negates much of the cynicism felt by the other three types (Dempsey, 1999).

It is interesting to note that none of these operational styles focuses on problem solving and community partnerships, although optimists come the closest. Operating under the first three styles may lead to aggressive police behavior because of the lack of trust perceived by these officers between themselves and the community.

Community policing focuses on quality-of-life issues and the needs of the people in the community. Officers who view their role as public servants and problem solvers may be less likely to respond to the community in a forceful, authoritative manner. Officers who have truly adopted the community policing philosophy will use their communication skills rather than physical force to resolve many situations. A "service" style may best represent the true community policing officer who relies on his or her ability to problem solve and communicate. He or she sees his or her role as community leader and helper, one who is a part of the community, rather than alienated from it. Service officers will help define policing for the new millennium and assist in reducing and preventing incidents of police violence.

Training

Kuykendall and Unsinger (1975, p. 275) identified three major objectives for a law enforcement training program: "to provide the newly hired peace officer with the basic skills necessary to successfully complete task assignments within the agency, to introduce the new officer into the work setting or environment, and to assist the officer in the further development of skills to meet a changing world and insure professional growth." It is imperative that police administrators and trainers keep these objectives in mind as they shape and guide the behaviors of officers.

Selecting individuals who already mirror the community policing philosophy simplifies the task of training. These officers already possess the basic skills that will enable them to successfully complete the tasks required from the department and the community. These officers will fit in much easier with a department that emphasizes community service and problem solving, so the task of training them to feel comfortable in their work setting is expedited.

Finally, these officers may be more responsive to the changing community and better able to adapt to the needs of a diverse citizenry. Professional growth will likely be more readily accepted and sought after because a college education is part of their background. Therefore, an officer who is selected because of his or her college education and problem-solving and critical thinking skills will likely expedite the entire "new officer socialization process." Those who do not possess these characteristics will likely extend the training process, thus slowing their ability to successfully function within the community.

Training that takes place within an academy setting, as well as in-service training, can influence the attitudes and behaviors of officers. Training that focuses on defensive tactics and firearms sends a certain message to the officers as does training that focuses on proactive, service activities and interpersonal communication. A balance between these topics will ensure that officers are fully prepared for the variety of situations they will encounter on the street (see Chapter 6 for a thorough discussion of the relationship between training and police violence).

Police officers must be trained in a wide range of subjects including the proper use of weapons, defensive tactics, and report writing. But too often these subjects are stressed at the expense of communication skills and problem solving. Without a clear balance between an enforcement mentality and one of service, officers may develop a deep mistrust of the people they serve.

It is important for an officer to constantly be aware of his or her surroundings as well as the people with whom he or she comes into contact. A person may become aggressive and present a threat to the officer at any moment. Officers must be able to deal with people in a civilized manner, however, while maintaining a healthy dose of suspicion.

Properly trained officers who have studied a balanced range of subjects will view the public differently than those whose training emphasizes combat and physical responses to varied situations. Balance is the key to developing skills in officers, skills that will meet the needs of the community they serve and better incorporate the community policing philosophy into their everyday encounters.

THE COMMUNITY POLICING PHILOSOPHY

Many misconceptions exist regarding the definition of community policing. Some police officers define it as a program to bridge the gap between the police and citizens they serve. Others see it as being "soft on crime" and think it should be placed in a special unit within the department, while others define it as a specialized program to improve public relations. It seems that each department and each officer have their own definitions of community policing, which ultimately creates confusion on the part of patrol officers.

Fortunately, there is agreement on the basic concepts, despite the many definitional issues that must be addressed. As such, community policing has been operationalized through many different programs. Robert Trojanowicz is considered by many to be the guiding force in defining and operationalizing community policing. Sadly, he passed away in 1994, but his legacy lives on. His definition of community policing gives a clear picture of what it is all about. Trojanowicz and Bucqueroux (1990, p. 7) wrote, "Community policing is a new philosophy of policing, based on the concept that police officers and private citizens working together in creative ways can help solve contemporary community problems related to crime, fear of crime, social and physical disorder, and neighborhood decay."

Community policing is also an organizational strategy designed to encourage participation by patrol officers in many management decisions that affect the way officers identify and assess issues encountered during their daily patrols. The key to understanding community policing is to view it as a *philosophy*. A philosophy is what guides officers—it is an attitude, a behavior, a way of looking at their job, but also a way of looking at those they serve. Instead of seeing citizens as the enemy and, as such, not to be trusted, citizens are viewed as "customers who should be shown a measure of respect and afforded a commitment to service" (Trojanowicz et al., 1998, p. 256). This orientation toward service offers officers alternatives to the militaristic and/or enforcement focus of traditional policing in which officers incited situations as opposed to defusing them.

Community policing is proactive, whereas traditional policing is more reactive. Community policing is concerned with issues that affect the quality of life in an area, such as physical and social decay. Probably one of the most important concerns of community policing is citizens' fear of crime. Fear of crime keeps many citizens behind locked doors. They may not feel safe in their community because this fear is their reality. Reported crime rates may be low, but residents will be less likely to venture outside and be more likely to have a negative perception of police officers if they perceive that the crime rate is high. Much of the fear can be dispelled by police officers walking through the community and making it a point to have positive interaction with residents.

Many citizens fear not only crime but also the police. Violent behavior as well as verbal abuse instills fear in citizens; trust levels are reduced, and the gap between police officer and citizen widens. Community policing can effectively deal with both of these issues through closer contact with the people being served.

To better understand the philosophy of community policing, Trojanowicz and Bucqueroux (1994) created the Nine P's of Community Policing. First and foremost, it is a **philosophy.** It is not a program or tactic, but an attitude that guides behavior; one might express it as a paradigm in which police officers operate. **Personalized** policing is the second "p." The police focus on establishing a more intimate relationship with the people served. Development of trust is a by-product of this intimacy. **Police** follows as the next "p." It must be stressed that community policing involves all the enforcement activities of traditional policing. Community police officers must arrest, write citations, and use force when necessary. Community policing *is* policing as most define it: enforcement and authority. **Patrol** is another important "p." It describes the types of activities in which community officers may engage. These activities include foot patrol, horse patrol, bike patrol, and so on, which differ from the traditional vehicular means of covering one's beat. The squad car has helped alienate the public from the police. These other types of patrol offer a way to build a more personalized relationship with the community by allowing closer contact with the public. **"Permanent"** stresses the idea that officers should be permanently assigned to an area in order to facilitate relationship building. **Place** is related to "permanent" as officers need the opportunity to become intimately familiar with the area they patrol. Relationships cannot be properly built if officers are rotated in and out of a particular beat at every shift change. Stability is essential.

Proactivity is vital to the community policing philosophy. Officers still react and respond to calls, but proactively try to prevent incidents from occurring in the first place. Officers are more aggressive when it comes to analyzing community concerns. Rather than merely react to a call for assistance, proactive officers move beyond a quick fix into problem solving. **Problem solving** is at the heart of community policing. It is one of the many reasons why the selection of appropriate personnel is essential. Community police officers must be problem solvers; they must be able to critically assess an area or situation and develop and act on solutions. Before I reveal the final "p," the significance of problem solving in relation to community policing dictates further discussion of the topic.

The SARA approach is one component of problem solving. SARA is an acronym for what has been termed problem-oriented policing. Scanning is the initial examination of the problem. Analysis takes the initial examination a step further by critically exploring the issue; for example, crime can be reduced by making a neighborhood safer, whether it be by installing more lighting in a poorly lit area or cleaning up trash in a vacant lot. **Re**-sponse involves working with various groups to assemble a plan of action to address the problem. **A**ssessment is the final component of SARA. This step requires a complete assessment of the response to determine if it has made an impact. SARA is not complete without the assessment phase for it provides the foundation for further responses to community concerns.

The final "p" in Trojanowicz and Bucqueroux's Nine P's of Community Policing is **partnership,** which ties all the "p's" together. Community policing cannot be successfully adopted if a partnership does not exist between the people and the police. Each has a role to play, and each role is important to the success of community policing. In a partnership, each partner has a say in how to deal with the issues; it is a matter of equity in the relationship. Some officers find it difficult to think in these terms; they do not like the idea of giving up their role as all-knowing leaders with all of the power and control. These types of officers may be more likely to resolve issues through the use of excessive force because they hold onto an "us vs. them" mentality.

VIOLENCE PREVENTION

How can incidents of police violence be prevented? There is no simple answer to this question. As Champion and Rush (1997, p. 355) suggested, "No amount of democratic policing can seemingly abate or divert violence, and to be sure, America is a violent country." Does this mean that we should not rely solely on the police to control violence, but instead purchase weapons and protect ourselves? It appears as if we are doing just that, as evidenced by the record number of firearms purchases during the early to mid-1990s (Champion & Rush, 1997). Understanding how, and if, arming oneself fits in with community policing is but one of the many challenges faced by police departments.

Those who are called to serve and protect must do just that. If citizens fear the police and lack trust, is there any hope of solving the problems, including police violence, that plague our communities? The key, I believe, lies in the community policing philosophy and the proper selection of quality personnel to serve as police officers. Understanding the community policing philosophy, and subsequently adopting and operationalizing it, can help ensure that police violence will not be tolerated.

The following suggestions are offered to assist in the reduction and prevention of police violence:

1. When recruitment is taking place, make certain that prospective candidates are aware that the department operates under the community policing philosophy. This will help eliminate the candidate who is seeking a power trip.
2. Make the community aware of the philosophy that drives the department, and enlist residents' support by involving them in crime prevention activities and quality-of-life issues.
3. Select only those candidates who have critical thinking and problem-solving skills. Candidates who have a college degree often bring with them these skills and abilities. College-educated officers have had the opportunity to interact with people of different cultures, making them better suited to patrol the streets of our

communities. These individuals are also better able to handle their discretionary power and have a variety of options to use in any given situation.

4. Select only those candidates who possess good communication skills, both written and verbal. Verbal communication, when properly used, can de-escalate many situations, resulting in less use of physical force. Police officer candidates who cannot express themselves verbally may likely resort to the use of physical force for lack of options.

5. Once candidates have been hired, continue to promote the community policing philosophy through in-service training. Incorporate the philosophy throughout the entire department; include the concepts in the patrol division, dispatch, and administration. Specialized units such as SWAT, Tactical Response Teams, and K-9 must also adopt and exhibit the philosophy in their duties. If each member of the department does not adopt the philosophy, its implementation will be hampered. Police academies must also incorporate the philosophy throughout their curriculum. The National Police Corps Program is attempting to do this and has established academies throughout the country that operate under the community policing philosophy.

6. Continue contact with residents and community leaders as this is vital to develop a sense of trust between the police and the community. Make the community more aware of the activities that involve the police. Establish civilian police academies that can help to educate residents regarding the situations that officers confront on a daily basis. These academies can make the citizen more aware of the dangers that officers face and the policies, procedures, and laws that must be a part of each decision made on the street. With a better view of police work, citizens can begin to understand policing at a much higher level than is portrayed on television.

To demonstrate the capability of community policing to reduce violence in society, consider riot prevention approaches. Riots and rumors go hand in hand. For example, Allport and Postman (1947) suggested that no riot ever happens without the assistance of rumor, and Lee and Humphrey (1967) described how rumor enters into the violence found in riots. Lee and Humphrey suggested that step one of riot development involves stories of the misbehavior or harmful acts of the hated out-group (e.g., street talk along the lines of "Six white officers put two Mexicans in the hospital because they couldn't speak English"). Step two involves the general rumor expanding into something larger, likely along the lines of some retaliatory act (e.g., "Something bad is going to happen to the cops on Main Street tonight"). The final stage involves the actual riotous behavior, with rumors sustaining the excitement. How can community policing approaches nonviolently prevent a riot?

For starters, riots usually begin when a history of tension exists between groups, and it is difficult for a department to change public opinion once a reputation has developed. It is hoped that in a potential riot situation, community policing approaches would proactively address the tension, thus immediately reducing the likelihood of a riot. The situation could also be improved by effectively communicating with the public. Whether it is through the media, or simply spreading the word on the street as to what exactly happened, and how the issue will be addressed, the situation could likely be defused by informing everyone as to the facts of the case. Police administrators must remember the power of communication and should not wait until tensions flare, or a riot occurs, before they address the public.

Finally, departments could avoid such situations through properly recruiting, hiring, and training qualified officers who would abstain from harmful behavior. This could be done, however, with or without a community policing approach.

Community policing can have an impact on violence, particularly juvenile violence. "Breaking the cycle of violence" should be high on the priority list of any police department's agenda. Potter and Kappeler (1998) stated that many violent teens are violently victimized and/or subject to acts of violence on a fairly regular basis. As such, Trojanowicz et al. (1998, p. 239) recommended that police problem-solving efforts should attempt to identify "pockets of violence" and respond "through enforcement, education, and community action." They stated, "The police must help organize neighborhoods to help fight those elements which are directly and indirectly associated with violent acts" (p. 239). They suggested a violence prevention approach involving police departments offering recreational, civic, and cultural opportunities for youths in high-risk areas. In accordance with Hirschi's (1969) social control theory, such outlets may go a long way in deterring youths from becoming involved in delinquent, specifically violent, behavior.

Although the earlier example involving the potential of community policing efforts to prevent a violent riot demonstrates how the media can assist law enforcement in violence prevention, many criticize the media for negatively influencing viewers' behaviors (e.g., Levine, 1999; Murray, 1999), going so far as to suggest that the media should be censored (e.g., Kristol, 1995; Liebowitz, 1999). Specifically, Miller and Hess (1994, p. 36) suggested that

> The media emphasizes violence, constantly carrying news of murder, rape, and assault. It seems that if a movie or television program is to succeed, at least three or four people must meet a violent death or suffer some physical injury. The average cartoon that children watch contains more violence than most adults realize. Children learn that violence is acceptable and justified under some circumstances. . . . Citizens expect the police to prevent (societal) violence, but the police cannot do it alone. Individuals must come together to help stop violence and in so doing can build a sense of community.

Of significant importance to community policing is public perception of crime and the effectiveness of crime-fighting efforts by police departments.

The onus is on police departments to work closely with local media to help ensure that crime prevention and crime-fighting efforts are adequately portrayed, but police unions (if they so choose) may want to work with media outlets at the national level. For example, Kappeler, Blumberg, and Potter (1996) argued that sensationalized law enforcement shows and violent and bizarre crime news reports contribute to the public's perception, specifically their fear, of crime. In response, Trojanowicz et al. (1998, p. 125) suggested that

> Such reporting has a chilling effect on people's sense of security. Community policing dictates that the police appeal to the news media for more balanced reporting and that the police participate more carefully in media productions. Although crime news is extremely popular, the police should attempt to have the media include more human interest stories about the

police and the community. These types of stories may foster a greater sense of security and help reduce the fear of crime.

Police administrators may counter the media's potential claim of the First Amendment right to freedom of speech through, among other things, appropriately approaching the media with sound evidence regarding how their participation and cooperation will help reduce violence in society.

Addressing media violence will have a large impact on preventing violence, particularly among young children. Along those lines, a strong community policing approach would entail ensuring that children are not perpetrators, witnesses, or victims of violence at school. Several unfortunate incidents of school-related violence (e.g., Columbine, not to mention the tragic deaths occurring at a Fort Worth church) have shaken our communities, leading some to believe that children can no longer avoid violence. In addressing the issue of community policing and school violence, Kipper (1996) suggested that law enforcement officials and school administrators must recognize the "concept that the school is the community and the community is the school" (p. 26).

Trojanowicz et al. (1998) suggested that community policing officers (CPOs) should work with school officials to develop school programs to prevent drug use, crime, and violence. They believed that CPOs should be more involved in investigating school-related crimes, with greater cooperation between police departments and schools with regard to exchanging information. For the sake of a more effective fight against juvenile violence in schools, schools should discontinue their historical practice of internally handling serious incidents, while police departments should provide school systems with information on arrests of juveniles charged with serious offenses. Much work remains, despite the progress being made regarding the exchange of juvenile violence-related information between police agencies and schools. In summing up the situation, Kipper (1996, p. 31) suggested: "Law enforcement must proactively address the possibility of school crime and violence. By making the schools an integral part of our community policing objective, we will enhance our credibility within our cities and towns. The real winners, however, will be our children."

A primary concern regarding youth violence involves the relationship between gangs and violence. Dart (1992) is among the many who noted the seriousness of gang-related activity, particularly as it relates to violence, in suggesting, "Violence perpetrated by street gangs is a principal—if not major—social affliction affecting American communities today. In the last decade of the 20th century, gangs exist in virtually every community . . . in every metropolitan area" (p. 96; see Shelden, Tracy & Brown, 2001, for elaboration of gang-related violence, and Miller & Hess, 1998, Chapter 11, for elaboration of community policing and gangs). Although they may not attend school, youth gang members often recognize schools as part of their turf and use this outlet to recruit, assault, and intimidate students. As such, many departments have adopted gang enforcement and gang resistance programs. For example, the Los Angeles Police Department's GREAT (Gang Reporting Evaluation and Tracking) system helps officers keep tabs on gang activity; the Racine (Wisconsin) Police Department's Gang Crime Diversion Program (GCDP) and the Austin (Texas) Police Department's Citizens Helping Austin Neighborhood Gang Environment (CHANGE) program focus on providing alternatives to gang involvement. In discussing community policing and special populations, Trojanowicz et al. (1998) addressed the unique challenges gangs represent for law enforcement and communities, adding that the mere existence of gangs demonstrates the limitations of traditional law enforcement efforts. They suggested that "Community policing appears to be the only viable way to confront the gang problem. Even then, departments must develop comprehensive programs that cut across a variety of fronts" (p. 248).

Among other things, it is hoped that educating children regarding the impacts and effects of violence will help address the root of the problem, thus increasingly the likelihood that young children will avoid violence now and later in their lives.

CONCLUSION

Among other things, violence by and against police officers can be reduced with better-educated and more highly trained officers, proper recruitment and selection of officers, and the building of a trusting relationship between the police and the community. When citizens view the police as partners and vice versa, improvements can be made in the current state of police-community relations. Citizens who trust police officers are more willing to assist the police with crime prevention and crime control efforts, and they develop a sense of empowerment through positive interaction with the police.

Police violence is a problem that could be addressed through more proactive responses. One way to do this is through adoption of the community policing philosophy because it offers alternatives to dealing with problems above and beyond an aggressive show of force. As noted by Trojanowicz et al. (1998, p. 256), community policing "attempts to focus on real problems, whereas traditional policing generally attended to symptoms of problems." Selecting personnel who appreciate and support community policing is essential. College-educated officers are often better prepared to accept and practice the concepts of community policing. Today's police officer must be a problem solver and view each citizen as a partner.

Continued training and practical application of the principles of community policing make the philosophy become real for officers. Community policing offers a broader approach to dealing with the problems plaguing our communities by offering long-term solutions rather than short-term fixes. It offers police officers alternatives to dealing with the citizens and situations they encounter. Community policing helps ensure the selection of quality personnel who are concerned with community problems, not just law enforcement activities and "catching the bad guys." An impact can be made in reducing the occurrence of police violence through diligent prosecution of violent offenders; enhanced recruitment, selection, and training practices; and adopting the community policing philosophy. However, community policing works only if all officers within the department embrace the philosophy. As we have recently seen in departments around the country, it takes only one unethical officer to destroy years of efforts to establish positive police-community relations.

Investing in the community through addressing youth violence should be of great concern to any police department. The saying "Today's youth are tomorrow's future" takes on added significance when today's youth are faced with, and commit, acts of violence on an unfortunate and unacceptably regular basis. The media's role in violence prevention (as it affects both juveniles and adults) should also not be overlooked. Whereas some may discredit the impact of the media in shaping, influencing, and perpetuating violence, we have little to lose by more effectively structuring portrayal of crime and the police in all forms of media. Freedom of speech and individual rights must certainly receive due consideration, but it can be argued that freedom from violence is more important to our society.

The media, however, are not solely to blame for violence in our society. Innumerable factors contribute to violence. A violence prevention strategy that relies on police officers simply responding to violent acts and making arrests is short-sighted and ineffective. The following statement by Trojanowicz et al. (1998, p. 242), although specifically targeting juveniles, largely sums up the current state of community policing:

> Community policing substantially expands the police role regarding juveniles. In the past, the police merely monitored trouble areas and detained juveniles who committed criminal acts. Community policing requires that the police work with a variety of public and private agencies throughout the community identifying problems and developing solutions to them.

It will take a community effort to reduce violence and all forms of crime in our society. We all must contribute. Effectively adopting and implementing a community-oriented policing approach signifies an effort by police departments to shift away from traditional crime-fighting approaches, and demonstrates their willingness to make the effort to help bridge the gap. Now, we must ensure that these departments effectively make the transition to community policing and encourage the community to cooperate and participate.

REFERENCES

ALLPORT, G., & POSTMAN, L. (1947). *The psychology of rumor*. New York: Henry Holt.

ARTHUR, J., & CASE, C. (1994). Race, class and support for police use of force. *Crime, Law and Social Change, 2,* 167–182.

BLACK, D., & REISS, A. (1967). *Patterns of behavior in police and citizen transactions*. Field Surveys III, Studies in Crime and Law Enforcement in Major Metropolitan Areas (Vol. 2). Washington, DC: U.S. Government Printing Office.

BLUMBERG, M. (1997). Controlling police use of deadly force: Assessing two decades of progress. In R. Dunham & G. Alpert (Eds.), *Critical issues in policing: Contemporary readings* (3rd ed.). Prospect Heights, IL: Waveland Press.

BRODERICK, J. (1987). *Police in a time of change* (2nd ed.). Prospect Heights, IL: Waveland Press.

CARTER, D. (1984). Theoretical dimensions in the abuse of authority by police officers. *Police Studies, 7*(4), 224–236.

CARTER, D., & RADELET, L. (1999). *The police and the community* (6th ed.). Upper Saddle River, NJ: Prentice Hall.

CARTER, D., & SAPP, A. (1992). College education and policing: Coming of age. *FBI Law Enforcement Bulletin, 1:* 8–14.

CARTER, D., SAPP, A., & STEPHENS, D. (1989). *The state of police education: Policy direction for the 21st century*. Washington, DC: Police Executive Research Forum.

CHAMPION, D., & RUSH, G. (1997). *Policing in the community*. Upper Saddle River, NJ: Prentice Hall.

CHEH, M. (1995). Are lawsuits an answer to police brutality? In W. Geller & H. Toch (Eds.), *And justice for all: Understanding and controlling police abuse of force* (pp. 233–259). Washington DC: Police Executive Research Forum.

CONYERS, J. (1981, January/February). Police violence and riots. *The Black Scholar, 2–5.*

DART, R. (1992, October). Chicago's "flying squad" tackles street gangs. *The Police Chief, 96–104.*

DEMPSEY, J. (1999). *An introduction to policing* (2nd ed.). Belmont, CA: West/Wadsworth.

FRIDELL, L., & PATE, A. (1997). Use of force: A matter of control. In M. L. Dantzker (Ed.), *Contemporary policing: Personnel issues and trends* (pp. 217–256). Boston: Butterworth-Heinemann.

FRIEDRICHS, D. (1996). *Trusted criminals.* Belmont, CA: Wadsworth Publishing.

FYFE, J. (1987). *The Metro-Dade police/citizen violence reduction project.* An unpublished report submitted to the Metro-Dade Police Department by the Police Foundation.

GELLER, W., & KARALES, K. (1981). *Shootings of and by Chicago police.* Chicago: Chicago Law Enforcement Study.

GILLIGAN, J. (1992). *Violence: Our deadly epidemic and its causes.* New York: Putnam.

GLENSOR, R., PEAK, K., & GAINES, L. (1999). *Police supervision.* Boston: McGraw-Hill.

GRANT, J., & GRANT, J. (1995). Officer selection and the prevention of abuse of force. In W. Geller & H. Toch (Eds.), *And justice for all: Understanding and controlling police abuse of force* (pp. 151–162). Washington, DC: Police Executive Research Forum.

GRAVES, F., & CONNOR, G. (1992). The FLETC use of force model. *The Police Chief, 59,* 56–58.

HIRSCHI, T. (1969). *Causes of delinquency.* Berkeley: University of California Press.

KANIA, R., & MACKEY, W. (1977). Police violence as a function of community characteristics. *Criminology, 15*(1), 27–48.

KAPPELER, V., BLUMBERG, M., & POTTER, G. (1996). *The mythology of crime and criminal justice* (2nd ed.). Prospect Heights, IL: Waveland Press.

KIPPER, B. (1996, June). Law enforcement's role in addressing school violence. *The Police Chief,* 26–31.

KLOCKARS, C. (1980). The Dirty Harry problem. *Annals of the American Academy or Political and Social Science, 452,* 33.

KRISTOL, I. (1995). Media violence should be censored. In C. Wekesser (Ed.), *Violence in the media: Current controversies* (pp. 53–56). San Diego, CA: Greenhaven Press.

KUYKENDALL, J., & UNSINGER, P. (1975). *Community police administration.* Chicago: Nelson-Hall.

LEE, A., & HUMPHREY, N. (1967). *Race riot.* New York: Octagon Books.

LEVINE, M. (1999). Media violence harms children. In W. Dudley (Ed.), *Media violence: Opposing viewpoints* (pp. 28–36). San Diego, CA: Greenhaven Press.

LIEBOWITZ, H. (1999). Government regulations restricting media violence may be necessary. In W. Dudley (Ed.), *Media violence: Opposing viewpoints* (pp. 70–76). San Diego, CA: Greenhaven Press.

LYNCH, M., MICHALOWSKI, R., & GROVES, W. B. (2000). *The new primer in radical criminology: Critical perspectives on crime, power and identity* (3rd ed.). Monsey, NY: Criminal Justice Press.

MILLER, L., & HESS, K. (1994). *Community policing: Theory and practice.* St. Paul, MN: West.

MILLER, L. S., & HESS, K. M. (1998). *The police in the community: Strategies for the 21st Century* (2nd ed.). Belmont, CA: Wadsworth.

MURRAY, J. (1999). Studies have established that media causes violence. In W. Dudley (Ed.), *Media violence: Opposing viewpoints* (pp. 43–48). San Diego, CA: Greenhaven Press.

NATIONAL INSTITUTE OF JUSTICE. (1996, November). Understanding use of force by and against the police (Exhibit 3, p. 5). Washington, DC: Office of Justice Programs.

NEW YORK STATE COMMISSION ON CRIMINAL JUSTICE AND THE USE OF FORCE. (1987). Report to the governor (Volumes I–IV). New York: New York State.

O'ROURKE, W. J. (1971). Should all policemen be college trained? *The Police Chief, 38*(12), 36.

POTTER, G., & KAPPELER, V. (1998). *Constructing crime.* Prospect Heights, IL: Waveland Press.

RADELET, L., & CARTER, D. (1994). *The police and the community* (5th ed.). New York: Macmillan.

REIMAN, J. (2001). *The rich get richer and the poor get prison* (6th ed.). Needham Heights, MA: Allyn and Bacon.

SHELDEN, R., TRACY, S., & BROWN, W. (2001). *Youth gangs in American society* (2nd ed.). Belmont, CA: Wadsworth.

SKOLNICK, J. (1975). *Justice without trial: Law enforcement in a democratic society.* New York: Wiley.

SYKES, R. E., & CLARK, J. (1975). A theory of deference exchange in police-civilian encounters. *American Journal of Sociology, 81,* 584–606.

TOCH, H. (1995). The catalytic situation in the violence equation. *Journal of Applied Social Psychology, 15*(2), 105–123.

TROJANOWICZ, R., & BUCQUEROUX, B. (1990). *Community policing: A contemporary perspective.* Cincinnati, OH: Anderson.

TROJANOWICZ, R., & BUCQUEROUX, B. (1994). *Community policing: How to get started.* Cincinnati, OH: Anderson.

TROJANOWICZ, R., KAPPELER, V., GAINES, L., & BUCQUEROUX, B. (1998). *Community policing: A contemporary perspective* (2nd ed.). Cincinnati, OH: Anderson.

WESTLEY, W. (1970). *Violence and the police: A sociological study of law, custom, and morality.* Boston: MIT.

9

The International Dimensions of Violence and the Police

Richard H. Ward

❖

INTRODUCTION

Violence both by and against the police varies greatly among countries depending on a number of factors including history; geography; ethnic, racial, and religious differences, and philosophy regarding the role of police in social control. Whereas similarities among countries exist in events and situations that may provoke police brutality, the most significant determinate of police violence is the country's form of government. Police in totalitarian countries use torture and force virtually uncontrolled as a means of maintaining a government's power. This is not the case in a democracy.

It is more difficult to find a single determinate for the cause of violence against the police. In some countries, such as France and South Korea, a long history of social protest frequently takes the form of attacks against the police; in others, only specific issues or situations result in the police periodically being the target of violence.

Just as the United States developed many criminal justice traditions from English common law and from early versions of policing in England, other countries find that their law enforcement and social control strategies were adopted from the countries of which they were formerly colonies. Colonial powers such as England and France, as well as Spain and Portugal, were influential toward the end of the 18th century; Egypt, China, and Africa were also powerful historically.

Studying history and developing a better understanding of other cultures reveals that violence by and against the police is not a new phenomenon. For example, a description of police conduct in Dublin, Ireland, in 1881 is not altogether different from reports of police brutality in many countries around the world today:

> The police drew their batons, and the scene, which followed beggars description. Charging headlong into the people, the constables struck right and left, and men and women fell under their blows. No quarter was given. The roadway was strewn with the bodies of the people. . . . All was confusion, and naught could be seen but the police mercilessly *batoning* people. (O'Connor, 1889, p. 469)

Violence by police and attacks on police continue to be widespread; both are causes for serious concern. In trying to identify the root causes of violence by law enforcement officers, the political structure of the country and the organization of the police must be considered. In its 1999 annual report, Amnesty International found human rights violations in at least 147 countries, many of which involve police and security forces (Chan, 2000). Human Rights Watch reported in 1997:

> Human Rights Watch's experience throughout the Americas and in other areas of the world has demonstrated that police violence is not an inevitable response to criminality. Nor is it irrevocably linked to poverty or unequal wealth distribution. Without doubt, poverty and social injustice are important factors that help explain the context in which police violence arises, but cannot alone explain significant differences in the incidence of police abuse, not only among nations, but also among the political subdivisions within given nations. (Human Rights Watch/Americas, 1997, p. 13)

A totalitarian country has, at least theoretically, one form of government and one philosophical approach, whereas a democratic country or republic has many political influences and differences of opinion among politicians, who serve by ballot rather than by the point of a gun. Although the police forces from each form of government may be similar, the philosophies differ. In England, for example, police officers do not generally carry firearms and their philosophy is that the police serve the public and that individual rights are important. Police in China do not carry firearms, either, but their philosophy is that the police serve the masses and that the individual is less important than the community as a whole.

A centralized police service emphasizes commonality in approaching the public, and the police view their job as being the same everywhere. In a decentralized system, policing is more likely to differ by region, whether it is a city or a town. Local control may take many forms, and police discretion may vary significantly. James Q. Wilson, in his book *Varieties of Police Behavior* (1968), and Jerome Skolnick, in *Justice Without Trial* (1966), identified different styles of policing in the 1960s and the different role that police play in various jurisdictions in handling similar cases in different ways. Through comparative research, many differences emerge about police forces around the world; some of the most disturbing concern the issue of violence.

The proliferation of weapons in many countries has had an impact on all forms of violence. In response, some countries, such as England and Norway, are increasing the availability of firearms to police who were heretofore largely unarmed.

The policies of government toward the use of force account for many differences in violence by and against the police. Evidence of death squads (frequently consisting of off-duty officers), "ethnic cleansing" units, and other types of violence-prone paramilitary police organizations is nonexistent in Western society. These types of organizations are more likely to exist in military dictatorships and in repressive regimes or dictatorships.

Nevertheless, even in the United States, police use of force is not fully understood. One observer concluded, "The impact of differences in police organizations, including administrative policies, hiring, training, discipline, and use of technology, on excessive and illegal force is unknown. Research is needed in this area" (Adams, 1999, p. 11). In their groundbreaking work on deadly force, William A. Geller and Michael S. Scott (1992, p. 23) noted: "Perhaps the greatest pitfall in interpreting studies on the use of deadly force is attempting to compare data from different jurisdictions."

These observations are no less true when attempting to understand and compare violence by and against the police on the international level. In addition to the factors enumerated by Geller and Scott, socioeconomic and demographic characteristics as well as cultural and political differences in various countries must be taken into account.

COMPARISONS—POLICE OF THE WORLD

At first glance, one of the major differences among police agencies is the different uniforms officers wear, whether it is the high hat of the British bobby, the scarlet red shirts of the Canadian mounted police, the traditional plastic caps of the Spanish carabinieri, or the berets of the Egyptian police. But the differences do not stop there.

In focusing on violence, generalizations and stereotypes frequently contribute to misunderstanding. There are, for example, perceptions among many Americans that Northern Ireland is an extremely violent country, that the Middle East is unsafe and crime is rampant, and that human rights violations in China impact a large part of the population. Such perceptions are incorrect, as are the perceptions by citizens in these and other countries that violent crime in the United States is rampant and foreigners are unsafe in our major cities. Thus, it is important, when studying the phenomenon of violence, to realize that in most countries violence has little direct impact on the vast majority of the population. There are exceptions. Ethnic and religious violence in some countries has been widespread and is frequently carried out by the police or the military. In countries such as the former Yugoslavia, the Congo (formerly Zaire), and Guatemala, violence has been much more commonplace than in other countries.

In some countries, such as Colombia, Sri Lanka, and Iraq, the government supports dissident groups covertly; police often initiate the violence and government officials are behind the attacks. Two of the most notorious examples occurred in South Africa during apartheid and in Guatemala, where thousands of suspected dissidents were murdered and buried in unmarked graves.

The police departments of some countries have reputations for violence, but it is often difficult to measure or discern not only levels of violence but also the extent to which a culture of violence exists within the police department. Assuming that the organization and philosophy of a police department has a strong impact on violence, the following descriptive analysis illustrates the causative factors of violence by police.

Although it is generally assumed that there is less violence by the police in developed countries, a report by Amnesty International found that human rights violations and police brutality existed in 27 of 34 countries surveyed in Europe and Central Asia. According to Brian Phillips of Amnesty International, "Police brutality and impunity is a situation one finds across the board in Europe." The report also noted that there were 65 deaths in police custody in 1998, and a "disproportionate number [were] from ethnic minorities" (Lawless, 2000).

It is difficult to develop cross-national comparisons of statistical data. In his research on cross-national crime, Jerome L. Napolitan (1997, pp. 23–25) pointed out that police may underreport or overreport certain crimes because of the influence of political pressure, differing legal systems and definitions, and the willingness or unwillingness of the public to report crime. There are also many differences in crime statistics between developed and developing countries. This is especially true when trying to understand police use of force and brutality data.

Figure 9–1 illustrates variables associated with police violence. In a totalitarian regime the police are likely to have minimum restraints regarding the use of force, and citizens generally are reluctant to protest police behavior. In a democratic society there may be varying degrees of acceptance of the use of force by police, but it is less likely that organizational violence or violence by a large number of officers will go undetected for any length of time.[1] In transitional governments—which include governments under siege because of a large separatist movement, terrorism, organized criminal activity, or other destabilizing influences—police activities may vary.[2]

A Typology of Police Violence Internationally

Form of Government

Totalitarian
Democratic
Transitional

Organizational Behavior

Individual
Group
Force

Determinant Variables

Political crisis
Minority focus
Crime-related
Incident-motivated (e.g. demonstration)
Citizen-compounded (e.g. dispute, drunk)
Psychological dysfunction
Fear factor
Errors and mistakes

FIGURE 9–1

Organizational behavior is defined here as acts by individual officers, acts by a relatively small group of officers, and acts by entire police forces in which certain levels of violence or excessive force may be commonly accepted.

Determinant variables seek to explain what might prompt the use of force. During a political crisis, especially when police are viewed as solely responsible to the government, the use of force to contain opponents is more likely to be accepted. This will be influenced by the actions of the opposition, who may be using violence to provoke the police. Excessive force against minorities, ethnic groups, or immigrants is perhaps one of the most common examples of what some view as acceptable force.

Crime-related actions are based either on the use of force against suspects in particularly heinous crimes, to gain a confession or punish an offender, or on a growing crime problem that fosters public acceptance of excessive force by the police. Incident-motivated violence is generally related to police activity at demonstrations, labor strikes, or other large-scale threatening situations. Citizen-motivated excessive force is likely to occur when an officer is threatened, provoked, or assaulted. In many cases this is likely to be a situational response. Psychological dysfunction refers to those officers who are by nature brutal or sadistic and who use force as a form of gratification or enjoyment. The fear factor refers to officers acting out of fear, and errors or mistakes are simple misjudgments on the part of the police.

Using such a model, it is possible to generalize regarding the types of violence likely to be most common in different countries. A numerical or statistical comparison must also consider the demographics of the country. Although it would be gratifying to say that police brutality does not exist in a country, some form of police brutality is present everywhere; no excessive force is a goal, not a reality. It is unlikely that police will ever reach a point in which the use of force is never necessary to maintain social order. The point at which it becomes excessive is the fulcrum that divides brutality and the acceptable use of force. History, as well as current events, indicates that many countries are moving away from the indiscriminate use of force. This is certainly true in the United States with respect to the use of deadly force.

The size and organization of a police force within a country may have an impact on violence and the police. Jurisdictions may differ significantly in the way they handle violent threats and the use of force. The United States, for example, has a police service that is much more autonomous than the police forces of the vast majority of other countries. The average size of a police force in the United States was 36.7 police officers in 1989. Canada had the next smallest force in size with an average of 114 police officers. This compares with India where the average size of a force is 40,506. In Great Britain, excluding London, where police forces were consolidated in the 1960s, the average size is 2,349 (*Police and Constabulary Almanac*, 2000, p. 515). Further comparisons of national figures show variations in where police are concentrated in a country. As Bayley (1994, p. 37) noted, "Very large cities, as one would expect, have the heaviest concentrations. New York City had 282 persons per officer in 1990, Tokyo 289, London 256, and Montreal 216."

Who the police report to, whether it be to the central government or to a smaller jurisdiction, is likely to impact the way in which social control is exercised, as well as the feelings of a particular community toward the police. Little data exist, however, to support the notion that the size of a force is directly related to violence if the ratio of officers to population served is considered.

VIOLENCE AGAINST THE POLICE

The use of violence against the police is, in some ways, correlated with actions of the police in using excessive and deadly force. Among the common conditions that contribute to violence against the police are:

- Violent demonstrations and riots
- High crime rates in which violence is common
- Ethnic, religious, or racial conflict
- Drug-related crime
- Retaliation against the police for perceived wrongs
- Widespread availability of firearms
- Policing alcohol-related activities

Student riots in South Korea and demonstrations in France have been characterized by attacks on the police. Firebombs and Molotov cocktails have been used frequently in South Korea in demonstrations. Throughout the world, one of the most common settings for violence is a demonstration as tempers run high. Soccer (or football) violence in Europe has become so highly organized that European police services maintain databanks on potential suspects. Groups and individuals travel from one country to another, intent on violence. They are often armed with knives, clubs, and other weapons designed to maim or kill.

In those countries where crime rates are high, the use of force against the police is not uncommon. In the Philippines, bank robbers armed with automatic weapons have killed or wounded numerous police officers. A similar situation exists in South Africa.

During the height of conflict in Northern Ireland, police were frequently the targets of violent attacks. In some instances, new recruits to the Provisional Irish Republican Army (PIRA) were expected to kill a police officer as a form of initiation into the group.[3]

In Brazil, the proliferation of drug-related crime and turf wars between gangs in Rio de Janeiro has become a serious problem. Human Rights Watch has observed, "Confrontations between the police and drug traffickers [predominantly in the shantytowns] have often been marked by indiscriminate shootings" (Human Rights Watch/Americas, 1997, p. 33). The result has sometimes been the killing of innocent bystanders.

In Colombia, police are often singled out by drug cartels for being too aggressive, or unwilling to accept bribes to look the other way. Either the police or their families are warned that failure to cooperate may result in retaliation.

The widespread availability of firearms in many countries has increased the likelihood of violence against the police. Well-organized terrorist groups frequently cooperate with rogue countries that supply them weapons. In the 1980s, Libya supplied weapons and explosives to the Provisional Irish Republican Army (PIRA) (Taylor, 1997, p. 335). The Palestinian Liberation Organization (PLO) received support from India's government, as well as from numerous other groups (Mulgrew, 1988, p. 203). At the same time the Indian government was a main source of weapons and training to the Tamil movement in Sri Lanka. The list goes on, and the outcome continues to be the use of readily available weapons to attack police.

A REGIONAL ANALYSIS

A complete analysis of violence by and against police on the international level is beyond the scope of this chapter. The annual reports on human rights by Human Rights Watch, Amnesty International, and the U.S. State Department provide a more complete review of the phenomenon of violence. The following material provides a broad spectrum analysis, using representative countries as a means of examining the police and violence in a global context. The United States is not included in this chapter because it is covered elsewhere in this text.

The Americas

The Canadian police service consists of a number of independent police forces in the larger towns and cities, and a national force, the Royal Canadian Mounted Police (RCMP), that has a long tradition of service to the community. With the exceptions of Quebec, where a French Canadian separatist movement has fostered demonstrations, and of numerous complaints by Indians (i.e., native Canadians) of excessive force, the Canadian police maintain a close relationship with the public. Individual allegations of police brutality have been rare. The alleged beating of a homeless man in 1999 by two officers, and an alleged cover-up of another brutality complaint by high-ranking officers, however, sparked a protest by a civil rights group that resulted in more than 100 arrests ("Chief Launches Probe," 1999; Boshra and Van Praet, 2000).

Many of the countries in Latin and South America have long histories of violence, as Amnesty International's (1999d) report noted:

> Torture, ill treatment and murder by police and security forces, and armed groups acting with their support and acquiescence, continued to be rife in the region. Such violations were reported in Argentina, Belize, Bolivia, Chile, Colombia, Dominican Republic, Ecuador, El Salvador, Guatemala, Guyana, Haiti, Honduras, Jamaica, Mexico, Paraguay and Venezuela.

This report also addressed the deaths of hundreds of people killed in Brazil by police and death squads with close ties to government-supported security forces. The Brazilian police service has had a long history of violence against the civilian population. Of particular concern are so-called "specialized military police."[4] A study of police brutality by Human Rights Watch/Americas between December 1995 and March 1997 found large differences in the rates of police killings between Rio de Janeiro and Sao Paulo. The report attributed these differences to the individual policies of the police in each of these cities. The report was critical of a policy in Rio de Janeiro that offered "bravery promotions or pay bonuses" to officers involved in shootings, many of which may be questionable. Between 1995 and February 1996 military police killed an estimated 201 people in Rio de Janeiro, and "examination of the police and coroner's reports in many of these cases suggest that rather than shoot-outs, these are cases of summary executions" (Human Rights Watch/Americas, 1997, p. 15).

The election of President Vincente Fox in Mexico in 2000 marked the first major change in the Mexican government in 71 years. Mexico's background of police brutality includes torture, death, and violence associated with corruption and drug trafficking. One of the major themes of Fox's platform was an overhaul of law enforcement. Observers of police in Mexico, however, cautioned that a strong civil service system and organized crime's control of many local police forces would make this a difficult task. Police in Mexico have been accused of murder, torture, forceful shakedowns (extortion), and a broad range of economic crimes, many associated with drug trafficking.

In Colombia the ongoing conflict between the drug cartels and the government has resulted in the deaths of numerous civilians, as well as police and drug runners. As many as 1,000 civilians have lost their lives in recent years, many of them tortured by police prior to their deaths (Amnesty International, 1999d).

The use of excessive force has been attributed to many factors. In Brazil, four categories of excessive force by police were identified by Human Rights Watch (1997, pp. 16–17), with a fifth category referring to the "disappearance" of individuals known to be in police custody. The four categories are

1. Police use of deadly force in raids on shantytowns
2. Individual instances that suggest inappropriate use of deadly force
3. Extrajudicial executions in crime-related actions that do not appear to justify the use of deadly force
4. Off-duty vendettas or provocation-related incidents (Human Rights Watch/Americas, 1997, pp. 16–17).

Observers of policing in Brazil note that police violence is endemic and has a long history. Obi Ebbe (2000, p. 19) pointed out that "The middle and ruling classes have established uses of force as a means to subordinate the poor." Many of the violent deaths in Brazil have been committed by death squads, vigilantes, and so-called "extermination groups." At least one estimate indicates that in the early 1990s about 200 of these types of groups roamed Brazil (Brooke, 1992).

Add to these categories the violence associated with drug activities, and we find many similarities in police actions to the rest of South America. Closely associated with these forms of violence is the use of torture in criminal investigations. Few countries in South America have access to sophisticated investigative technology, and training is lacking; therefore, the police frequently resort to torture and intimidation to gain confessions.

Western Europe

The police services of Western Europe have developed well-trained law enforcement officials out of strong democratic systems. Nevertheless, issues of excessive force continue to plague the police in many European countries. The police of England, however, have a generally favorable reputation when it comes to complaints of excessive force or brutality. Because the average police constable in England does not carry a firearm, complaints against the police regarding questionable shootings have usually been limited to the actions of specialized units.

Organizationally, the police service in England consists of 43 separate police units, referred to as constabularies; the Metropolitan Police Department, the largest force with about 26,300 police personnel; and the City of London Police Force, a relatively small force operating mainly in the business district. Each of the constabularies has some degree of autonomy from the central government, but the Home Secretary sets a number of policies that impact all forces. These include training standards, salary, and conditions of employment.

English police are well trained and new recruits complete a 24-month program at a regional academy. Although firearms are not common, about 10% of officers are trained in the use of handguns, and an increasing number of investigators and officers on patrol are now armed. Senior officers at different ranks attend various courses at the Police College at Bramshill.

English police are usually drawn from the middle class, most are white, and few have college degrees. The concept of higher education for police is relatively new in England. There is no lateral entry in the police service, and senior officers must make their way through the ranks. Chief constables and the commissioners of the Metropolitan Police Department and the City of London Police Force are selected by review boards, which include representatives of the community that they will serve. Traditionally, the English police have had a close relationship with the public. In the early 1800s concerns arose about the use of excessive force to exert confessions and thus use of excessive force was prohibited:

> Whenever a person is brought to the station on a charge of felony, the Inspector or other officer on duty, will not on any account suffer any statement in the nature of a confession, to be extracted from the person charged, either by the Police Constables concerned in the case, or by any other person. (Metropolitan Police, 1837)

Following a number of incidents involving police brutality and allegations of excessive force in the early 1970s, the Metropolitan Police Commissioner, Sir Robert Mark, established a special unit known as A-10 to deal with citizen complaints. At least one historian described this as "perhaps the most important change at Scotland Yard for a century" (Critchley, 1978, p. 325).

Police conflict with minority groups from former British colonies, however, has increasingly engendered complaints about police treatment. A number of major incidents have recently occurred, resulting in mob violence and allegations of excessive force by the police. Also, soccer violence prompted the government to enact emergency laws in 2000 to restrict known offenders from attending local matches and traveling to matches abroad ("World Briefing," 2000, p. 5).

Research on the subject of police violence in England is sparse, and the ability to identify justifiable use of force versus unjustifiable force is difficult. One of the earlier efforts to study police brutality in England compared the number of citizen complaints over time with the number of officers. The author concluded that a 25% increase in complaints with a relatively stable force size required further examination. However, the author also found that the number of assaults recorded in the general population had also increased significantly. In fact, when these figures were compared with complaints against police for assault, the percentages were closely correlated (see Table 9–1) (Box, 1983, pp. 87–89).

Much of the violence against the police in England is committed by so-called "soccer hooligans" and, to a lesser degree, by participants in special-interest group demonstrations, such as animal rights groups. In addition, there appears to be a growing trend

TABLE 9–1 Increases in Recorded Indictable Assault, Wounding Offenses Compared with Increases in Recorded Complaints Against the Police for Assault, England and Wales, 1970–1980

Year	Assault Offenses Recorded	Percent +/- 1970 = 1,000	Rate/1,000 Adult Population	Percent +/- 1970 = 1,000	Assault Complaints Against Police	Percent +/- 1970 = 1,000	Rate/1,000 Police Officers	Percent +/- 1970 = 1,000
1970	39,266	100	1.26	100	1,093	100	1.2	100
1974	61,878	158	2.01	159	1,982	181	2.1	175
1977	80,609	205	2.59	205	2,888	264	2.9	242
1980	95,601	342	3.03	240	3,069	280	2.6	217

Source: Box, Steven. (1983). *Power, crime and mystification.* New York: Tavistock Publications, p. 89. Used with permission.

toward attacks on the police by drunks or angry citizens. In the Northumbria Constabulary in the city of Newcastle, the number of "brutality against police" attacks increased significantly during the first 5 months of 2000. On one beat with a large concentration of nightclubs, 49 attacks on police occurred. Since only 39 attacks occurred throughout the rest of the force, speculation is that the nightclubs materially affected the high number of attacks (Jones & Manson, 2000).

In contrast to the popular public support of the police in England, the Royal Ulster Constabulary (RUC) in Northern Ireland finds itself caught up in the long-standing political and religious struggle between Catholics and Protestants. For much of the earlier history of this conflict following separation of the island, the police were viewed as an arm of the British government. This has changed in the past decade as the police cracked down on militants of both sides. As the country moves slowly toward a peace accord, the police have become a major political issue, criticized by both sides.

Nevertheless, in recent years, complaints against the police have dropped. Citizen complaints to the Independent Commission for Police Complaints (2000) dropped from 5,545 in 1987–1988 to 4,222 in 1998–1999. Complaints of assault by police dropped from 2,119 to 1,778, and for unlawful arrest or detention from 504 to 224.

Critics would argue, though, that the issue is not so much the number of complaints, but rather the number that are substantiated. Very few of the complaints handled in 1998–1999 were substantiated (6), most were unsubstantiated (895), and a large number were withdrawn (274) or were incapable of being investigated (274). Fifty were informally resolved (Independent Commission for Police Complaints, 2000).[5]

Perhaps the number of deaths attributed to the police depicts a more accurate view of the police force in Northern Ireland. From 1990 to 1994, 20 deaths were attributed to the police. Between 1995 and 2000, there were five deaths involving police and none in 1999 (Royal Ulster Constabulary, 2000a).

For many years the police have been the target of radical extremists, and they have frequently been accused of overreacting. In many incidents they have. Although attacks on the police have increased over the 10-year period between 1990 and 1999, police deaths attributed to the security situation have declined. During the same period, the number of injuries to civilians, most of which did not involve the police, has fluctuated, while the number of civilian deaths has declined in the last 5 years (see Table 9–2).

The Northern Ireland situation is unique with regard to most Western countries, but it is illustrative of the dangers facing police in an area of civil strife, particularly when they are the focal point of violence by extremist groups. The danger is further compounded by the availability of firearms and other weaponry. In responding to violence, the police frequently draw on heavier firepower or weapons, and as noted earlier, may react more quickly than police in countries where public order is well established.

In contrast to the close relationship that generally exists between the police and the public in England, the French police are closely aligned with the government and are more likely to be tolerated than admired by citizens. In recent years the police have made strong efforts to develop a closer sense of cooperation with the public. A form of community policing was introduced in the 1990s, and training has placed greater emphasis on the prevention of excessive force. Furthermore, the French government has introduced new legislation to strengthen individual rights and handle complaints against the police.

TABLE 9–2   **Injuries and Deaths to Police and Civilians in Northern Ireland Due to Security Situation, 1990–1999**

Year	Injuries to the Police	Deaths of Police	Civilian Injuries	Civilian Deaths
1990	214	7	478	49
1991	139	5	570	75
1992	148	2	598	76
1993	147	3	824	70
1994	170	3	937	56
1995	370	1	554	8
1996	459	0	905	14
1997	357	3	730	17
1998[a]	384	1	1,094	53
1999	395	0	553	7

[a]1998 marked a series of bombings after voters in Northern Ireland and the Irish Republic approved a peace agreement between the British and Irish governments. The Omagh car bombing on August 15, 1998, killed 28 people and injured more than 330.

Source: Royal Ulster Constabulary (2000a, July 5). *Deaths due to the Northern Ireland security situation.* [Online] Available: http://www.ruc.police.uk/press/statistics/deaths2.htm. Royal Ulster Constabulary (2000b, July 5). *Injuries as a result of the Northern Ireland security situation: 1968–2000.* [Online] Available: http://www.ruc.police.uk/press/statistics/injury2.htm.

In January 1999, shortly after fatal shootings by police officers of unarmed civilians, a draft law was introduced to create the *Conseil supérieur de la déontologie et de la sécurité* (csds) to oversee the working and implementation of codes of practice governing the different police forces and the gendarmerie. The minister of justice presented a series of draft laws aimed at a radical overhaul of the justice system. These included measures to confer a greater degree of independence on public prosecutors and to reinforce the principle of presumption of innocence (Amnesty International, 1999b).

Many allegations of police use of excessive force in Europe are related to the increasing number of illegal immigrants who have moved from Eastern Europe and Asia, seeking refuge or better living conditions. In a number of incidents, police have been accused of handling demonstrations with excessive force, including widespread use of tear gas and water cannons.

In Germany, where a decentralized police system as well as a national police service exist, the police have had numerous confrontations with legal and illegal immigrants in many parts of the country. When the Berlin Wall came down in late 1989, unifying the country, Germany was faced with two markedly different cultural and political traditions that came into conflict. The rise of the neo-Nazi or skinhead movement in East Germany frequently made police the targets of violent demonstrators.

Continuing allegations of police brutality have been common in Spain, where a Council of Europe committee on antitorture alleged that the national police, the Civil Guard (*Guardia Civil*), and the autonomous Basque police commonly use excessive force against civilians. According to one news account, "The committee said it had reports of female detainees having been raped and others having had plastic bags put over their heads to suffocate them in 1997 and 1998" ("Spain Dismisses Accusations," 2000).

Eastern Europe

For more than half a century, Eastern Europe was dominated by the former Soviet Union, and many of the countries in this region retain characteristics of the Soviet police state. Russia itself is today facing an internal crisis with regard to the police. Corruption, violence, and a breakdown of the old social structure have contributed to an increased level of hostility between the police and the public.

Russia, faced with economic decline and the rise of organized crime, evinces a demoralized police service that has turned to various forms of extortion and the use of excessive force in dealing with a beleaguered public. The conflict with Chechnya has contributed to a series of terrorist attacks in Moscow and attacks on police at demonstrations. The police, or Militia (MVD), use torture to gain confessions, and the rapid turnover of Internal Affairs ministers has contributed to a lack of planning and direction. In many parts of the country, police are poorly paid, many waiting months for a paycheck. The result has frequently been chaos.

Any examination of police brutality on the global scene must include atrocities in the former Yugoslavia, where ethnic and religious violence has torn the region asunder. The conflicts in Bosnia, and more recently in Kosovo, illustrate the tremendous power of the police under authoritarian leadership. Crimes carried out by the Serbian police forces in Bosnia and Kosovo in the 1990s are well documented. But, it is important to note that vicious acts were committed by both sides in the Balkans, each more horrible than the last. Despite a United Nations (UN) tribunal and the indictment of numerous individuals for acts of cruelty almost beyond human imagination, there continue to be ongoing reports of violence by all sides, even, at times, by the UN peacekeepers.

A report by Amnesty International (1998, p. 43) regarding a "marked increase in police and military actions" concluded that as of February 28, 1998, hundreds of murders in Kosovo had occurred, and "many of these appear to have been extrajudicial executions." Among the reported activities on the part of the police were brutal beatings with truncheons; punching and kicking; electric shocks; rape; murder; assassination; hostage taking; and "disappearances" of citizens believed to be killed by the police. The report also cited numerous attacks by the Kosovo Liberation Army (KLA) against police and military targets (Amnesty International, 1998).

In many ways these examples of police brutality lie at the end of a spectrum of violence committed by authorities. Actions taken against large groups of civilians are not solely limited to Kosovo; they have become part of a trend associated with separatist movements in many countries under siege. Of particular relevance in such scenarios is the deep-seated hatred that frequently exists between ethnic and religious groups. The term "ethnic cleansing" has roots in many countries and may be compared with the "killing fields" of Cambodia and with ethnic and tribal strife in several African countries.

Africa

Political turmoil in numerous African countries has resulted in a series of atrocities carried out by police and military authorities in countries such as Rwanda, the Congo, Zimbabwe, Nigeria, and Uganda. In many respects, it is impossible to make a distinction between police and military units. For example, the Hutu militia primarily carried out widespread massacres in Rwanda. In the Congo, thousands of Hutu refugees who had fled there were systematically massacred by members of the AFDL (*Alliance des forces democratique pour la liberacion du Congo*) as well as by mercenaries and forces of other countries (Amnesty International, 1997). Although the subject of violence during conflict between armed groups is beyond the scope of this chapter, it is important to recognize that in such conflict the police are frequently involved as participants in support of the existing government. Caught in the middle are innocent civilians and, in the case of Africa, many refugees fleeing from violence.

One of the countries most notorious for the use of excessive force is South Africa. The apartheid period was one of the most publicized examples of outright criminal activity sponsored by the government and carried out by the police. Excesses ranged from murder of dissidents to the day-to-day use of force by the police. Caught in the middle were black police officers who were frequently beaten or killed by citizens (Thompson, 1990, p. 231).

In the 1980s the government of South Africa moved to suppress dissent and unrest and proclaimed a state of emergency. One account detailed life under martial law:

> To reestablish control of the black population, the government resorted to bannings, arrests, detentions, and treason trials. Police interrogators tortured victims, and unidentified persons who were widely believed to be members of the security police assassinated antiapartheid activists inside and outside South Africa. On February 12, 1987, Adtriaan Vlok, minister of law and order, admitted that 13,300 people, a high proportion of whom were children, had been detained under the emergency regulations; unofficial estimates ran as high as 29,000. On March 2, 1987, Vlok said that 43 people had died in police custody. (Thompson, 1990, p. 236)

With the end of apartheid and the election of Nelson Mandela, sweeping reforms were undertaken, and many government and police officials were subsequently found guilty of numerous criminal acts. In 1995 the new government of Nelson Mandela formed the Truth and Reconciliation Commission, which was charged with investigating crimes committed during apartheid by the previous government, the police, and other groups, such as the African National Congress (ANC). One of the unique aspects of the Commission was its ability to grant amnesty to individuals who had committed politically motivated crimes if they confessed to their actions.

Revelations of the Commission included a long list of violent acts committed by the police against citizens, many involving murder and torture. Critics of the Commission's activities focused on the granting of amnesty to numerous government and police officials who had admitted to killing dissidents ("Half Truth," 2000).

Today, violence in South Africa has turned mainly to gang killings and assaults on a beleaguered police force. Allegations that police may be part of terror campaigns, or may be afraid to take action against gangs, are abundant. In Cape Town, bomb attacks and murders have occurred as a result of strife between ethnic and racial gangs. In 1996 a group of Muslims, calling itself People Against Gangsterism and Drugs (PAGAD), began to take the law into their own hands, lynching and burning one gang leader to death. PAGAD has also allegedly been responsible for a number of attacks on the police, injuring seven officers in one bomb attack in 1999 ("Cops and Bombers," 2000).

A national force polices Nigeria, but despite reform efforts following 16 years of military rule, the country continues to be the subject of numerous police abuses. In addition to reports of disappearances, the 1999 U.S. State Department Report on Human Rights noted that "Army, police and security force officers regularly beat protesters, criminal suspects, detainees and convicted prisoners." According to the report, the government has taken steps to reduce police violence, however, and a number of senior officials have been dismissed or arrested (U.S. State Department, 2000, p. 2).

Despite reform, arrests in Nigeria continue to be an ongoing problem. In Lagos, police reportedly shot and killed at least seven persons during a riot in April 1999; in August 1999, police fired on a group of demonstrating college students, killing six. Police, military, and anticrime units have been accused of many extrajudicial killings while attempting to arrest criminals. There have been reports of deaths of suspects in police custody and numerous reports of excessive force by police attempting to extort money. There have also been reports of threats and the use of force against journalists by police—one journalist was allegedly beaten to secure a confession and letter of apology (U.S. State Department, 2000, pp. 4–10).

Middle East

Understanding violence in the Middle East, so frequently associated with terrorism, is complicated by many Americans' misperceptions of Arab culture and the Muslim religion. With the exception of the state of Israel, Muslims are in the majority throughout the Middle East. Within the region, conflicts contribute to some government-sponsored or dissident violence in Algeria, Iraq, Iran, and Yemen. In other countries, such as Egypt, Saudi Arabia, Lebanon, Tunisia, Bahrain, and Kuwait, the use of torture, brutality, and coercive force to control dissidents and gain confessions has been reported (Amnesty International, 1999e).

The Egyptian police structure is centralized, with the largest contingent of officers being stationed in Cairo. Perhaps the most significant difference between police in Egypt and in the United States is a clear distinction between officers (those at and above the rank of lieutenant) and subordinates. Officers receive training in the police academy for four years, but for lower ranks, the training is much less.

Although Egypt is predominantly a Muslim country, its legal system is generally secular and based on civil law, particularly as it relates to common crimes. In capital cases and investigations involving political dissidents, Egyptian police have historically been accused of using torture. In a recent case involving a murder investigation, the Egyptian Organization for Human Rights alleged that hundreds of citizens were arrested and tortured by the police in an effort to solve a double homicide ("Egyptian Copt," 2000).[6] Amnesty International reports:

In Egypt, torture of political prisoners continued to be systematic in the headquarters of the infamous State Security Investigations (SSI) headquarters in Cairo and branches throughout the country, as well as in police stations and sometimes in prisons. The most common methods of torture were electric shocks, beatings, suspension by the wrists or ankles and burning with cigarettes. There were also various forms of psychological torture, including death threats and threats of rape or sexual abuse of the detainee or female relatives. (Amnesty International, 1999a)

Israel, a small country with a population of almost six million, has a national police service that was formed in 1948 following the founding of the state. The Israel National Police (INP) is based on the English model, and, in addition to its responsibility for controlling crime and maintaining order, has responsibility for internal security. Since its independence, Israel has been threatened by most of the Arab states in the region, and terrorism has been an ongoing and consistent source of concern. Five police districts and 13 subdistricts report to a police commissioner. The border police and the Civil Guard, two nontraditional police units, have primary responsibility for internal security and the prevention of terrorism.

The Israeli police have had a notorious reputation for the way in which they handle Palestinian and other Arab citizens. In the 1980s the Israeli government, recognizing growing concern about police misconduct, and responding to media and external pressures, began to focus on the topic. In February 1993, police officials "admitted publicly that brutality was indeed a problem." At a press conference, a report entitled "The Police Force and Police Brutality" was released. The report documented 1,800 complaints of police misconduct involving 2,700 police officers in 1992. In 1992, responsibility for the investigation of citizen complaints was transferred from the police to the Department of Internal Investigations of the Ministry of Justice. The result was that "police officers accused of criminal offenses are prosecuted and tried in regular courts, whereas officers accused of non-criminal offenses have their cases heard in the Police Disciplinary Court" (Bensinger, 1998, pp. 45–46). According to Israel National Police statistics, police use of excessive force declined from 300 officers facing indictment in 1995 to 229 in 1997 (Ebbe, 2000).

Asia

The police, or public security officers, of the People's Republic of China (PRC) draw on a history of more than 50 years following the victory of Mao Tse-tung's forces against those of Chiang Kai-shek in 1949. Any understanding of police violence in China, though, must be traced back hundreds, even thousands, of years and take into consideration the unique cultural and historical experiences of the Chinese under despotic and conquering rulers. The use of torture and force by occupying forces is vividly illustrated by Japan's occupation of China prior to and during World War II, with perhaps the most savage example being the so-called "rape of Nanjing."

Following the repressive regime of the Kuomintang government under Chiang Kaishek, China underwent a series of government purges, carried out primarily by the police; it has been estimated that more than a million people were killed under the Mao government. Torture and brutality were common, culminating in the Cultural Revolution from 1966 to 1976 that severely crippled the country.

However, as Dutton (1992, p. 3) pointed out, "It must be made clear from the outset that policing in the classical sense [in China] did not rely solely on the coercive power of the state." He suggests that close family relationships and an intricate social control system in many ways fostered self-policing, concluding, "Indeed, given the severity of punishments meted out by successive governments once cases became 'public,' it is generally agreed by most scholars that families and communities would try to deal with recalcitrants internally rather than hand over authority to the harsh regime of the law" (Dutton, 1992, p. 3).

China's open-door policy, inaugurated by Deng Xiaoping in the late 1970s, following the visit of U.S. President Richard Nixon to Beijing, marked the beginning of a new era of reform. Of particular importance has been the establishment of a new body of criminal law and criminal procedures, along with new education and training models for police. But change has not come easily, and despite greater control of the police, serious examples of repression and violence by the public security forces continue.

Amnesty International's 1999(c) Human Rights Report illustrates some of the problems:

> Many cases of torture were reported by unofficial sources. Three men, Zhou Guiyi, Xiao Beizhou and Yu Li, were beaten to death by police in Hubei's Xinzhou County between April 1997 and February 1998. The families of the three men received compensation, but no action was taken to bring those responsible to justice. Abdul Helil, a Uighur detained in the xuar for leading a demonstration in Gulja in February 1997, was reportedly tortured after arrest to force him to confess to "crimes" and denounce friends. In mid-1998, he was reportedly held in the prison of the 4th Division of the Xinjiang Production and Construction Corps, a military-run institution, where he continued to be ill-treated. Zhu Shengwen, the Vice-Mayor of Harbin, Heilongjiang province, alleged he was tortured to force him to confess to corruption. He said he was punched, had his arms twisted and wrenched, and was repeatedly given electric shocks with an electric baton. In April he was sentenced to life imprisonment. No investigation into his allegation of torture was known to have been carried out. In October Li Jiayong, a member of the New Testament Church in Shandong province, reportedly died in police custody. The police reportedly claimed he had committed suicide by jumping out of a window, but private sources believed he had died as a result of torture. He had been detained and badly beaten twice before. There was no independent inquiry into his death.
>
> Local media also reported cases of torture and ill-treatment. In March [1998] a newspaper revealed that police in Guangdong province had kept a farmer chained inside a two-square-metre iron cage for five years as punishment for attacking an officer. The day after the newspaper report, the man was set free. The Guangdong authorities subsequently set up a commission to investigate the incident. In June, for the first time in China, an official publication published figures for the number of people who had been tortured to death in custody in previous years: 126 people had died in such circumstances in 1993 and 115 in 1994. (Amnesty International, 1999c)

Imagine a centralized police service with more than one million officers. The Ministry of Public Security in China oversees this massive operation that is based on centrally developed policies and a standardized training curriculum. The Public Security University in Beijing educates more than 4,000 young officers, many of whom will become future leaders in the larger departments, known as provincial or bureau organizations. Entry to the national university is competitive, and graduates of the 4-year program receive the equivalent of bachelor's degrees. Each of China's 34 provinces and regions also maintains one or more police academies, in which training is dictated by the type of assignment the officer will receive. These programs range from 2 to 4 years.

The majority of police are unarmed and responsible for traditional policing duties. The census police carry out one nontraditional duty: keeping track of citizens living in their areas of responsibility.[7]

Since the Cultural Revolution, the police have been actively developing programs designed to gain public confidence. However, the vast size and population of China presents unique problems that result in differences in various regions or cities with regard to the use of force. The police are agents of the government, and much of the criticism related to brutality is related to the suppression of dissidents. A case in point is police handling of a group known as Falun Gong, following a government pronouncement that the group is a political organization and not a "health improvement" group.[8]

Police in China have used violence against minorities in many of the autonomous regions such as Tibet. In some instances, the police use torture to conduct investigations or to obtain confessions. In predominantly Muslim regions that border Muslim countries, there have been ongoing acts of sabotage or terrorism; the police crackdown in these regions has been harsh.

In the 1990s China revised its criminal laws and criminal procedures, placing great emphasis on the rights of individuals who are suspects or who are in custody. Still, there is a great difference between what is written and what actually occurs on the street. Nevertheless, in certain cases, police officers have been charged with abuse of authority. For example, two Chinese police officers were found guilty of torturing a robbery suspect to death in an effort to secure a confession. The suspect was handcuffed to a water pipe for 3 days and was deprived of food and water. A court in Guizhou issued a suspended death sentence to one officer and life imprisonment to the other ("Man Dies," 2000).

The Criminal Procedure Law of China states:

> The people's courts, the people's procuratorates and the public security agencies shall safeguard the procedural rights to which participants in proceedings are entitled according to the law. . . . Participants in proceedings shall have the right to file charges against judicial, procuratorial and investigatory personnel whose acts infringe on their citizens' procedural rights or subject their persons to indignities. (Zhou, 1998, p. 3)

For a country of more than one billion people that is rapidly emerging from Third World status to that of a major global power, China has made significant strides in modernizing its police service. In this context, it is worthwhile to note that even in Hong Kong, which is viewed as having one of the most professional police services in Asia, examples of police violence are not unknown:

> In May [1998] four police officers were sentenced to between four and six months' imprisonment for torturing a suspect. The four were accused of attempting to force Yiu So-man to admit to possessing heroin by stuffing a shoe in his mouth, pouring water into his nose and ears until he fainted, and threatening to throw him off a balcony.

> In August [1998] a police officer with a history of mental health problems was convicted of manslaughter for shooting and killing detainee Chan Kwok-keung in Aberdeen police station

in 1997. Police pledged to enhance measures to identify unfit officers. Legislators argued that the implementation of long-delayed safeguards for detainees might have prevented the incident. (Amnesty International, 1999c)

The Hong Kong police force, which was under the command of a British governor until the colony was returned to China in 1997, displays many of the characteristics associated with police forces that developed under British colonialism. These police forces display a professional approach that is absent in neighboring countries and in countries that were colonized by more oppressive nations.

In Malaysia, a country made up of Muslims and ethnic Chinese, the police have generally had a reputation as a progressive, well-trained organization. Modeled on the British police service, Malaysia's police overcame earlier years of turbulence under the current leadership of Prime Minister Mahathir bin Mohamad (elected 1981). However, numerous allegations of brutality and torture followed the arrest of former deputy prime minister Anwar Ibrahim in April 1999.

A human rights group reported that it was investigating 132 complaints, most of them related to the Ibrahim arrest. The head of the human rights group said that most senior police officers "told him they believe in freedom of assembly and constitutional rights" ("Malaysian Rights," 2000). But there is often a problem with the practical difficulty of policing demonstrations, he added. In Malaysia, a group of three people is an illegal assembly if they refuse to follow police orders to disperse.

SOCIAL CONTROL AND THE POLICE

In attempting to understand violence by and against the police throughout the world, we must recognize several influences beyond historical development, culture, and training. One such influence is the form of government; significant distinctions exist between police agencies in democratic versus totalitarian countries. There are frequently major differences in how victims of excessive force are treated; minorities, political dissidents, and perpetrators of certain types of crime, such as rape, are likely to elicit different levels of violence by the police in different countries. In addition, the media, government, and watchdog groups play varying roles in scrutinizing police behavior.

Some of these variables are also present in various parts of the United States, particularly during periods of turmoil, such as the Vietnam War and civil rights eras. Police in different countries are faced with different social problems, varying public attitudes toward police and crime, and even significant threats to the government. Although there can be no justification for brutality or other forms of abuse, it is necessary to be aware of all these elements that form the basis for police behavior in order to combat police violence.

If a government is accepting or supportive of police violence, then it is unlikely that any intervention to reduce police violence will be successful. However, there is a significant distinction to be made between renegade or dysfunctional, violence-prone individual police officers and a climate of excessive force throughout an organization.

A comprehensive analysis of police-related violence in countries discussed earlier in this chapter, using the typology in Figure 9–1, offers some basis for comparison (see Table 9–3).

TABLE 9–3 Country Analysis—Levels of Police Violence

Form of Government	Canada	Colombia	England	France	No. Ireland	Russia	Yugoslavia	Egypt	Nigeria	Saudi Arabia	U.S.
Totalitarian											
Democratic											
Strong	X		X	X				X			X
Weak		X			X	X			X		
Transitional							X				
Hereditary—e.g., Kingdom										X	
ORGANIZATIONAL BEHAVIOR											
Individual	X		X	X	X	X	X	X	X		X
Group of officers		X			X	X	X	X	X	X	
Most of force		X				X	X	X	X		
DETERMINANT VARIABLES											
Political crisis	X		X		X	X	X	X		X	X
Minorities[a]	X	X	X	X	X		X			X	X
Crime-related	X	X				X			X	X	
Incident-motivated[b]	X		X	X	X			X	X	X	X
Citizen-motivated	X	X	X	X	X				X	X	X
Psychological dysfunction					X		X				
Fear factor	X	X			X	X	X	X			
Mistakes and Errors	X	X	X	X	X	X	X	X	X	X	X

[a]Includes immigrants

[b]Includes demonstrations and sports violence

Although the form of government and organizational factors are generally understood, a number of the determinant variables listed in Table 9–3 require further explanation. A determinant variable is the primary influence behind violence by police in a specific country. There will be overlapping variables that contribute to violence and, in some cases, more than one contributory factor. For example, political violence generally includes demonstrations or riots in which mobs or protesters attack police.

Minority-defined focus is discrimination against a particular group based on racial or ethnic differences. In such cases, there is likely to be systematic violence used by the police against members of these groups.

Crime-related violence means the use of violence by police to counter a crime wave or a particularly sensitive crime. Such violent activities may involve a large part of a police force as part of a strict enforcement policy, or small groups or individuals who are reacting to criminal activity. It may relate, for example, to gang activity or the murder of a police officer.

Incident-motivated violence usually occurs at demonstrations that get out of control. There is less likely to be a sustained policy against any single group. Excessive force may be a reaction to unlawful activities, such as rock or bottle throwing by some members of the protesting group. Sports violence falls into this category.

Citizen-motivated (or compound) violence is police overreaction to a physical assault by a citizen or group of citizens. The officer goes beyond the limits of reasonable force, and in some cases may actually retaliate against the offender in a harsh way.

Despite the increasing use of psychological testing and improved training, especially in Western and developed countries, individuals with pathological tendencies toward violence do become members of police forces. Psychological dysfunction refers to those individuals who enjoy being brutal, or who use force as a compensating mechanism for other deficiencies.

The fear factor in policing should not be overlooked in assessing the use of violence. Police encounter stress-producing situations, and their profession is laced with uncertainty. Some individuals may turn to the use of force unreasonably out of fear, or because they acted too quickly.

One of the most common instances of excessive force, particularly the use of deadly force, occurs when a police officer perceives a danger that does not exist. Often the officer believes that an individual is armed, but no weapon is later found. Unfortunately, such cases continue to be problems throughout the world, and police can make mistakes that result in serious injury or death.

CONCLUSIONS

Police violence is, unfortunately, common throughout the world, although more so in some countries than in others. The level and extent of police violence is influenced dramatically by political, geographical, and cultural differences. Violence ranges from the mistaken use of force to pathological torture or killing by individuals who are psychologically unsuited to police work. In between is a broad range of behavior that results in the use of force, in varying degrees and in differing situations. Of particular concern is violence against minority, ethnic, or religious groups, or against those who are protesting for one reason or another. When an officer crosses the line between the justifiable use of force and excessive force, he or she is committing a violent act. This also holds true for citizens who move from peaceful demonstrations or disagreements with the police to the use of force or violence against the police.

There is little doubt that police in a repressive regime—as opposed to a democracy—are more likely to use violence as a form of social control; there is no law except that of the police. However, violence by and against the police occurs all too frequently in developed and democratic countries as well. In such countries, a legal system should address such abuses. Regrettably, even in democratic countries, there may well be systematic use of violence, especially against racial or ethnic minorities.

It appears that police violence is less prevalent in countries whose populations are primarily homogeneous. Police violence in such countries tends to be more individualistic, based in some measure on situational incidents rather than innate hostility against a particular group. This is particularly true in Scandinavian countries and a few countries in South America, such as Costa Rica.

There does not appear to be a strong correlation between violence and organizational structure. National police forces are not altogether different from decentralized forces. There is evidence of systematic violence in both forms of organization.

Ultimately, several factors do appear to have an impact on the use of violence, the first being the government's political structure and political philosophy. Where a government takes a strong stand against the use of excessive force, there is generally going to be less violence. But this is often offset by other factors, such as rising crime or serious public disorder.

Interestingly, the level of police education and training appears not to be a significant factor when measuring instances of police violence. Training, education, and experience are certainly key components of a professional police service; however, there is yet little proof when comparing police violence on an international scale that it occurs much less where higher levels of education among officers are required.

Little data are available regarding violence against the police on an international level. In some countries, the police are targets of extremists and criminals. In other countries, the police are the victims of violent protests, riots, or mob action at various events. In the United States, "an average of 222 police officers were killed each year during the 1970s, including a record high 271 in 1974. The annual fatality figure then dropped in the 1980s to 188, followed by another steep decline to 155 officer deaths each year in the 1990s ("Century of Sacrifice," 2000). Some attribute this decline to better training, but this is not clear. For example, it is estimated that in some countries "25% of police officers have received no basic police training at all" (Hazenberg, 2000). Data show that firearms assaults against police actually remained stable or increased between 1978 and 1990 (Geller & Scott, 1992). But little data have addressed how many more officers might have died were it not for improved medical procedures; this is worth further exploration.

On an international level, there are also vast differences in the number of officers assaulted or killed. In the 1990s, for example, police in South Africa were six times more likely to be killed than police in the United States (Geller & Scott, 1992, p. 79). In some countries, the relationship between the police and minorities is so strained that violence is in the air at almost any confrontation. The axiom that "violence begets violence" is particularly true in countries in which the police and the community are in conflict with one another. Finally, because many police deaths are attributed to firearms, the availability of such weapons must be considered in making cross-national comparisons.

Perhaps the most significant variable in reducing violence—of all types—is recognition that the rule of law must be the deciding factor in solving conflicts and bringing miscreants to justice. This is not easy to accomplish, particularly in developing countries and those involved in domestic turmoil. The best hope for the future rests in the development of effective and just legal systems that do not discriminate. All countries of the world need to continue to work toward this goal.

NOTES

The author would like to express his appreciation to Cindy Moors, whose research was invaluable in preparation of the chapter, and to Jane Buckwalter for her insightful comments and assistance.

1. There are, of course, exceptions to this where the public is likely to be in favor of, or tolerant of, actions against certain individuals or minority groups. For example, where the crime rate is high, the public is more likely to support heavy-handed police strategies.
2. Examples include countries where there is large-scale political violence, such as Sri Lanka and Chechnya; those threatened by crime, such as Colombia and Russia; and those where the political structure is in question, such as Northern Ireland.
3. Based on several of the author's interviews between August 1988 and March 1996. See also Peter Taylor (1997). *Behind the Mask: The IRA and Sinn Fein* (New York, TV Books); and Chris Ryder (2000). *Inside the Maze: The Untold Story of the Northern Ireland Prison Service* (London: Methuen).
4. Specialized military police units were initially established as "shock units" in Brazil's war on terrorists and subversives. Military police officers on duty came under laws that made it impossible to prosecute them (see Human Rights Watch/Americas, 1997, pp. 22–23).
5. Resolution figures do not agree because of overlapping years.
6. Christian Copts are a religious group numbering an estimated 10 million people in Egypt.
7. There is also a relatively large number of so-called Armed Police, who are part of the army and have responsibility for guarding government facilities, protecting officials, and controlling crowds at times. The majority of Armed Police, however, are conscripts who usually serve for 2 years. The closest comparison with the United States is that of the National Guard, which a governor can call out in times of political upheaval.
8. There is much disagreement as to the role and motives of the Falun Gong movement. Its leader, a former police officer, immigrated to the United States and has been described as a secretive individual whose organization is more political than it is purported to be.

REFERENCES

ADAMS, K. (1999). What we know about police use of force. In National Institute of Justice, *Use of force by police*. Washington, DC: U.S. Department of Justice. (NCJ 176330, pp. 1–14).

AMNESTY INTERNATIONAL. (1997). *Democratic Republic of Congo: Deadly alliances in Congolese forests*. New York: Author.

AMNESTY INTERNATIONAL. (1998). *Kosovo: The evidence*. London: Author.

AMNESTY INTERNATIONAL. (1999a). *Human rights report: Egypt*. London: Author.

AMNESTY INTERNATIONAL. (1999b). *Human rights report: France*. London: Author

AMNESTY INTERNATIONAL. (1999c). *Human rights report: People's Republic of China*. London: Author.

AMNESTY INTERNATIONAL. (1999d). *Human rights report: South American region*. London: Author.

AMNESTY INTERNATIONAL. (1999e). *Human rights report: The Middle East and North Africa*. London: Author.

BAYLEY, D. (1994). *Police for the future*. New York: Oxford University Press.

BENSINGER, G. (1998). *Justice in Israel: The criminal justice system* (3rd ed.). Huntsville, TX: Office of International Criminal Justice.

BOSHRA, B., & VAN PRAET, N. (2000, March 16). Anti-brutality protest turns ugly. *The (Montreal) Gazette*.

BOX, S. (1983). *Power, crime, and mystification*. New York: Tavistock Publications.

BROOKE, J. (1992, November 8). Looting Brazil. *New York Times*, pp. 31–33, 42, 45, 70.

CENTURY OF SACRIFICE: POLICE DEATHS PEAKED IN 70'S—NOW ON STEADY DECLINE. (2000). *Memorial news: Newsletter of the National Law Enforcement Officers Memorial Fund*, 1.

CHAN, E. (2000, June 15). U.S., 146 other countries labeled as rights violators, *Chicago Tribune*. [On-line]. Available: http://www.chicagotribune.com/news/nationworld/article/0,2669,SAV-0006150254,ff.html.

CHIEF LAUNCHES PROBE OF 4 COPS. (1999, December 31). *The (Montreal) Gazette*.

COPS AND BOMBERS: SOUTH AFRICA'S CAPE TOWN STRUGGLES TO COPE WITH CRIME AND WOULD-BE "SELF-PROTECTION" GROUPS. (2000, February 7). *Time, 155*(5). Lexis-Nexis Academic Universe.

THE CRIMINAL PROCEDURE LAW OF THE PEOPLE'S REPUBLIC OF CHINA. (1998). Huntsville, TX: Office of International Criminal Justice. (Z. Zhou Trans.)

CRITCHLEY, T. (1978). *A history of police in England and Wales* (Rev. ed.). London: Constable London.

DUTTON, M. (1992). *Policing and punishment in China: From patriarchy to "the people."* England: Cambridge University Press.

EBBE, O. (2000). *Comparative and international criminal justice systems: Policing, judiciary, and corrections* (2nd ed.). Boston: Butterworth-Heinemann.

EGYPTIAN COPT GETS 15 YEARS HARD-LABOR IN HIGH-PROFILE MURDER CASE. (2000, June 5). *Agence France Press*. Lexis-Nexis Academic Universe.

HOFFMAN, M. (1989). *The world almanac and book of facts*. New York: World Almanac Books.

GELLER, W., & SCOTT, M. (1992). *Deadly force: What we know*. Washington, DC: Police Executive Research Forum.

HALF TRUTH. (2000, June 17). *The Economist*. Lexis-Nexis Academic Universe.

HAZENBERG, A. (2000). The police and human rights in Europe: How does your service measure up against those in Europe. *Interpol: International criminal police review* (Number 480, p. 12). Lyons, France: Interpol.

HUMAN RIGHTS WATCH/AMERICAS. (1997). *Police brutality in urban Brazil*. New York: Author.

INDEPENDENT COMMISSION FOR POLICE COMPLAINTS. (2000, July 7). *Complaint statistics*. [On-line]. Available: http://www.ruc.police.uk/press/statistics/complaints.htm.

JONES, P., & MANSON, R. (2000, May 27). Town's police face most danger. *The Sentinel (Stoke)*. Lexis-Nexis Academic Universe.

LAWLESS, J. (2000, April 5). Amnesty report says European nations guilty of rights abuses. *The Associated Press*. Lexis-Nexis Academic Universe.

MALAYSIAN RIGHTS WATCHDOG STILL PROCESSING COMPLAINTS. (2000, June 5). *Agence France Press*. Lexis-Nexis Academic Universe.

MAN DIES FROM POLICE BRUTALITY IN CHINA. (2000, January 6). *Agence France Press*. Lexis-Nexis Academic Universe.

METROPOLITAN POLICE, POLICE ORDERS (1837, November 3). In Wilbur R. Miller (1977), *Cops and bobbies: Police authority in New York and London, 1830–1870* (Metropolitan Police Records 7/5, vol. 284, p. 76). Chicago: University of Chicago Press.

MULGREW, I. (1988). *Unholy terror: The Sikhs and international terrorism*. Toronto: Key Porter Books.

NAPOLITAN, J. (1997). *Cross-national crime: A research review and sourcebook.* Westport, CT: Greenwood Press.

O'CONNOR, T. (1889). *The Parnell movement; With a sketch of Irish parties from 1843.* New York: Benzinger Brothers.

POLICE AND CONSTABULARY ALMANAC. (2000). Oxford: R. Hagell & Co.

ROYAL ULSTER CONSTABULARY. (2000a). Deaths due to the Northern Ireland security situation. [On-line]. Available: http://www.ruc.police.uk/press/statistics/deaths2.htm.

ROYAL ULSTER CONSTABULARY (2000b). Injuries as a result of the Northern Ireland Security Situation: 1968–2000. [On-line]. Available: http://www.ruc.police.uk/press/statistics/injury2.htm.

SKOLNICK, J. (1966). *Justice without trial: Law enforcement in a democratic society.* New York: Wiley.

SPAIN DISMISSES ACCUSATIONS OF POLICE BRUTALITY. (2000, April 13). *Deutsche Press-Agentur.* Lexis-Nexis Academic Universe.

TAYLOR, P. (1997). *Behind the mask: The IRA and Sinn Fein.* New York: TV Books.

THOMPSON, L. (1990). *A history of South Africa.* New Haven, CT: Yale University Press.

TONRY, M., & MORRIS, N. (1989). *Modern policing.* Chicago: University of Chicago Press.

U.S. STATE DEPARTMENT. (2000, February 25). 1999 country reports on human rights practices: Nigeria. [On-line]. Available: http://www.state.gov/www/global/human_rights/1999_hrp_report/nigeria.html.

Wilson, J. Q. (1968). *Varieties of police behavior: The management of law and order in eight communities.* Boston: Harvard University Press.

WORLD BRIEFING: BRITAIN: CURBING HOOLIGANS. (2000, July 5). *New York Times*, p. A5.

10

Future Directions in Police Violence: What to Expect

Gene Stephens

INTRODUCTION

Violence is as American as cherry pie, or so said black activist Stokely Carmichael. Violence by, against, and sanctioned by police has been well documented in the preceding pages as well as by a plethora of researchers over the years (e.g., Bayley, 1998; Dubofsky, 1975; Spitzer, 1981). What can we expect in the 21st century: more of the same, new types and reasons for violence, or a real trend away from violence by and against police and in society in general?

Based on my 30 years experience as a *futurist* specializing in the future of criminal justice and police in particular, it would appear that the answer is all of the above—and, in chronological order, I hope. That is, more of the same for the next few years, followed by a short period of *new* violence, and finally a *real* decrease in violence by and against police, reflecting a turn away from violence in the social system—worldwide—all within this first decade of the new millennium (if we are lucky).

I am hedging a little, but the timetable could be altered by the tactics of the coming social changes as mentioned earlier as well as by the methods adopted by the new breed of terrorists and organized crime gangs. Bayley (1998) put it well when he noted that community-oriented policing and problem-oriented policing definitely can slow police violence but could be derailed if group violence—stemming from inequities in race, class, and ethnicity—escalates. Police might be expected to revert to their quasi-military 20th-century model. Bayley believed the bunker mentality also might be adopted if terrorists and organized crime use modern technology, which affords more potential destructiveness on the part of criminals and police.

As I am a bit more of an optimist, it appears to me that the last hurrah of endemic violence likely will occur, but it will only sidetrack temporarily, not alter the direction already established for a less violent future. Still, let us look at the three periods postulated: *more of the same, new violence, and less violence.*

MORE OF THE SAME

The police have been an instrument of the social elites for most of their existence in the United States—beginning in the second quarter of the 19th century. Industrialists learned early that they inflamed the passions of the masses when they used private police to batter, beat, and sometimes kill workers who dared to try to organize, or worse yet, strike. As public police became available, the industrialists began calling on these public servants to do their strike busting, but under the guise of enforcing the law—keeping the streets clear, stopping property damage, and quelling public disturbances (Dubofsky, 1975; Spitzer, 1981).

These early public police were born into a violent period, as Americans moved west to the lawless frontier, while back in the East, police were expected to uphold the status quo in the face of riots brought on by huge economic and ethnic disparities (Peak & Glensor, 1996). Police in the East were forced to cope with violence, often pitting them against hostile citizens in the communities, while out in the West the sheriffs and marshals became folk heroes, largely based on tales of their no-nonsense use of force against outlaws and gunfighters on the frontier.

The importance of this frontier period cannot be overemphasized, as it set the tone for policing even to this day. The eastern police officer by the end of the 19th century began to adopt the western sheriff as a role model, and this "take charge," "accept no back talk" attitude permeated many agencies.

As police were absorbed into neighborhood precincts, they often tried to "rule their beats" at the "end of a nightstick" and through use of "curbstone justice" (Peak & Glensor, 1996). The blue brotherhood or police subculture evolved from this "we vs. they" militaristic model. Crank (1998) suggested that the model is intrinsically linked with violence. The thinking goes something like this: We protect our own. It is a war out there; it's us against them. Always cover for another officer. Don't back down. Always have superior firepower. Use it!

Bayley (1994) stated that police "go to work as if they were going to war" (p. 70). Just getting dressed—bulletproof vest, club, gun, and often riot gear and visored helmet—sets the mood for war. The irony, of course, is that 90% of police work is service, and even when confrontation does occur, no more than 5% of incidents involve use of physical force (Bayley, 1994). Thus police prepare for war, but their major role is to make and keep the peace in nonviolent ways.

In his *Monster: The Autobiography of an L.A. Gang Member,* Kody Scott (1993) alleged that gangs in Los Angeles considered the police as just one more gang, sometimes acting on its own, but often choosing sides in gang conflict to further its own interests. Scott claimed that sometimes police would tell his gang where to find rivals and even suggest how to eliminate them.

Police-citizen encounters in low-income, minority-dominated communities have become stereotyped as violent in nature, and one form of popular music—rap—was spawned in large part as a new form of protest. Police have quite naturally been incensed by lyrics in rap songs such as "Cop Killer" by Ice-T, but Ehrenreich (1992) argued that many black youths believe it is police who create and indulge in anarchy and violence, citing the nearly 10,000 reports of police brutality recorded annually by the U.S. Department of Justice by the 1990s.

Sayles (1999) insisted that corruption and brutality go hand in hand. He found that officers often confess that their first steps across the line to break the rules were to commit acts of brutality. By showing a willingness to abuse offenders in custody, they hoped to prove to other officers that they were tough cops who could be trusted. They also used violence to demonstrate dominance and authority over the citizenry in their patrol district and to punish those they feared would otherwise evade justice in the courts. Finally, some simply enjoy the power and thrills they gain from violent action (Sayles, 1999).

One peculiar police phenomenon that can lead even normally by-the-book officers to get involved in violent encounters is the police chase. For example, after a July 2000 incident in which Philadelphia police chased a suspect, television cameras provided the nation with a view of 10 officers surrounding the suspect and beating and kicking him as he lay on the ground ("Suspect beaten on video," 2000). Police said that during the chase the suspect stole a police car and shot at them, hitting one officer in the thumb. Later it was found that another officer had shot the officer during the "frantic chase."

Analyzing the chase later, criminologist James Fyfe of Temple University called the incident "the police version of the bench clearing brawl" (Michaels, 2000, p. 5A). Geoffrey Alpert of the College of Criminal Justice at the University of South Carolina commented: "The normal pursuit is going to have an enormous adrenaline dump and raise the heart rate and expectations of the officers. Excessive force is certainly not the order of the day, but you'll find it at the end of a pursuit more than any other type of police work" (Michaels, 2000, p. 5A). Hans Toch, criminologist at State University of New York-Albany, added: "All of a sudden you have umpteen cars responding, and you get this kind of mob psychology. . . . This was blue rage" (Michaels, 2000, p. 5A).

One suggestion made by Alpert and others is to remove pursuing officers from the call before the actual arrest, turning the custodial procedures over to less involved, less adrenaline-pumped officers.

In 1985 in *Tennessee v. Garner*, the U.S. Supreme Court ruled on police violence that "the use of deadly force to apprehend an apparently unarmed, non-violent fleeing felon is an unreasonable seizure under the fourth amendment." In more recent years, overreaction by police against minor offenders, suspects, and even bystanders has resulted in civil liability lawsuits and public demonstrations. The combination has led many police departments to change their training focus to emphasize violence reduction, resistance, or avoidance through communication and restraint. Interactive role-playing and simulation have been used to show officers how to apply tactical knowledge to avoid situations that will likely result in violence (Alpert & Dunham, 1997).

Of equal concern is violence by police against citizens they have been called to help. Imagine that parents call police to quell a violent outburst by their mentally disturbed teenager; police arrive and after a momentary standoff shoot the youth when he lunges at them with a knife. The police reasoning: We must meet lethal force with lethal force. We have no real alternative. The truth is that police have been slow to adopt alternatives, often arguing that if the "bad guy" or the deranged person has lethal force and is prepared to use it, police must have lethal force and authority to use it also.

In recent episodes, a sharp contrast has been drawn between demonstrators or drunk or drugged disorderly persons being confronted by police carrying stun guns, compressed air-beanbag weapons, or rubber or plastic bullets and being confronted by police using standard-issue lethal weapons. (Less-than-lethal weapons will be discussed later in the "Less Violence" section.)

The real issue emerging for the next few years is whether police and the citizenry (including public offenders) are ready to turn away from the "crime and crime fighting on the frontier" mentality that dominated the 20th century (Bailey & Hale, 1998; Stephens, 1996a). Two major political battlegrounds will be the key indicators here: guns and capital punishment.

The ebb and flow between gun owners/users/advocates and gun control advocates continues, and as long as guns are widely available and glorified, there is little chance of violence by and against police being reduced substantially. The gun is an integral element of the frontier law enforcer model that police adopted and the public accepted. Only when the public and police turn away from this approach (evidence suggests that this is happening in many areas) will violence abate significantly.

Capital punishment is another barometer, as the willingness of citizens to use police powers to put fellow citizens to death—whatever the crime and circumstances—brutalizes society and inherently implies that violence is an acceptable means of problem solving. The long-term outlook likely will include a moratorium and even an end to use of the death penalty, but not for some time yet.

Meanwhile, the gun culture and state-sanctioned death message is being heard loud and clear by the nation's crime-prone adolescents. Lest they miss it, consider the 200,000 acts of violence and 20,000 murders the average American witnesses on television by age 18 (Canon, 1993; Digital age data, 2000).

Another factor in near-future violence is simple demographics: The teenage population in the United States will increase some 30% during the first decade of the 21st century (Bureau of the Census, 1995). This does not have to mean more violence as some criminologists have forecast (Fox, 1996), but without major change in the way American society nurtures, rears, and socializes its youth and meets their needs, more violence might well be expected. Luckily, care and concern for children is growing, but whether nationwide support will keep pace with their needs is yet to be determined.

Still another factor is the "state of anomie" many Americans find themselves in as the new economic system—based on creating and processing information rather than producing tangible products—displaces workers, many of whom find themselves unprepared technologically and emotionally to take advantage of the new system (Stephens, 1996b, 1998a, 1998b). Whereas more jobs exist than ever before with still more on the horizon, many people are simply not ready for the change. In such times of great expectations with little direction in how to achieve them, frustration and fear lead to confrontation and violence. Hate, antigovernment sentiment, and anti-immigrant sentiment—as they are now increasing—in such times, and the expression of anomie is often violent, even terroristic. Militias and hate groups are examples of these phenomena.

Possibly the most difficult trend to reverse will be the desensitization to the consequences of violence seen in many children as they are besieged daily by violence in all mass media as well as in electronic games. Characters die often without any apparent suffering and without any physical or social consequences depicted. Police are portrayed in the media as tough (macho) crimefighters who "must" violate the rules and use violence to catch and punish violators of the law. Police violence in this context is seen as critical to protecting the public (Bailey & Hale, 1998; Kappeler, Blumberg, & Potter, 2000).

This media portrayal not only influences public perceptions about real police work but greatly impacts police officers as well. Most police departments require only a high school diploma as a prerequisite for the job, and despite nearly half a century of readily available police science and criminal justice college programs for police, the average officer still starts to work with only a high school diploma. Where does this candidate get his or her idea about what the job entails—the real character of police work? Research indicates it is from the media (particularly TV and movies) and from often embellished stories from family, friends, and police officers they meet (Bailey & Hale, 1998; Barak, 1994). Whereas the young officer will eventually learn that constant excitement and the violent exercise of power is not the true character of the job, he or she likely will begin with the TV version of reality and find it enhanced by the curricula and tenor of police training, including the stories and informal learning he or she gains in the field as a probationary officer. For example, when I was a newspaper reporter on the police beat, I would often attend morning roll calls as a good time to find and question officers. A few days after Clint Eastwood's original *Dirty Harry* movie debuted, I observed numerous young officers at roll call confronting fellow officers while snarling the "do you feel lucky, well do you?" dialogue from the film. Until this socialization process changes (as it is changing in places) throughout the police establishment, violence by police likely will not diminish substantially.

NEW TYPES OF VIOLENCE

The information technology and biotechnology age has arrived, and with it come new opportunities and methods to commit violence. We will even need to reconsider the definition of violence. If a community is dependent on the Internet for its commerce, communication, and indeed its health and welfare, is being cut off from the web by a blackmailer or terrorist then a violent act? Should cloning a copy of oneself (but without a brain or nervous system)—to be used for spare parts—be deemed a violent crime? These situations and many similar ones may be occurring by the end of this first decade of the 21st-century.

Information technology will provide both police and offenders with many new tools. For example, constant surveillance technology that allows us to watch and listen to anyone anywhere without his or her knowledge can be used to protect, control, or terrorize citizens (Kushner, 1998; Stephens, 1998a). Offenders—from angry individuals to terrorists—can use computers to crash airplanes, to kill patients by overdose or allergic reaction, or to track and destroy unsuspecting victims for malice or profit. Computers can be programmed to allow elevators to fall, to release toxic chemicals, to explode nuclear reactors, to overheat electrical circuitry and start fires, and much more. Violence can be committed by detonating explosives remotely from halfway around the world, using electronic signals carried to the target by the Global Positioning System (GPS) satellites (Stephens, 1998a).

Talented computer crackers (malevolent individuals seeking profit, revenge, or terrorism) can reprogram computer systems to create explosions, meltdowns, blackouts, shutdowns, and much more, that can lead to serious injuries and deaths. Already police are counterattacking as cybercops surf the web in search of criminals from electronic con artists to pedophiles. The natural progression would be for police to use methods similar to crackers by reprogramming the computers of dissident individuals and groups to eliminate (even maim and kill) the suspected offenders (Stephens, 1995, 1998a).

One dreaded form of "violence" is identity theft, a crime that begins with the thief obtaining as little as a social security number or a single credit card number. With these, the offender can not only steal the victim's life savings and leave him or her deeply in debt but can indeed destroy the victim's creditworthiness, sanity, and ability to trust anyone again. What could be more violent? Would you rather someone threaten to beat you up or threaten to take your identity and all that you have?

In modern identity theft, the culprit clones credit cards, obtains new credit based on the victim's good credit, and sells the cards and identification to the highest bidder or poses as the victim and goes on a spending spree. Beyond this, the offender and his or her clients leave a long trail of unpaid bills and false statements in the name of the victim. Sometimes the offender intentionally destroys the capacity of the victim to recover by sending (now often by e-mail) nasty or mocking messages to creditors, employers, and friends of the victim he or she is imitating.

Many public offenders could say that police have been doing this to them for years—using "victimless" crime ordinance enforcement (e.g., vagrancy, blocking the sidewalk, public drunkenness) to remove them from the streets because of their profile (e.g., likely to be drug dealing, likely to be a neighborhood nuisance). Once incarcerated, even if for only 30 to 60 days, the offender cannot keep a job or pay bills; when this arrest-jail, arrest-jail procedure becomes a revolving door, the offender (victim?) can no longer find a job or legitimately support himself or herself and/or a family.

As commerce on the Internet expands, more identity theft can be expected, and as Internet access becomes critical to success and even life, being denied access will be a weapon for police to use against suspected offenders. The remaining question is whether computer-savvy offenders will turn the tables on police and use identity theft to destroy individual officers, or even ban together and go after a group of police.

New types of violence can also be expected in the rapidly expanding biological sciences. As biotechnology progresses, communicable diseases or deadly genetically engineered microorganisms can be released into air and/or water supplies to disable or kill millions, or released in a room to kill or disable a single individual or small group. This technology can be used against police (e.g., to wipe out a precinct headquarters) or by police (e.g., to eliminate a gang or dissident group).

Using low-tech applications of biotechnology, police and their prey might smear their bullets with deadly biomaterial (similar to pygmies who soaked their blowgun darts in poison) or might modify nonlethal weapons by replacing knockout chemicals and gases with toxic chemicals, microorganisms, and gases.

In the not-too-distant future, biochips (organic computers) will be implanted in the neural systems of humans to receive, store, and use massive amounts of information. As individuals increasingly rely on these internal computers to run their daily lives, a new crime—mindstalking—can be expected (Stephens, 1992, 1995, 1989a). Here the cracker breaks into the organic computer and alters or erases the individual's biochip. Messages can be sent (e.g., "Electronically transfer all your money to me or die"; "Do as I say or I'll erase all of your memory") to terrorize, or commands can be inserted ("Increase data processing speed a millionfold"; "Cease breathing") to disable or kill. Again, talented cybercops would likely have the same skills and opportunities to use against suspected offenders.

One special type of police violence could emerge from a natural progression of the current electronic monitoring of probationers and parolees (Stephens, 1996a, 1998a). Already the monitors are being tracked by GPS to allow more flexibility and closer scrutiny of these persons. For example, the probationer may be allowed to follow a preset path from home to work to after-work counseling and/or treatment and back to home. In the next few years, the monitors can be expected to be implanted in the offender, opening the way for electrodes to be attached to make the system self-policing. If the offender strays from approved locations, electroshock would be automatically administered until the offender returns to acceptable areas. To protect the person from unauthorized intrusion, encryption of monitors likely will be used. Police, however, will likely be considered a "trusted third party" and thus will be given the encryption "key," especially with probable cause to believe the person is involved in new criminal activity (Stephens, 1995). Police then could use the implanted electrodes to control the suspected offender—a new form of violence.

Finally, in the search for better weapons for police, one avenue that has been explored involves ultrasound (Stephens, 1996a). A continuum of sound could be used to disable, kill, and even disassemble individuals. At lower levels, a loud grating sound would make the receiver cover his or her ears or run to escape, while at somewhat higher levels, a seemingly unheard sound would produce unconsciousness; at still higher levels it would destroy the brain and internal organs and kill recipients; and at the highest levels, it would dematerialize the individual or group, leaving only a puddle of remains. Whereas such technology cannot now be used at the street level because it is not unidirectional, it may be developed for other purposes (e.g., to quell prison riots). Once developed, such weaponry likely would result in unauthorized use by and against police.

Much of this new technology can be delivered by drones (unmanned remotely controlled aircraft) (Stephens, 1998a), which reduces the danger to the initiating party, thus making violence a more appealing option.

We have only scratched the surface here of the many creative ways that both police and citizens may adapt emerging technology to respond violently to situations. It should be clear by this time that *there are no technological solutions* to the problem of violence in American society. All sides to any disagreement likely will have access to weapons and other means of wreaking violence against perceived enemies. An ever-escalating spiral of violence and counterviolence is indeed possible (some would say probable), but it is neither inevitable nor in the interest of Americans.

Reconsidering and pulling back from this future scenario might better serve all parties.

LESS VIOLENCE

At the same time that new methods of violence are evolving, there are signs that Americans are tired of the violence and are increasingly seeking alternatives and even exercising restraint. The best indicator may be the dramatically decreasing crime rate—including violent offenses—that started in the mid-1990s and continued into the 21st century (Federal Bureau of Investigation [FBI], 2000). Although pockets of modest increases appeared, overall the crime rate decreased significantly during this period (Johnson, 2000; Lynn, 2000; Sniffen, 2000), to the point that some researchers postulated that U.S. society in the year 2000 was *safer than at any other time in its history* (Kappeler et al., 2000).

Ironically, violent confrontations and reactions by and against police also were prominent in the news during this period (Stephens, 2000a). Again, however, statistics on police-citizen violent encounters belied the perception that such incidents were on the increase. Even amidst the headlines and frequent telecasts of violent confrontations from Los Angeles to Philadelphia and New York, official reports indicated that such incidents overall significantly decreased during this period.

Consider this interpretation: Crime news is a staple of the media, and crime decreased substantially, leaving a potential void for the media. Thus, added coverage of significant incidents, such as violent police-suspect encounters, was both possible and desirable from the media's perspective. Second, new technology in the hands of the public (e.g., the camcorder) increased access and documentation of such incidents and provided dramatic visuals for the media. Third, with crime less of a problem, the public was more likely to turn its attention to the violence by some offenders and by the police: Protecting society from the protectors was balanced against protecting society from the offenders. Finally, parents, educators, and social service providers (among others) began banning together in a movement to curb violence in society—particularly gun violence. The most visible gun culture in the nation has been in the police departments in every community.

Thus, a feasible scenario for the future—based on extrapolation of these trends—would be that the acceptability of violence as a means of solving problems will become increasingly unacceptable as America (finally) becomes more civilized.

Changes in U.S. justice—from community-oriented policing (COP) to restorative justice—are already well under way, and, if continued, will provide an environment increasingly hostile to violence (Stephens, 1996a, 1996b, 1998b, 1999). Consider the following scenario as we move toward peace and less violence.

Police departments across the nation develop COP or problem-oriented policing (POP) and truly understand and adopt the attendant philosophy and methods—proactive focus on preventing crime; community assessment of the needs and tasks necessary to identify and solve crime-breeding situations; creation and maintenance of public-private-community partnerships to get the job done; and attention to the development, nurturing, and maintenance of an inclusive community focus. Here the police are an integral part (not an appendage) of a broad communitywide network and thus less likely to act or be seen as independent agents of social control. Catching criminals would be replaced by preventing crime and crime-breeding situations as the major focus of police (Stephens, 1996b, 1998b, 1999, 2000b).

Under restorative justice, the movement away from criminal courts toward offender-citizen mediation and arbitration or other alternative dispute resolution (ADR) programs will escalate. Soon adversary proceedings will be limited to stranger-to-stranger predatory incidents (e.g., serial offenders, career criminals), which represent only a small percentage of reported crime (e.g., all murders and rapes together represent less than 1% of reported crime) (FBI, 2000).

Prisons will be reserved for individuals truly dangerous to society, instead of being used to punish primarily minority and poor defendants, based on a belief in retribution and deterrence. All others found guilty of offenses via ADR systems will be required to pay restitution to their victims, provide service to their community, and reform themselves via community-based education and restoration programs.

Meanwhile, the well-established movement to save America's youth at risk (Stephens, 1997) will continue to build on its already impressive record—from creating and providing nonviolent conflict resolution and character-building programs to all school districts to harnessing tutors, mentors, counselors, and health care specialists to serve increasing numbers of these children in need. The obvious next step will be to fortify these civic-private-public partnerships into a network to serve all of America's young people—a task already under way. Part of the nonviolent program—supported by curriculum developed and made available by the American Bar Association (ABA, undated)—is to teach students, teachers, counselors, other school staff, bus drivers, and so on, how to resolve conflict without weapons or any type of violence. In places where this has been instituted properly, violence and disciplinary problems have decreased dramatically (Stephens, 1997).

If violence is no longer acceptable to parents and children, then how can police sustain it? To rebut the argument that lawbreakers will still exist and many will choose to use violence to achieve their ends, it is clear that technology will provide new tools that both police and offenders can and likely will utilize. As violence becomes increasingly socially unacceptable, all will be under pressure to find alternative methods, even to commit crimes and to incapacitate offenders.

An effort nearing conclusion—the Less-Than-Lethal Weapons Initiative coordinated by the National Institute of Justice (NIJ, 1993)—will provide alternatives to lethal force by police. The goal is to provide law enforcers with an array of weapons (and eventually a single all-purpose weapon) that can quell a suspect or disorderly citizen without seriously injuring or killing him or her. Since police have insisted that they have equal or superior stopping power to the lawbreakers, such a weapon(s) must be instantaneous and effective to be acceptable.

Among the weapons that have been developed and tested are the thermal gun, which raises the body temperature of the person shot to 107 degrees, disabling him or her; the net gun, which enmeshes the suspect in a net; the velocity-controlled gun, which allows the police to shoot rubber, plastic, and even wooden bullets at less-than-lethal velocity to disable the individual; the sticky foam gun, which spreads a substance over the suspect that immediately sticks him or her in place; and the dart gun, which dispenses disabling chemicals or gas on impact ("Darts," 1996).

The weapons closest to having the mandatory immediate stopping power are the sticky foam and dart guns, but the first requires a long cleanup period afterward and the second is not fully perfected as chemicals or gases that might seriously injure or kill one person might not even stop another. Still, it appears that in the near future new chemicals and/or gases that meet the instantaneous requirement will be developed (possibly using bioengineering) and less-than-lethal weapons will be widely available and effective. As has been found in other societies, when police turn away from use of violence, the public and offenders tend to follow, and a trend toward societal nonviolence is established (Kappeler et al., 2000).

Although it would be preferable to end on this happy note, the truth is that the thin blue line will be difficult to change. Many in policing are already on the road to a nonviolent future, but others will neither embrace nor accept such a change.

One group on the front line of the new frontier in policing—preventing crime and violence by intelligent use of emerging technology and partnerships with the public—is members of Police Futurists International (PFI) (*http://www.policefuturists.org/*). Begun by graduates of Special Agent William L. Tafoya's Future of Policing class for the National Academy (i.e., local and state law enforcement officers) students at the FBI Academy, the Internet-linked and future-savvy group has expanded to a worldwide membership. PFI also meets jointly with the World Future Society each year—conducting panels on topics such as the future of policing, cyberpolicing, and community policing trends.

Still, acceptance of nonlethal weapons and emphasis on prevention of crime and violence will face many obstacles—some of which were mentioned earlier. Chief among them is the war model image many police jealously embrace. For the high school graduate who joins the police as a means of upward mobility, the crimefighter role is compelling and fills his or her need (possibly even lust) for power—over his or her own life and over others. Sayles (1999) stated:

> The police believe themselves to be the only real crimefighters. There are other agencies, either public or private (e.g., prosecutors, courts, probation, crime watch programs), which the police view as merely ancillary. Only the police are the real guardians of justice—everyone else is just playing at it. (p. 156)

Because of the paramilitary nature of police, the blue brotherhood is strong. Police have a mutual experience as all start at the bottom, go through the same training, and survive the same probationary period. Through this process, each officer learns what fellow officers expect—what is acceptable behavior among police. Many retreat into this enveloping police subculture, often ignoring, or at least making secondary, their duty to the public they are sworn and paid to serve. They develop cynicism and an "us vs. them" bunker mentality that justifies violence in the "war on crime" (Sayles, 1999; Sparrow, Moore, & Kennedy, 1990).

It is a lot to overcome, but police accreditation, higher education requirements, additional training, peace model–oriented training, and salary and promotion guidelines stressing proactive prevention of crime and violence are under way, as well as citizen groups supporting the changes both in police and other justice arenas. For example, the Commission on Accreditation for Law Enforcement Agencies, jointly sponsored by the International Association of Chiefs of Police (IACP), the National Sheriffs Association, the National Organization of Black Law Enforcement Executives (NOBLE), and the Police Executive Research Forum (PERF), has established accreditation standards for law enforcement agencies that stress prevention, interagency cooperation and coordination, and citizen interaction. The Police Association for College Education (PACE) in Alexandria, Virginia, promotes adoption of a college degree as an entry-level requirement for police. The Community Policing Consortium in Washington, D.C., coordinates police-citizen links, and the Center for Law Enforcement Ethics in Richardson, Texas, provides "Train the Trainer" programs that encourage the inclusion of ethics in basic police training everywhere. Citizen initiatives have led to formation of organizations such as the Center for Restorative Justice and Peacemaking at the University of Minnesota and the Victim Offender Mediation Association (VOMA) in New Smyrna Beach, Florida.

Finally, if public pressure for violence abatement by and against police continues, emerging technology will offer assistance in other areas, but at a price to civil liberties—privacy in particular. One reason both police and suspects choose violence quickly as a response to confrontation is that both sides believe they are likely to "get away with it." For police, it usually comes down to the officer's word against that of the suspect, and for the accused, there was a substantial chance he or she could escape custody and evade charges. The latter is borne out by crime statistics, as for years only 1 of 5 reported index crimes (i.e., homicide, rape, assault, robbery, burglary, larceny, motor vehicle theft, and arson) has resulted in an arrest (FBI, 2000). Whereas violent crime clearance by arrest is higher than this average for all index crimes, other data indicate that most crimes—at least 2 out of 3—are not even reported to police (Bureau of Justice Statistics, 2000). Thus the offender—at least statistically—likely will not be detected or captured.

This likelihood of escape plays a prominent role in suspects' willingness to flee from police on foot or in vehicles, precipitating the police pursuit. Often—particularly when the police do not know the identity of the individual being chased and/or the person is in a stolen vehicle or one that is not registered in his or her name—escape of pursuing officers indeed means escape from custody and charges. Police realize this and often are willing to take chances that endanger themselves, the chased suspect, and the general public in order to capture the person "not showing proper respect for the law." Thus violent confrontation and the escape/chase becomes pragmatic for both the pursuer and the pursued. Current police pursuit policies in most agencies require that officers break off a pursuit when the danger to the public (e.g., high speeds in heavy traffic) outweighs the danger from the suspect if not apprehended. This, of course, is a judgment call, and in practical terms, the adrenaline-pumped, agitated, and excited officers in the chase seldom make such a decision voluntarily, and often even ignore or pretend not to receive a radio call from a superior officer to desist.

The truth is, with current and emerging technology, there is little reason for high-speed pursuit and confrontation. Most patrol cars already are equipped with in-car video equipment to record pursuit and stops, and some cars already have robots that can be dropped from car to roadway to run under the pursued car and by radio signal shut down the electronic equipment on board, effectively disabling the vehicle and ending the chase. Soon electromagnets or microwaves will be used from the patrol car to disable the pursued car ("Darts," 1996). Another avenue is to have helicopters follow the pursued vehicle and provide information that allows police to intercept the car without need for pursuit (Stephens, 1996b).

Ahead is technology that will provide for automated highways: cars on major thoroughfares will be placed on autopilot and pulled along by computer chips in the roadway that communicate with chips placed in the vehicles. Already such a system is being tested on a strip of Interstate 15 in San Diego County (Chelsea, 1996). As automated highways increase, all vehicles will be outfitted with chips to make them compatible with the roadway. One ancillary product of the system is that all vehicles will be identifiable via the implanted chip, thus eliminating their anonymity. Police will be able to obtain an instant ID even without physically seeing the car, thanks to GPS tracking. Other emerging technology will allow authorities to take pictures to identify the driver, using high-resolution cameras from police satellites fitted with GPS technology. Suspects will not be able to evade being constantly watched and tracked; *there will be no escape from "Big Brother."*

At the same time, patrol cars are already being outfitted with cameras and similar technology, meaning police will be constantly under surveillance with all actions recorded (Wald, 1999). It will no longer simply be the officer's word against the suspect's. When violence occurs, the tape or digital record will tell the tale. Anonymous violence by police or suspect will be rare indeed.

CONCLUSION

Whether police violence waxes or wanes in the future is dependent on whether violence remains widely acceptable as a method of conflict resolution in American society. I have explored the likely scenarios of a short-term increase in violence, new types of violence, and a long-term diminishment of violence. This future is based on extrapolation of trends already under way, but trends are malleable to factors as diverse as major events, socioeconomic change, and technological adaptation. In the 1980s, for example, when President Ronald Reagan and Press Secretary Jim Brady were shot by John Hinckley, two trends were altered. The "not guilty by reason of insanity" verdict on Hinckley's case led to a new plea and verdict "guilty but mentally ill" being adopted widely; furthermore, the federal "Brady Bill" was passed requiring registration of handguns. In addition, Brady established handgun control as a counterbalance for the National Rifle Association (NRA), leading to background checks and waiting periods to purchase guns in most states. Socioeconomic changes also influence trend directions as crime responds to the changes in the U.S. economy, and new technologies such as the Internet and genetic engineering lead to new directions in both crime and crime fighting.

The bottom line is that violence by and against police will reflect violence in society or at least perceived violence. A warning here: Perceptions of violence in society change slowly and are more a product of popular culture (Bailey & Hale, 1998) than of reality. That is, the media are the primary players in creating social reality in the United States, and even as violence has waned to the point that some say the United States is safer than ever before in its history, reporting of violence in the media has actually increased (Bailey & Hale, 1998; "Crime wave sweeps," 1997), raising the fear and anxiety levels that have kept violence a feasible and acceptable response in a society many see as out of control.

Thus, the answer to police violence will require bringing social and empirical reality about violence into congruence, probably a prerequisite to making violence socially unacceptable.

REFERENCES

ALPERT, G. P., & DUNHAM, R. G. (1997). *Policing urban America* (3rd ed.). Prospect Heights, IL: Waveland Press.

AMERICAN BAR ASSOCIATION. (undated). *The standing committee on dispute resolution*. Washington, DC: Author.

BAILEY, F., & HALE, D. (1998). *Popular culture, crime, and justice*. Belmont, CA: Wadsworth.

BARAK, G. (Ed.). (1994). *Media, process, and the social construction of crime: Studies in newsmaking criminology*. New York: Garland.

BAYLEY, D. H. (1994). *Police for the future*. New York: Oxford University.

BAYLEY, D. H. (1998, November/December). Ideas in American policing. *Society*, 16–19.

BUREAU OF THE CENSUS. (1995). *Current population, U.S. population reports, U.S. population estimates by sex, race, and Hispanic origin: 1992 to 2050*. Washington, DC: Author.

BUREAU OF JUSTICE STATISTICS. (2000). *Criminal victimization in the United States, 1998*. Washington, DC: U.S. Government Printing Office.

CANON, C. M. (1993, July/August). Honey, I warped the kids. *Mother Jones*, 176–181.

CHELSEA, M. K. (1996, November 4). Robots of the road. *Time*, 76–78.

CRANK, J. P. (1998). *Understanding police culture*. Cincinnati, OH: Anderson.

CRIME WAVE SWEEPS NETWORKS' NEWSCASTS. (1997, November 7). *USA Today*, p. A3.

DARTS, SMART GUNS AMONG THE OPTIONS. (1996, May 20). *USA Today*, p. A3.

DIGITAL AGE DATA. (2000). In G. Stephens (Ed.), *Criminal justice in perspective* (p. 105). Columbia: University of South Carolina Press.

DUBOFSKY, M. (1975). *Industrialism and the American worker, 1865–1920*. Arlington Heights, IL: Harlan Davidson.

EHRENREICH, B. (1992, July 20). . . . or is it creative freedom. *Time*, 98.

FEDERAL BUREAU OF INVESTIGATION. (2000). *Crime in the United States 1999: Uniform crime reports*. Washington, DC: U.S. Government Printing Office.

FOX, J. A. (1996, March). *Trends in juvenile violence*. Washington, DC: Bureau of Justice Statistics.

JOHNSON, K. (2000, May 8). Serious crime down again: 7% dip in '99. *USA Today*, p. A1.

KAPPELER, V. E., BLUMBERG, M., & POTTER, G. W. (2000). *The mythology of crime and criminal justice* (3rd ed.). Prospect Heights, IL: Waveland Press.

KUSHNER, H. W. (Ed.). (1998). *The future of terrorism: Violence in the new millennium*. Thousand Oaks, CA: Sage.

LYNN, G. (2000, May 8). Homicides up in a few places. *USA Today*, p. A1.

MICHAELS, D. (2000, July 16). Police in beating ignore tenets, analysts say. *Dallas Morning News*, p. 5A.

NATIONAL INSTITUTE OF JUSTICE. (1993, March). *NIJ Initiative on less-than-lethal weapons*. (NCJ 133523). Washington, DC: Author.

PEAK, K. J., & GLENSOR, R. W. (1996). *Community policing and problem solving: Strategies and practices*. Upper Saddle River, NJ: Prentice Hall.

SAYLES, S. L. (1999). Is there a distinct subculture of police? Yes. In J. C. Sewell (Ed.), *Controversial issues in policing*. Boston: Allyn and Bacon.

SCOTT, K. (1993). *Monster: The autobiography of an L.A. gang member*. New York: Atlantic Monthly Press.

SNIFFEN, M. J. (2000, May 8). FBI reports longest streak of reduction in serious crime. *The (Columbia, SC) State*, pp. A1, A5.

SPARROW, M. K., MOORE, M. H., & KENNEDY, D. M. (1990). *Beyond 911: A new era for policing*. New York: Basic Books.

SPITZER, S. (1981). The political economy of policing. In D. F. Greenberg (Ed.), *Corrections and punishment*. Beverly Hills, CA: Sage.

STEPHENS, G. (1992, November/December). Crime and the biotech revolution. *The Futurist, 26*(6), 38–42.

STEPHENS, G. (1995, September/October). Crime in cyberspace: The digital underworld. *The Futurist, 29*(5), 24–28.

STEPHENS, G. (1996a). Humanizing twenty-first century justice: Balancing "freedom to" and "freedom from." In K. W. Hunter & T. C. Mack (Eds.), *International rights and responsibilities in the future*. Westport, CT: Praeger.

STEPHENS, G. (l996b). The future of policing: From a war model to a peace model. In B. Maguire & P. F. Radosh (Eds.), *The past, present, and future of American criminal justice*. Dix Hills, NY: General Hall.

STEPHENS, G. (l997, March/April). Youth at risk: Saving the world's most precious resource. *The Futurist, 31*(2), 31–38.

STEPHENS, G. (l998a). Cyber-biotech terrorism: Going high tech in the 21st century. In H. W. Kushner (Ed.), *The future of terrorism: Violence in the new millennium*. Thousand Oaks, CA: Sage.

STEPHENS, G. (l998b, July/August). Thinking globally, acting locally: Bringing peace to everyone's hood. *Crime & Justice International, 14*(18–19), 9–10, 32–33.

STEPHENS, G. (1999, November). Preventing crime: The promising road ahead. *The Futurist, 33*(9), 29–34.

STEPHENS, G. (Ed.). (2000a). *The American criminal justice system*. Columbia: University of South Carolina Press.

STEPHENS, G. (2000b). A futures perspective on leadership development. In T. D. Anderson (Ed.), *Every officer is a leader: Transforming leadership in police, justice, and public safety*. Boca Raton, FL: St. Lucie Press.

SUSPECT BEATEN ON VIDEO DIDN'T SHOOT OFFICER. (2000, August 8). *The (Columbia, SC) State,* p. A4.

TENNESSEE V. GARNER, 471 U.S. 1, 105 S. Ct. 1694, 85 L. Ed. 2d 1 (1985).

WALD, M. L. (1999, May 30). "Black box" for cars reveals accidents' details. *The (Columbia, SC) State,* p. 16.

11

Policing and Violence in Review:

Perspectives from the Practitioner Turned Academic/Practitioner

M. L. Dantzker

INTRODUCTION

Throughout the history of policing there has been violence by and against the police, and every day you can find such stories as these:

- California officer on medical leave apparently commits suicide in patrol car behind station house
- Police wound 25-year-old after car chase across two Missouri counties
- Plainclothes officers shoot suspect after wild shoot-out in pizza shop
- New Orleans deputies on desk duty after pliers used on suspect.

Although such violence is not a new phenomenon, anytime such activities occur, and especially if they are caught on videotape, much is said about them. Pundits, whether they are academics, media personalities, ordinary community members, or police practitioners, often have something to offer, be it to defend the police or to criticize. Neither this chapter nor the text as a whole is meant to do either. We have attempted to do nothing more than offer perspectives and documented information as to why violence occurs, whether it is by the police or against the police. The focus of this chapter is to offer the author's personal experiences and pontifications on police violence and to summarize the text.

PERSONAL PERSPECTIVES

My first awareness of police violence (by the police) was a result of media reports of the 1968 Democratic National Convention. Despite being an adolescent, I was very cognizant of what I was witnessing on the television—police officers freely striking out at protesters regardless of who they were or what they had done. Although I was being raised to respect police officers and their powers, these scenses provided me with doubts and concerns of hypocrisy of the "protective" value of the police. Today, I often cite this example as the time when, perhaps, not only an adolescent but the nation as a whole became more aware of the violent prospects of policing and police officers. However, despite what I had seen, for years to come I would remain respectful, even fearful, of the police and their powers, never truly understanding their position in society until I donned a uniform and badge.

In 1981 I became a police officer in a midwestern city of approximately 60,000 people (which included a state university campus). Because of state laws at the time that allowed officers to begin working the streets prior to completing the police academy, I was out on patrol before I had any formal preparation, placed with a veteran officer who was going to "show me the ropes." Hence began my socialization to policing that would continue through a 10-week academy less than two months later.

Throughout the initial training period much of what I would learn revolved around the quasi-military mentality that strongly reinforced the police "need to be in control" and police loyalty, "support your brethren officers, regardless." Unfortunately, this latter "stance" would come under great strain (within a few months after I graduated from the academy) on my first witnessing of "curbside justice," administered by not one but several fellow officers on an individual who had punctured the tires of a patrol car as it was parked at a local restaurant (the officers were inside on break).

Although I did not take part in this event, I also did nothing to stop it (something I would later criticize other officers for not doing in similar situations). After the subject was transported to the jail, and I was washing the blood off and out of the unit I was assigned to, I did, however, make it known that I was not very pleased with what I saw and probably would have a difficult time in court supporting the "official" story. Unfortunately, as the years progressed and I spent more time on the streets, not only did I observe other such events but actually participated in a few, too. The idea of "curbside justice" eventually meant more to me than when I first began my career. Of course, my response was usually in response to an attack on my person or fellow officer, or at the end of a car or foot pursuit that would be the catalyst for the violent response.

On leaving police work for the classroom full-time as an academic, my perspectives and views began to return to those I had when I first began in policing. Reading of or viewing police brutality in such cases as Rodney King, Malice Green, Amadou Diallo, or Abner Louima, I would criticize and often second-guess those officers who had been involved in these events, forgetting what it was like to be in their positions. It was not until I returned to policing as a reserve officer that I remembered what it was like to be on the streets in a position in which I could be a target of or the purveyor of violence. However, the difference for me today, in contrast to that young rookie officer in 1981, is that I can better relate to the responses from both the citizens and police with respect to the use of violence. Unfortunately, relating and understanding are not the same. As this text has demonstrated, understanding police violence is very difficult. Thus, all we can hope is that by reading and discussing the information offered, students of policing will take a broader view of how and why police violence occurs.

IN REVIEW

The attempt to understand police violence has long involved a cultural, socialization, or training approach. Perhaps, however, other forces are at work that have been given little to no attention. In Chapter 1, Paul B. Stretsky offers a different perspective by looking at police violence as a result of what he refers to as "political economy."

Stretesky begins by explaining how he uses a model that examines policing from historical, materialistic, and dialectical perspective. In general he suggests viewing police violence in reference to the larger social and economic conditions and the development of the police for "social order" as our society changed from an agricultural to a capitalistic economy. As he notes, our shift from feudalism to capitalism created new social problems that required some "force" of control. He reinforces this by offering a historical examination that takes us from the English frankpledge system to the watch system to a proactive approach; that is, we went from policing being decentralized to centralized, primarily because of capitalist forms of production. This change had implications for police violence because policing, whether in its initial form of private police or in the modern public police, was called on to protect capitalist interests during times of strikes and other labor unrest.

Stretesky continues to reinforce his position through discussion of police development in England, where class issues were prevalent and police officers hired by the London Metropolitan Police had to agree to give up their class ties, and police development in the United States, beginning with colonial America and slave patrols. Industrial America needed police units (private and public) to deal with immigrants and organized labor (with violence if need be). Similarly, the Texas Rangers were formed to deal with Mexicans and Indians (often in a violent manner). Basically, early American police came out in force to repress strikes, maintain order, ensure racial oppression, and control threatening populations.

From industrialization to the age of reform, Stretesky suggests that despite paid police not being popular and often targets of violence, as well as being purveyors of violence, increased training and greater controls of the police aided in decreasing violence—but violence did not disappear, especially in poor and minority areas. The 1960s was the pivotal time for recognition of police violence and the need for better controls, which led to national commissions and legislation that required increased training and education of officers. Today, he offers that violence still exists, especially against the poor, the unemployed, and minority/nonwhite groups, but training, policies, and community relations have had some positive effects on lessening police violence. He closes by suggesting that, despite all the changes, police violence can be viewed as a result of stages of economic development.

Whether it is a matter of economics or not, violence by and against policing exists. To better understand this phenomenon, Jason T. Carmichael and David Jacobs, in Chapter 2, examine the literature of violence used by and against the police. They begin by supporting Stretesky's position that police use force to control and maintain order and to enforce legal directives. However, they take a modern view of the situation by first offering how the use of violence is being regulated by the courts with such cases as *Tennessee v. Garner* (1985) (use of deadly force) and *Graham v. Connor* (1989) (use of excessive force) and how the police are subject to lawsuits. Their chapter continues with an examination of the police use of nondeadly force for which they advise there is limited research. Carmichael and Jacobs note that the research that does exist looks at officer characteristics and situational effects, and that findings indicate that nondeadly force is used in a majority of situations in which officers encounter resistance.

Their review then examines the research on deadly force. Again, Carmichael and Jacobs advise that the research is limited and also tends to focus on officer characteristics for which there seem to be no identifiable predictors, and to focus on race for which findings do suggest that deadly force may be used disproportionately against minorities. However, they indicate that said research offers the conventional belief that minorities commit more violent crimes, which leads to problems (i.e., violent confrontations with the police).

Carmichael and Jacobs continue with a review of research examining killings of police officers in multiple jurisdictions. Although they report that the studies vary sharply, a consistent finding was that killings of officers in cities where blacks have more political and economic influence than whites are reduced.

After further review of research of violence against police officers, Carmichael and Jacobs offer both a micro and macro view. Among other findings, from a microlevel, they report that nonlethal assaults against police officers are often due to an offender being intoxicated. At the macrolevel, research indicates that there have been reductions in both nonlethal and lethal assaults, but the cause(s) why are not clear because of the difficulties in analyzing such events. In conclusion, according to the research they reviewed, Carmichael and Jacobs offer that control of police violence requires political control through relevant state and federal laws, department policies about the use of force, and hiring officers who are more community-oriented than crime-oriented.

Since we all interpret what we see or read differently, more than one view is expected about understanding policing and violence. In Chapter 3, Robert P. McNamara starts with two examples of more current and better-known acts of police violence—the cases of Diallo and Louima—in his attempt to explain officers as offenders and as victims. This exploration begins with violence by the police.

McNamara suggests that violent acts by the police are rooted in the subcultural and socialization aspects of policing. Expounding on the works of Crank, he offers that violence can be viewed as a result of morality, masculinity, and solidarity, each of which is a response to both external threats (e.g., danger) and internal threats (e.g., administrative lack of concern) and develop through socialization.

With respect to morality, McNamara claims that police officers possess a high-mindedness and see themselves as protectors of morality, which legitimizes and justifies their use of force against those who violate "social morality" (e.g., the laws). Masculinity refers to an issue of bravery that would be diminished if force (violence) was not used on occasion. Solidarity is the loyalty and authority shared by police officers that reinforces use of force or protects those who use force against those deemed as deserving of such treatment.

McNamara's description of socialization mirrors the experiences of all police officers: academy, field training, and probation, during which the officer learns expectations, rules, and behaviors that are reinforced, including those supporting violent behavior.

However, he offers up the nature versus nurture debate as to whether police officers are made or born and how much of a role the subculture plays in police violence. His bottom line regarding police use of violence is that it is difficult to explain why officers become violent or brutal.

As McNamara points out, explaining violence by police officers is difficult; so, too, is explaining violence against officers. Although he offers a variety of theories (subculture of violence, differential association, and frustration-aggression) as a means to explain this behavior, ultimately he concludes that the "why" behind violence against police officers remains elusive.

Through the first three chapters, the information provided allowed us to look at policing and violence from a broader perspective with suggestions that violence is the result of political economy or socialization, although the research offers minimal support. However, there was a brief mention of situational possibilities, an explanation more readily acceptable to someone like myself. What is meant by situational factors and their relationship to policing and violence is explored in Chapter 4 by Ronald Burns and Charles Crawford. With their chapter, they address the ability of situational factors to explain (1) police violence, (2) the research, and (3) several real-life accounts.

Starting with police use of force, Burns and Crawford reaffirm previous chapters' findings of the difficulty in accurately measuring the number of incidents of police use of force. They offer an explanation of Sherman's five levels of analyses or explanations—organizational, community, legal, individual, and situational—before embarking on their devoted discussion of the situational explanations.

Situational factors in policing, according to Burns and Crawford, refer to the characteristics and behaviors of the suspects involved in the encounter and the structural characteristics found in the immediate vicinity and nature of the incident. This explanation suggests that police officer response (violence) is a result of several factors present at the time of his or her encounter with a citizen. For example:

> An alarm at a local sporting goods store is activated. Officers, on their arrival, find that it appears to have been burglarized, and some handguns may have been stolen. The information is broadcast over the radio. Checking the area near the store, two other officers come across an individual carrying a backpack who starts to run when he sees the officers. The officers pursue on foot and eventually draw and aim their weapons at the suspect, advising him to "freeze" as he is cornered in a backyard. Here's the situation for the officers: possible burglary suspect (felony), believed to be carrying several handguns (potential for danger), tried running from officers (pursuit adrenaline), and any move perceived to be a threat (i.e., going for a weapon) could cause one or both officers to shoot. Fortunately, the suspect cooperated and no force was necessary, which was good because the suspect was actually a teenager who had been burglarizing vehicles in the wrong place at the wrong time. (*This is a true event that happened to me during my rookie year.*)

According to the situational explanation, had the suspect done something other than follow the officers' commands, violence may have been warranted. This is supported by the literature; as Burns and Crawford explained, the more consistent factors identified that lead to police violence in a situation relate to the suspect.

According to Burns and Crawford, the research on situational explanations of police violence suggests that individual traits such as race, class, and ethnicity as well as gender tend to be related to police use of force. Furthermore, they indicate that the individual's behavior can affect use of force, that is, if the suspect is aggressive or resisting, has used or is under the influence of drugs or alcohol, or is committing a violent offense. They also acknowledge the research's findings related to structural factors. These factors include how the officer enters a situation (reactive versus proactive), whether the encounter is in private or public with bystanders, the time of day, the presence of other officers, and whether it is a domestic situation. All are related to whether the officer may use force.

In closing, Burns and Crawford discuss the use of force continuum and force factor as two ways of addressing how much force an officer should use. This is followed by a brief discussion of the reality of the use of force for which officers may receive training in an academy, but force takes place in the real world and does not always fall within the training or continuum parameters. The fact remains that there may be a variety of reasons why an officer uses force, each of which stems from the encounter with the suspect.

Police violence may be viewed as verbal or physical and can range from minimal invasion to death. Although there are probably numerous accounts of limited police violence, there are fewer accounts of police officers using deadly force. However, it is often those deadly force encounters that receive the most attention. Steven E. Reifert, in Chapter 5, takes us through a discussion of the police use of deadly force using three realistic scenarios to discuss the literature. His ultimate goal is to focus on the intentional acts of deadly force and why the officer used it. In discussing deadly force, he warns that there are three issues to consider: (1) the reliability of the information, (2) the push to overcome any resistance to using deadly force, and (3) the lack of information and research regarding the inability or intentional resistance to using deadly force.

Reifert begins by expanding earlier discussions on how we measure use of force, particularly the use of deadly force. As he notes, it is a source of controversy due to inadequate or inaccurate sources, inconsistency in reporting, and the difficulty in measuring it. Despite these shortcomings, we know that police officers occasionally use deadly force. To better understand why, he suggests it is because police officers are taught to kill.

It is believed that most humans have a natural reluctance to killing. Police training attempts to overcome that reluctance through operant conditioning, much in the same manner as the military trains soldiers. This is done through the use of simulators, which place officers in positions in which they must decide to shoot or not. One of Reifert's arguments is that police officers are trained simply to respond with deadly force whenever necessary rather than seek alternatives to its use. This leads to his explanation of shooting incidents as being the result of scripted behavior or cultural factors.

Scripted behavior, according to Reifert, may be social situational, which develops over time, or may be deadly force, which reflects training. The social situational script results from a collecting of numerous "scripts" in which the officer has either observed or participated in activities that could call for the use of deadly force. The deadly force script has four phases: anticipation, entry/initial contact, information exchange, and final frame. From the cultural perspective, Reifert reiterates previously discussed ideas of nature versus nurture (socialization versus predisposition) and the "code of silence" as they relate to use of deadly force.

In closing, Reifert advises that police officers, as humans, have an aversion to kill, but are sometimes placed in a situation in which deadly force is the only option. On the other hand, an attempt is made to overcome the aversion through operant conditioning. The downside is that alternatives to the use of deadly force are seldom offered.

Training continues to be a major issue for policing. As suggested in the previous discussion, training may very well be a catalyst for use of deadly force. This argument is countered to some degree in Chapter 6 by Kenneth W. Flynn who focuses strictly on training and police violence.

Flynn starts by discussing the difference between education and training with education being viewed as the sharing of knowledge or being instructed or taught, whereas training is the practical instruction of how to use the knowledge. As with earlier authors, Flynn, too, supports the idea of socialization that occurs through training in a police academy. Rather than focus on the socialization aspect, however, he focuses on the training component.

Flynn suggests that use of force training is important, and should teach officers how to effectively and safely do their jobs within legally proscribed confines. He advocates more than just an operant response, giving verbal judo as an alternative that should be taught. He continues by discussing training standards, highlighting his state's mandatory 104 hours, which includes laws, concepts, the mechanics of arrest, and firearms. He explains further how his agency devotes 93 additional hours to use of force topics. Despite the number of hours his agency provides for use of force training, he does not necessarily believe that it is enough and advocates continued in-service training to include civil liability issues.

Use of force can be taught through classroom, role-playing, hands-on, and field activities. Flynn states that training should focus on making decisions to use force, what force is, the abuses and excessive use, and why to use force. Concurring with other authors, he discusses the use of force continuum and how his agency trains officers with it. He concludes that training is an essential response to use of force and perhaps the curbing of violence by police officers.

The examination of violence by police officers often revolves around issues of physical brutality or use of deadly force. However, one form of potential use of violence often ignored is the police pursuit. Matt Welch, in Chapter 7, explores police pursuits as one form of violence not to be ignored. He begins by stating that since Moses' day there have been pursuits. In examining this topic, he divides pursuits into three types: pursuit of time (e.g., a high-priority response); pursuit of a compliant subject (e.g., stopping someone on a traffic violation); and pursuit of the noncompliant subject (e.g., the high-speed evader), which tends to offer the greatest degree of violence.

Welch identifies air, boat, motorcycle, and other modes of pursuit, in addition to the standard vehicular pursuit. The key issues he identifies with pursuits are life, money, and lawyers, indicating that the major issue is liability. Welch points out that injury or death from a pursuit could be deemed the result of officer negligence. However, for an officer to be negligent, the following must be proved:

1. The officer owed the injured party a duty not to engage in certain conduct.
2. The officer's actions violated that duty.
3. The officer's negligent conduct was the proximate cause of the accident.
4. The suing party suffered actual and provable damages. (Schofield, 1988)

Welch continues his discussion with a closer look at the numbers related to police pursuits. He reports that little research exists that looks at the actual costs of pursuits; more research exists on loss of property, but it is still limited and we must accept the findings with caution; loss of life is not as high as perceived; the initiation of pursuits often starts from attempted traffic stops; the person most often responsible for a pursuit is a male in his early to mid-twenties; and more research is needed.

Welch advocates the need for clear department policies through operant conditioning. He offers a comparison of two agencies he worked for and notes that many agencies do have policies. Still, he warns that the existence of a policy does not necessarily prevent dangerous pursuits from happening. He concludes his discussion by offering several causes of officer-initiated pursuits such as the adrenaline rush, the thrill, and stress. Solutions offered include policies, training, and technology. In sum, he advocates that police pursuits, as a form of violence, are an important concern and should be further addressed because they can lead to serious injury, loss of life, and destruction of property.

To this point, it appears that whether police violence is due to socialization, cultural or situational factors, or training, it exists, and little has been offered to truly understand why or how to control it. Perhaps it is not simply a question of a proscribed solution but more of a need for change in policing, particularly in the interaction of police officers and community members. The perspective offered in Chapter 8 by Rhonda K. DeLong is the relationship of violence as it pertains to community policing.

DeLong begins, as the majority in this text have, by trying to explain police violence. She suggests that it may simply be the response for justice. It is her position that community policing is central to the prevention of police violence because it requires the building of trust without which violence occurs.

Prior to addressing the community policing aspect, DeLong discusses whether the use of force is ever really necessary. As with those before her, she advises that before using deadly force, officers must consider the subject's ability and opportunity to cause serious harm and jeopardy to others. She believes the limiting of force can be accomplished through recruitment, selection, and training of officers. She suggests that we tend to recruit the wrong individuals. DeLong claims that policing recruits those with a military background (who may possess a mentality for violence), and this often limits the number of females; that selection of 21-year-olds raises an issue of maturity (suggesting a minimum age of 25); and that limited educational requirements has its own set of implications (suggesting that college education has a more positive influence on police use of violence). As in previous chapters, she also reiterates the effect and influence current training methods have on officers.

Overall, DeLong's major focus is on community policing, and she describes this philosophy using Trojanowicz and Bucqueroux's Nine P's. Ultimately, she advocates that police use of violence can be addressed through community policing because this approach changes policing through recruitment, selection, training, community awareness, communication, and continual contact. She concludes that community policing will lead to a decrease in police violence.

Because this text is geared for use in the United States, the emphasis has been on policing and violence in this country. As with many other topics, however, much can be learned through comparisons. Police violence is no different. Although we cannot celebrate the existence of police violence in other countries, we can welcome the opportunity to study it as a means of perhaps better understanding police violence in our country. To assist us in this matter, Richard H. Ward in Chapter 9 looks at dimensions of violence and the police from an international perspective.

Ward offers that in comparing police use of violence by country, the most significant determinant is the country's form of government, although finding a single determinant for use of violence against the police is much more difficult. To study police use of violence he offers the following typology:

Form of Government

totalitarian, democratic, or transitional

Organizational behavior

individual, group, or force

Determinant variables

political crisis, minority focus, crime-related, incident-motivated, citizen-compounded, psychological dysfunction, fear factor, errors and mistakes

Regarding the use of violence against the police, Ward suggests that in some ways it is correlated with the actions of the police (e.g., demonstration response).

Although they will not be discussed again here, Ward provided a regional analysis of violence, looking at the Americas, Western Europe, Eastern Europe, the Middle East, and Asia. The United States is left out of these analyses because the bulk of the text is devoted to violence in the United States. Ultimately, he concludes that police violence is common throughout the world, varies from a simple mistake to systematic torture, and may be explained by form of government, organizational behavior, or various variables. However, few data are available about violence against police officers.

Unequivocally, violence by and against the police exists throughout the world. Of course, of concern here is its existence in the United States. On a daily basis we can find reports of its use by and against police officers. The question is: Where does it end? The answer to this question is addressed by Gene Stephens in Chapter 10, as he ponders the future directions in police violence.

According to Stephens, in the 21st century we can expect three things pertaining to police violence (in this order):

1. more of the same
2. new types of violence
3. a real trend away from violence by and against police officers

Stephens suggests that violence could get worse before its gets better. As policing maintains its current approach to dealing with citizens and training, there appears to be no reason for violence to dissipate. He also suggests that as long as society remains prone to violence, and it is perpetuated through certain mediums (i.e., the media), the police will continue to respond accordingly.

Regarding new types of violence, Stephens points out how technology, in particular, will create "computer violence" and a need for new responses by police. Furthermore, technology will provide nonlethal weaponry that will assist in reducing violence.

Finally, Stephens believes that a real trend away from violence will occur because of community policing, restorative justice, and nonlethal weaponry. Still, he offers that the future will be based on major events, socioeconomic change, and technological adaptation. Ultimately, he advises that violence by and against the police will reflect violence in society or at least perceived violence.

In closing, there is still much to learn about policing and violence. This text offers differing views and perspectives that I hope will encourage people to think more seriously about this important issue in our country, policing and violence.

REFERENCES

SCHOFIELD, D. (1988, May). Legal issues of pursuit driving. *FBI Law Enforcement Bulletin,* 23–30.